AROUND SEPTEMBER,
I'M GOING ON A TRIP
TO GUAM WITH A FRIEND.
DONATIONS GLADLY
ACCEPTED.
THX.

空 知 英 秋

Hideaki Sorachi

I got this letter from my big sister...

Hideaki Sorachi was born on May 25, 1979, and grew up in Hokkaido, Japan. His ongoing series, *GIN TAMA*, became a huge hit when it began running in the pages of Japan's *Weekly Shonen Jump* in 2004. A *GIN TAMA* animated series followed soon after, premiering on Japanese TV in April 2006. Sorachi made his manga debut with the one-shot story *DANDELION*!

GIN TAMA VOL. 4
SHONEN JUMP ADVANCED Manga Edition

STORY & ART BY HIDEAKI SORACHI

Translation/Matthew Rosin, Honyaku Center Inc.
English Adaptation/Drew Williams
Touch-up Art & Lettering/Steve Dutro
Cover & Interior Design/Sean Lee
Editor/Annette Roman

Printed in the U.S.A.

Published by VIZ Media, LLC
P.O. Box 77010
San Francisco, CA 94107

10 9 8 7 6 5 4 3 2
First printing, January 2008
Second printing, June 2017

www.viz.com

THE WORLD'S MOST
CUTTING-EDGE MANGA

www.shonenjump.com

Vol. 4

Exaggerate the Tales of Your Exploits by a Third, so Everyone Has a Good Time

STORY & ART BY
HIDEAKI SORACHI

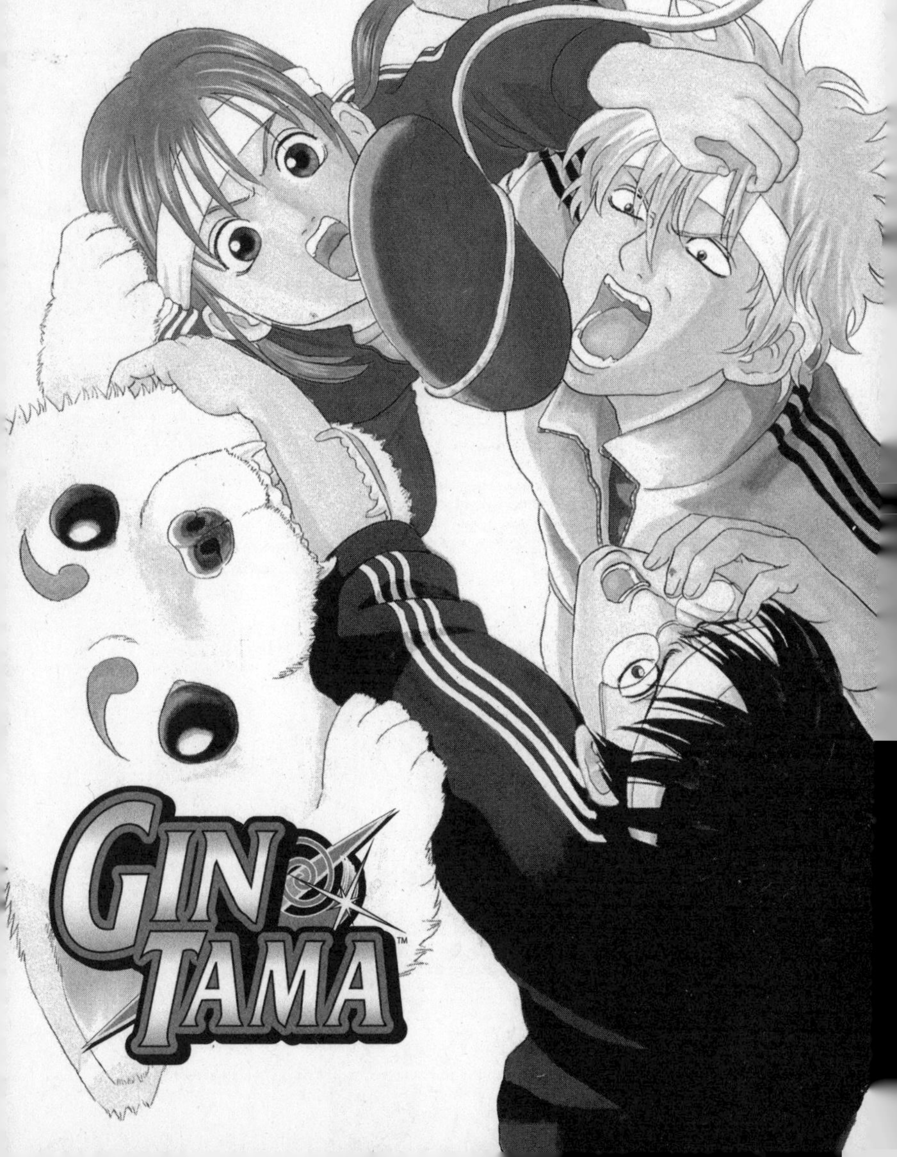
GIN TAMA™

Cast of Characters

Yorozuya Members

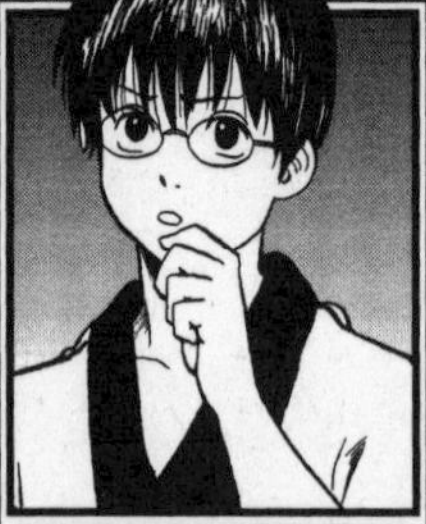

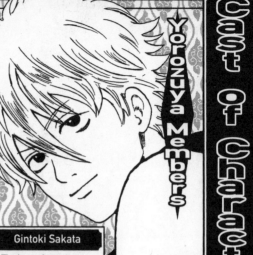

Shinpachi Shimura

Works under Gintoki in an attempt to learn about the samurai spirit, but has been regretting his decision recently. Also president of idol singer Tsu Terakado's fan club.

Gintoki Sakata

The hero of our story. He needs to eat something sweet periodically or he gets cranky. He commands a powerful sword arm but is one step away from diabetes. A former member of the exclusionist faction which seeks to eliminate the space aliens and protect the nation.

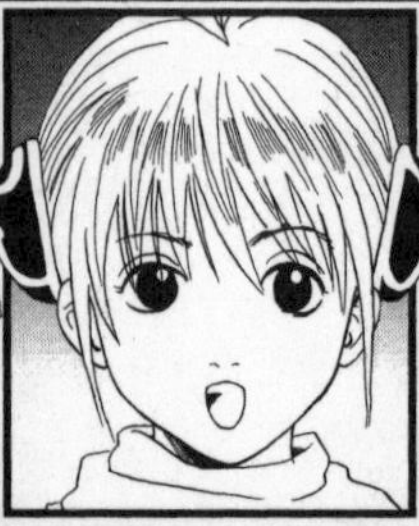

Kagura

A member of the "Yato Clan," the most powerful warrior race in the universe. Her voracious appetite and often inadvertent comic timing are unrivalled.

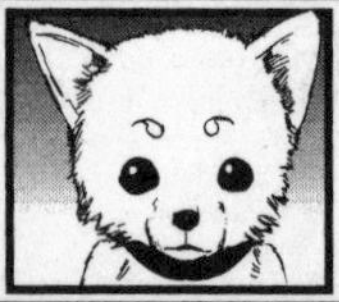

Sadaharu/animal

A giant space creature kept as a pet in the Yorozuya office. Likes to bite people (especially Gintoki).

Shinsengumi Members

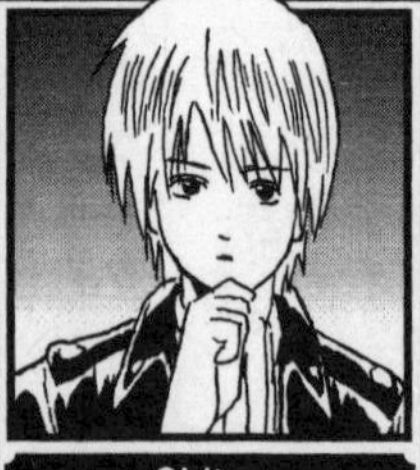

Okita

The most formidable swordsman in the Shinsengumi. His jovial attitude hides an utterly black heart. He wants to take over as the Vice-Chief.

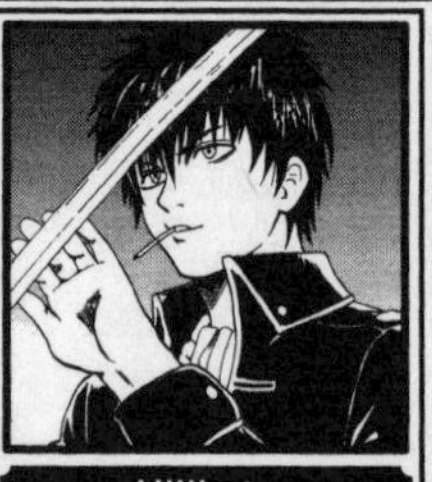

Hijikata

Vice-Chief of the Shinsengumi, Edo's elite Delta Force police unit. His cool demeanor turns to rage the moment he draws his sword. The pupils of his eyes always seem a bit dilated.

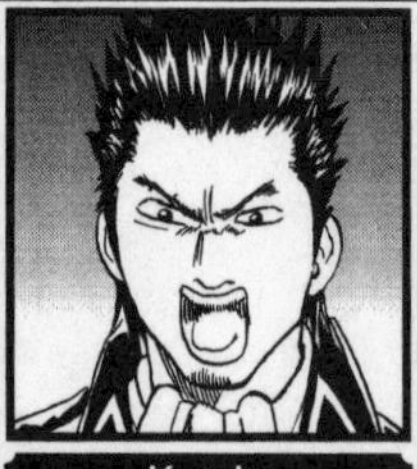

Kondo

Chief of the Shinsengumi. A trusted leader, yet the insufferable stalker of Otae, Shinpachi's elder sister.

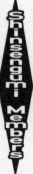

Other Characters

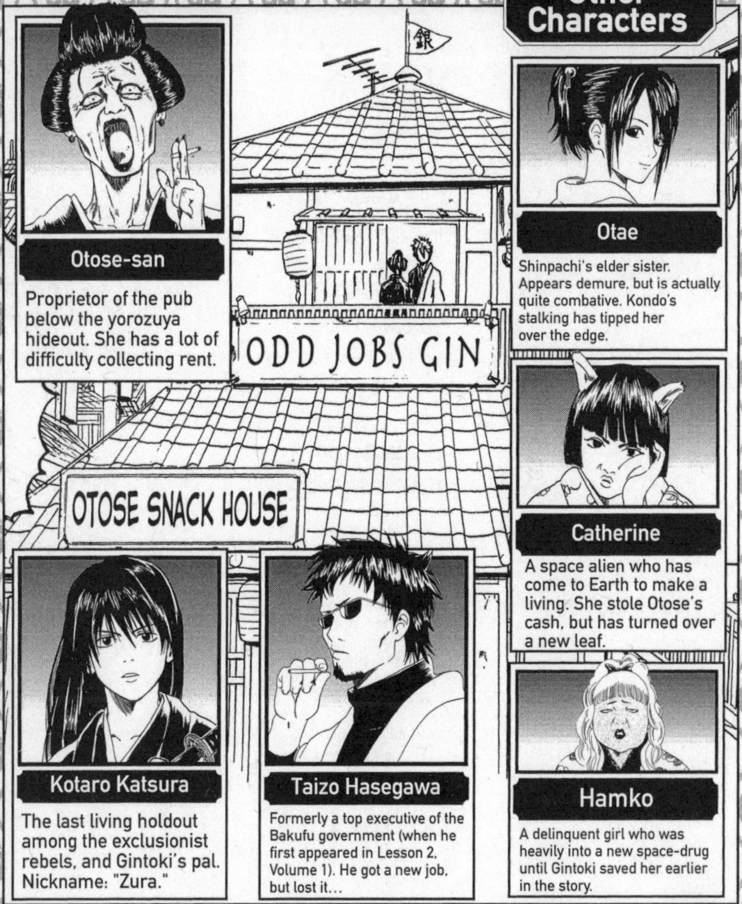
ODD JOBS GIN
OTOSE SNACK HOUSE

Otose-san

Proprietor of the pub below the yorozuya hideout. She has a lot of difficulty collecting rent.

Otae

Shinpachi's elder sister. Appears demure, but is actually quite combative. Kondo's stalking has tipped her over the edge.

Catherine

A space alien who has come to Earth to make a living. She stole Otose's cash, but has turned over a new leaf.

Kotaro Katsura

The last living holdout among the exclusionist rebels, and Gintoki's pal. Nickname: "Zura."

Taizo Hasegawa

Formerly a top executive of the Bakufu government (when he first appeared in Lesson 2, Volume 1). He got a new job, but lost it…

Hamko

A delinquent girl who was heavily into a new space-drug until Gintoki saved her earlier in the story.

The story thus far

In an alternate-universe Edo (Tokyo), extraterrestrials land in Japan and the new government issues an order outlawing swords. The samurai, who have reached the pinnacle of power and prosperity, fall into rapid decline.

Twenty years hence, only one samurai has managed to hold onto his fighting spirit: a somewhat eccentric fellow named Gintoki "Odd Jobs Gin" Sakata. A lover of sweets and near diabetic, our hero sets up shop as a *yorozuya*—an expert at managing trouble and handling the oddest jobs.

Joining "Gin" in his business is Shinpachi Shimura, whose sister Gin saved from the clutches of nefarious debt collectors. After a series of unexpected circumstances, the trio meet a powerful alien named Kagura, who becomes—after some arm-twisting—a part-time team member.

Lately, the various members of the yorozuya trio have dueled the Shinsengumi elite police for a prime cherry blossom viewing spot, helped out an alien "water spirit," meddled in a pop idol's love life, pimped Sadaharu on a TV game show, and been accused of arson… Suffice to say the yorozuya gang has been busy. What in the world will they foul up *this* time?!

WHAT THIS MANGA'S FULL OF vol. 4

Lesson 23
You Only Gotta Wash Under Your Armpits—Just the Armpits
7

Lesson 24
Exaggerate the Tales of Your Exploits by a Third, so Everyone Has a Good Time
27

Lesson 25
You Say *Kawaiiii* so Often, You Must Really Think You're Cute Stuff
47

Lesson 26
You Can Forget to Bring Spare Undies on a Voyage, but Don't Forget UNO
67

Lesson 27
When You're in a Fix, Keep on Laughing, Laughing…
91

Lesson 28
Oh, Yeah! Our Crib Is Number One!
111

Lesson 29
You Really Think You Can Study for Exams While Listening to Music?! Turn It off Already!
131

Lesson 30
It's Not the Bad Guys Who Cause Calamities, It's the Hyperactive Types
151

Lesson 31
Sons Only Take After Their Fathers' *Negative* Attributes
169

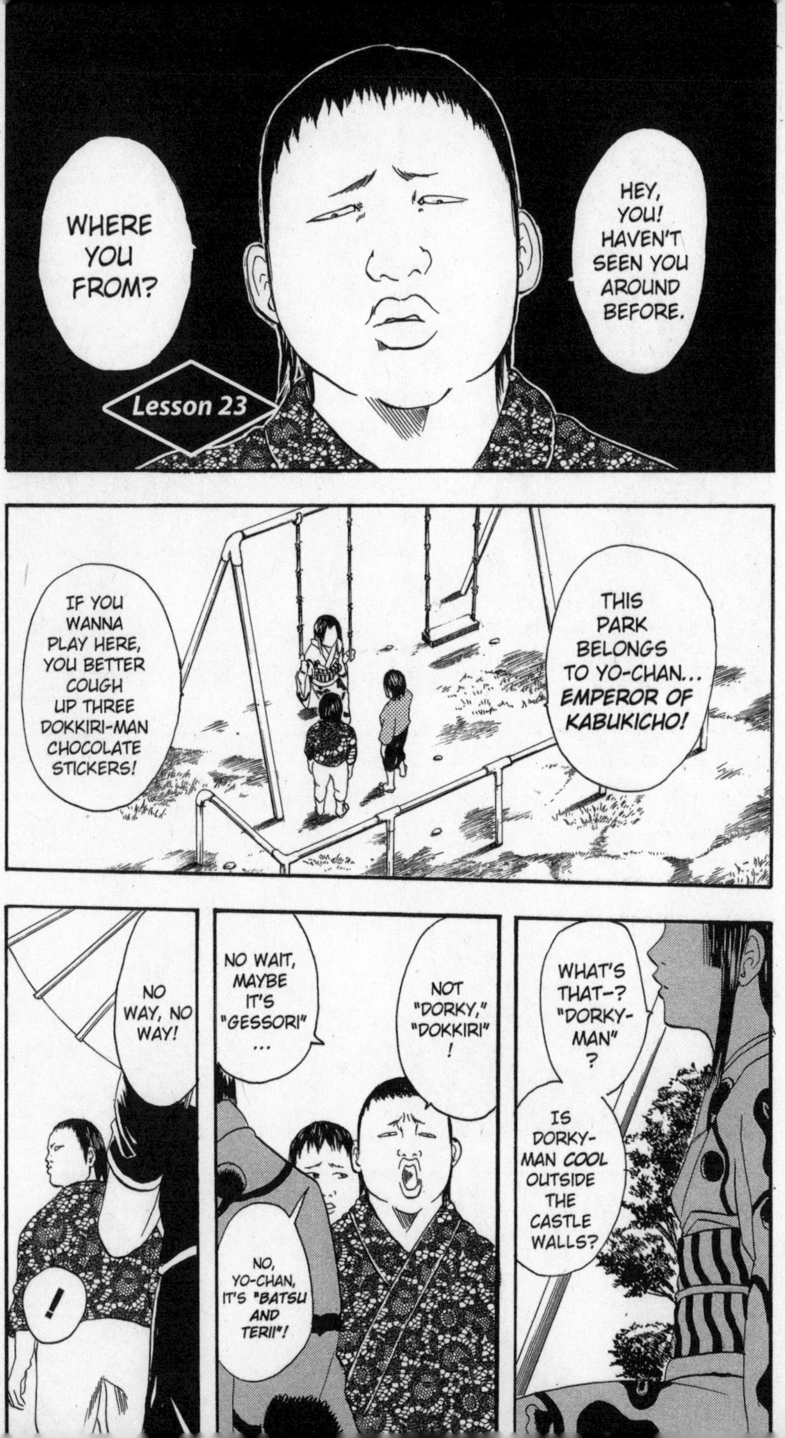
HEY, YOU! HAVEN'T SEEN YOU AROUND BEFORE.
WHERE YOU FROM?
Lesson 23
THIS PARK BELONGS TO YO-CHAN... EMPEROR OF KABUKICHO!
IF YOU WANNA PLAY HERE, YOU BETTER COUGH UP THREE DOKKIRI-MAN CHOCOLATE STICKERS!
WHAT'S THAT—? "DORKY-MAN"?
IS DORKY-MAN COOL OUTSIDE THE CASTLE WALLS?
NOT "DORKY," "DOKKIRI"!
NO WAIT, MAYBE IT'S "GESSORI"...
NO, YO-CHAN, IT'S "BATSU AND TERII"!
NO WAY, NO WAY!
!

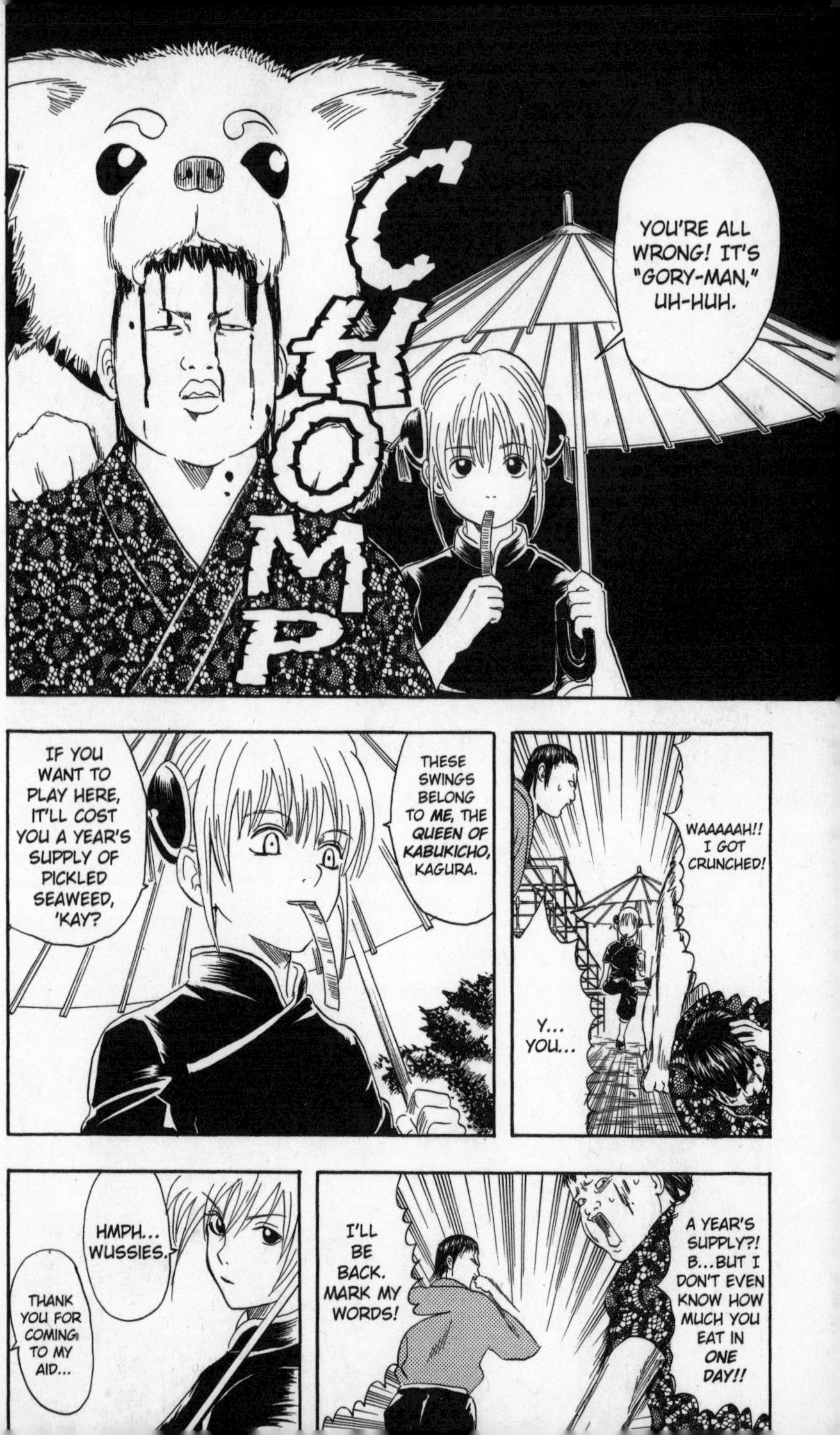
YOU'RE ALL WRONG! IT'S "GORY-MAN," UH-HUH.
CHOMP
WAAAAAH!! I GOT CRUNCHED!
Y... YOU...
THESE SWINGS BELONG TO *ME*, THE *QUEEN OF KABUKICHO*, KAGURA.
IF YOU WANT TO PLAY HERE, IT'LL COST YOU A YEAR'S SUPPLY OF PICKLED SEAWEED, 'KAY?
A YEAR'S SUPPLY?! B...BUT I DON'T EVEN KNOW HOW MUCH YOU EAT IN ONE DAY!!
I'LL BE BACK. MARK MY WORDS!
HMPH... WUSSIES.
THANK YOU FOR COMING TO MY AID...

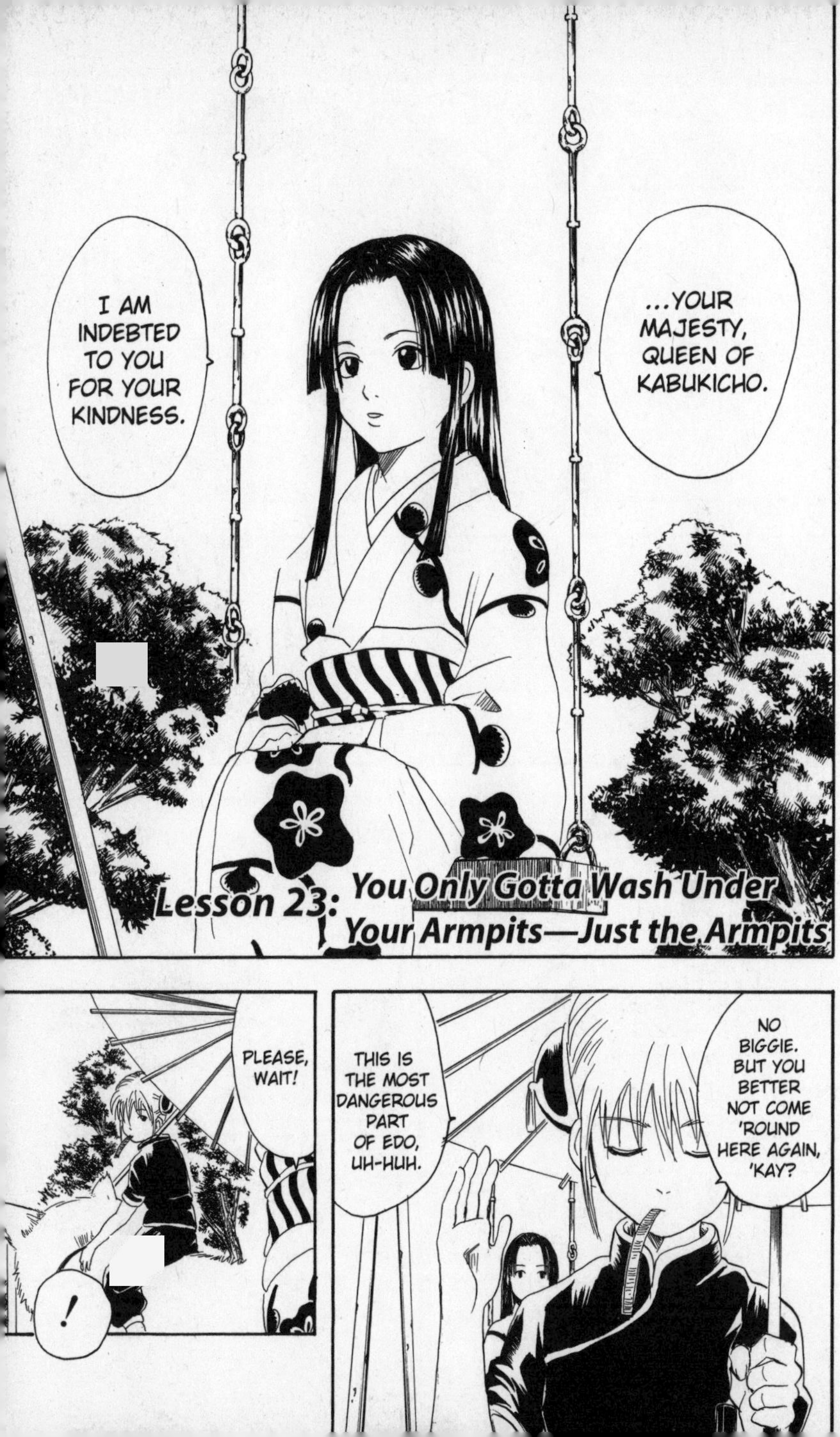
...YOUR MAJESTY, QUEEN OF KABUKICHO.
I AM INDEBTED TO YOU FOR YOUR KINDNESS.
Lesson 23: You Only Gotta Wash Under Your Armpits—Just the Armpits
NO BIGGIE. BUT YOU BETTER NOT COME 'ROUND HERE AGAIN, 'KAY?
THIS IS THE MOST DANGEROUS PART OF EDO, UH-HUH.
PLEASE, WAIT!
!

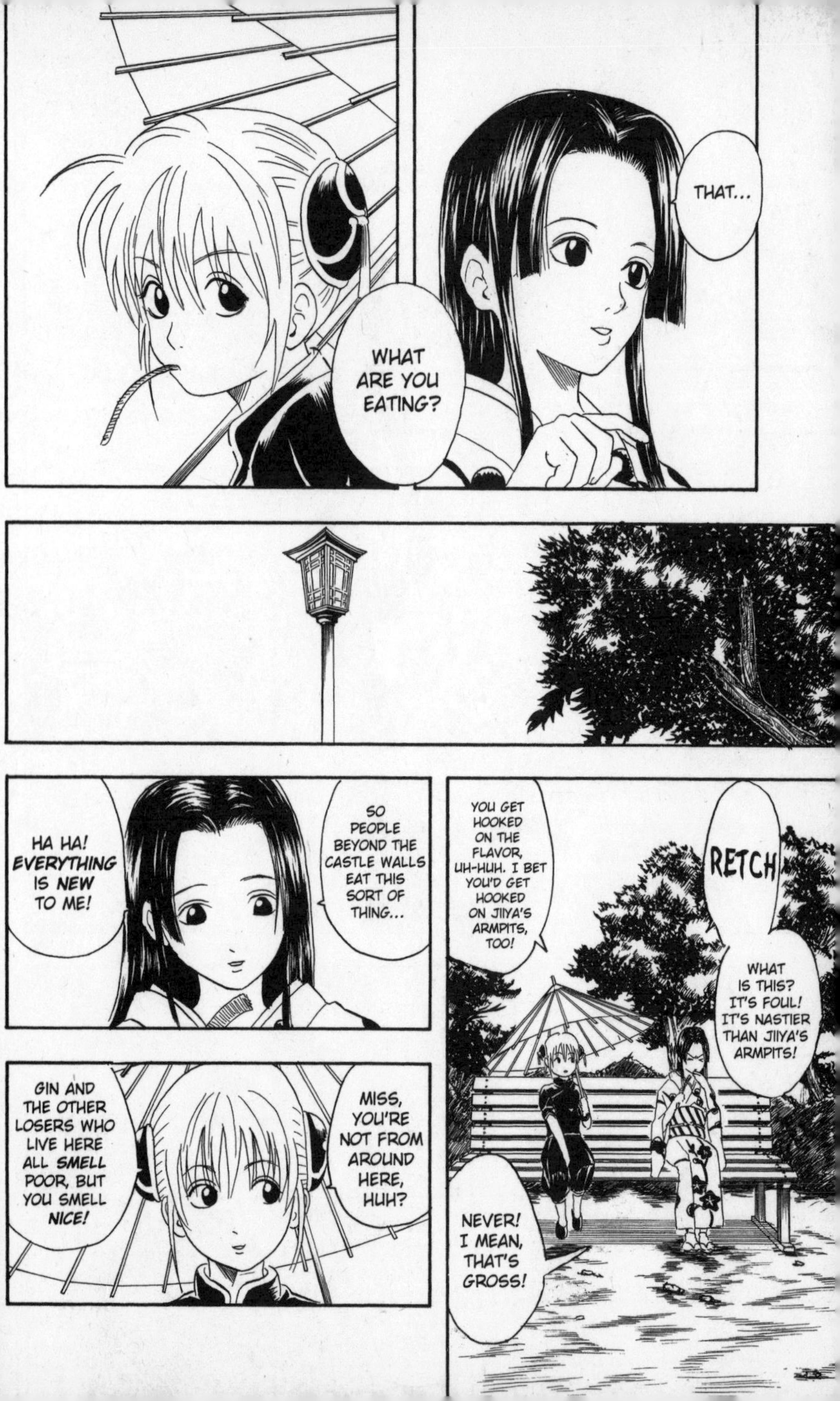
THAT...
WHAT ARE YOU EATING?
RETCH
WHAT IS THIS? IT'S FOUL! IT'S NASTIER THAN JIIYA'S ARMPITS!
YOU GET HOOKED ON THE FLAVOR, UH-HUH. I BET YOU'D GET HOOKED ON JIIYA'S ARMPITS, TOO!
NEVER! I MEAN, THAT'S GROSS!
SO PEOPLE BEYOND THE CASTLE WALLS EAT THIS SORT OF THING...
HA HA! EVERYTHING IS NEW TO ME!
MISS, YOU'RE NOT FROM AROUND HERE, HUH?
GIN AND THE OTHER LOSERS WHO LIVE HERE ALL SMELL POOR, BUT YOU SMELL NICE!

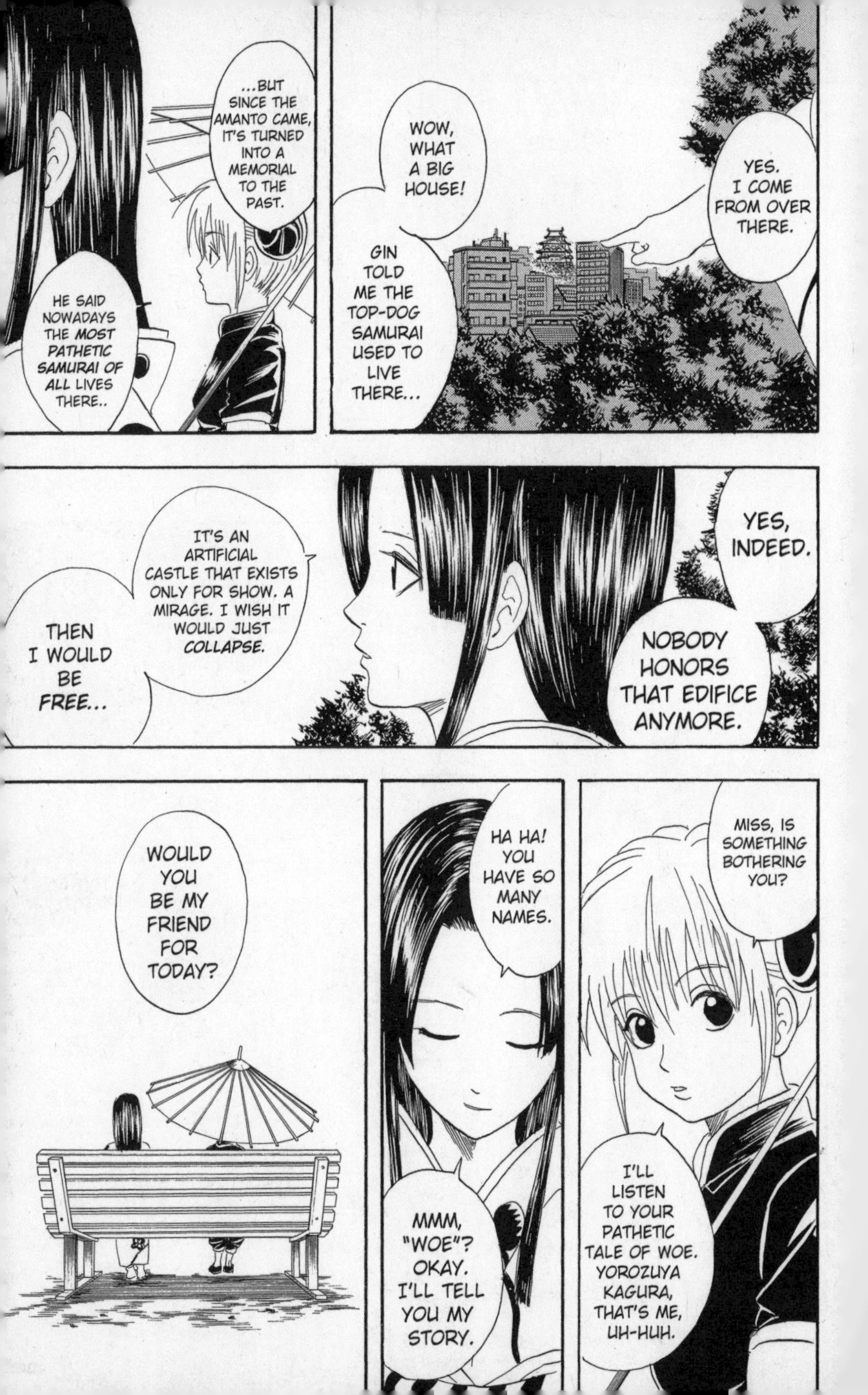
YES. I COME FROM OVER THERE.
WOW, WHAT A BIG HOUSE!
GIN TOLD ME THE TOP-DOG SAMURAI USED TO LIVE THERE...
...BUT SINCE THE AMANTO CAME, IT'S TURNED INTO A MEMORIAL TO THE PAST.
HE SAID NOWADAYS THE MOST PATHETIC SAMURAI OF ALL LIVES THERE..
YES, INDEED.
NOBODY HONORS THAT EDIFICE ANYMORE.
IT'S AN ARTIFICIAL CASTLE THAT EXISTS ONLY FOR SHOW. A MIRAGE. I WISH IT WOULD JUST COLLAPSE.
THEN I WOULD BE FREE...
MISS, IS SOMETHING BOTHERING YOU?
I'LL LISTEN TO YOUR PATHETIC TALE OF WOE. YOROZUYA KAGURA, THAT'S ME, UH-HUH.
HA HA! YOU HAVE SO MANY NAMES.
MMM, "WOE"? OKAY. I'LL TELL YOU MY STORY.
WOULD YOU BE MY FRIEND FOR TODAY?

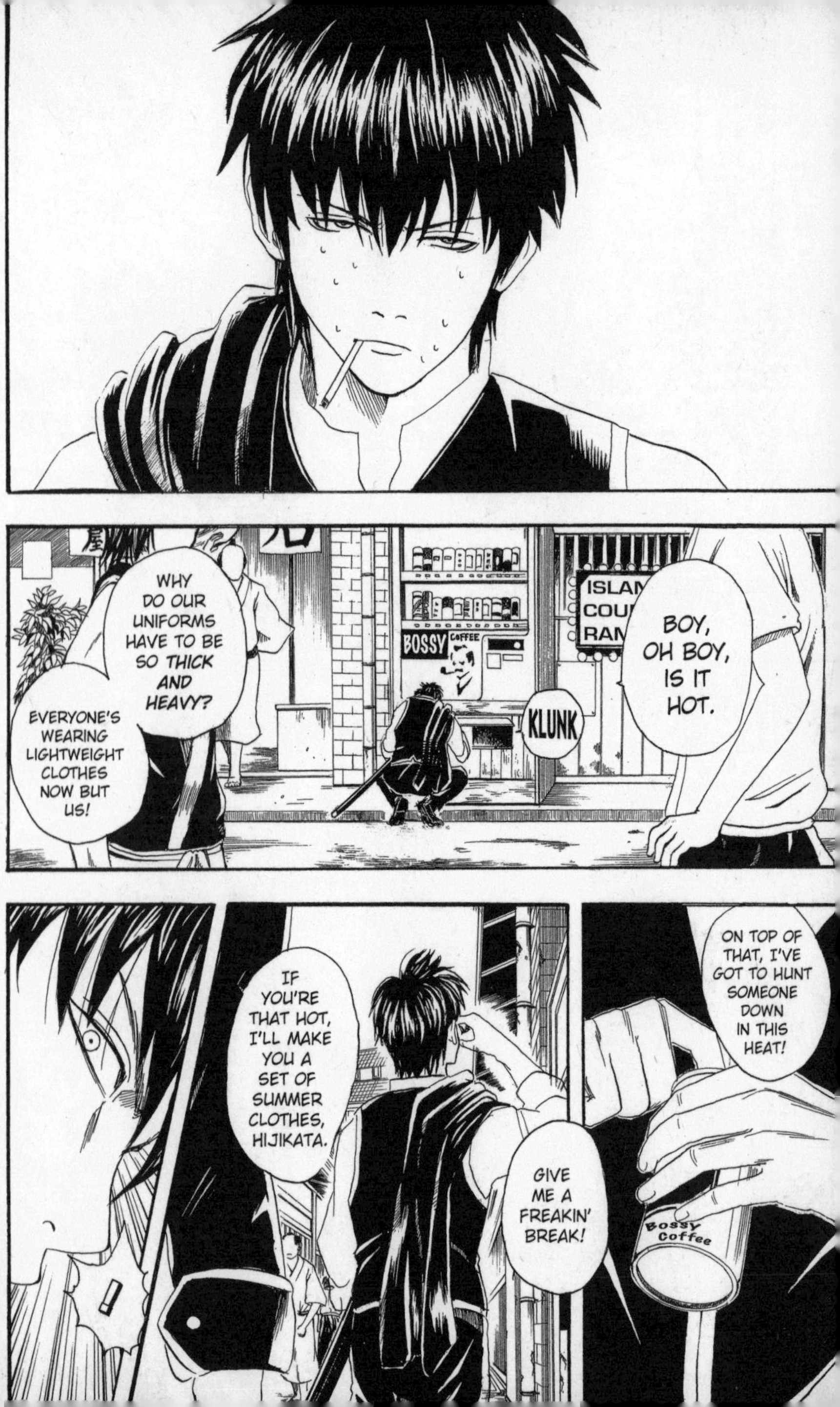
BOY, OH BOY, IS IT HOT.
KLUNK
BOSSY COFFEE
WHY DO OUR UNIFORMS HAVE TO BE SO THICK AND HEAVY?
EVERYONE'S WEARING LIGHTWEIGHT CLOTHES NOW BUT US!
ON TOP OF THAT, I'VE GOT TO HUNT SOMEONE DOWN IN THIS HEAT!
GIVE ME A FREAKIN' BREAK!
Bossy Coffee
IF YOU'RE THAT HOT, I'LL MAKE YOU A SET OF SUMMER CLOTHES, HIJIKATA.
!

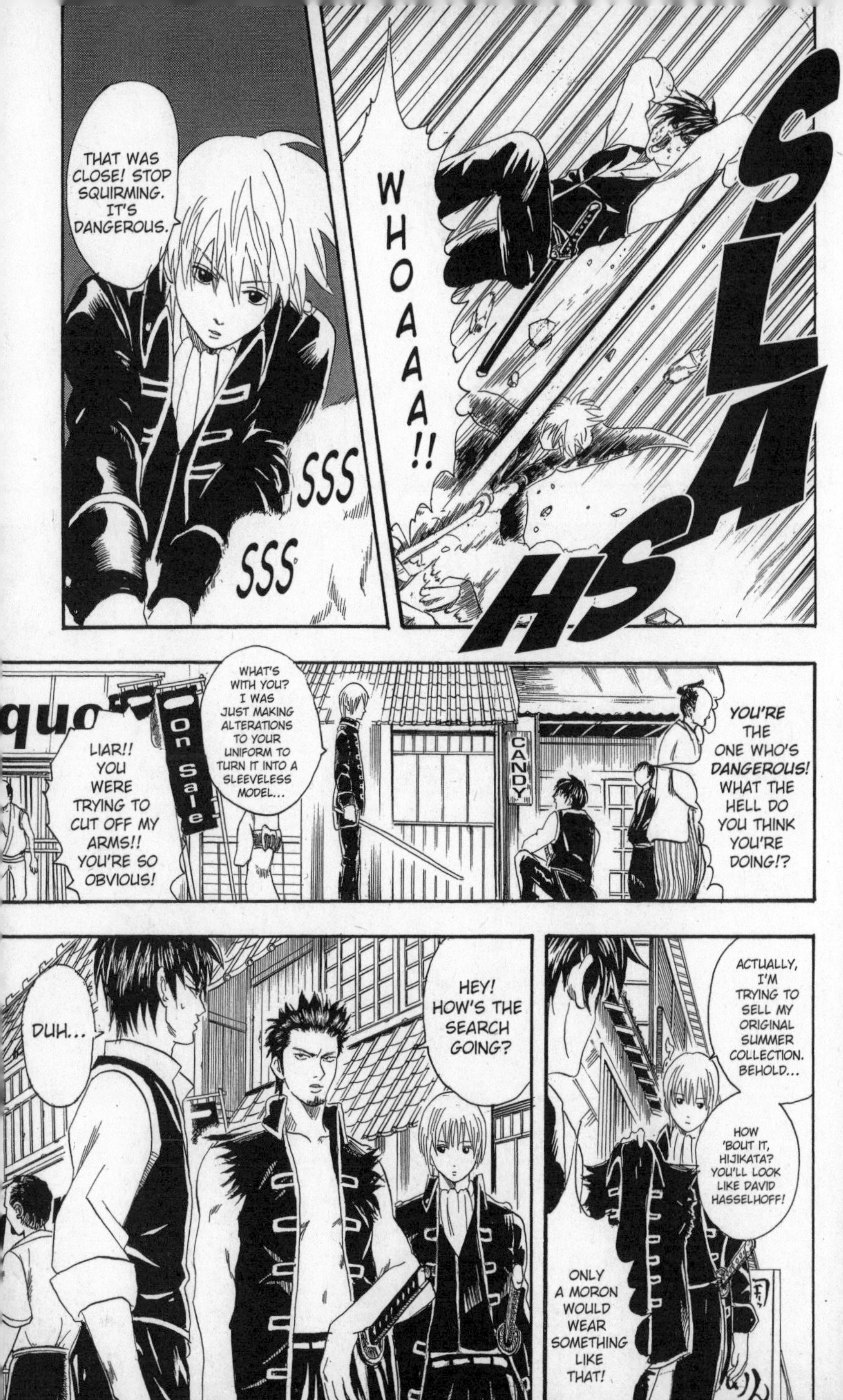
WHOAAA!!
SLASH
THAT WAS CLOSE! STOP SQUIRMING. IT'S DANGEROUS.
SSS
SSS
YOU'RE THE ONE WHO'S DANGEROUS! WHAT THE HELL DO YOU THINK YOU'RE DOING!?
CANDY
WHAT'S WITH YOU? I WAS JUST MAKING ALTERATIONS TO YOUR UNIFORM TO TURN IT INTO A SLEEVELESS MODEL...
On Sale
LIAR!! YOU WERE TRYING TO CUT OFF MY ARMS!! YOU'RE SO OBVIOUS!
quo
ACTUALLY, I'M TRYING TO SELL MY ORIGINAL SUMMER COLLECTION. BEHOLD...
HOW 'BOUT IT, HIJIKATA? YOU'LL LOOK LIKE DAVID HASSELHOFF!
ONLY A MORON WOULD WEAR SOMETHING LIKE THAT!
HEY! HOW'S THE SEARCH GOING?
DUH...

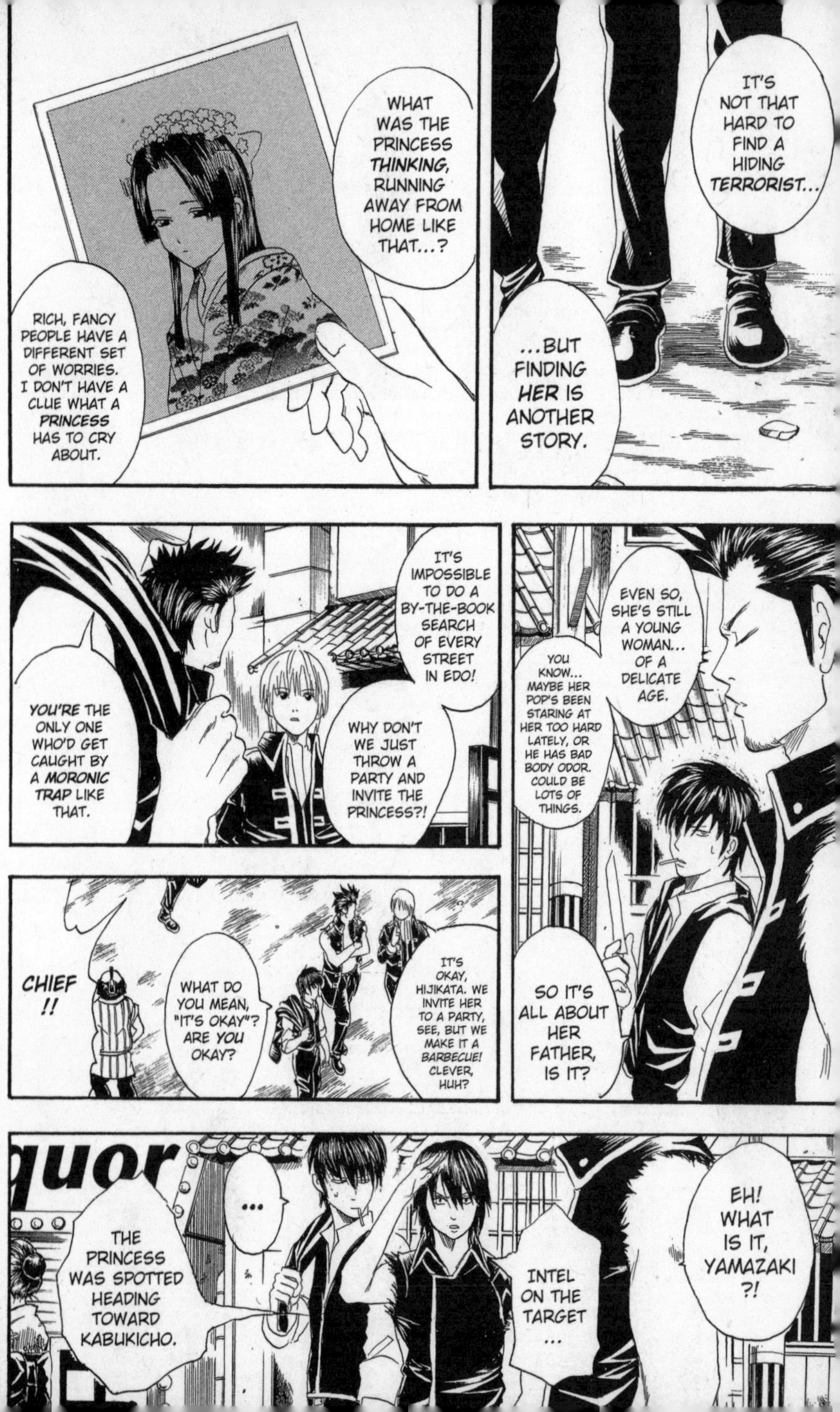
IT'S NOT THAT HARD TO FIND A HIDING *TERRORIST*...
...BUT FINDING *HER* IS ANOTHER STORY.
WHAT WAS THE PRINCESS *THINKING*, RUNNING AWAY FROM HOME LIKE THAT...?
RICH, FANCY PEOPLE HAVE A DIFFERENT SET OF WORRIES. I DON'T HAVE A CLUE WHAT A *PRINCESS* HAS TO CRY ABOUT.
EVEN SO, SHE'S STILL A YOUNG WOMAN... OF A DELICATE AGE.
YOU KNOW... MAYBE HER POP'S BEEN STARING AT HER TOO HARD LATELY, OR HE HAS BAD BODY ODOR. COULD BE LOTS OF THINGS.
SO IT'S ALL ABOUT HER FATHER, IS IT?
IT'S IMPOSSIBLE TO DO A BY-THE-BOOK SEARCH OF EVERY STREET IN EDO!
WHY DON'T WE JUST THROW A PARTY AND INVITE THE PRINCESS?!
YOU'RE THE ONLY ONE WHO'D GET CAUGHT BY A *MORONIC TRAP* LIKE THAT.
IT'S OKAY, HIJIKATA. WE INVITE HER TO A PARTY, SEE, BUT WE MAKE IT A BARBECUE! CLEVER, HUH?
WHAT DO YOU MEAN, "IT'S OKAY"? ARE *YOU* OKAY?
CHIEF !!
EH! WHAT IS IT, YAMAZAKI ?!
INTEL ON THE TARGET ...
...
THE PRINCESS WAS SPOTTED HEADING TOWARD KABUKICHO.
quor

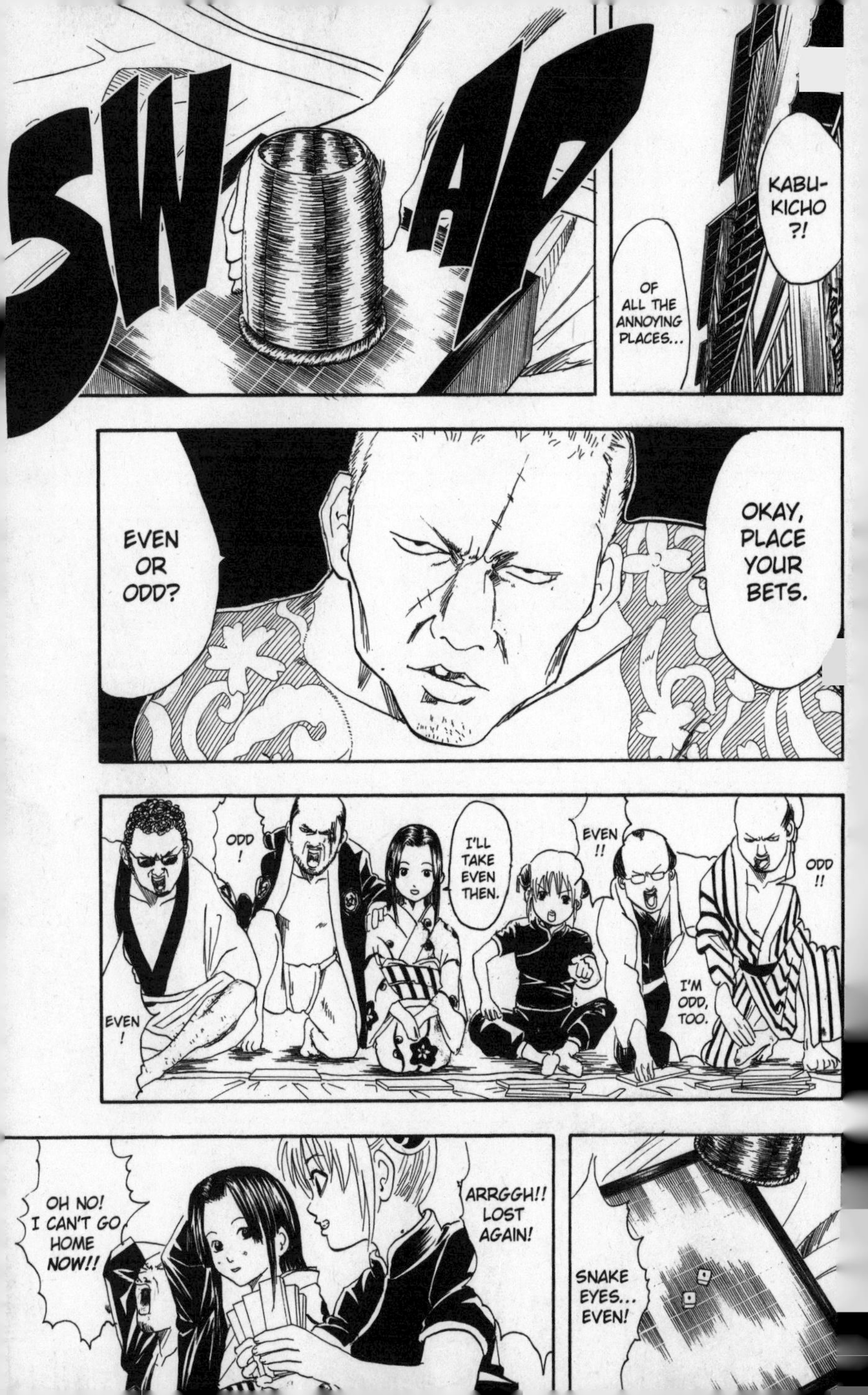
KABU-KICHO ?!
OF ALL THE ANNOYING PLACES...
SWAP
OKAY, PLACE YOUR BETS.
EVEN OR ODD?
ODD !!
EVEN !!
I'M ODD, TOO.
I'LL TAKE EVEN THEN.
ODD !
EVEN !
SNAKE EYES... EVEN!
ARRGGH!! LOST AGAIN!
OH NO! I CAN'T GO HOME NOW!!

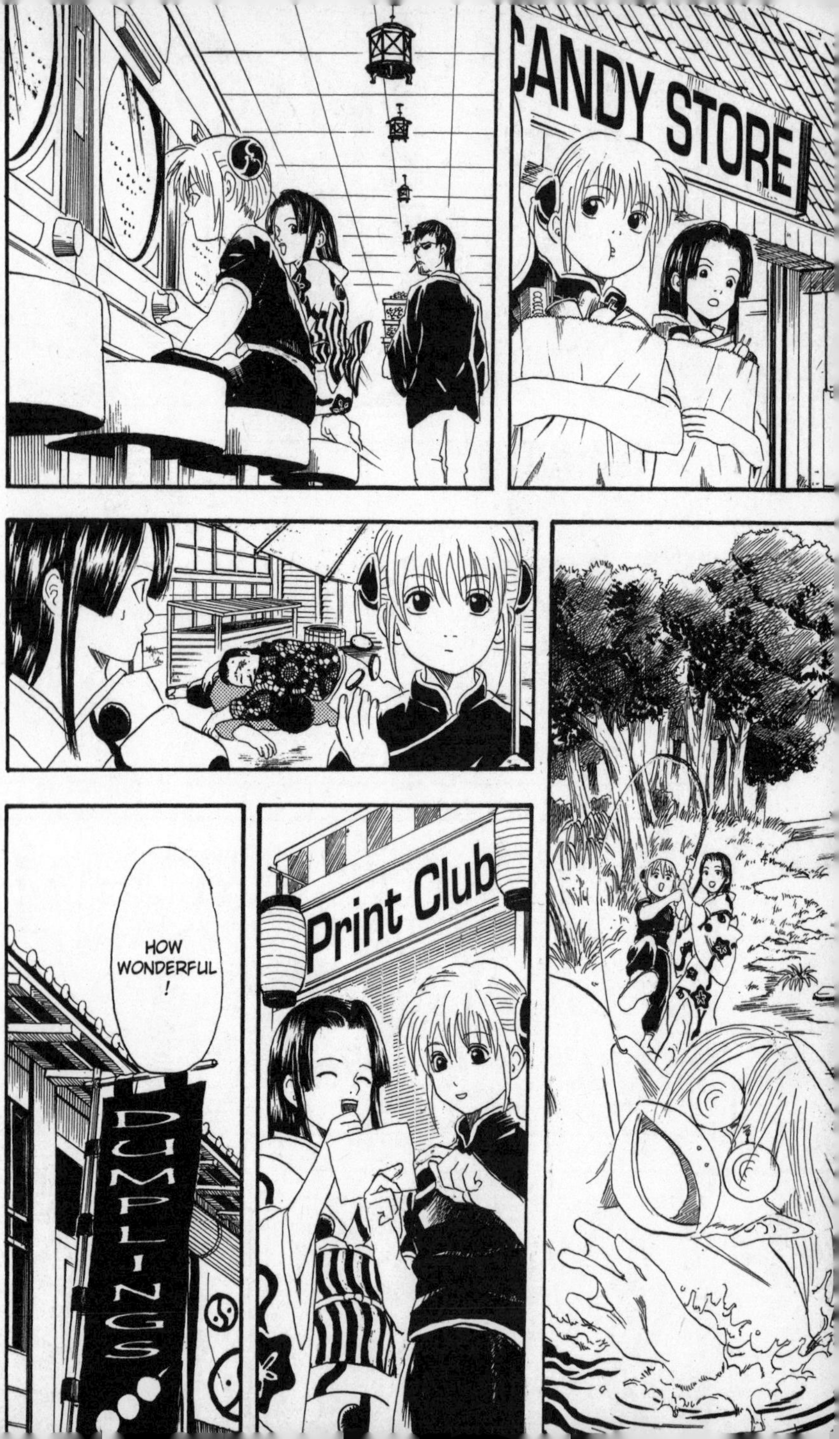
CANDY STORE
Print Club
HOW WONDERFUL!
DUMPLINGS

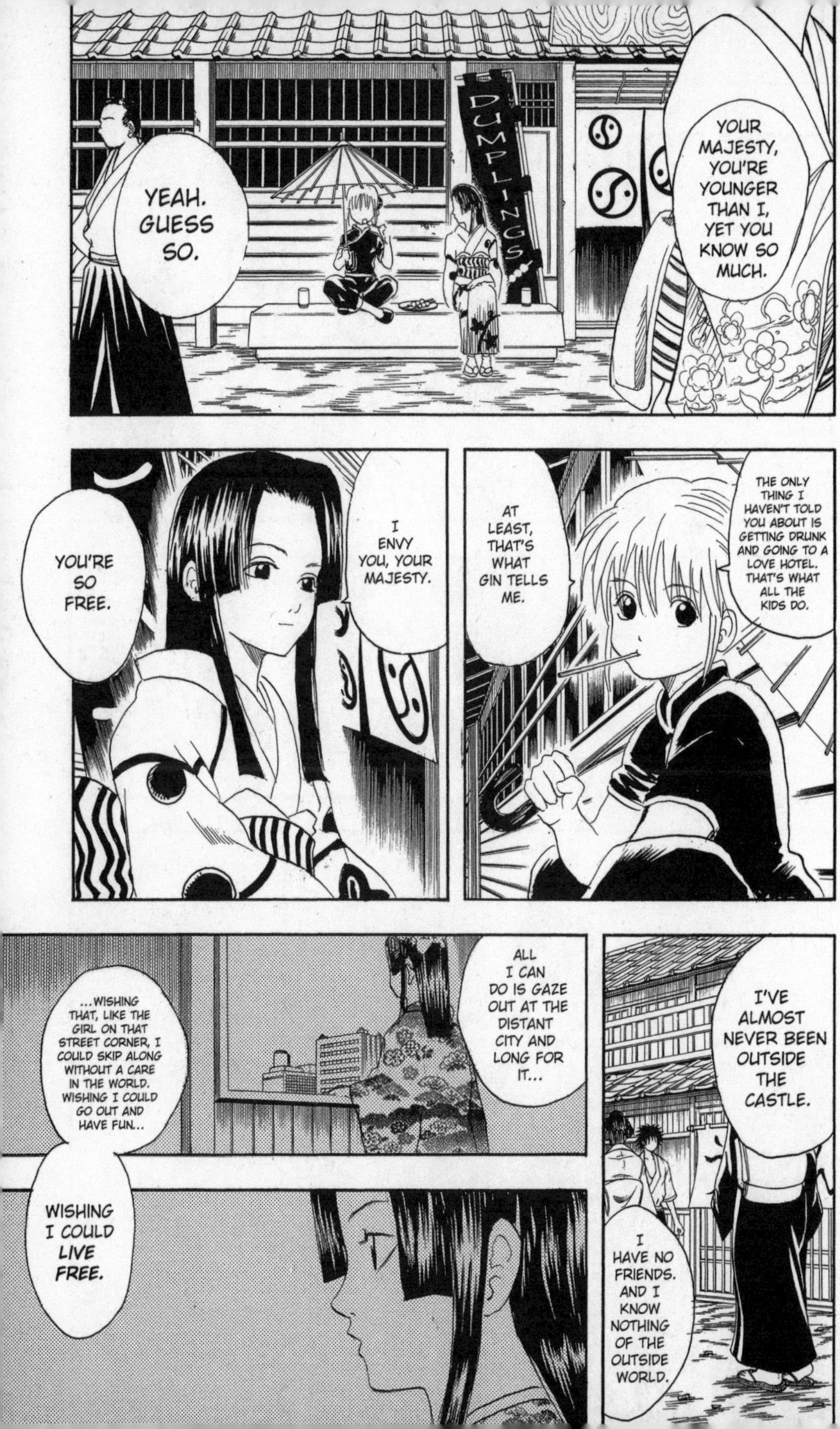
YOUR MAJESTY, YOU'RE YOUNGER THAN I, YET YOU KNOW SO MUCH.
YEAH. GUESS SO.
DUMPLINGS
THE ONLY THING I HAVEN'T TOLD YOU ABOUT IS GETTING DRUNK AND GOING TO A LOVE HOTEL. THAT'S WHAT ALL THE KIDS DO.
AT LEAST, THAT'S WHAT GIN TELLS ME.
I ENVY YOU, YOUR MAJESTY.
YOU'RE SO FREE.
I'VE ALMOST NEVER BEEN OUTSIDE THE CASTLE.
I HAVE NO FRIENDS. AND I KNOW NOTHING OF THE OUTSIDE WORLD.
ALL I CAN DO IS GAZE OUT AT THE DISTANT CITY AND LONG FOR IT...
...WISHING THAT, LIKE THE GIRL ON THAT STREET CORNER, I COULD SKIP ALONG WITHOUT A CARE IN THE WORLD. WISHING I COULD GO OUT AND HAVE FUN...
WISHING I COULD LIVE FREE.

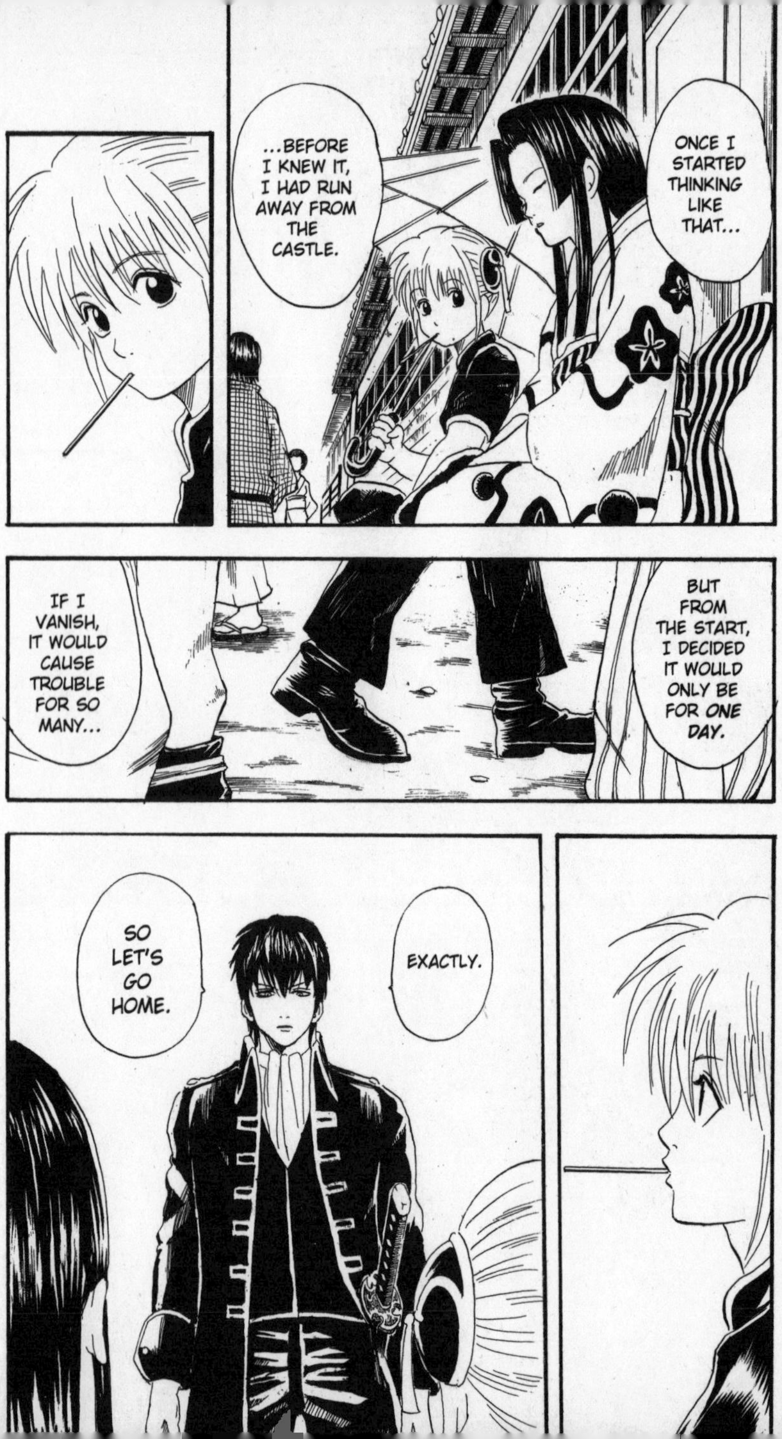
ONCE I STARTED THINKING LIKE THAT...
...BEFORE I KNEW IT, I HAD RUN AWAY FROM THE CASTLE.
BUT FROM THE START, I DECIDED IT WOULD ONLY BE FOR ONE DAY.
IF I VANISH, IT WOULD CAUSE TROUBLE FOR SO MANY...
EXACTLY.
SO LET'S GO HOME.

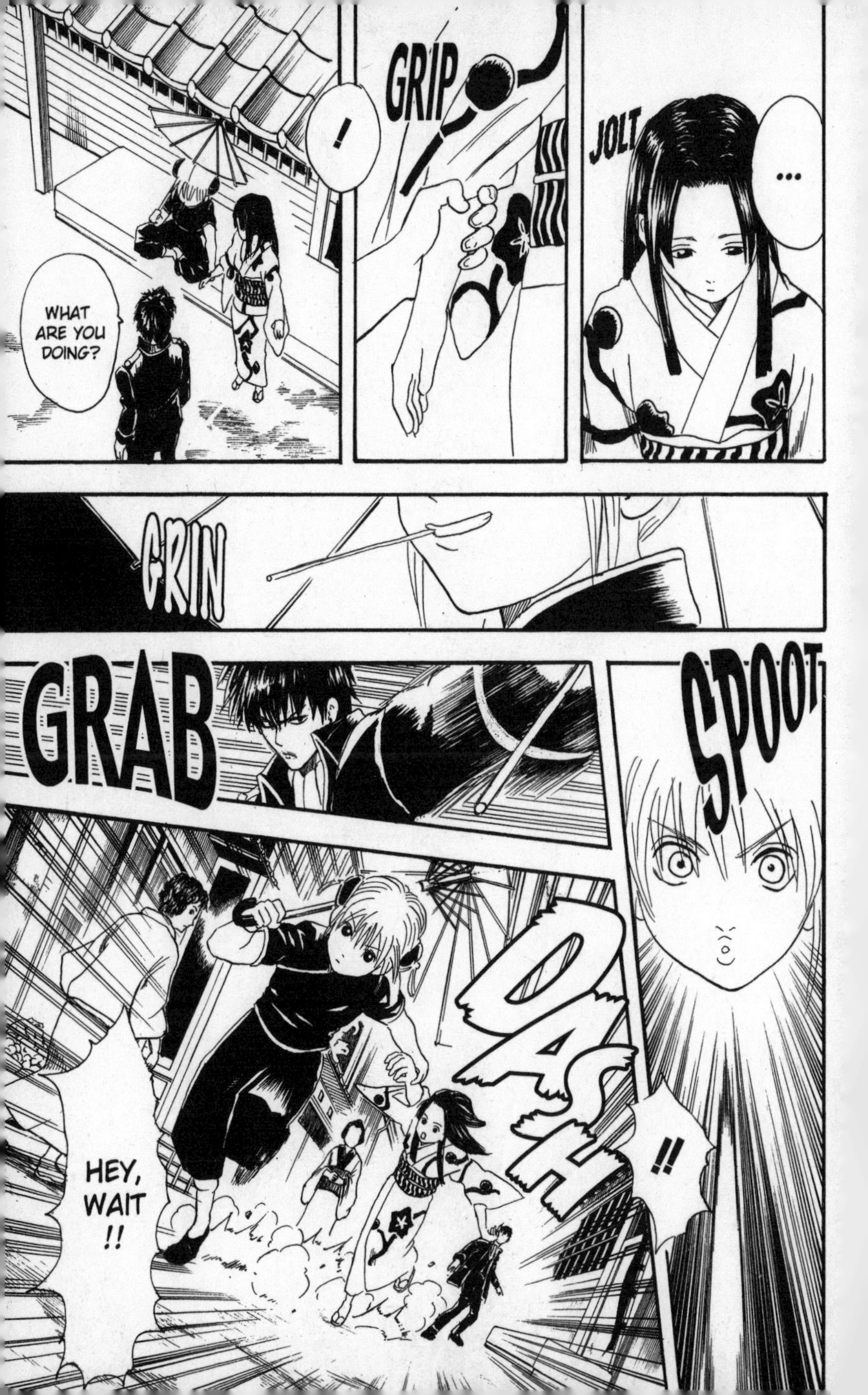
JOLT
...
GRIP
!
WHAT ARE YOU DOING?
GRIN
SPOOT
GRAB
DASH!!
HEY, WAIT!!

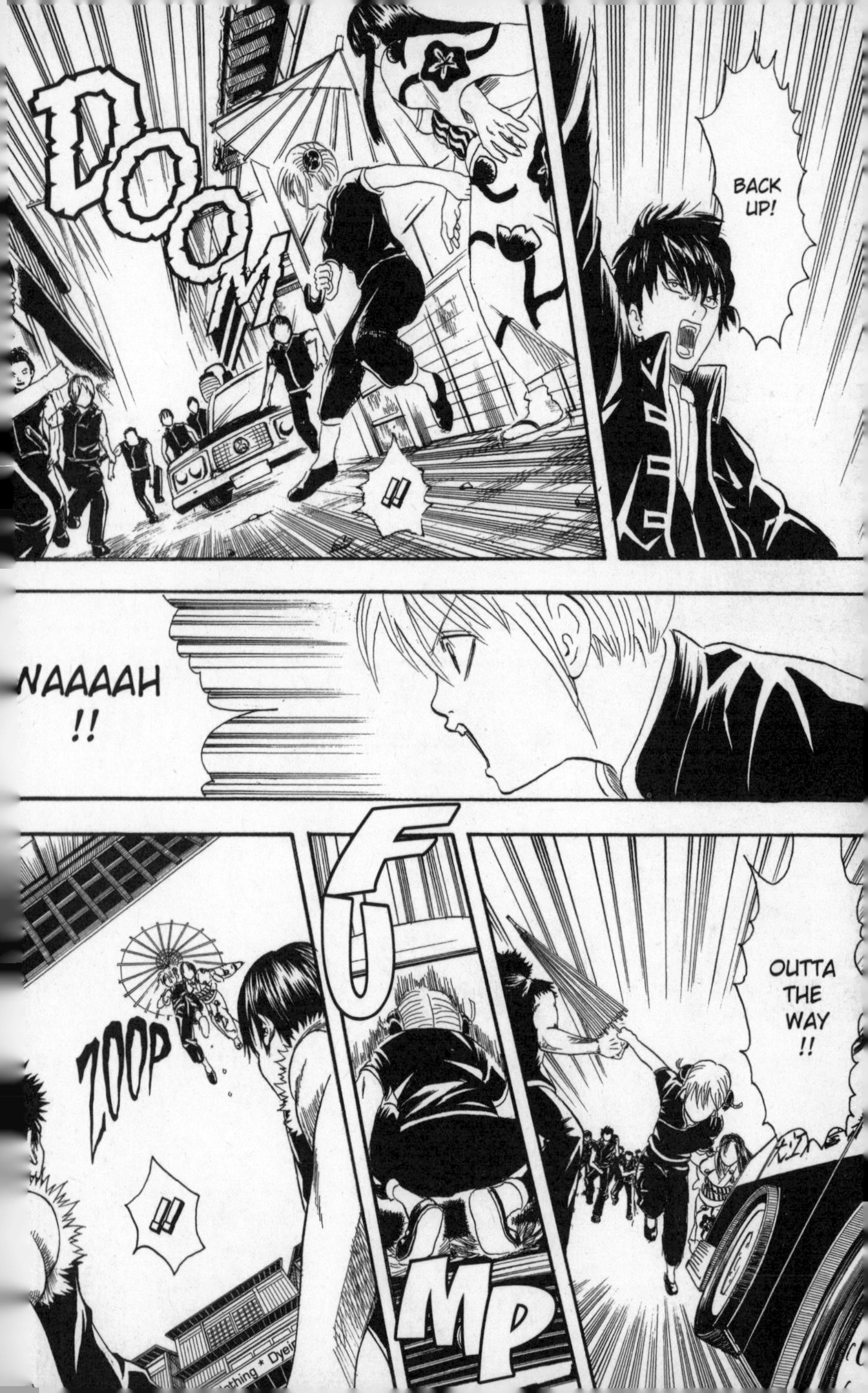
BACK UP!
DOOM
!!
NAAAAH !!
OUTTA THE WAY !!
FUMP
ZOOP
!!

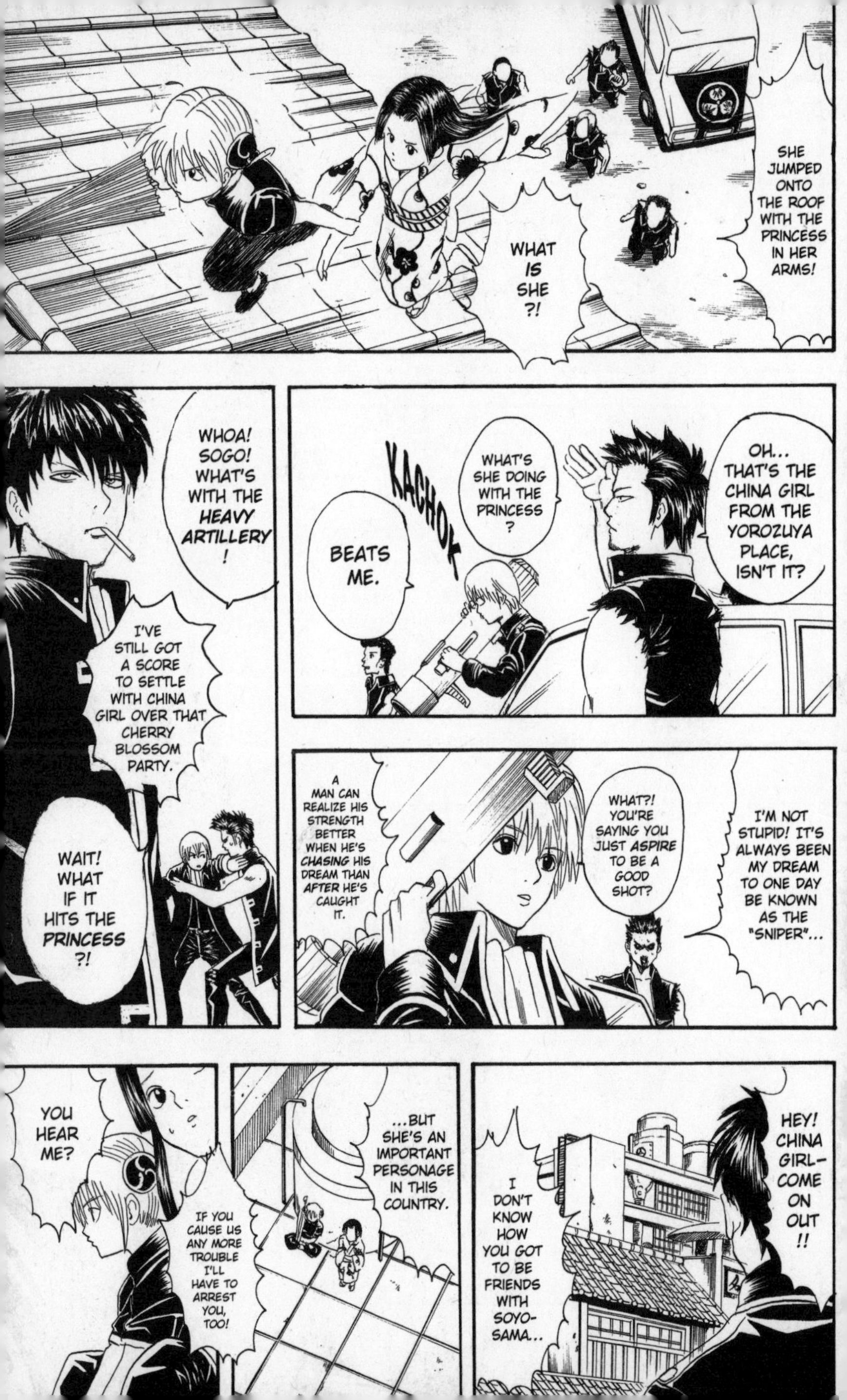
SHE JUMPED ONTO THE ROOF WITH THE PRINCESS IN HER ARMS!
WHAT IS SHE ?!
OH... THAT'S THE CHINA GIRL FROM THE YOROZUYA PLACE, ISN'T IT?
WHAT'S SHE DOING WITH THE PRINCESS ?
KACHOK
BEATS ME.
I'M NOT STUPID! IT'S ALWAYS BEEN MY DREAM TO ONE DAY BE KNOWN AS THE "SNIPER"...
WHAT?! YOU'RE SAYING YOU JUST ASPIRE TO BE A GOOD SHOT?
A MAN CAN REALIZE HIS STRENGTH BETTER WHEN HE'S CHASING HIS DREAM THAN AFTER HE'S CAUGHT IT.
WHOA! SOGO! WHAT'S WITH THE HEAVY ARTILLERY !
I'VE STILL GOT A SCORE TO SETTLE WITH CHINA GIRL OVER THAT CHERRY BLOSSOM PARTY.
WAIT! WHAT IF IT HITS THE PRINCESS ?!
HEY! CHINA GIRL— COME ON OUT !!
I DON'T KNOW HOW YOU GOT TO BE FRIENDS WITH SOYO-SAMA...
...BUT SHE'S AN IMPORTANT PERSONAGE IN THIS COUNTRY.
IF YOU CAUSE US ANY MORE TROUBLE I'LL HAVE TO ARREST YOU, TOO!
YOU HEAR ME?

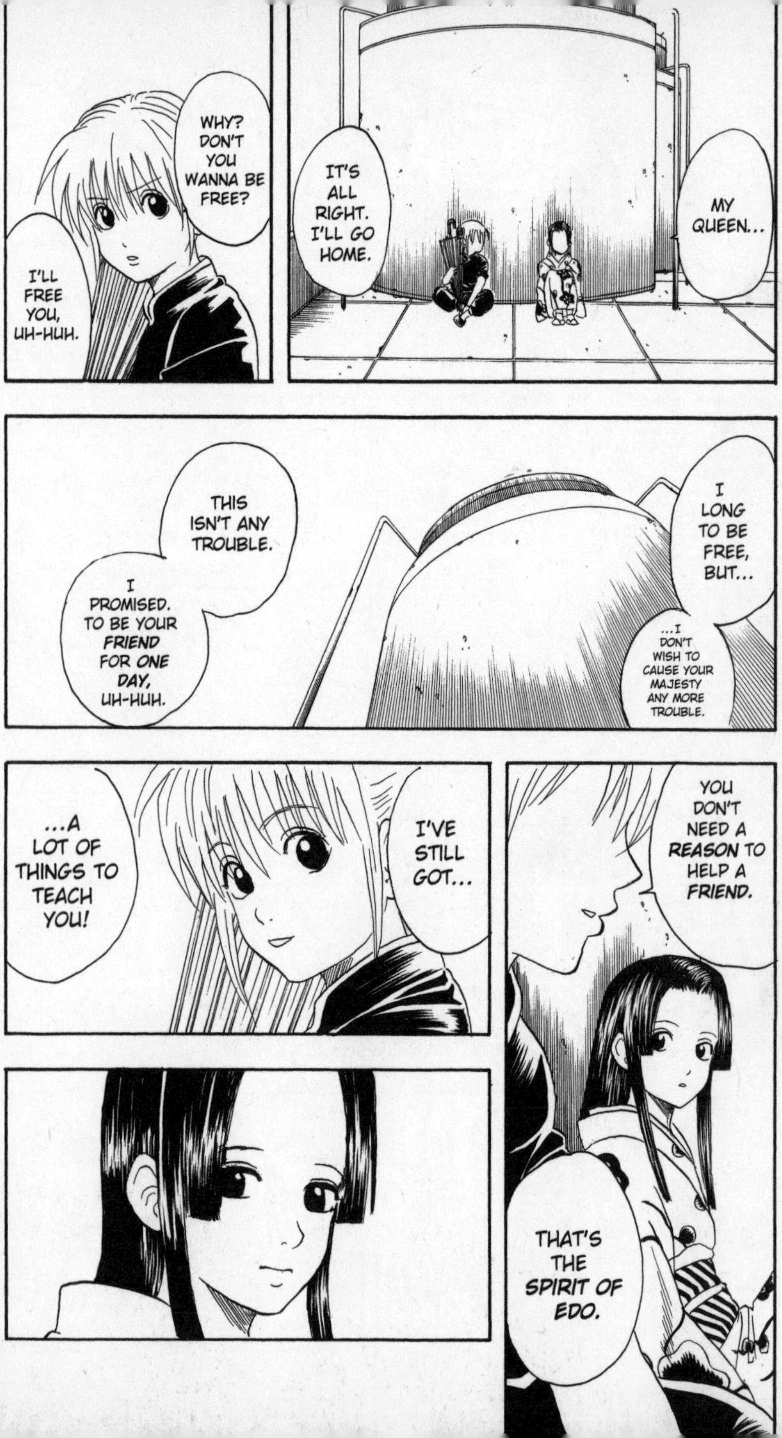
MY QUEEN...
IT'S ALL RIGHT. I'LL GO HOME.
WHY? DON'T YOU WANNA BE FREE?
I'LL FREE YOU, UH-HUH.
I LONG TO BE FREE, BUT...
...I DON'T WISH TO CAUSE YOUR MAJESTY ANY MORE TROUBLE.
THIS ISN'T ANY TROUBLE.
I PROMISED. TO BE YOUR FRIEND FOR ONE DAY, UH-HUH.
YOU DON'T NEED A REASON TO HELP A FRIEND.
THAT'S THE SPIRIT OF EDO.
I'VE STILL GOT...
...A LOT OF THINGS TO TEACH YOU!

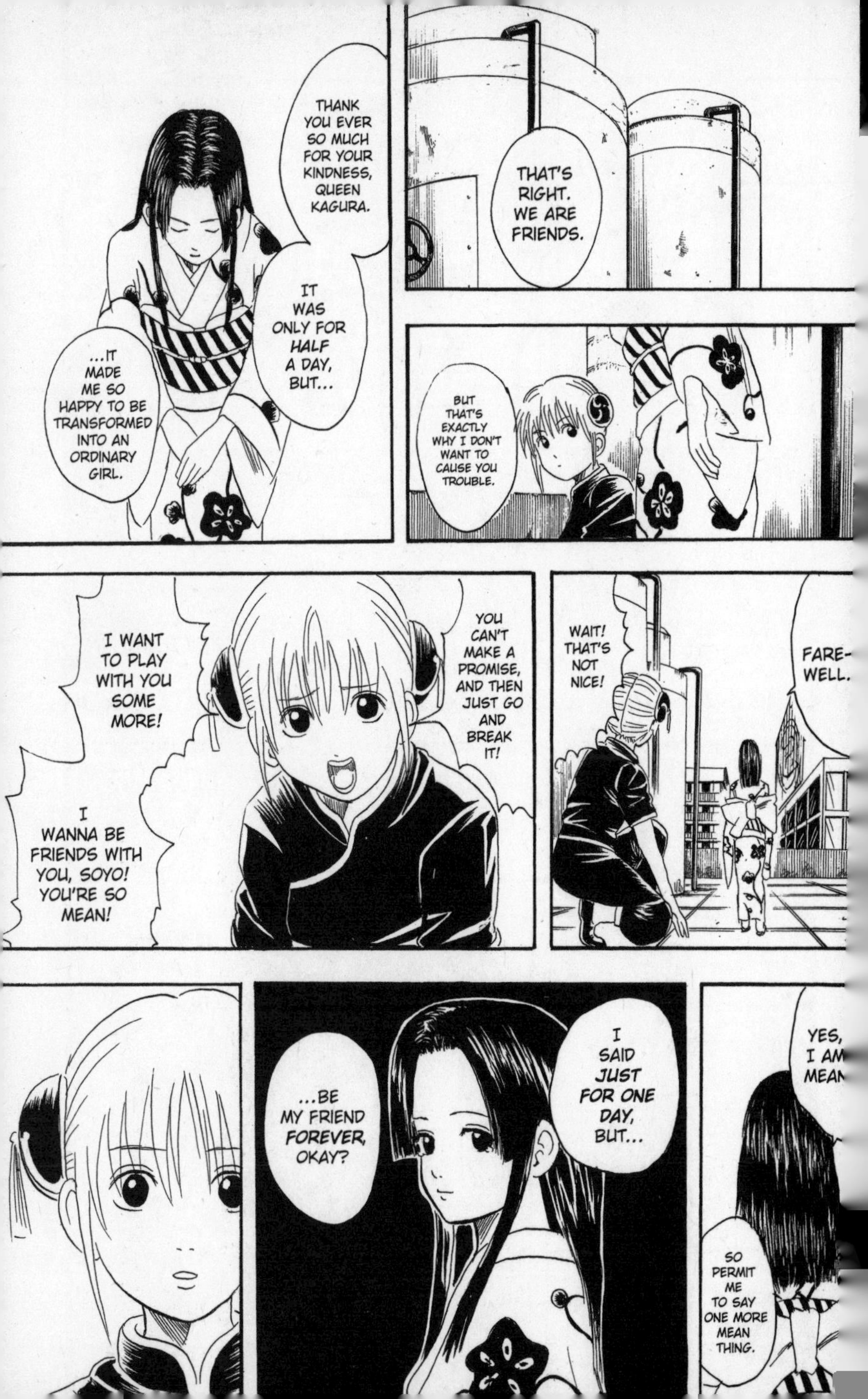
THAT'S RIGHT. WE ARE FRIENDS.
BUT THAT'S EXACTLY WHY I DON'T WANT TO CAUSE YOU TROUBLE.
THANK YOU EVER SO MUCH FOR YOUR KINDNESS, QUEEN KAGURA.
IT WAS ONLY FOR HALF A DAY, BUT...
...IT MADE ME SO HAPPY TO BE TRANSFORMED INTO AN ORDINARY GIRL.
FARE-WELL.
WAIT! THAT'S NOT NICE!
YOU CAN'T MAKE A PROMISE, AND THEN JUST GO AND BREAK IT!
I WANT TO PLAY WITH YOU SOME MORE!
I WANNA BE FRIENDS WITH YOU, SOYO! YOU'RE SO MEAN!
YES, I AM MEAN
SO PERMIT ME TO SAY ONE MORE MEAN THING.
I SAID JUST FOR ONE DAY, BUT...
...BE MY FRIEND FOREVER, OKAY?

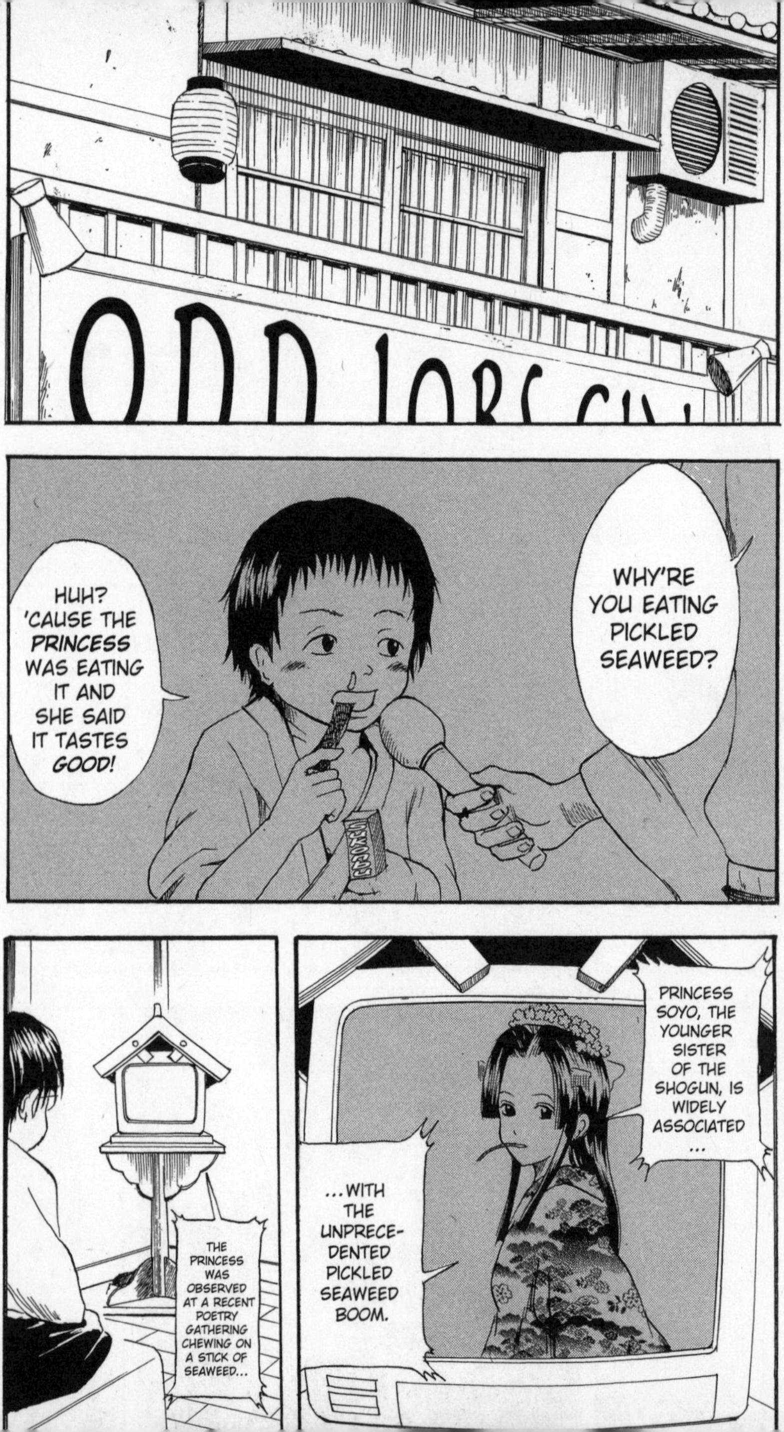
WHY'RE YOU EATING PICKLED SEAWEED?
HUH? 'CAUSE THE *PRINCESS* WAS EATING IT AND SHE SAID IT TASTES *GOOD!*
PRINCESS SOYO, THE YOUNGER SISTER OF THE SHOGUN, IS WIDELY ASSOCIATED ...
...WITH THE UNPRECE-DENTED PICKLED SEAWEED BOOM.
THE PRINCESS WAS OBSERVED AT A RECENT POETRY GATHERING CHEWING ON A STICK OF SEAWEED...

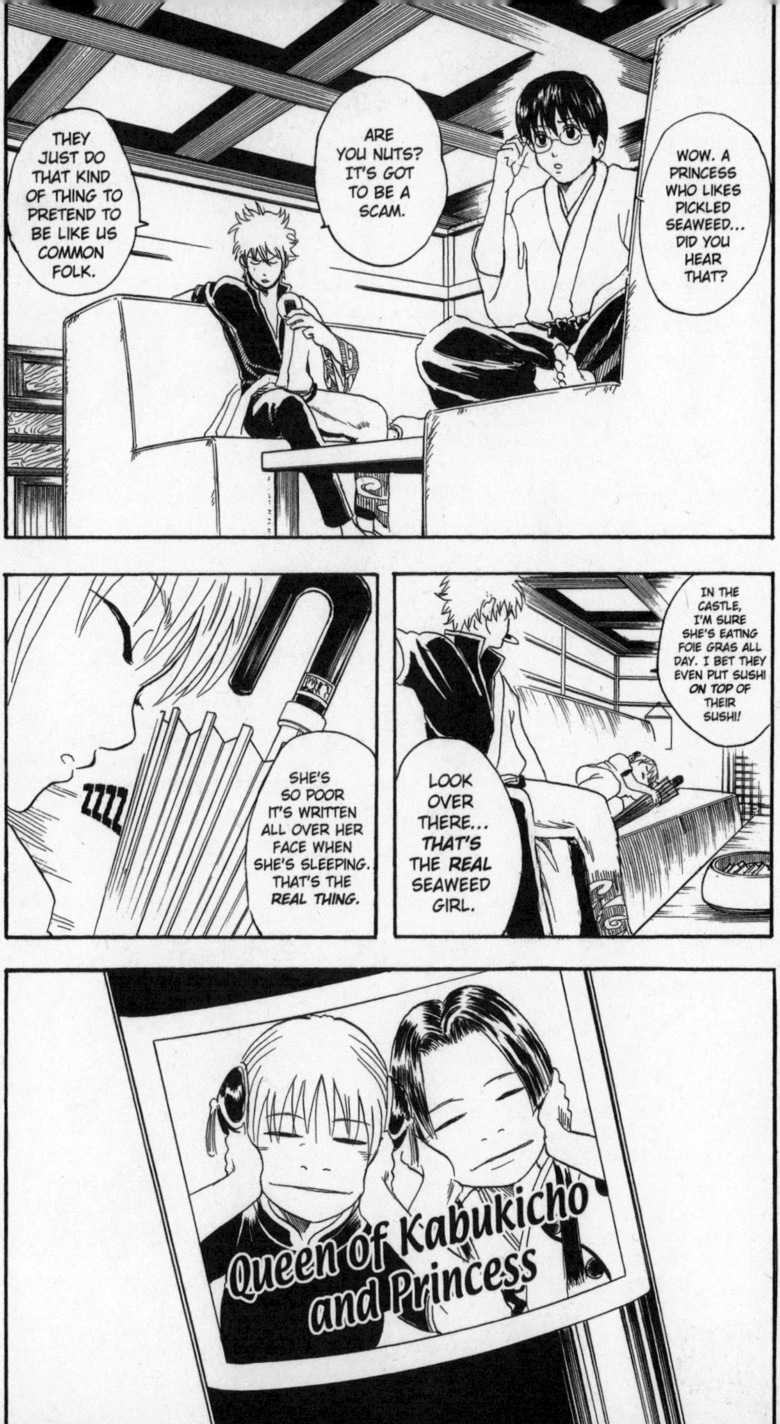
WOW. A PRINCESS WHO LIKES PICKLED SEAWEED... DID YOU HEAR THAT?
ARE YOU NUTS? IT'S GOT TO BE A SCAM.
THEY JUST DO THAT KIND OF THING TO PRETEND TO BE LIKE US COMMON FOLK.
IN THE CASTLE, I'M SURE SHE'S EATING FOIE GRAS ALL DAY. I BET THEY EVEN PUT SUSHI ON TOP OF THEIR SUSHI!
LOOK OVER THERE... *THAT'S* THE *REAL* SEAWEED GIRL.
SHE'S SO POOR IT'S WRITTEN ALL OVER HER FACE WHEN SHE'S SLEEPING. THAT'S THE *REAL THING.*
ZZZZ
Queen of Kabukicho and Princess

Thank you very much for purchasing Gin Tama volume 4. The manga has already been published for one year now. When I came to town and paid a visit to the editorial department just about a year ago, the Editor in Chief told me, "You're still young. You'll have another chance." Basically, he was saying I'd be put to death before I even got started. Also, at the New Year's party, I got pushed around by some hotshots. But take a look at this now, Mr. Hotshots, huh? Volume 4 is already out, see? You were all wrong, folks. (heh heh)

All right, everyone, your long-awaited special edition Q&A section will start in this volume.

Please read on.
sorachi

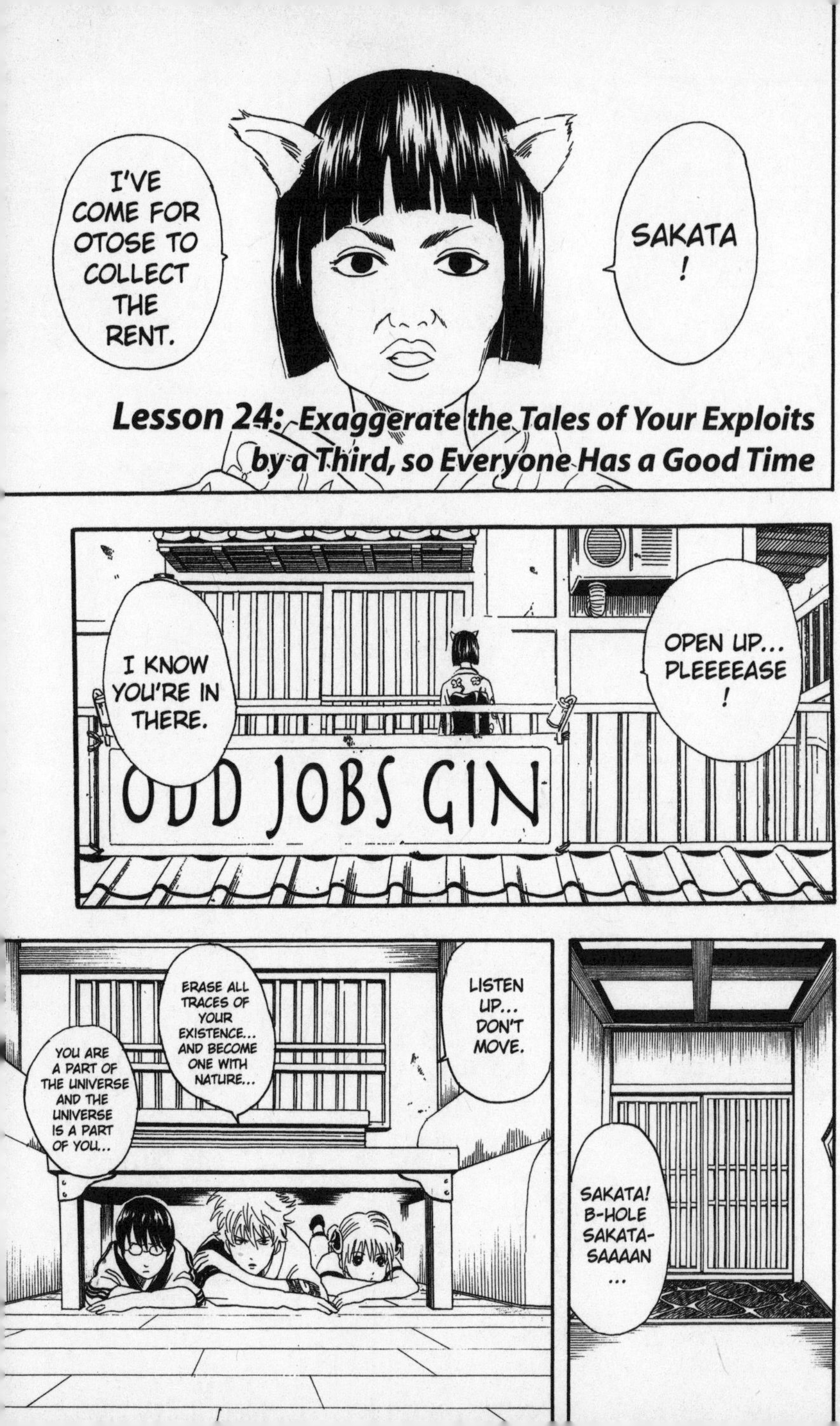
SAKATA !
I'VE COME FOR OTOSE TO COLLECT THE RENT.
Lesson 24: Exaggerate the Tales of Your Exploits by a Third, so Everyone Has a Good Time
OPEN UP... PLEEEEASE !
I KNOW YOU'RE IN THERE.
ODD JOBS GIN
SAKATA! B-HOLE SAKATA-SAAAAN ...
LISTEN UP... DON'T MOVE.
ERASE ALL TRACES OF YOUR EXISTENCE... AND BECOME ONE WITH NATURE...
YOU ARE A PART OF THE UNIVERSE AND THE UNIVERSE IS A PART OF YOU...

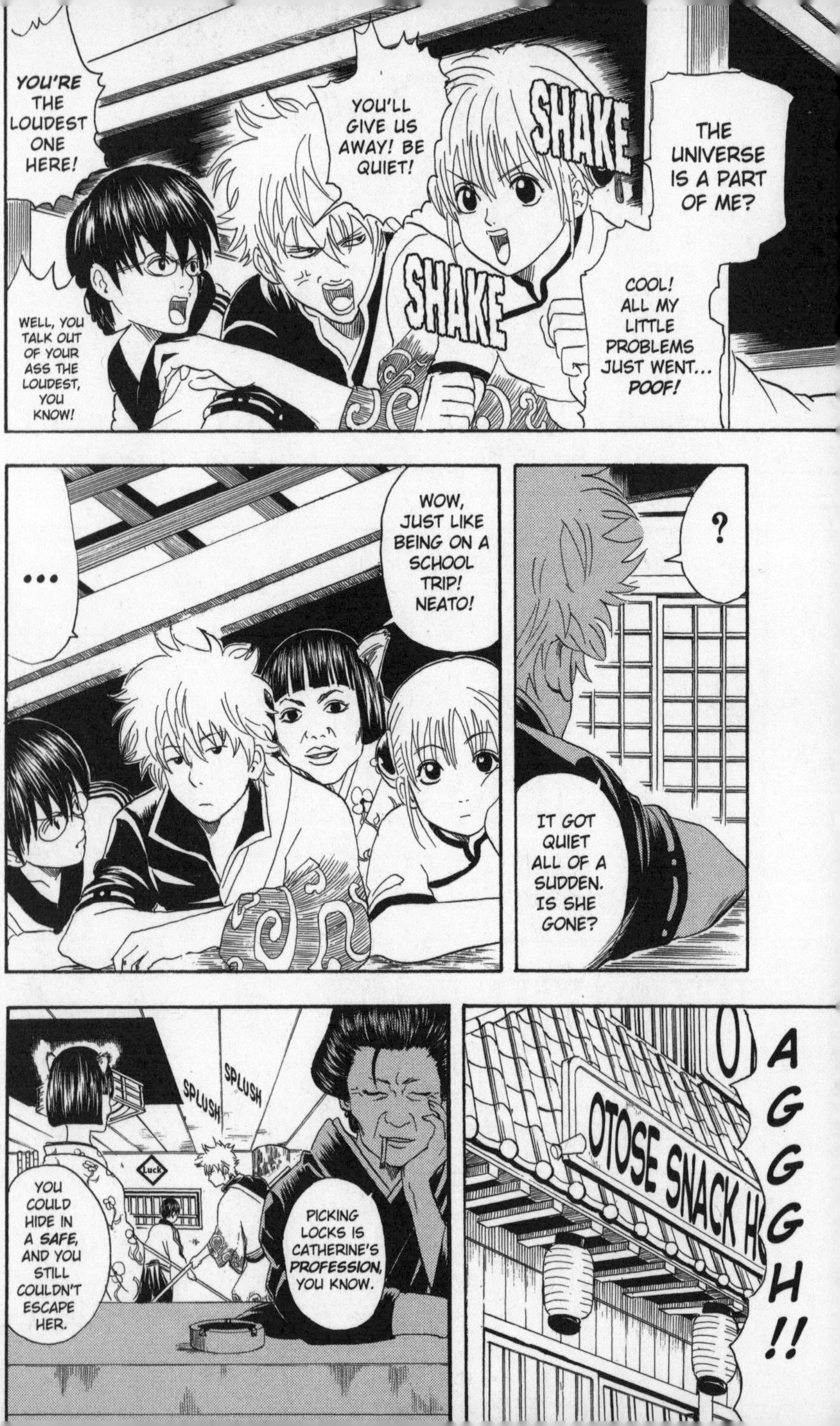
THE UNIVERSE IS A PART OF ME?
SHAKE
COOL! ALL MY LITTLE PROBLEMS JUST WENT... *POOF!*
YOU'LL GIVE US AWAY! BE QUIET!
SHAKE
YOU'RE THE LOUDEST ONE HERE!
WELL, YOU TALK OUT OF YOUR ASS THE LOUDEST, YOU KNOW!
?
IT GOT QUIET ALL OF A SUDDEN. IS SHE GONE?
WOW, JUST LIKE BEING ON A SCHOOL TRIP! NEATO!
...
OTOSE SNACK H
AGGGGH!!
PICKING LOCKS IS CATHERINE'S *PROFESSION*, YOU KNOW.
SPLUSH
SPLUSH
Luck
YOU COULD HIDE IN A *SAFE*, AND YOU STILL COULDN'T ESCAPE HER.

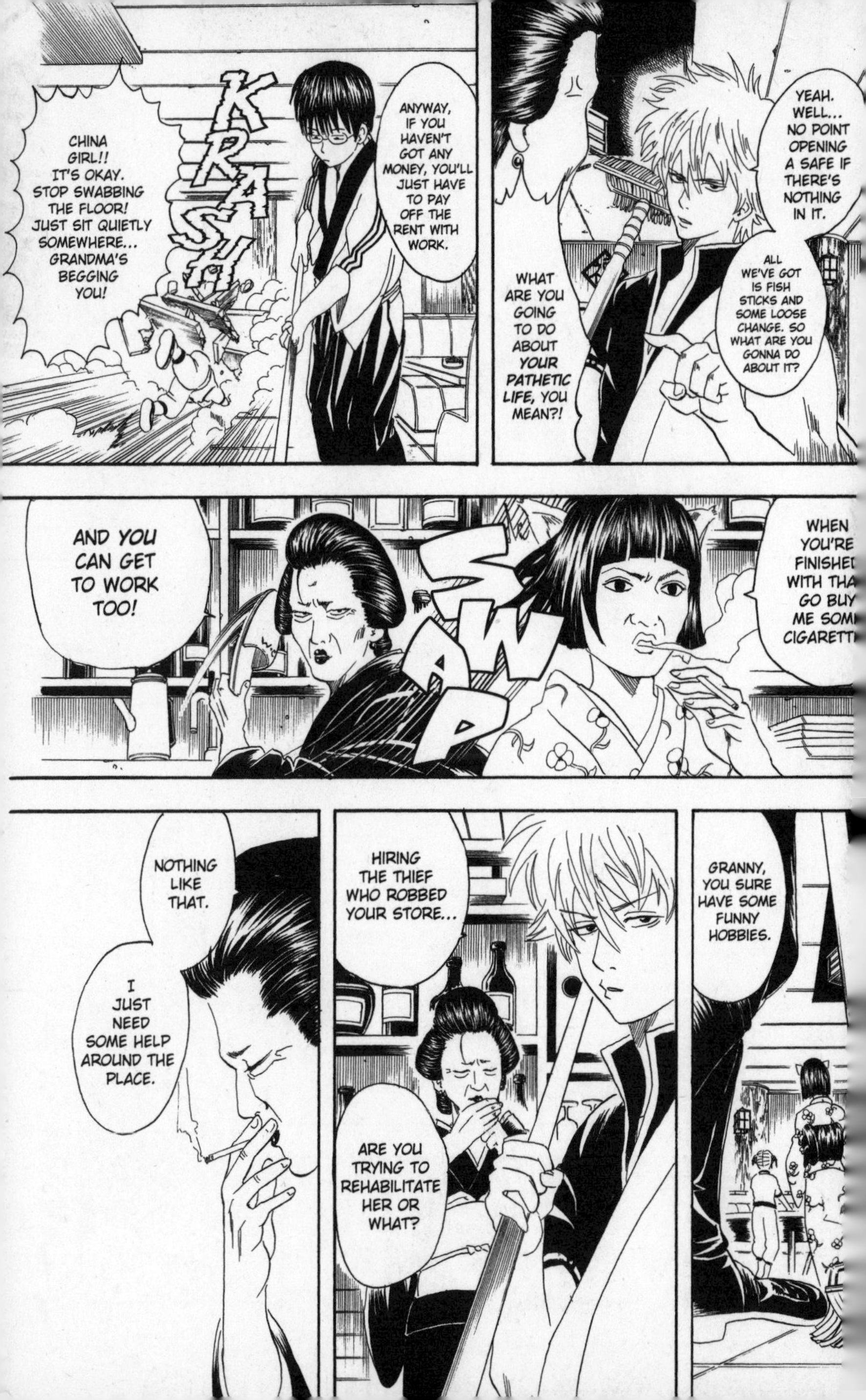
YEAH. WELL... NO POINT OPENING A SAFE IF THERE'S NOTHING IN IT.
ALL WE'VE GOT IS FISH STICKS AND SOME LOOSE CHANGE. SO WHAT ARE YOU GONNA DO ABOUT IT?
WHAT ARE YOU GOING TO DO ABOUT *YOUR* PATHETIC LIFE, YOU MEAN?!
ANYWAY, IF YOU HAVEN'T GOT ANY MONEY, YOU'LL JUST HAVE TO PAY OFF THE RENT WITH WORK.
KRASH
CHINA GIRL!! IT'S OKAY. STOP SWABBING THE FLOOR! JUST SIT QUIETLY SOMEWHERE... GRANDMA'S BEGGING YOU!
WHEN YOU'RE FINISHED WITH THA GO BUY ME SOM CIGARETT
SWAP
AND *YOU* CAN GET TO WORK TOO!
GRANNY, YOU SURE HAVE SOME FUNNY HOBBIES.
HIRING THE THIEF WHO ROBBED YOUR STORE...
ARE YOU TRYING TO REHABILITATE HER OR WHAT?
NOTHING LIKE THAT.
I JUST NEED SOME HELP AROUND THE PLACE.

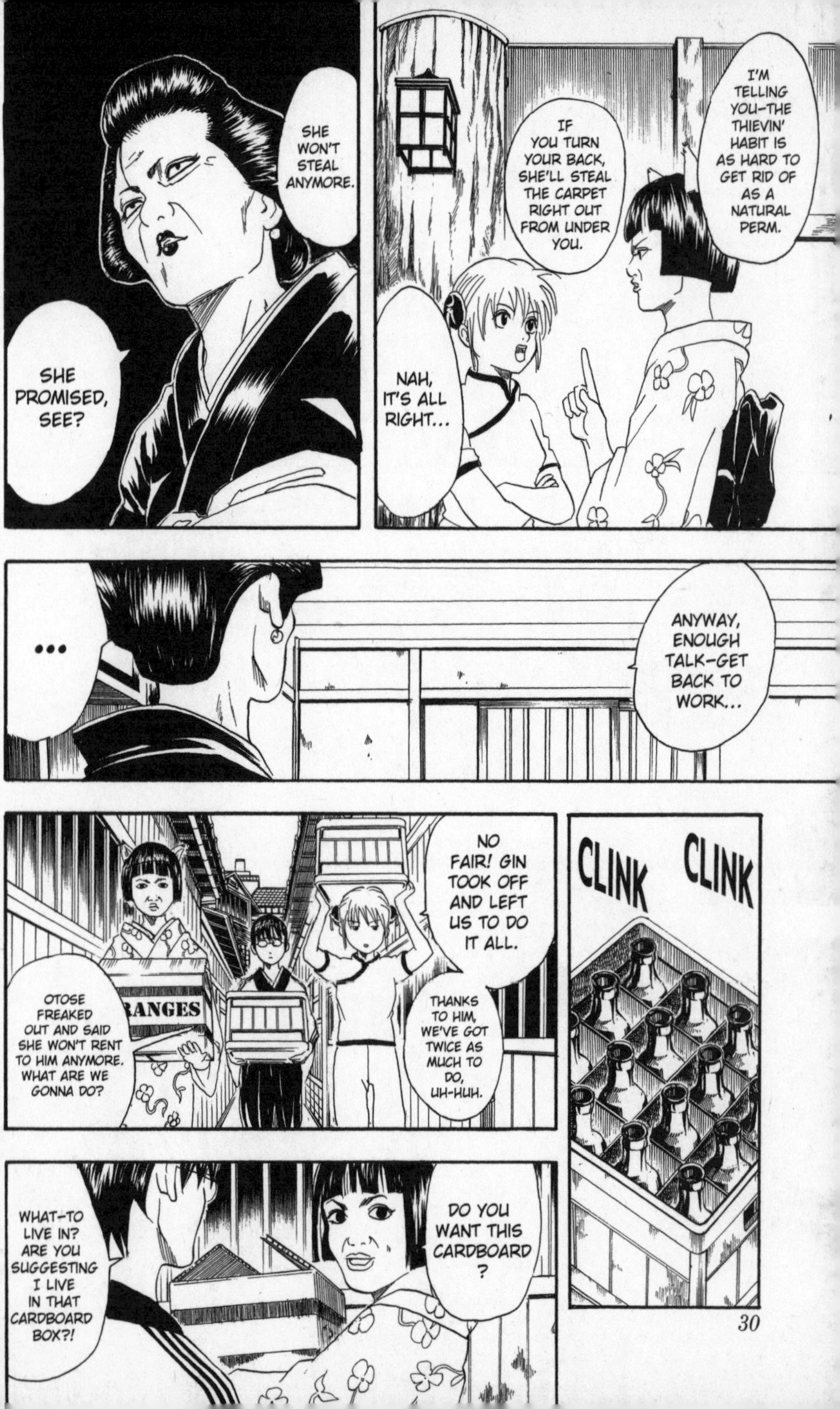
I'M TELLING YOU—THE THIEVIN' HABIT IS AS HARD TO GET RID OF AS A NATURAL PERM.
IF YOU TURN YOUR BACK, SHE'LL STEAL THE CARPET RIGHT OUT FROM UNDER YOU.
NAH, IT'S ALL RIGHT...
SHE WON'T STEAL ANYMORE.
SHE PROMISED, SEE?
ANYWAY, ENOUGH TALK—GET BACK TO WORK...
...
CLINK
CLINK
NO FAIR! GIN TOOK OFF AND LEFT US TO DO IT ALL.
THANKS TO HIM, WE'VE GOT TWICE AS MUCH TO DO, UH-HUH.
OTOSE FREAKED OUT AND SAID SHE WON'T RENT TO HIM ANYMORE. WHAT ARE WE GONNA DO?
DO YOU WANT THIS CARDBOARD ?
WHAT—TO LIVE IN? ARE YOU SUGGESTING I LIVE IN THAT CARDBOARD BOX?!

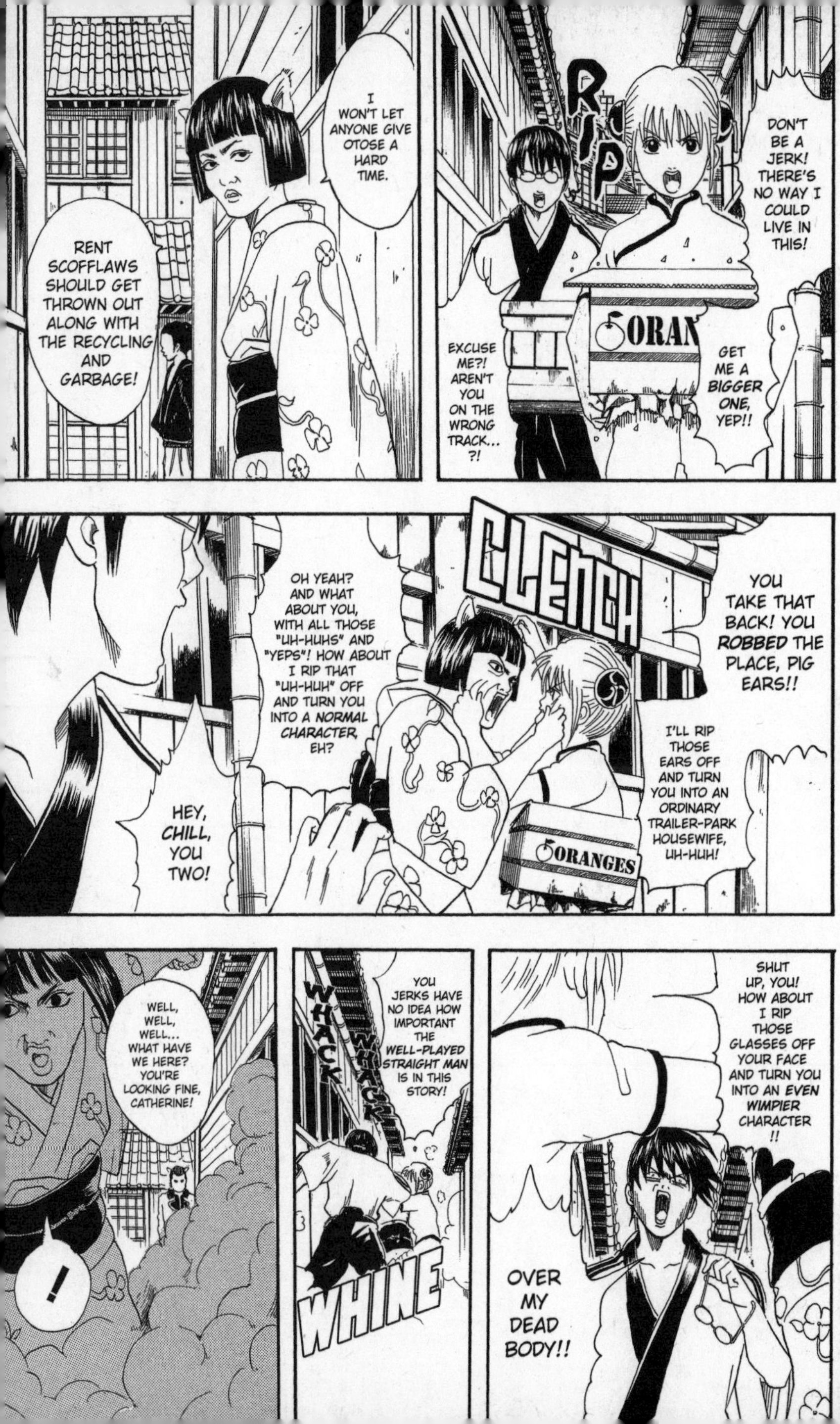
RIP
DON'T BE A JERK! THERE'S NO WAY I COULD LIVE IN THIS!
ORAN
GET ME A BIGGER ONE, YEP!!
EXCUSE ME?! AREN'T YOU ON THE WRONG TRACK...?!
I WON'T LET ANYONE GIVE OTOSE A HARD TIME.
RENT SCOFFLAWS SHOULD GET THROWN OUT ALONG WITH THE RECYCLING AND GARBAGE!
CLENCH
YOU TAKE THAT BACK! YOU ROBBED THE PLACE, PIG EARS!!
I'LL RIP THOSE EARS OFF AND TURN YOU INTO AN ORDINARY TRAILER-PARK HOUSEWIFE, UH-HUH!
ORANGES
OH YEAH? AND WHAT ABOUT YOU, WITH ALL THOSE "UH-HUHS" AND "YEPS"! HOW ABOUT I RIP THAT "UH-HUH" OFF AND TURN YOU INTO A NORMAL CHARACTER, EH?
HEY, CHILL, YOU TWO!
SHUT UP, YOU! HOW ABOUT I RIP THOSE GLASSES OFF YOUR FACE AND TURN YOU INTO AN EVEN WIMPIER CHARACTER!!
OVER MY DEAD BODY!!
WHACK
WHACK
YOU JERKS HAVE NO IDEA HOW IMPORTANT THE WELL-PLAYED STRAIGHT MAN IS IN THIS STORY!
WHINE
WELL, WELL, WELL... WHAT HAVE WE HERE? YOU'RE LOOKING FINE, CATHERINE!
!

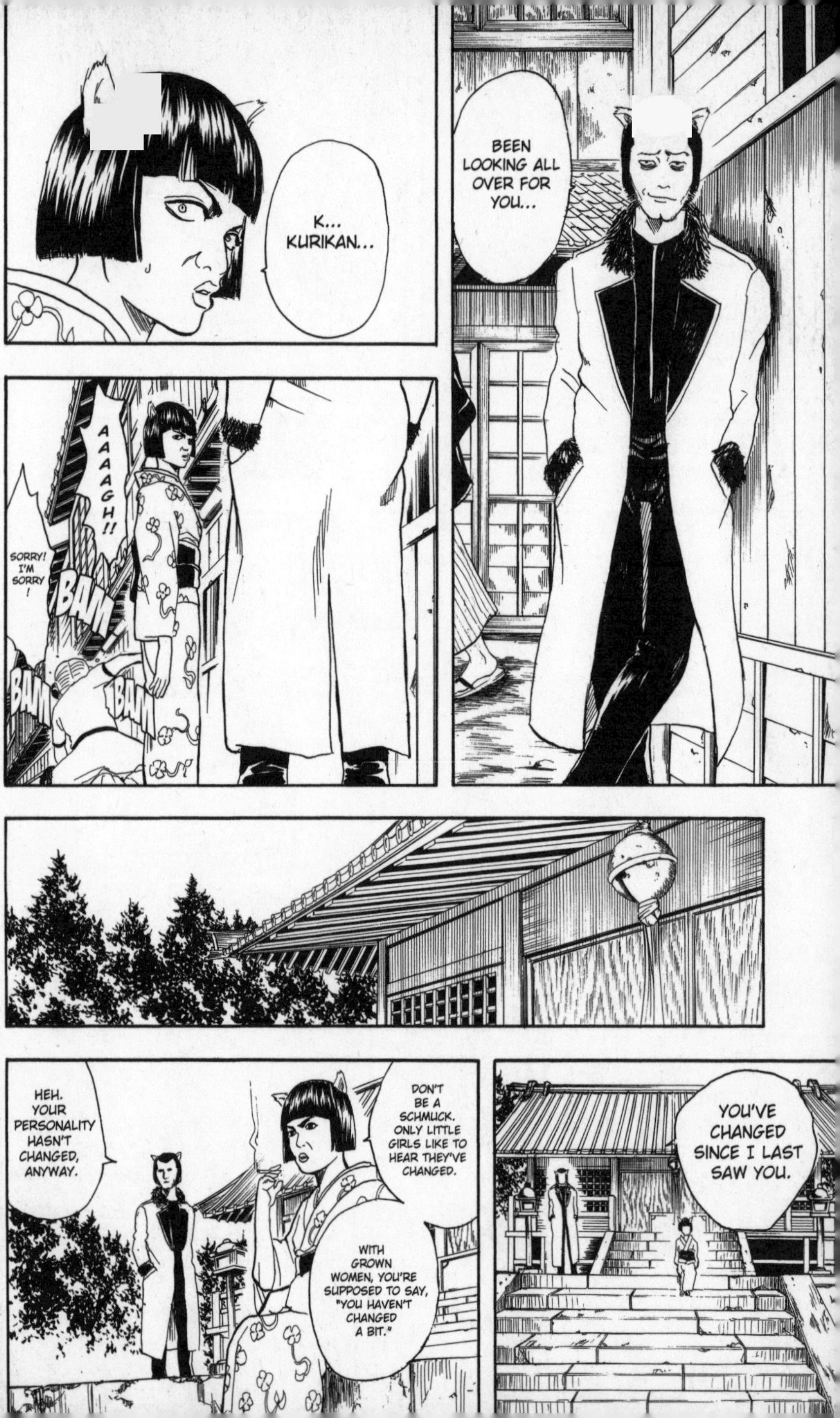
BEEN LOOKING ALL OVER FOR YOU...
K... KURIKAN...
AAAAAGH!!
SORRY! I'M SORRY!
BAM
BAM
BAM
YOU'VE CHANGED SINCE I LAST SAW YOU.
DON'T BE A SCHMUCK. ONLY LITTLE GIRLS LIKE TO HEAR THEY'VE CHANGED.
WITH GROWN WOMEN, YOU'RE SUPPOSED TO SAY, "YOU HAVEN'T CHANGED A BIT."
HEH. YOUR PERSONALITY HASN'T CHANGED, ANYWAY.

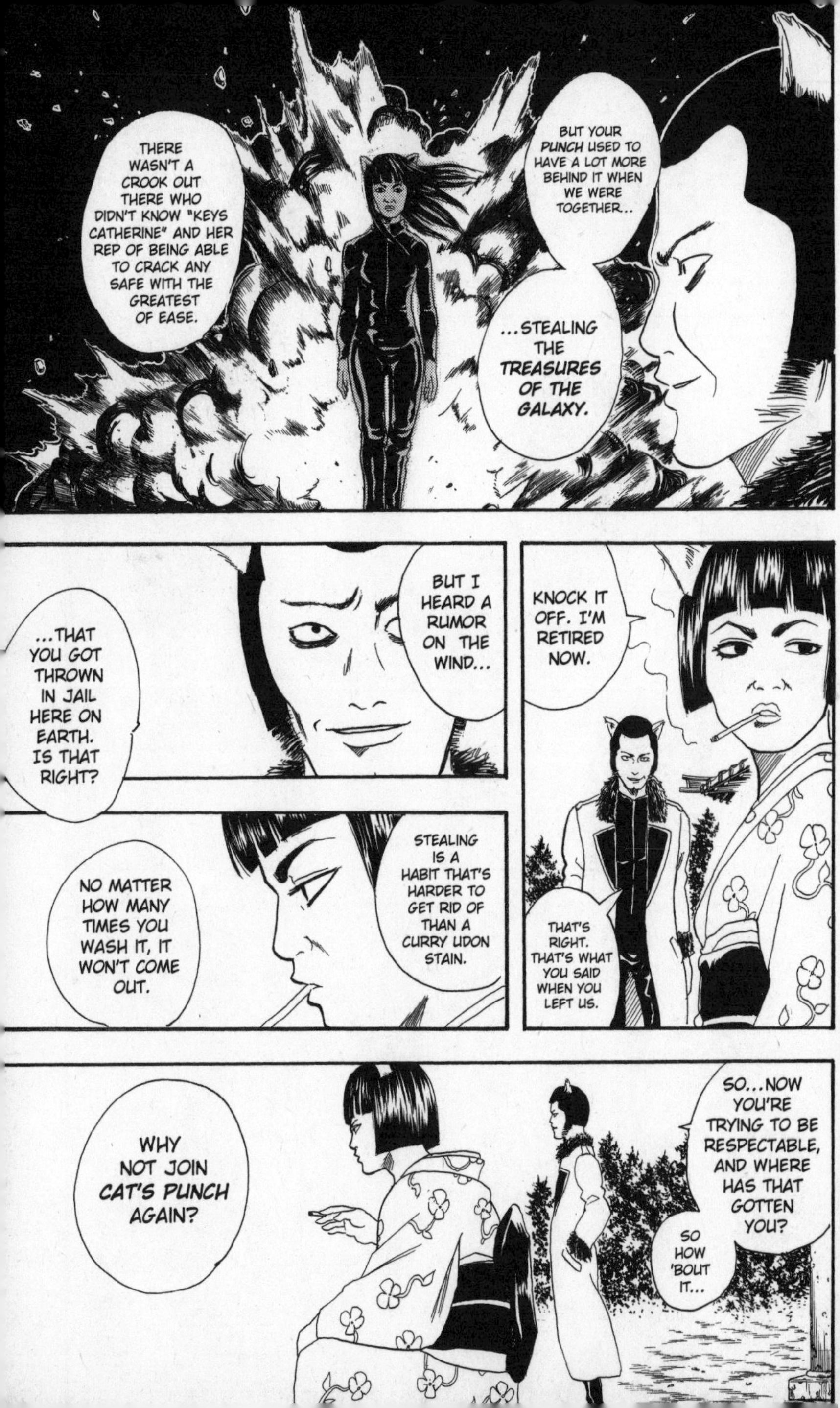
BUT YOUR PUNCH USED TO HAVE A LOT MORE BEHIND IT WHEN WE WERE TOGETHER...
...STEALING THE TREASURES OF THE GALAXY.
THERE WASN'T A CROOK OUT THERE WHO DIDN'T KNOW "KEYS CATHERINE" AND HER REP OF BEING ABLE TO CRACK ANY SAFE WITH THE GREATEST OF EASE.
KNOCK IT OFF. I'M RETIRED NOW.
THAT'S RIGHT. THAT'S WHAT YOU SAID WHEN YOU LEFT US.
BUT I HEARD A RUMOR ON THE WIND...
...THAT YOU GOT THROWN IN JAIL HERE ON EARTH. IS THAT RIGHT?
STEALING IS A HABIT THAT'S HARDER TO GET RID OF THAN A CURRY UDON STAIN.
NO MATTER HOW MANY TIMES YOU WASH IT, IT WON'T COME OUT.
SO...NOW YOU'RE TRYING TO BE RESPECTABLE, AND WHERE HAS THAT GOTTEN YOU?
SO HOW 'BOUT IT...
WHY NOT JOIN CAT'S PUNCH AGAIN?

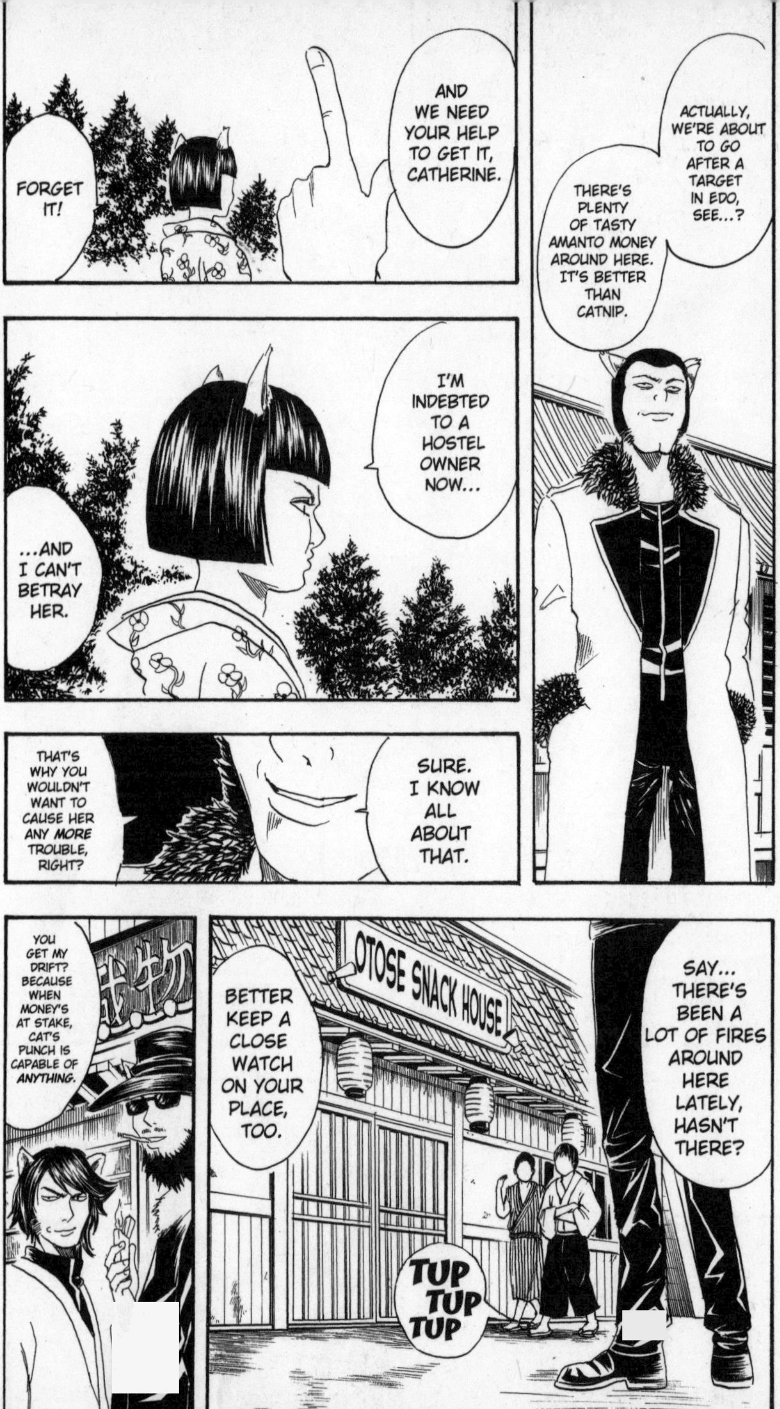
ACTUALLY, WE'RE ABOUT TO GO AFTER A TARGET IN EDO, SEE...?
THERE'S PLENTY OF TASTY AMANTO MONEY AROUND HERE. IT'S BETTER THAN CATNIP.
AND WE NEED YOUR HELP TO GET IT, CATHERINE.
FORGET IT!
I'M INDEBTED TO A HOSTEL OWNER NOW...
...AND I CAN'T BETRAY HER.
SURE. I KNOW ALL ABOUT THAT.
THAT'S WHY YOU WOULDN'T WANT TO CAUSE HER ANY *MORE* TROUBLE, RIGHT?
SAY... THERE'S BEEN A LOT OF FIRES AROUND HERE LATELY, HASN'T THERE?
OTOSE SNACK HOUSE
BETTER KEEP A CLOSE WATCH ON YOUR PLACE, TOO.
TUP TUP TUP
YOU GET MY DRIFT? BECAUSE WHEN MONEY'S AT STAKE, CAT'S PUNCH IS CAPABLE OF *ANYTHING*.

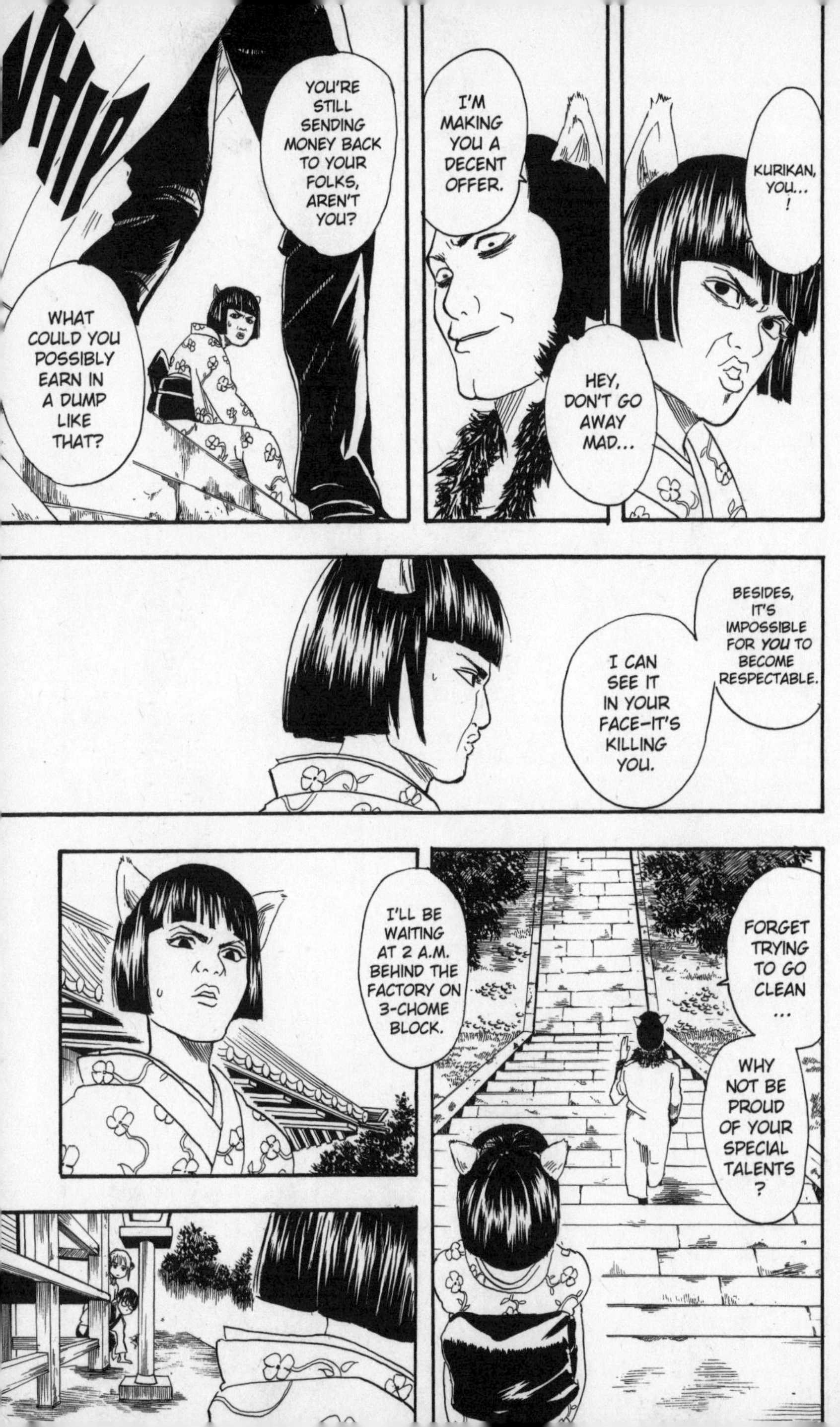
KURIKAN, YOU...!
HEY, DON'T GO AWAY MAD...
I'M MAKING YOU A DECENT OFFER.
YOU'RE STILL SENDING MONEY BACK TO YOUR FOLKS, AREN'T YOU?
WHAT COULD YOU POSSIBLY EARN IN A DUMP LIKE THAT?
BESIDES, IT'S IMPOSSIBLE FOR YOU TO BECOME RESPECTABLE.
I CAN SEE IT IN YOUR FACE—IT'S KILLING YOU.
FORGET TRYING TO GO CLEAN ...
WHY NOT BE PROUD OF YOUR SPECIAL TALENTS?
I'LL BE WAITING AT 2 A.M. BEHIND THE FACTORY ON 3-CHOME BLOCK.

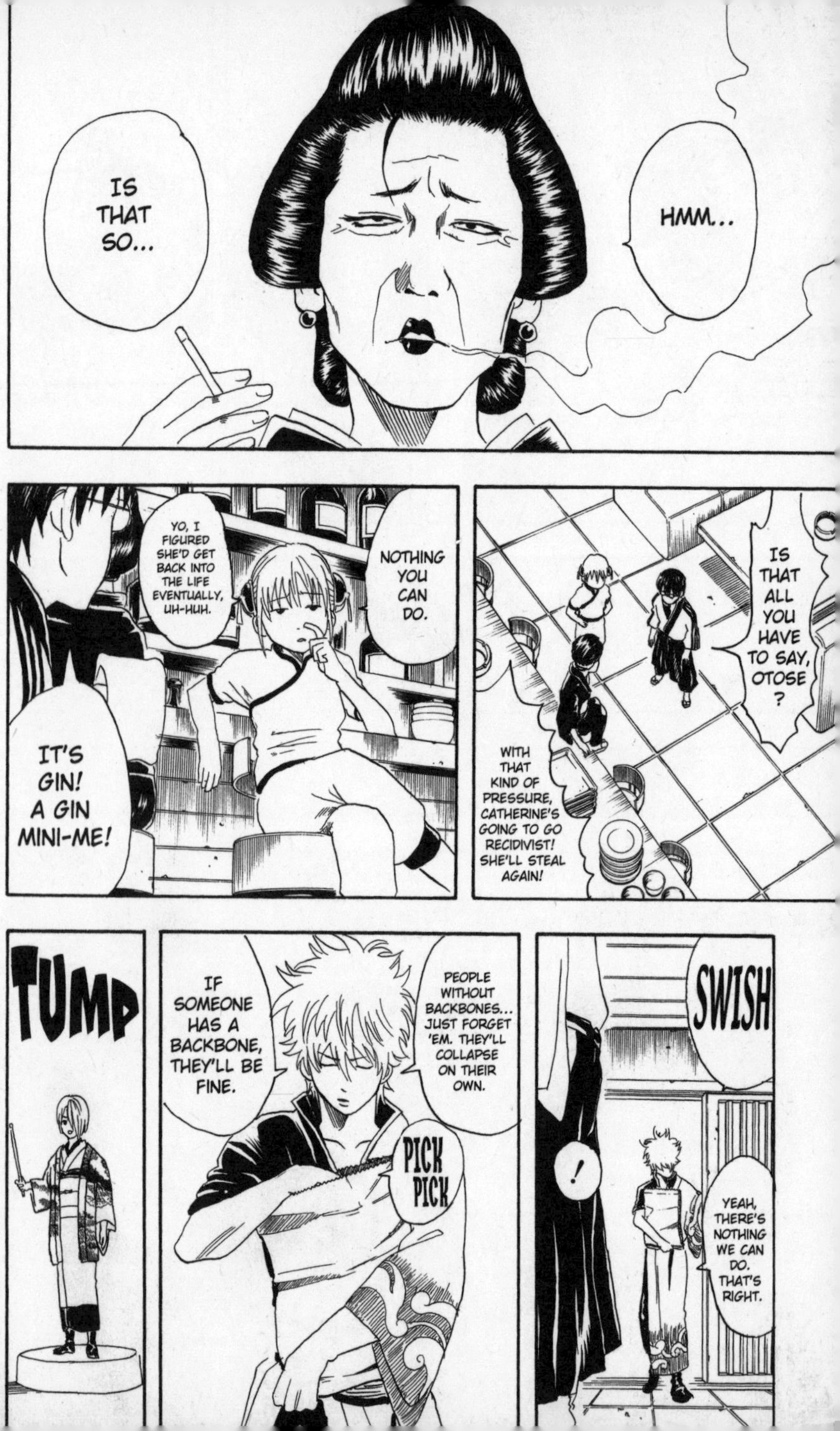
HMM...
IS THAT SO...
IS THAT ALL YOU HAVE TO SAY, OTOSE?
WITH THAT KIND OF PRESSURE, CATHERINE'S GOING TO GO RECIDIVIST! SHE'LL STEAL AGAIN!
NOTHING YOU CAN DO.
YO, I FIGURED SHE'D GET BACK INTO THE LIFE EVENTUALLY, UH-HUH.
IT'S GIN! A GIN MINI-ME!
SWISH
!
YEAH, THERE'S NOTHING WE CAN DO. THAT'S RIGHT.
PEOPLE WITHOUT BACKBONES... JUST FORGET 'EM. THEY'LL COLLAPSE ON THEIR OWN.
IF SOMEONE HAS A BACKBONE, THEY'LL BE FINE.
PICK PICK
TUMP

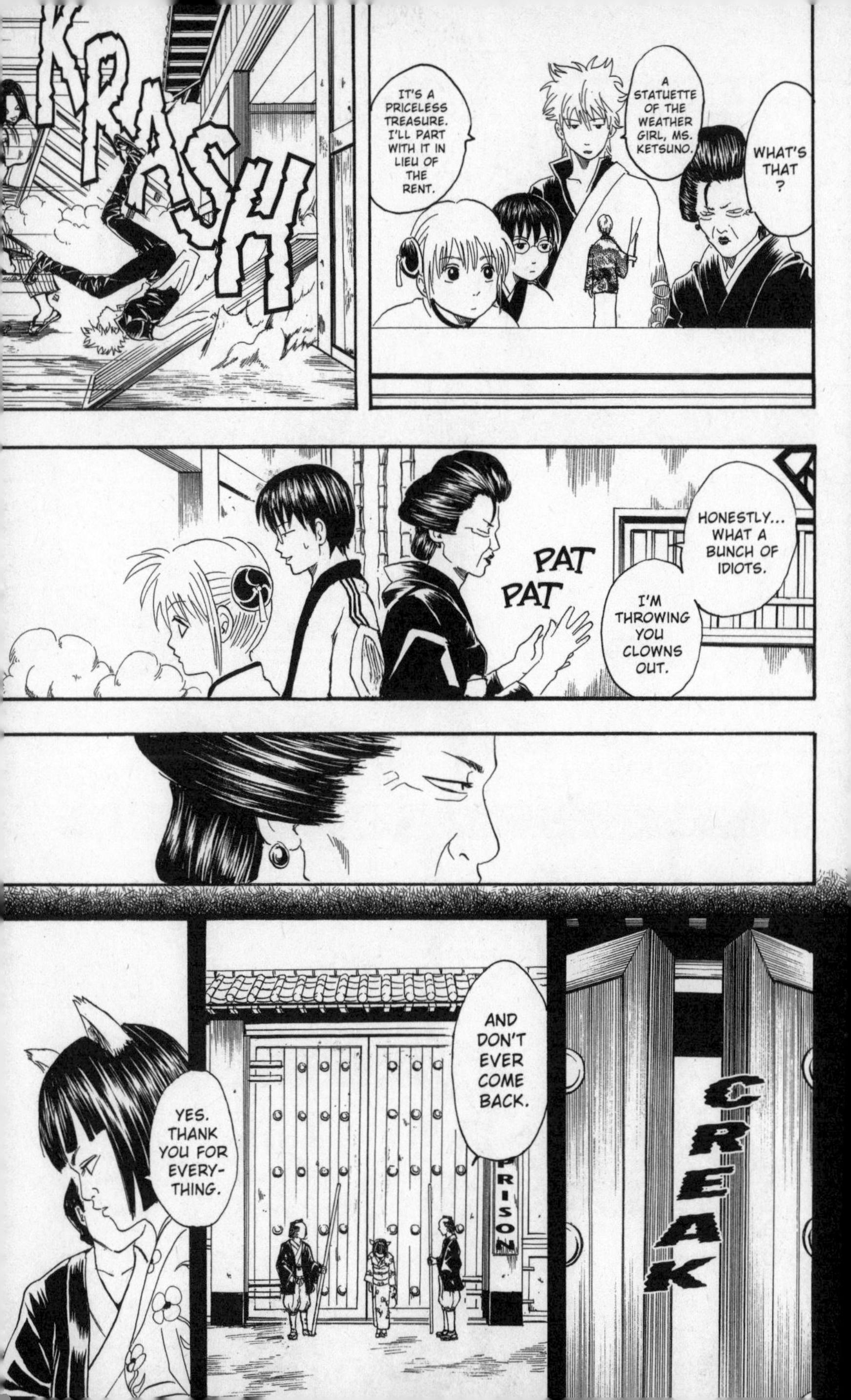
WHAT'S THAT?
A STATUETTE OF THE WEATHER GIRL, MS. KETSUNO.
IT'S A PRICELESS TREASURE. I'LL PART WITH IT IN LIEU OF THE RENT.
KRASH
HONESTLY... WHAT A BUNCH OF IDIOTS.
I'M THROWING YOU CLOWNS OUT.
PAT PAT
CREAK
AND DON'T EVER COME BACK.
PRISON
YES. THANK YOU FOR EVERY-THING.

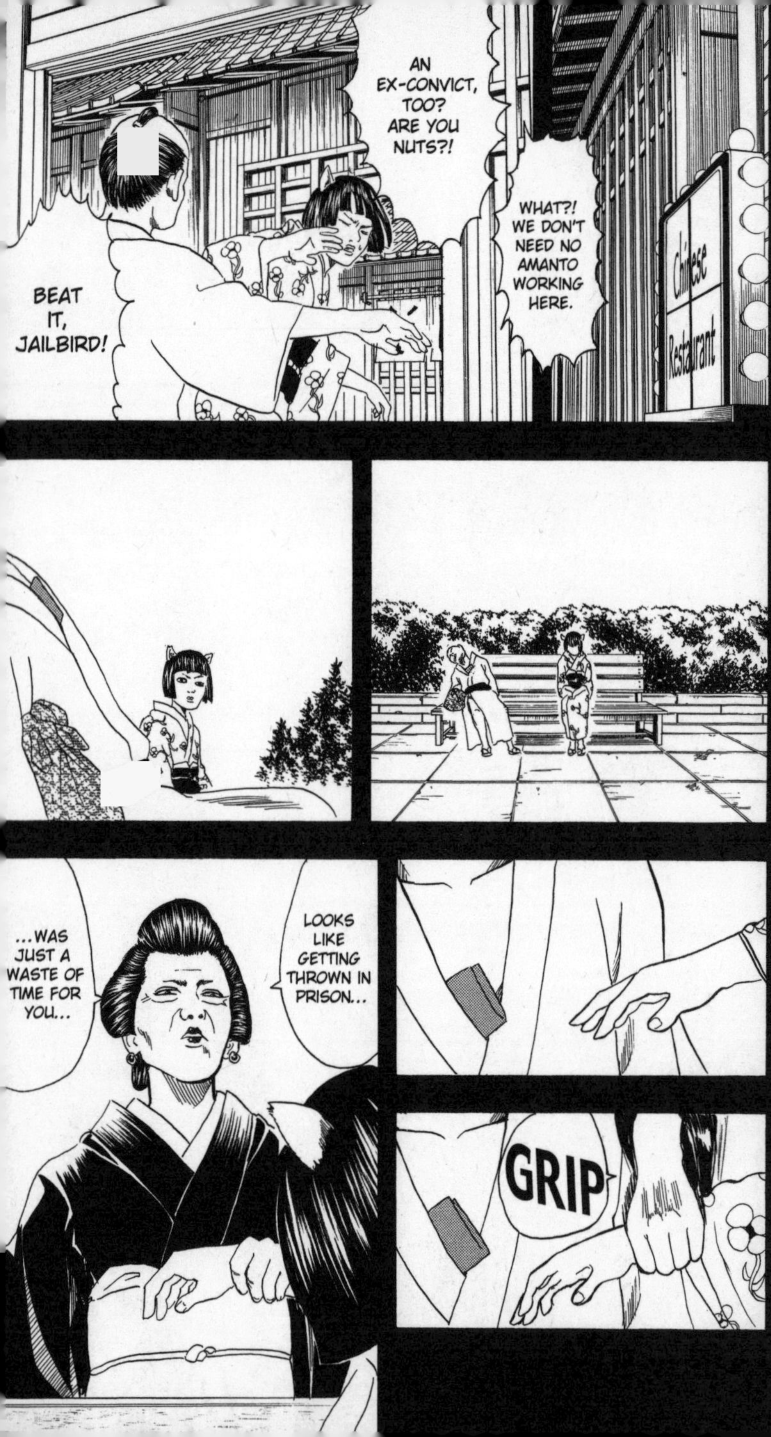
WHAT?! WE DON'T NEED NO AMANTO WORKING HERE.
Chinese Restaurant
AN EX-CONVICT, TOO? ARE YOU NUTS?!
BEAT IT, JAILBIRD!
GRIP
LOOKS LIKE GETTING THROWN IN PRISON...
...WAS JUST A WASTE OF TIME FOR YOU...

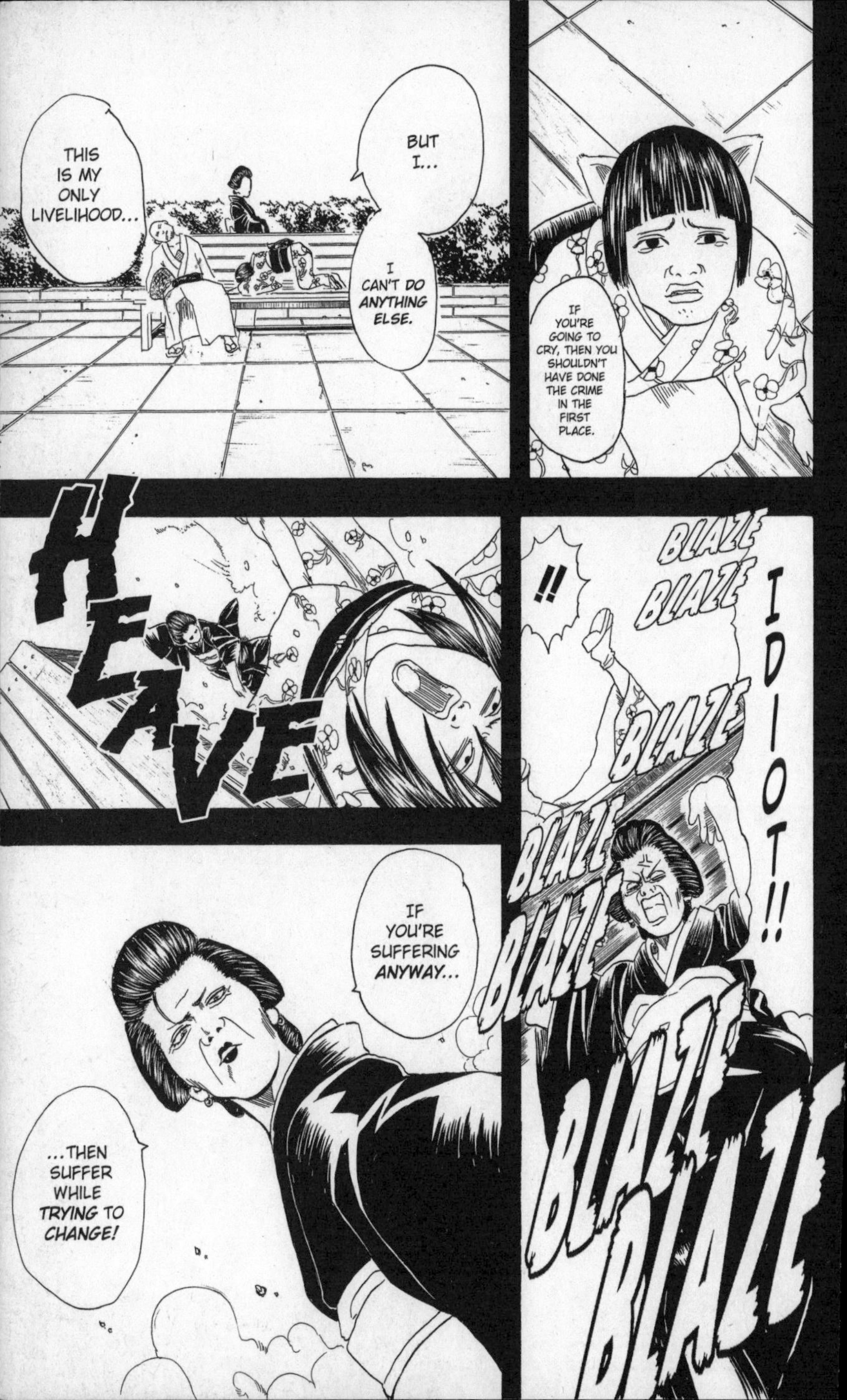
IF YOU'RE GOING TO CRY, THEN YOU SHOULDN'T HAVE DONE THE CRIME IN THE FIRST PLACE.
BUT I...
I CAN'T DO ANYTHING ELSE.
THIS IS MY ONLY LIVELIHOOD...
BLAZE
BLAZE
IDIOT!!
!!
BLAZE
BLAZE
BLAZE
BLAZE
HEAVE
IF YOU'RE SUFFERING ANYWAY...
...THEN SUFFER WHILE TRYING TO CHANGE!

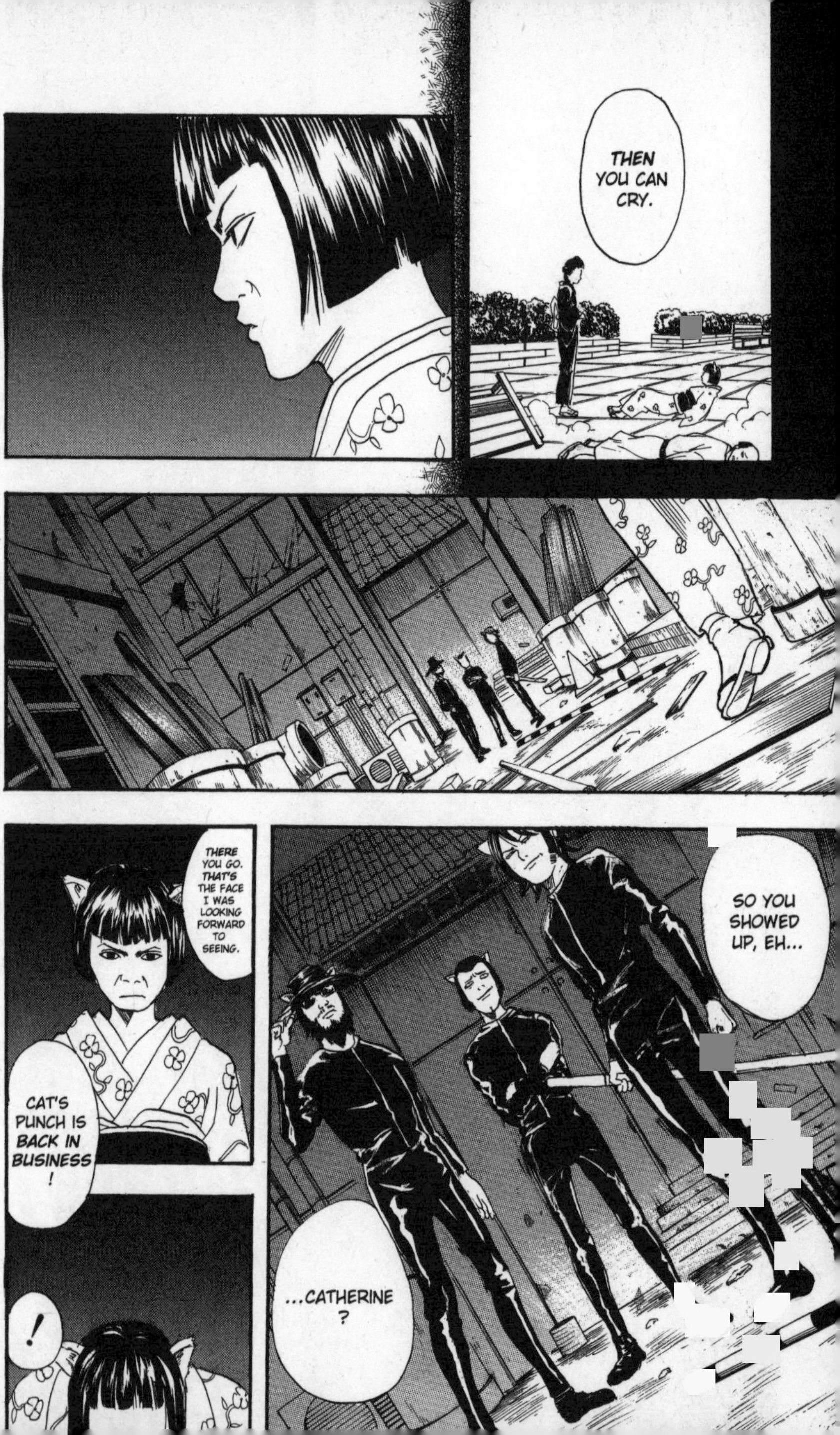
THEN YOU CAN CRY.
SO YOU SHOWED UP, EH...
...CATHERINE?
THERE YOU GO. THAT'S THE FACE I WAS LOOKING FORWARD TO SEEING.
CAT'S PUNCH IS BACK IN BUSINESS!
!

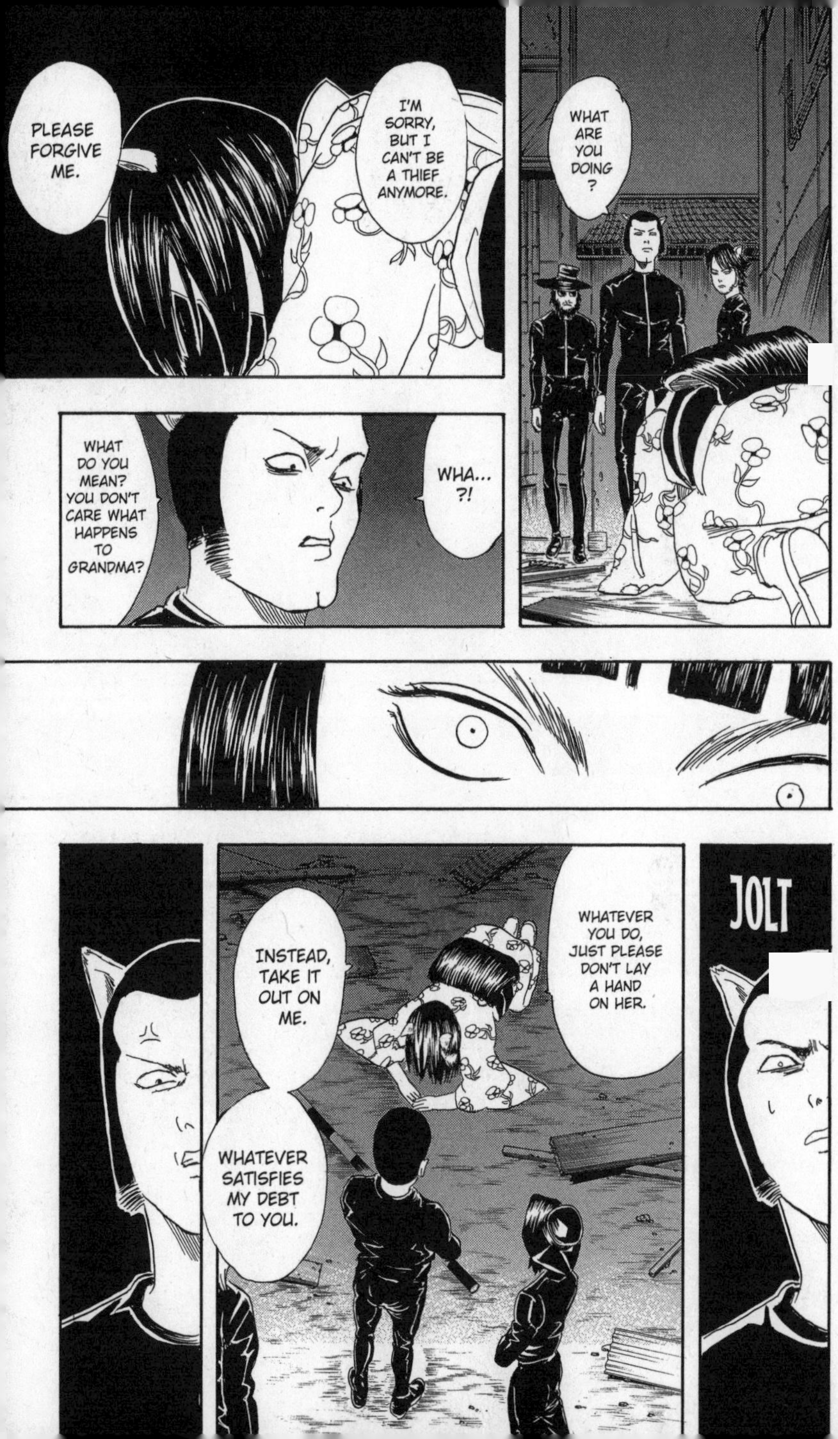
WHAT ARE YOU DOING ?
I'M SORRY, BUT I CAN'T BE A THIEF ANYMORE.
PLEASE FORGIVE ME.
WHA... ?!
WHAT DO YOU MEAN? YOU DON'T CARE WHAT HAPPENS TO GRANDMA?
JOLT
WHATEVER YOU DO, JUST PLEASE DON'T LAY A HAND ON HER.
INSTEAD, TAKE IT OUT ON ME.
WHATEVER SATISFIES MY DEBT TO YOU.

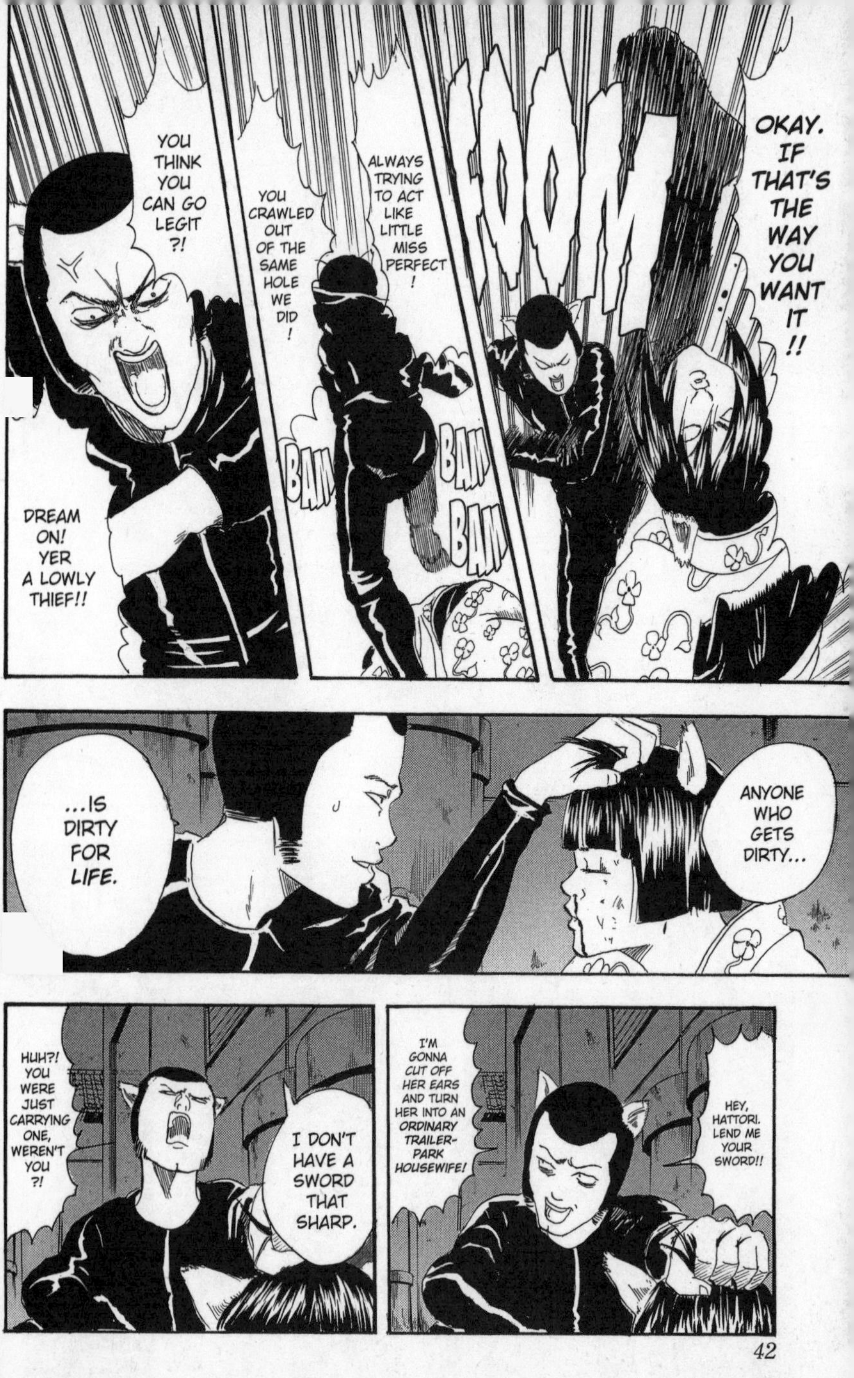
FOOM
OKAY. IF THAT'S THE WAY YOU WANT IT!!
ALWAYS TRYING TO ACT LIKE LITTLE MISS PERFECT!
YOU CRAWLED OUT OF THE SAME HOLE WE DID!
BAM
BAM
BAM
YOU THINK YOU CAN GO LEGIT?!
DREAM ON! YER A LOWLY THIEF!!
ANYONE WHO GETS DIRTY...
...IS DIRTY FOR LIFE.
HEY, HATTORI. LEND ME YOUR SWORD!!
I'M GONNA CUT OFF HER EARS AND TURN HER INTO AN ORDINARY TRAILER-PARK HOUSEWIFE!
I DON'T HAVE A SWORD THAT SHARP.
HUH?! YOU WERE JUST CARRYING ONE, WEREN'T YOU?!

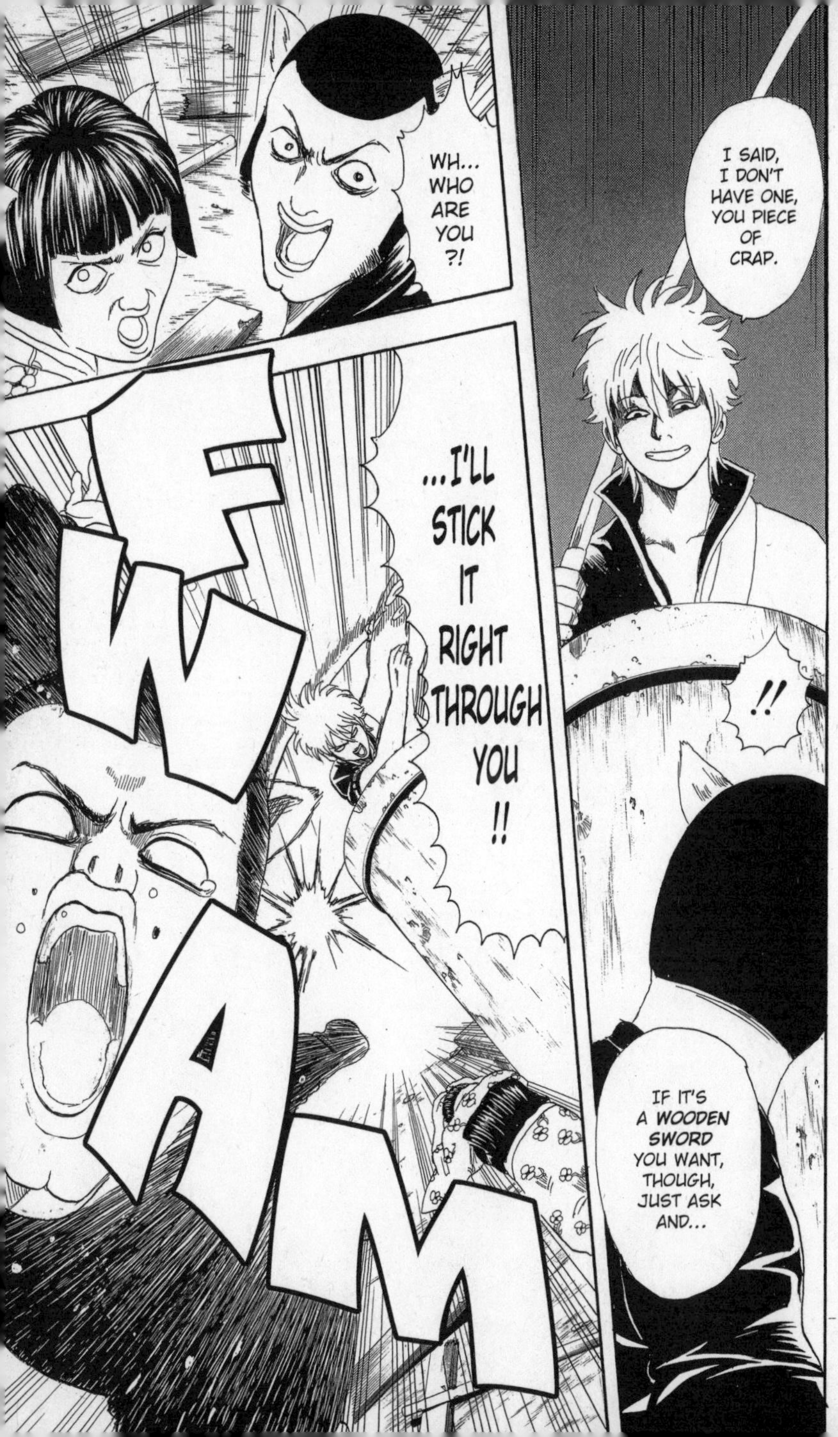
I SAID, I DON'T HAVE ONE, YOU PIECE OF CRAP.
!!
IF IT'S A WOODEN SWORD YOU WANT, THOUGH, JUST ASK AND...
WH... WHO ARE YOU ?!
...I'LL STICK IT RIGHT THROUGH YOU !!
WHAM

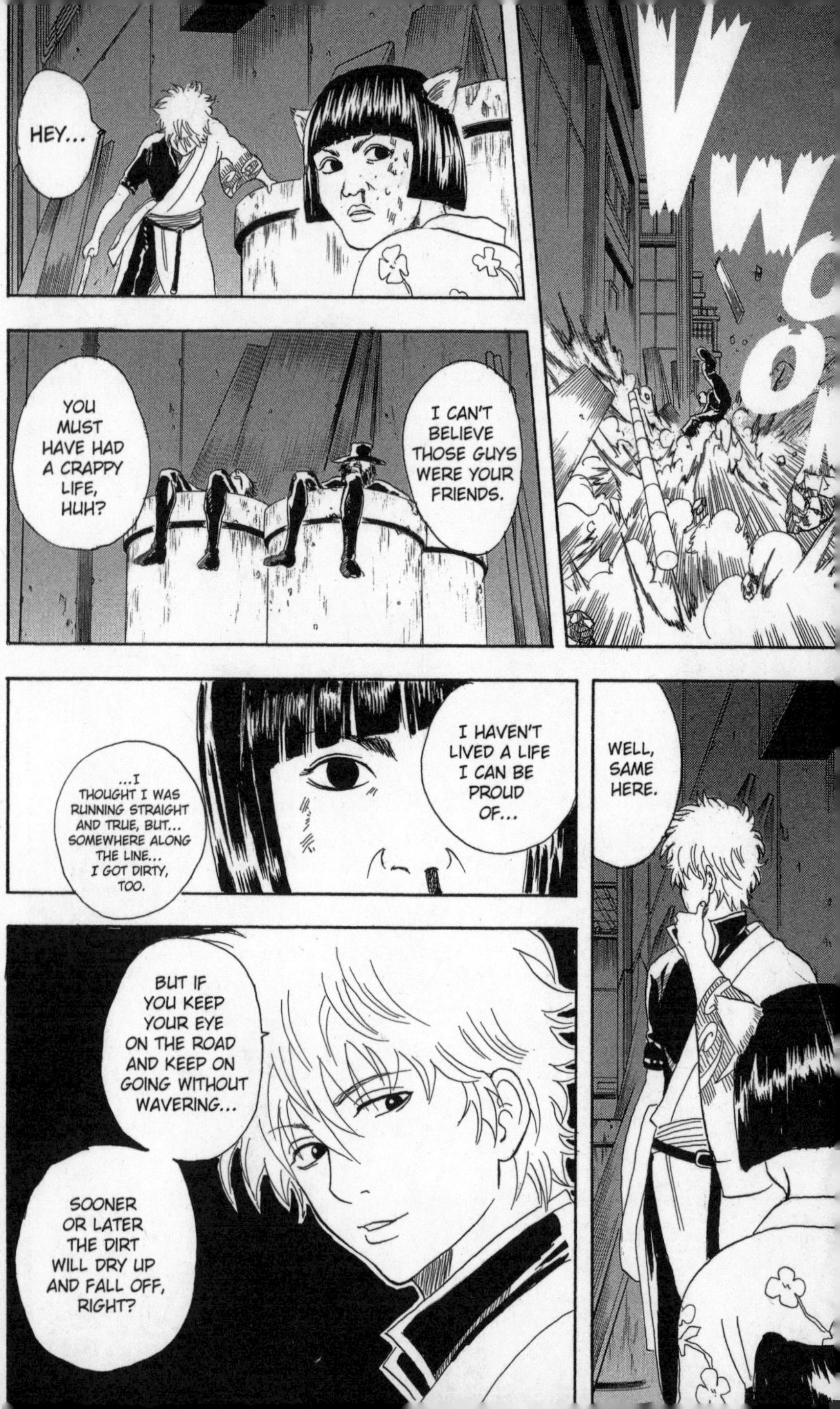
HEY...
I CAN'T BELIEVE THOSE GUYS WERE YOUR FRIENDS.
YOU MUST HAVE HAD A CRAPPY LIFE, HUH?
WELL, SAME HERE.
I HAVEN'T LIVED A LIFE I CAN BE PROUD OF...
...I THOUGHT I WAS RUNNING STRAIGHT AND TRUE, BUT... SOMEWHERE ALONG THE LINE... I GOT DIRTY, TOO.
BUT IF YOU KEEP YOUR EYE ON THE ROAD AND KEEP ON GOING WITHOUT WAVERING...
SOONER OR LATER THE DIRT WILL DRY UP AND FALL OFF, RIGHT?

READ THIS WAY

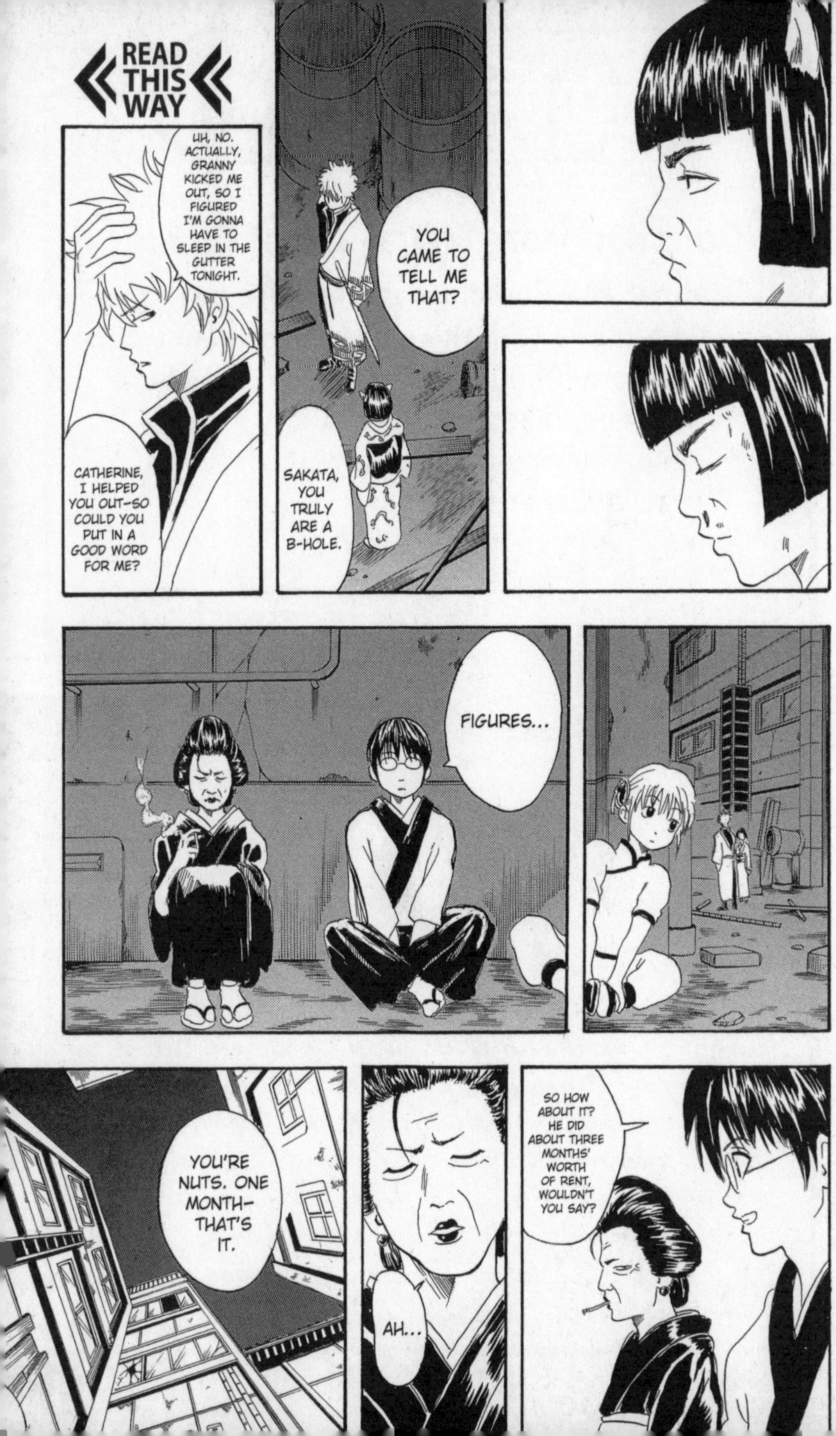
YOU CAME TO TELL ME THAT?
SAKATA, YOU TRULY ARE A B-HOLE.
UH, NO. ACTUALLY, GRANNY KICKED ME OUT, SO I FIGURED I'M GONNA HAVE TO SLEEP IN THE GUTTER TONIGHT.
CATHERINE, I HELPED YOU OUT–SO COULD YOU PUT IN A GOOD WORD FOR ME?
FIGURES...
SO HOW ABOUT IT? HE DID ABOUT THREE MONTHS' WORTH OF RENT, WOULDN'T YOU SAY?
AH...
YOU'RE NUTS. ONE MONTH–THAT'S IT.

Sorachi's Q&A
Hanging with the Readers #1

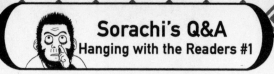

Question from Miwa-san of Osaka:

Hello there. Sorachi-san. If you're having a tough time with the extras, how about doing something like this...? Tell us where Gin sleeps, takes a bath, etc.
Please show us the layout of the Yorozuya's apartment.

Futon Closet (Kagura's bedroom)
Foyer
Hall
Kitchen
Toilet
Bath
Sofa
Table
Sofa
Japanese-style room
Veranda
Desk
TV

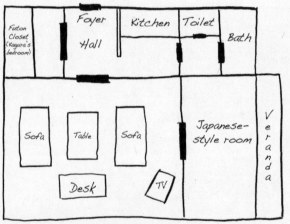

Gin-san sleeps in the Japanese-style room, or on the sofa, and sometimes doesn't even come home at night. Shinpachi sometimes stays overnight, and other times returns home instead. Kagura is like Doraemon [The manga space-cat character who sleeps in a futon closet—Ed. note]. Sadaharu sleeps wherever he wants.

(Q&A #2 is on page 66)

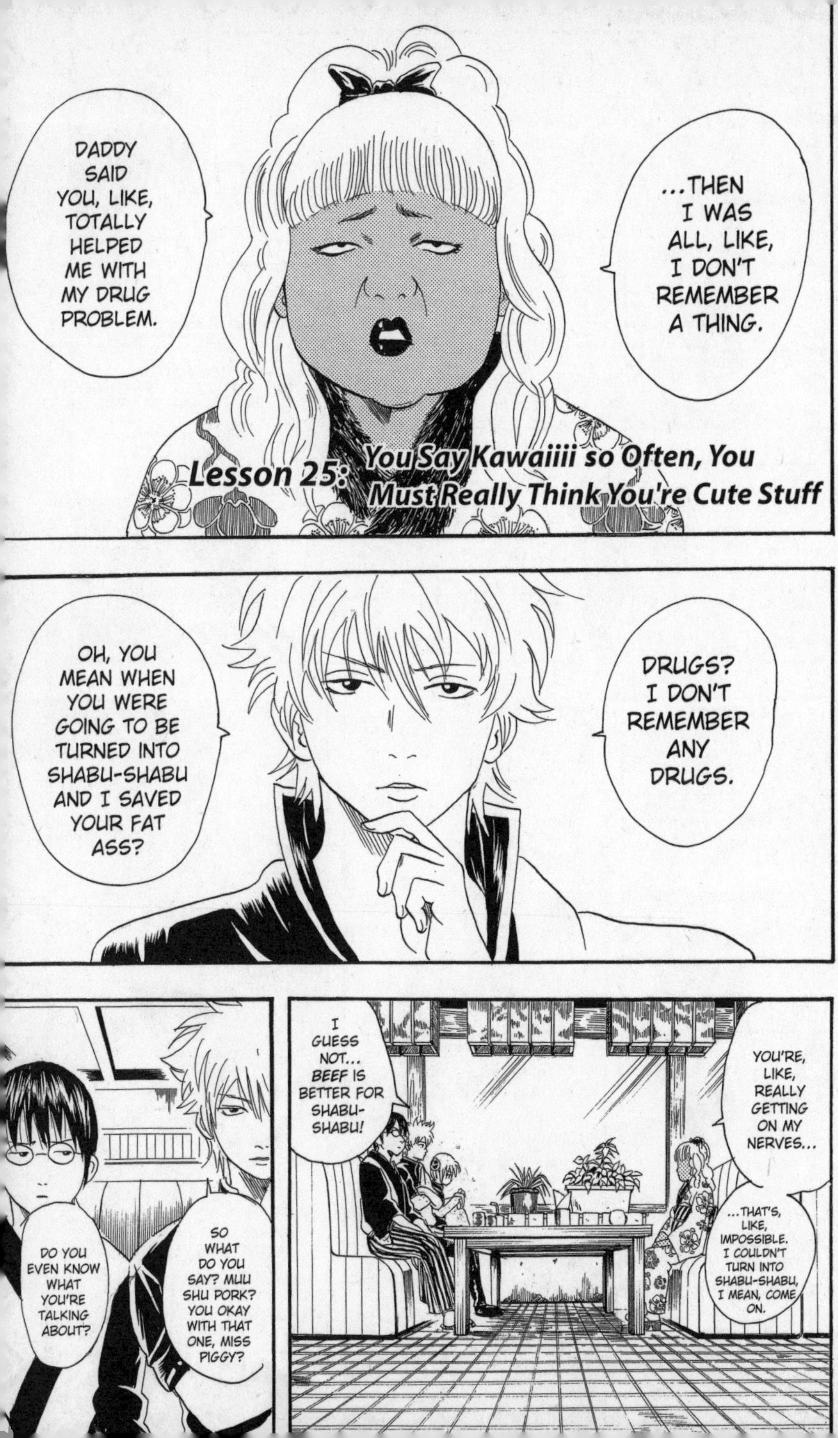
...THEN I WAS ALL, LIKE, I DON'T REMEMBER A THING.
DADDY SAID YOU, LIKE, TOTALLY HELPED ME WITH MY DRUG PROBLEM.
Lesson 25: You Say Kawaiiii so Often, You Must Really Think You're Cute Stuff
DRUGS? I DON'T REMEMBER ANY DRUGS.
OH, YOU MEAN WHEN YOU WERE GOING TO BE TURNED INTO SHABU-SHABU AND I SAVED YOUR FAT ASS?
YOU'RE, LIKE, REALLY GETTING ON MY NERVES...
...THAT'S, LIKE, IMPOSSIBLE. I COULDN'T TURN INTO SHABU-SHABU, I MEAN, COME ON.
I GUESS NOT... BEEF IS BETTER FOR SHABU-SHABU!
SO WHAT DO YOU SAY? MUU SHU PORK? YOU OKAY WITH THAT ONE, MISS PIGGY?
DO YOU EVEN KNOW WHAT YOU'RE TALKING ABOUT?

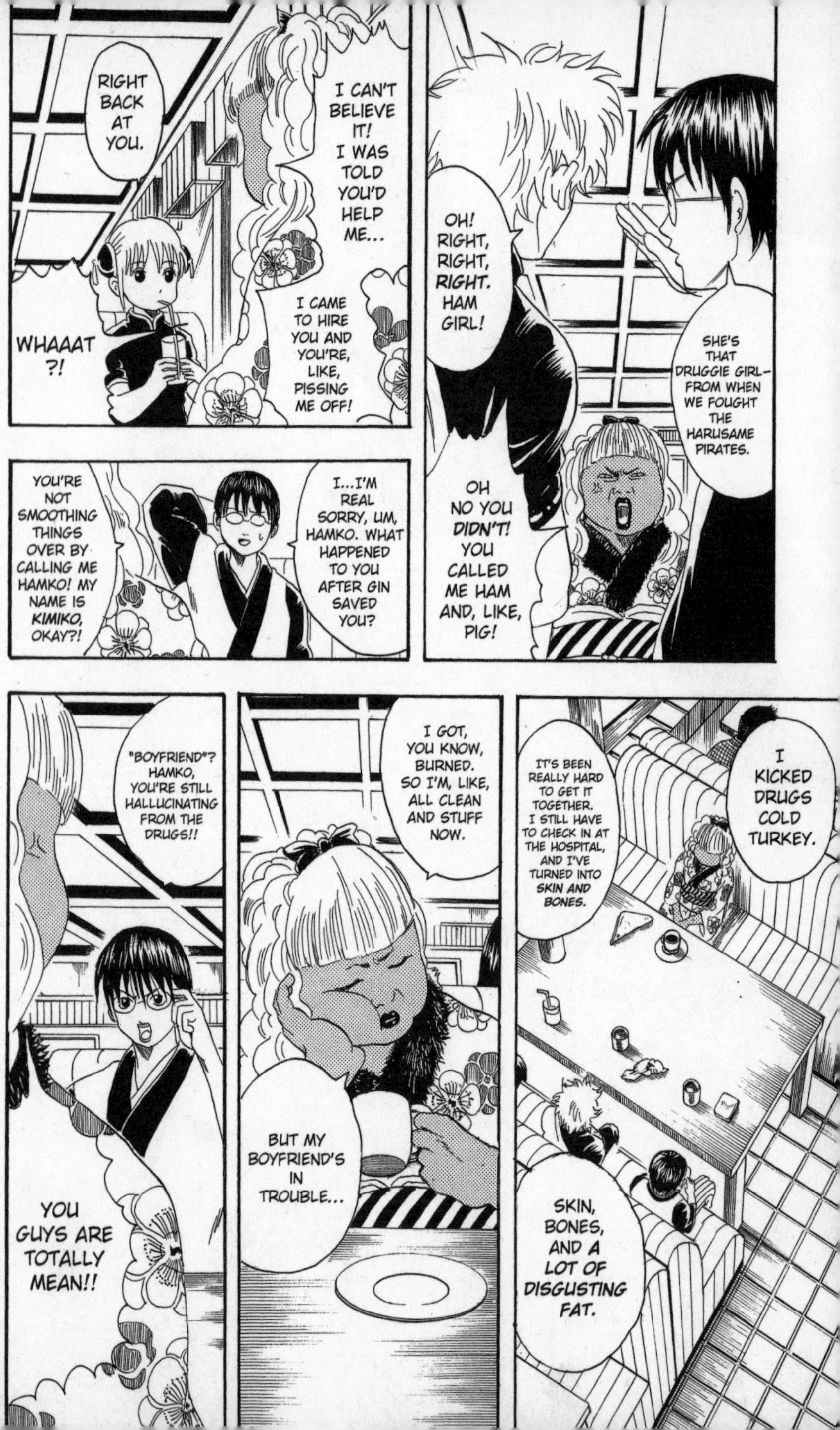
SHE'S THAT DRUGGIE GIRL—FROM WHEN WE FOUGHT THE HARUSAME PIRATES.
OH! RIGHT, RIGHT, RIGHT. HAM GIRL!
OH NO YOU DIDN'T! YOU CALLED ME HAM AND, LIKE, PIG!
I CAN'T BELIEVE IT! I WAS TOLD YOU'D HELP ME...
RIGHT BACK AT YOU.
I CAME TO HIRE YOU AND YOU'RE, LIKE, PISSING ME OFF!
WHAAAT?!
I...I'M REAL SORRY, UM, HAMKO. WHAT HAPPENED TO YOU AFTER GIN SAVED YOU?
YOU'RE NOT SMOOTHING THINGS OVER BY CALLING ME HAMKO! MY NAME IS KIMIKO, OKAY?!
I KICKED DRUGS COLD TURKEY.
IT'S BEEN REALLY HARD TO GET IT TOGETHER. I STILL HAVE TO CHECK IN AT THE HOSPITAL, AND I'VE TURNED INTO SKIN AND BONES.
SKIN, BONES, AND A LOT OF DISGUSTING FAT.
I GOT, YOU KNOW, BURNED. SO I'M, LIKE, ALL CLEAN AND STUFF NOW.
BUT MY BOYFRIEND'S IN TROUBLE...
"BOYFRIEND"? HAMKO, YOU'RE STILL HALLUCINATING FROM THE DRUGS!!
YOU GUYS ARE TOTALLY MEAN!!

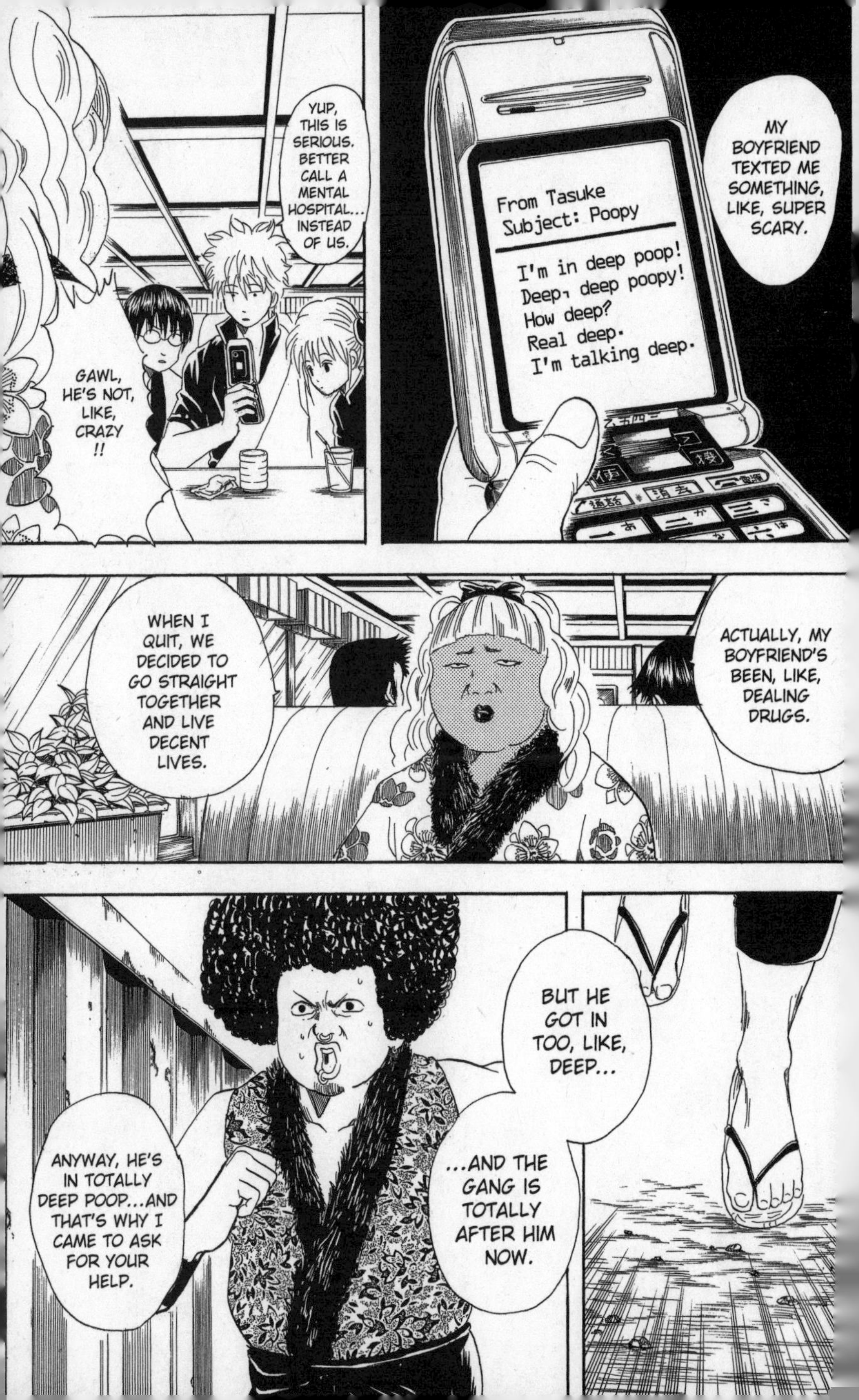
MY BOYFRIEND TEXTED ME SOMETHING, LIKE, SUPER SCARY.
From Tasuke
Subject: Poopy
I'm in deep poop!
Deep, deep poopy!
How deep?
Real deep.
I'm talking deep.
YUP, THIS IS SERIOUS. BETTER CALL A MENTAL HOSPITAL... INSTEAD OF US.
GAWL, HE'S NOT, LIKE, CRAZY !!
ACTUALLY, MY BOYFRIEND'S BEEN, LIKE, DEALING DRUGS.
WHEN I QUIT, WE DECIDED TO GO STRAIGHT TOGETHER AND LIVE DECENT LIVES.
BUT HE GOT IN TOO, LIKE, DEEP...
...AND THE GANG IS TOTALLY AFTER HIM NOW.
ANYWAY, HE'S IN TOTALLY DEEP POOP...AND THAT'S WHY I CAME TO ASK FOR YOUR HELP.

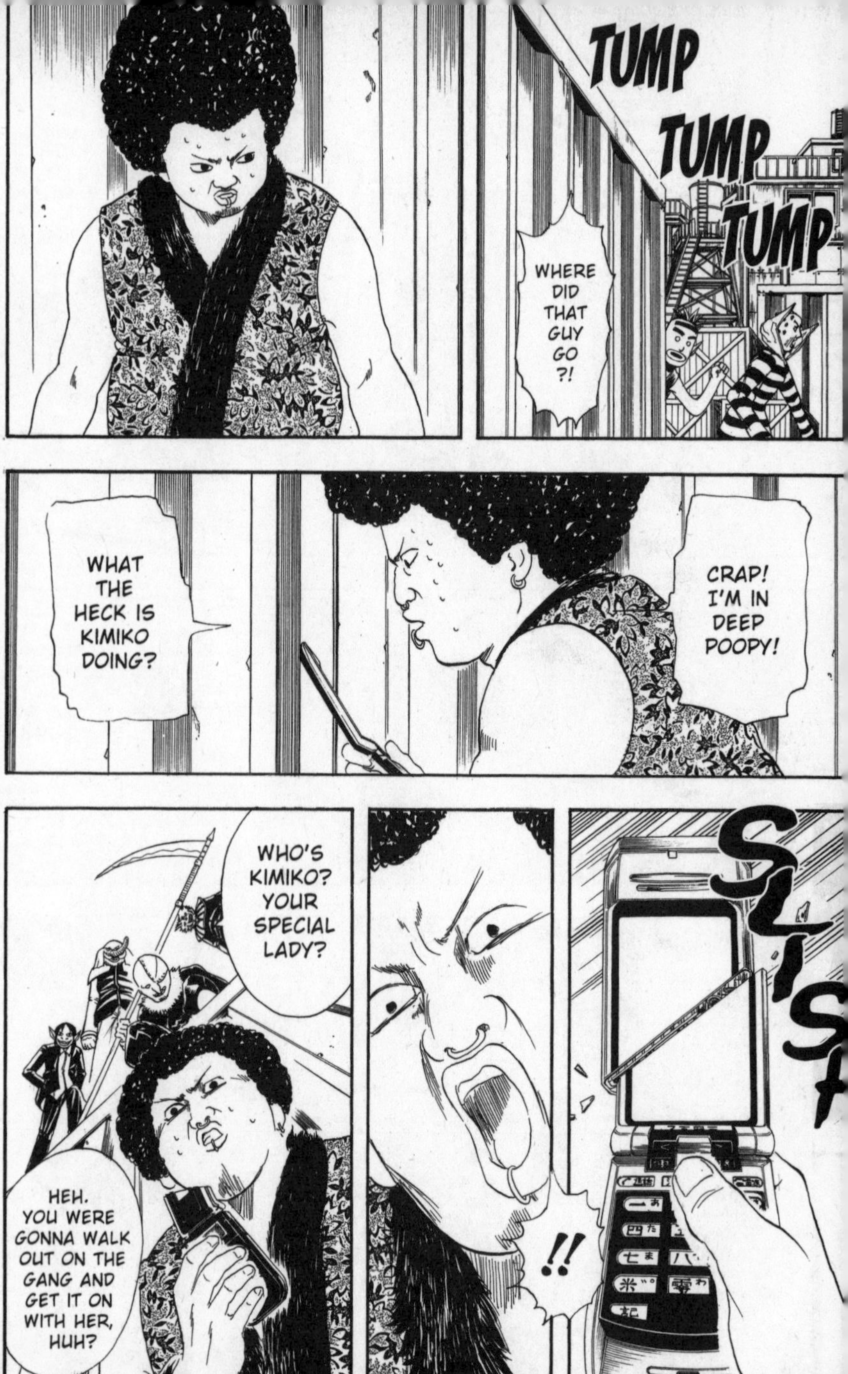
TUMP
TUMP
TUMP
WHERE DID THAT GUY GO?!
CRAP! I'M IN DEEP POOPY!
WHAT THE HECK IS KIMIKO DOING?
SLISH
!!
WHO'S KIMIKO? YOUR SPECIAL LADY?
HEH. YOU WERE GONNA WALK OUT ON THE GANG AND GET IT ON WITH HER, HUH?

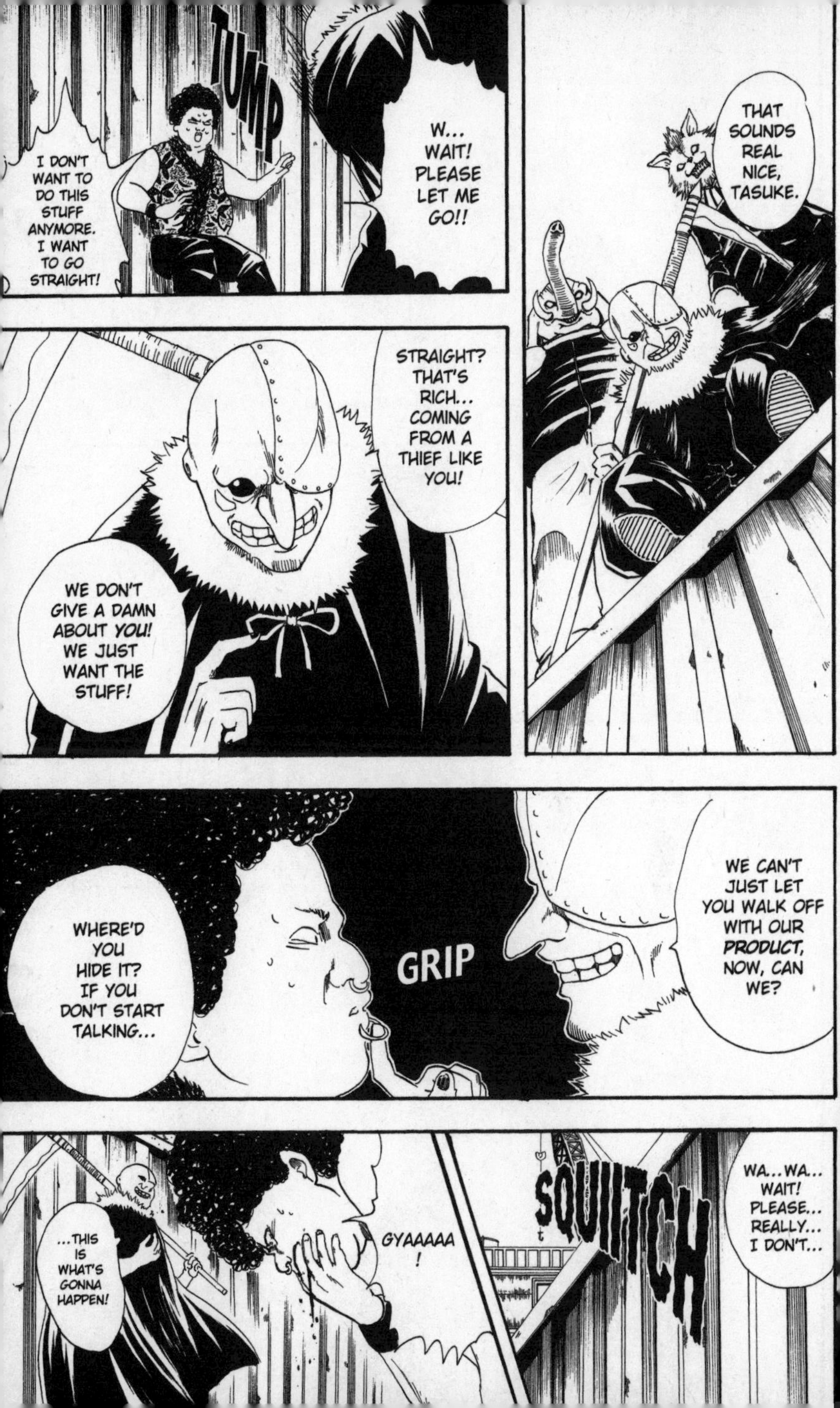
THAT SOUNDS REAL NICE, TASUKE.
TUMP
W... WAIT! PLEASE LET ME GO!!
I DON'T WANT TO DO THIS STUFF ANYMORE. I WANT TO GO STRAIGHT!
STRAIGHT? THAT'S RICH... COMING FROM A THIEF LIKE YOU!
WE DON'T GIVE A DAMN ABOUT YOU! WE JUST WANT THE STUFF!
WE CAN'T JUST LET YOU WALK OFF WITH OUR PRODUCT, NOW, CAN WE?
GRIP
WHERE'D YOU HIDE IT? IF YOU DON'T START TALKING...
WA...WA... WAIT! PLEASE... REALLY... I DON'T...
SQUIITCH
GYAAAAA!
...THIS IS WHAT'S GONNA HAPPEN!

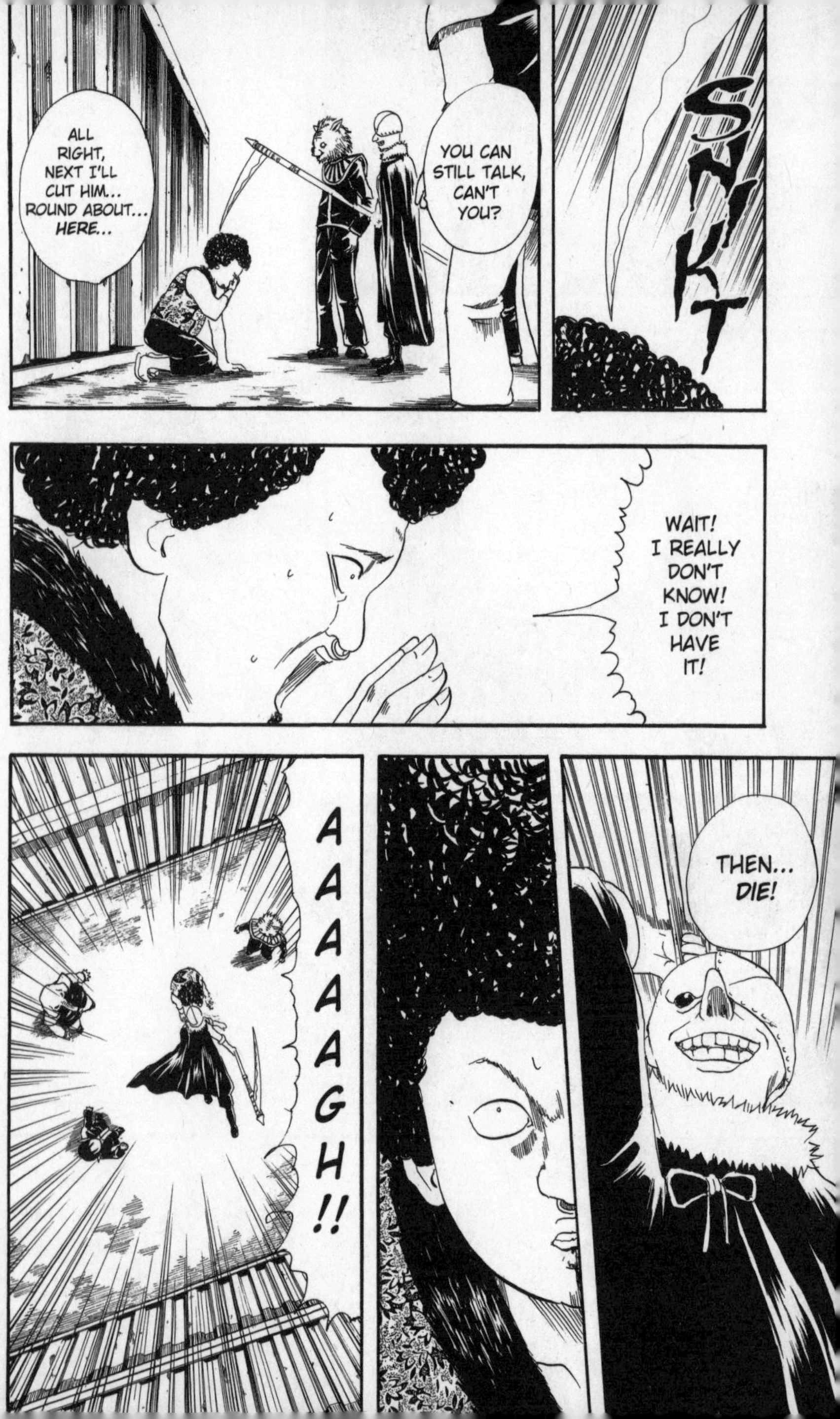
SHIKT
YOU CAN STILL TALK, CAN'T YOU?
ALL RIGHT, NEXT I'LL CUT HIM... ROUND ABOUT... HERE...
WAIT! I REALLY DON'T KNOW! I DON'T HAVE IT!
THEN... DIE!
AAAAAAGH!!

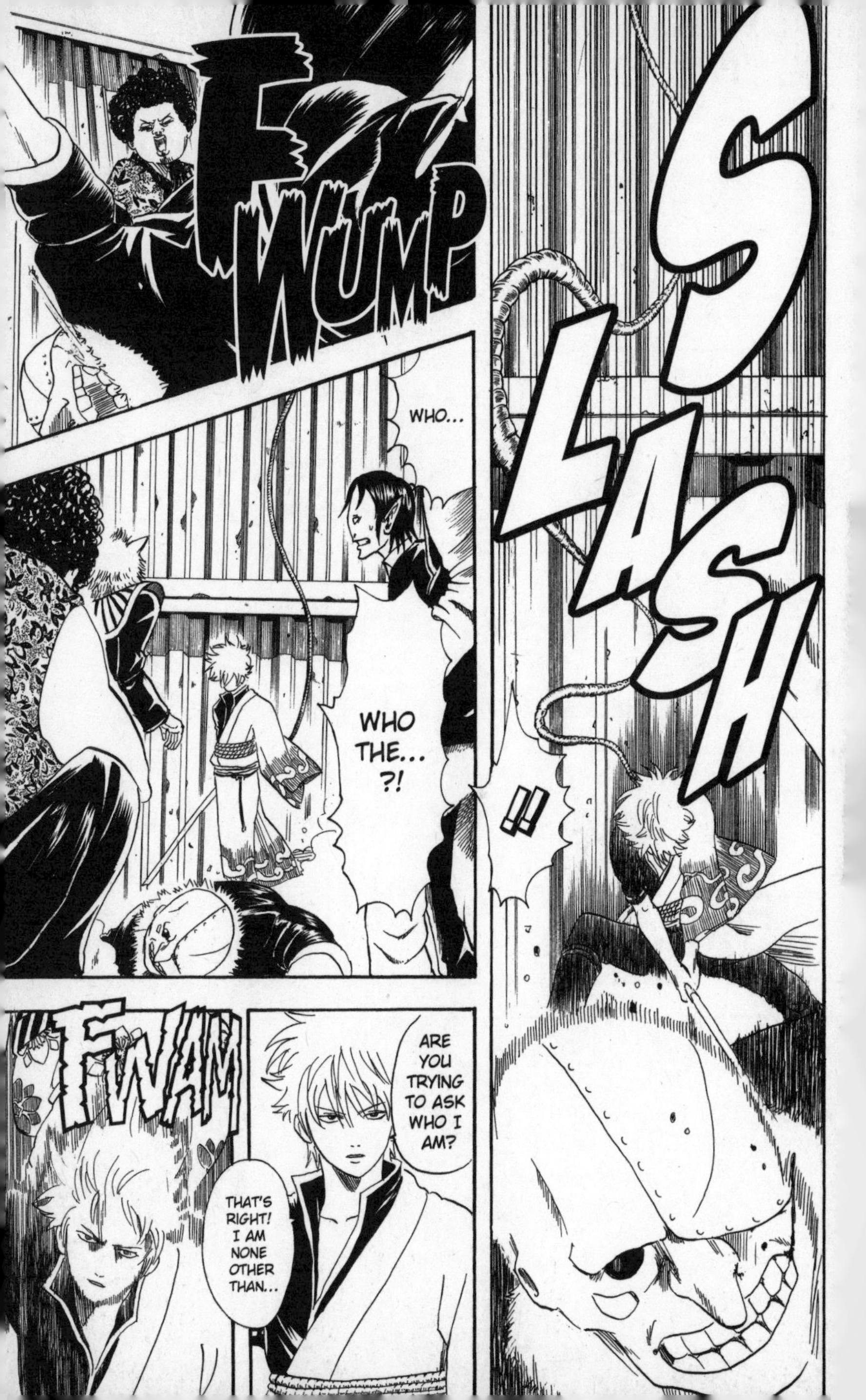
SLASH
!!
FWUMP
WHO...
WHO THE... ?!
ARE YOU TRYING TO ASK WHO I AM?
THAT'S RIGHT! I AM NONE OTHER THAN...
FWAM

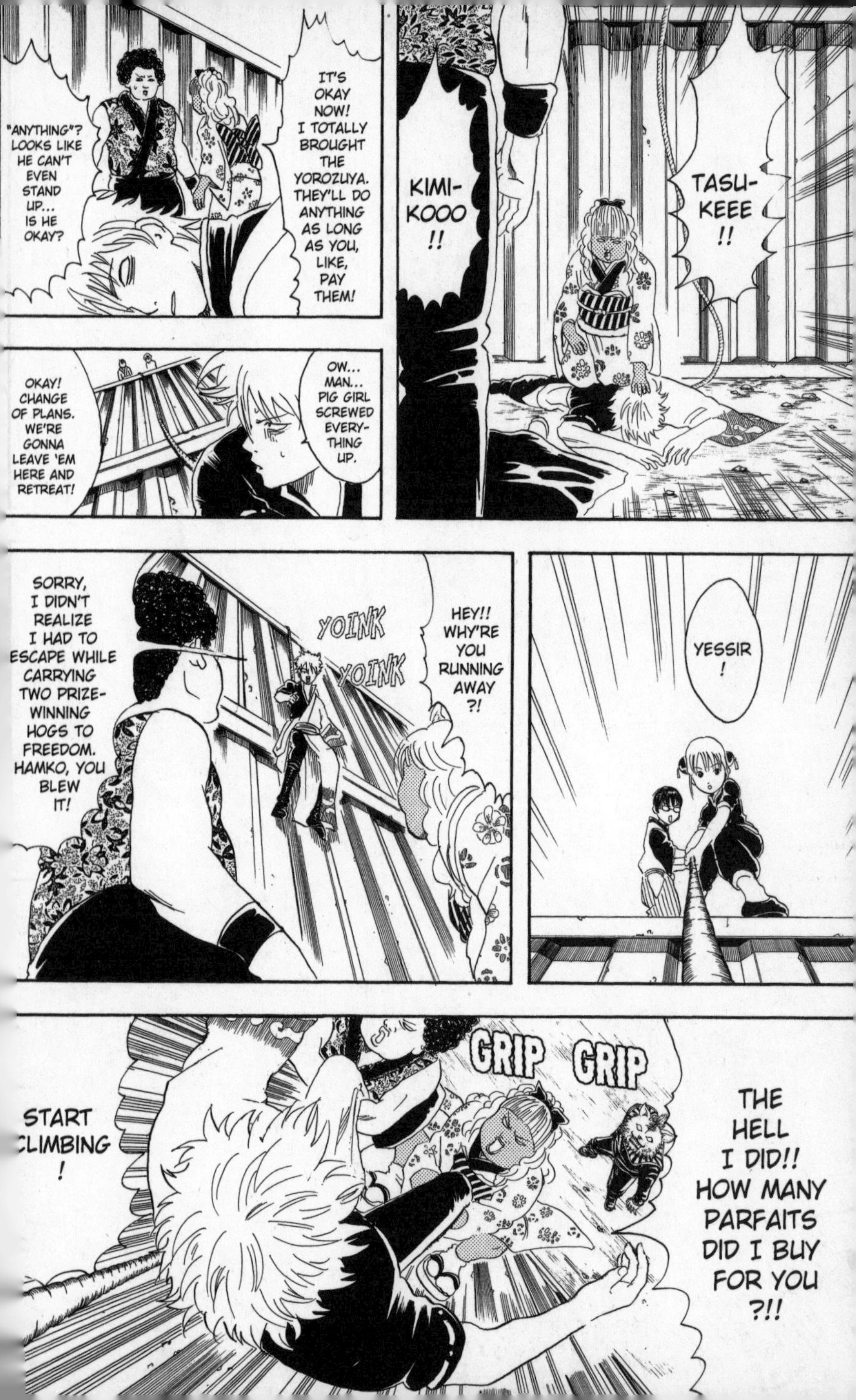
TASU-KEEE!!
KIMI-KOOO!!
IT'S OKAY NOW! I TOTALLY BROUGHT THE YOROZUYA. THEY'LL DO ANYTHING AS LONG AS YOU, LIKE, PAY THEM!
"ANYTHING"? LOOKS LIKE HE CAN'T EVEN STAND UP... IS HE OKAY?
OW... MAN... PIG GIRL SCREWED EVERYTHING UP.
OKAY! CHANGE OF PLANS. WE'RE GONNA LEAVE 'EM HERE AND RETREAT!
YESSIR!
HEY!! WHY'RE YOU RUNNING AWAY?!
YOINK
YOINK
SORRY, I DIDN'T REALIZE I HAD TO ESCAPE WHILE CARRYING TWO PRIZE-WINNING HOGS TO FREEDOM. HAMKO, YOU BLEW IT!
THE HELL I DID!! HOW MANY PARFAITS DID I BUY FOR YOU?!!
GRIP
GRIP
START CLIMBING!

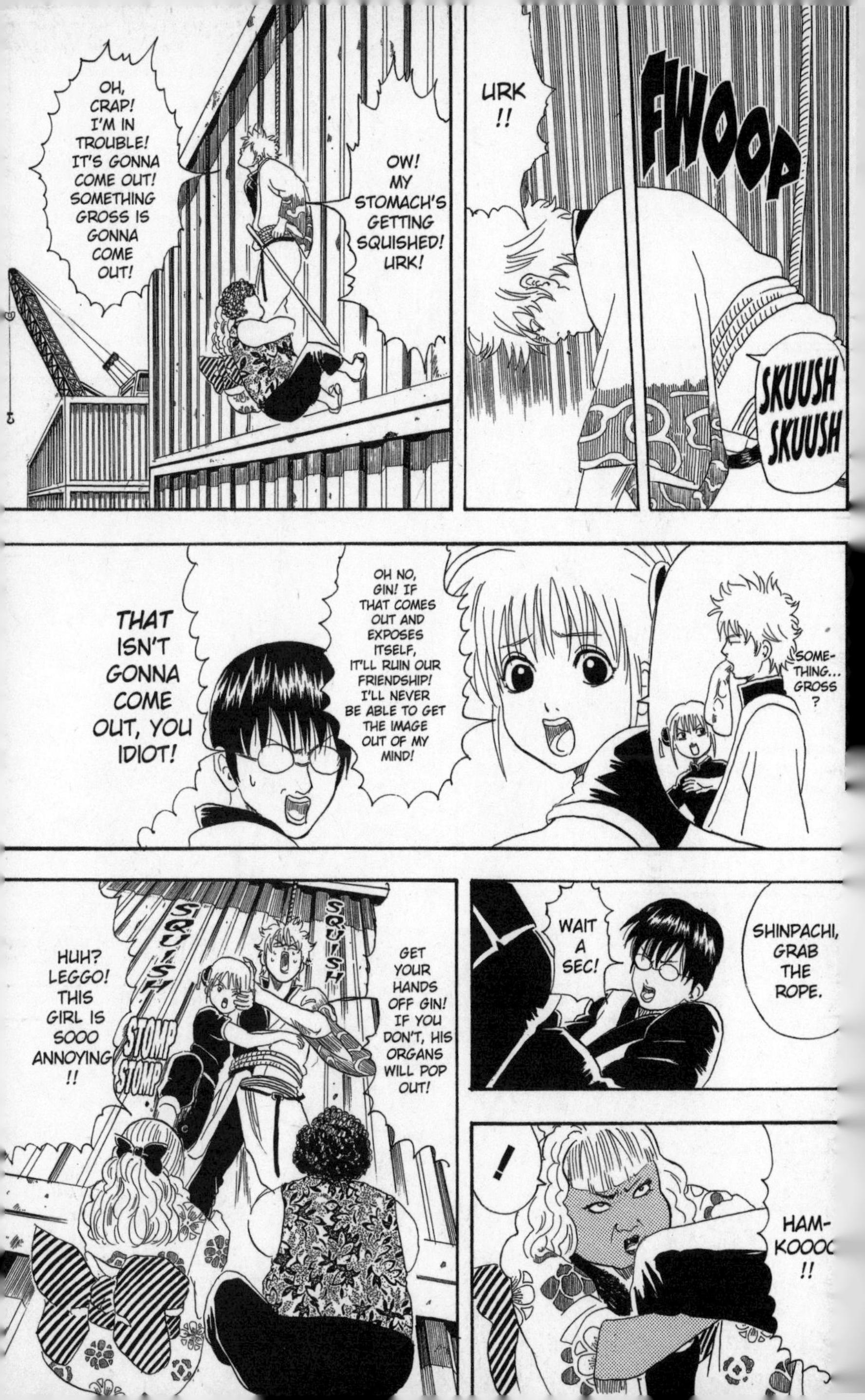
URK !!
FWOOP
SKUUSH SKUUSH
OW! MY STOMACH'S GETTING SQUISHED! URK!
OH, CRAP! I'M IN TROUBLE! IT'S GONNA COME OUT! SOMETHING GROSS IS GONNA COME OUT!
SOME-THING... GROSS ?
OH NO, GIN! IF THAT COMES OUT AND EXPOSES ITSELF, IT'LL RUIN OUR FRIENDSHIP! I'LL NEVER BE ABLE TO GET THE IMAGE OUT OF MY MIND!
THAT ISN'T GONNA COME OUT, YOU IDIOT!
SHINPACHI, GRAB THE ROPE.
WAIT A SEC!
HAM-KOOO !!
!
SQUISH
GET YOUR HANDS OFF GIN! IF YOU DON'T, HIS ORGANS WILL POP OUT!
SQUISH
HUH? LEGGO! THIS GIRL IS SOOO ANNOYING !!
STOMP STOMP

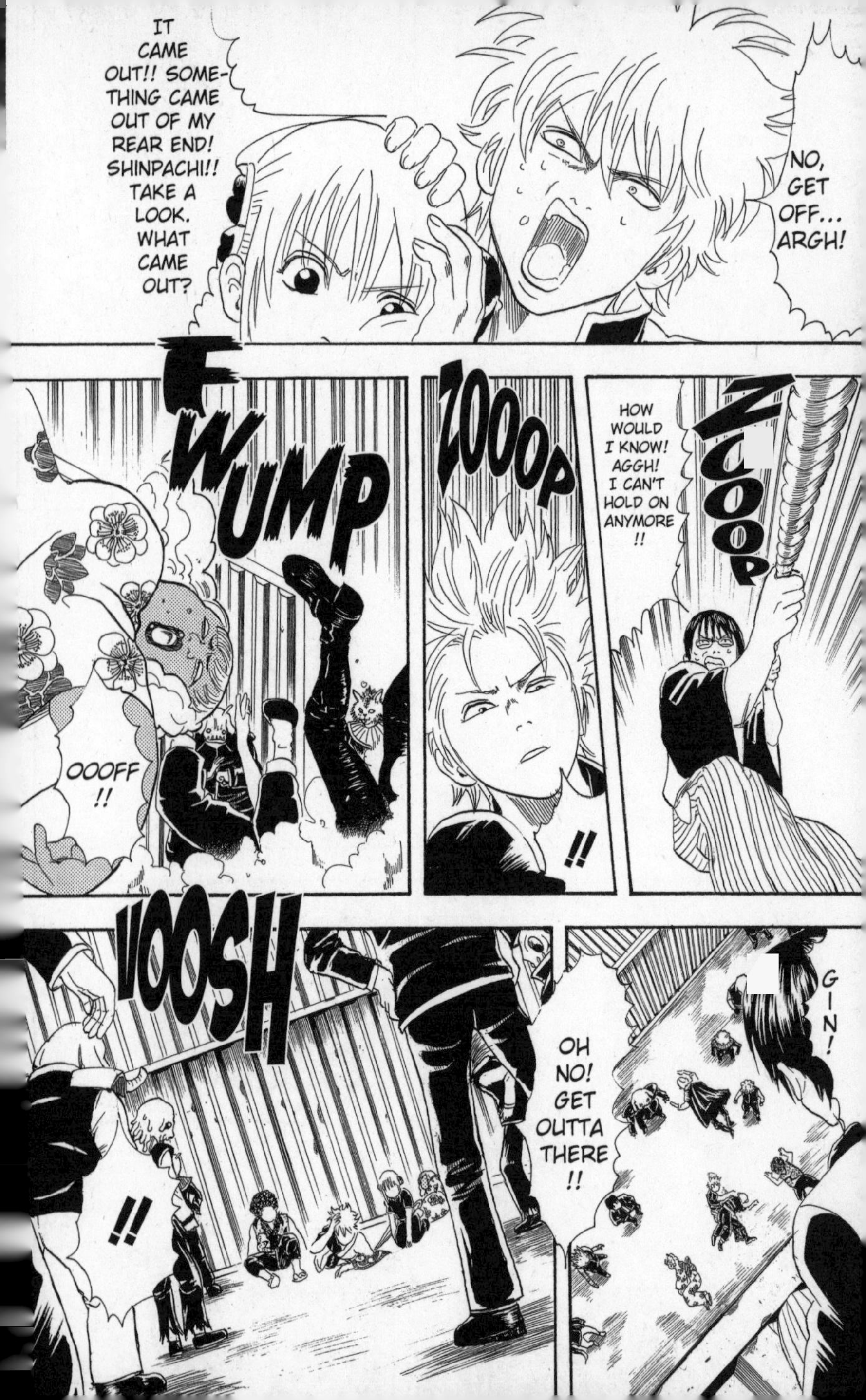
NO, GET OFF... ARGH!
IT CAME OUT!! SOME-THING CAME OUT OF MY REAR END! SHINPACHI!! TAKE A LOOK. WHAT CAME OUT?
ZOOOP
HOW WOULD I KNOW! AGGH! I CAN'T HOLD ON ANYMORE!!
ZOOOP
!!
FWUMP
OOOFF!!
GIN!
OH NO! GET OUTTA THERE!!
VOOSH
!!

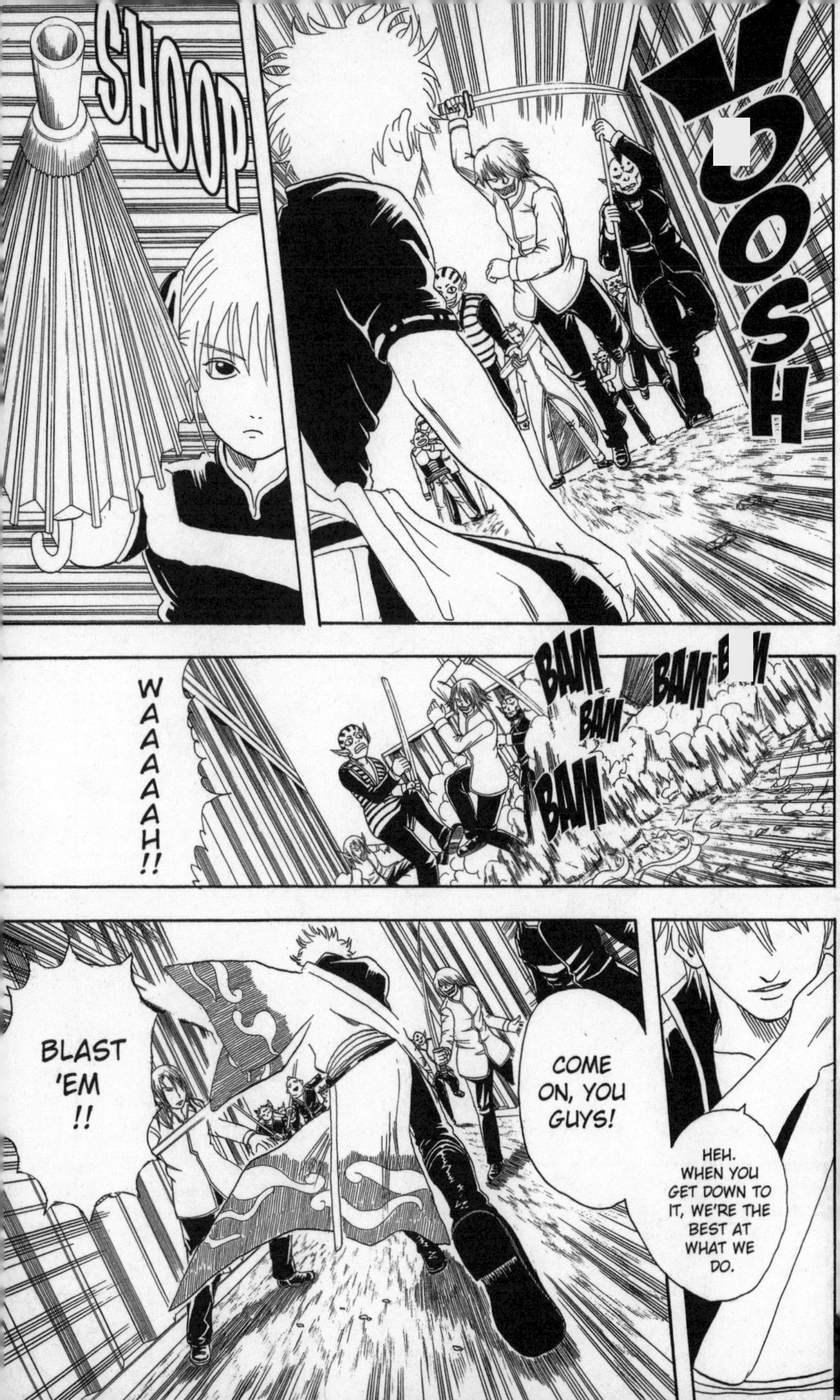
VOOSH
SHOOP
BAM
BAM
BAM
BAM
WAAAAAAH!!
HEH. WHEN YOU GET DOWN TO IT, WE'RE THE BEST AT WHAT WE DO.
COME ON, YOU GUYS!
BLAST 'EM !!

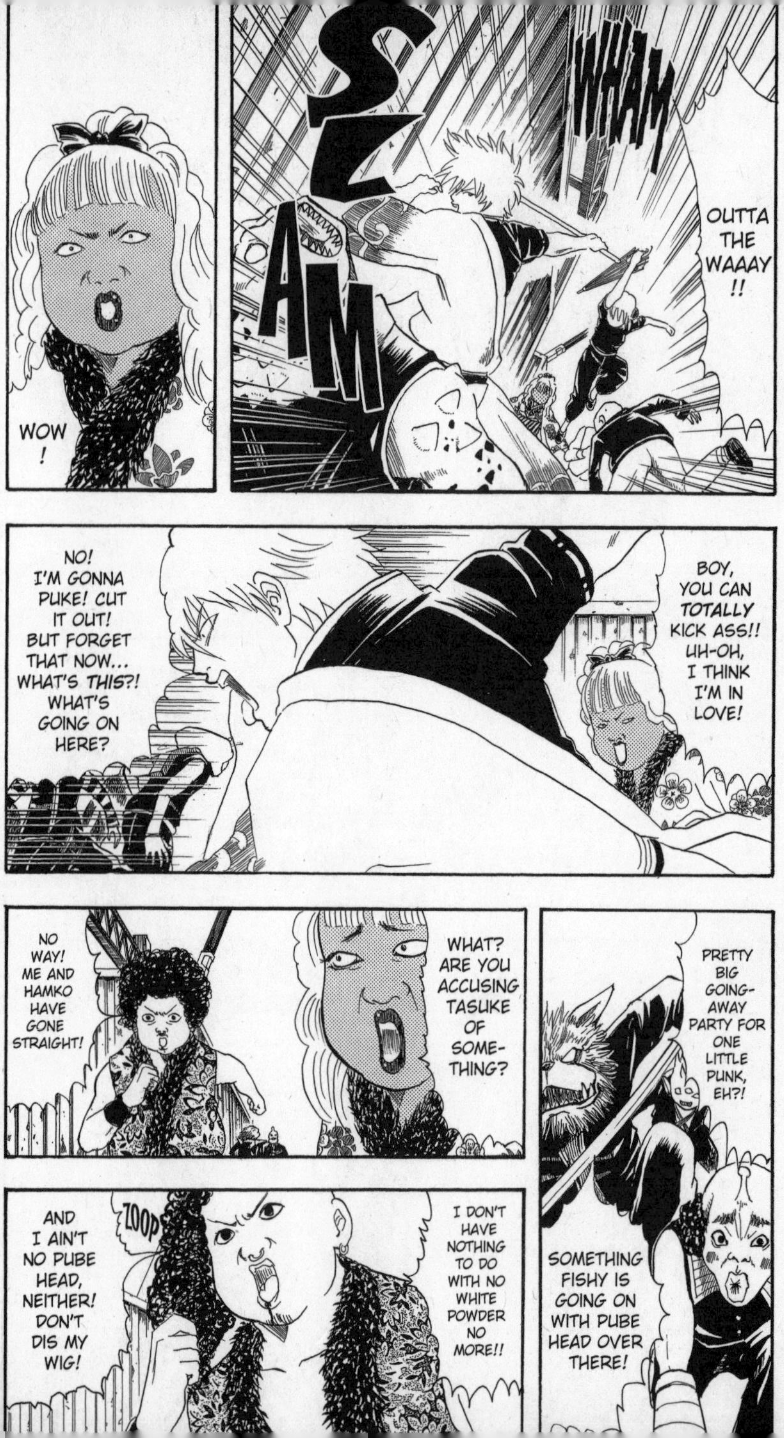
WHAM
SLAM
OUTTA THE WAAAY!!
WOW!
BOY, YOU CAN TOTALLY KICK ASS!! UH-OH, I THINK I'M IN LOVE!
NO! I'M GONNA PUKE! CUT IT OUT! BUT FORGET THAT NOW... WHAT'S THIS?! WHAT'S GOING ON HERE?
PRETTY BIG GOING-AWAY PARTY FOR ONE LITTLE PUNK, EH?!
SOMETHING FISHY IS GOING ON WITH PUBE HEAD OVER THERE!
WHAT? ARE YOU ACCUSING TASUKE OF SOME-THING?
NO WAY! ME AND HAMKO HAVE GONE STRAIGHT!
I DON'T HAVE NOTHING TO DO WITH NO WHITE POWDER NO MORE!!
ZOOP
AND I AIN'T NO PUBE HEAD, NEITHER! DON'T DIS MY WIG!

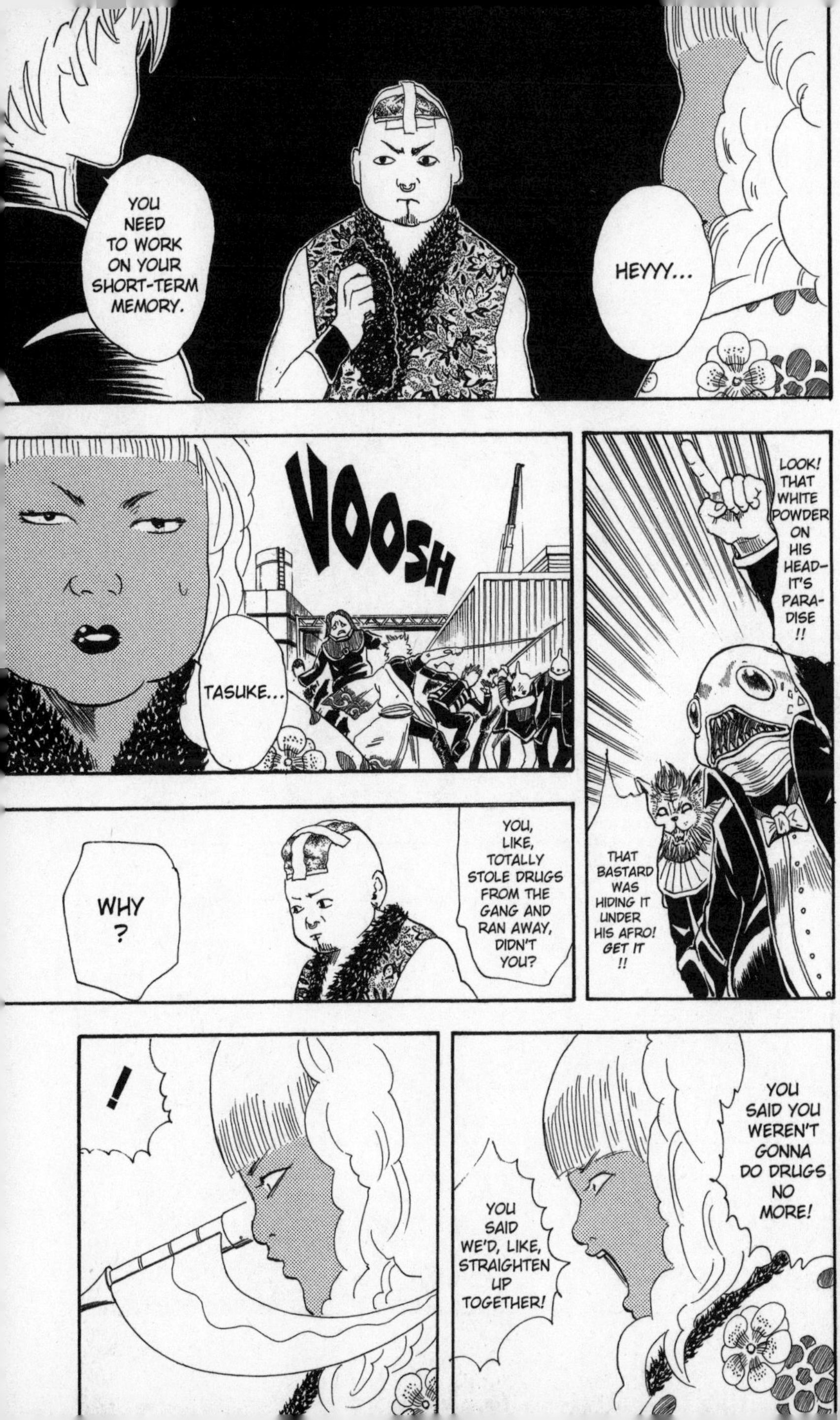
HEYYY...
YOU NEED TO WORK ON YOUR SHORT-TERM MEMORY.
LOOK! THAT WHITE POWDER ON HIS HEAD—IT'S PARADISE!!
THAT BASTARD WAS HIDING IT UNDER HIS AFRO! GET IT!!
VOOSH
TASUKE...
YOU, LIKE, TOTALLY STOLE DRUGS FROM THE GANG AND RAN AWAY, DIDN'T YOU?
WHY?
YOU SAID YOU WEREN'T GONNA DO DRUGS NO MORE!
YOU SAID WE'D, LIKE, STRAIGHTEN UP TOGETHER!
!

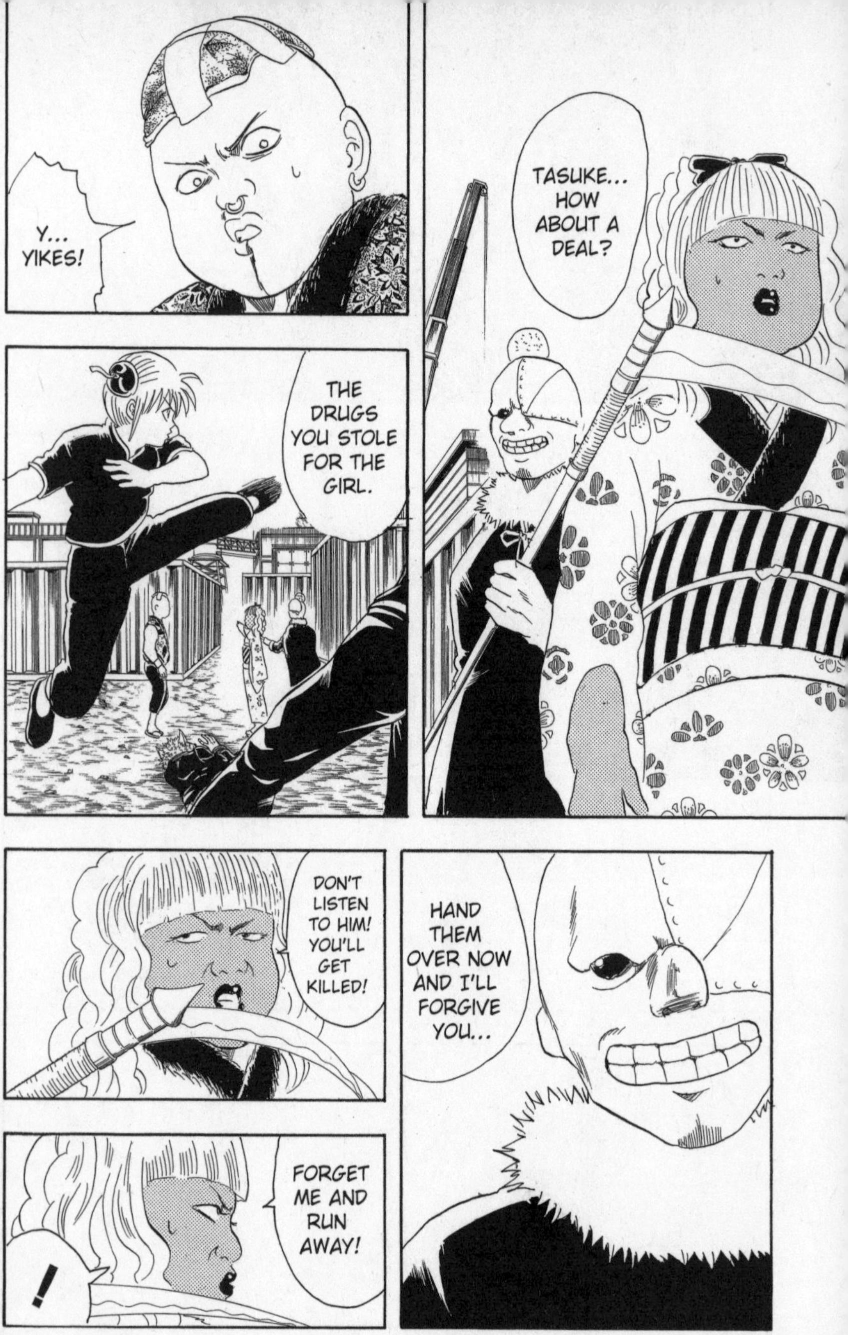
TASUKE... HOW ABOUT A DEAL?
Y... YIKES!
THE DRUGS YOU STOLE FOR THE GIRL.
HAND THEM OVER NOW AND I'LL FORGIVE YOU...
DON'T LISTEN TO HIM! YOU'LL GET KILLED!
FORGET ME AND RUN AWAY!
!

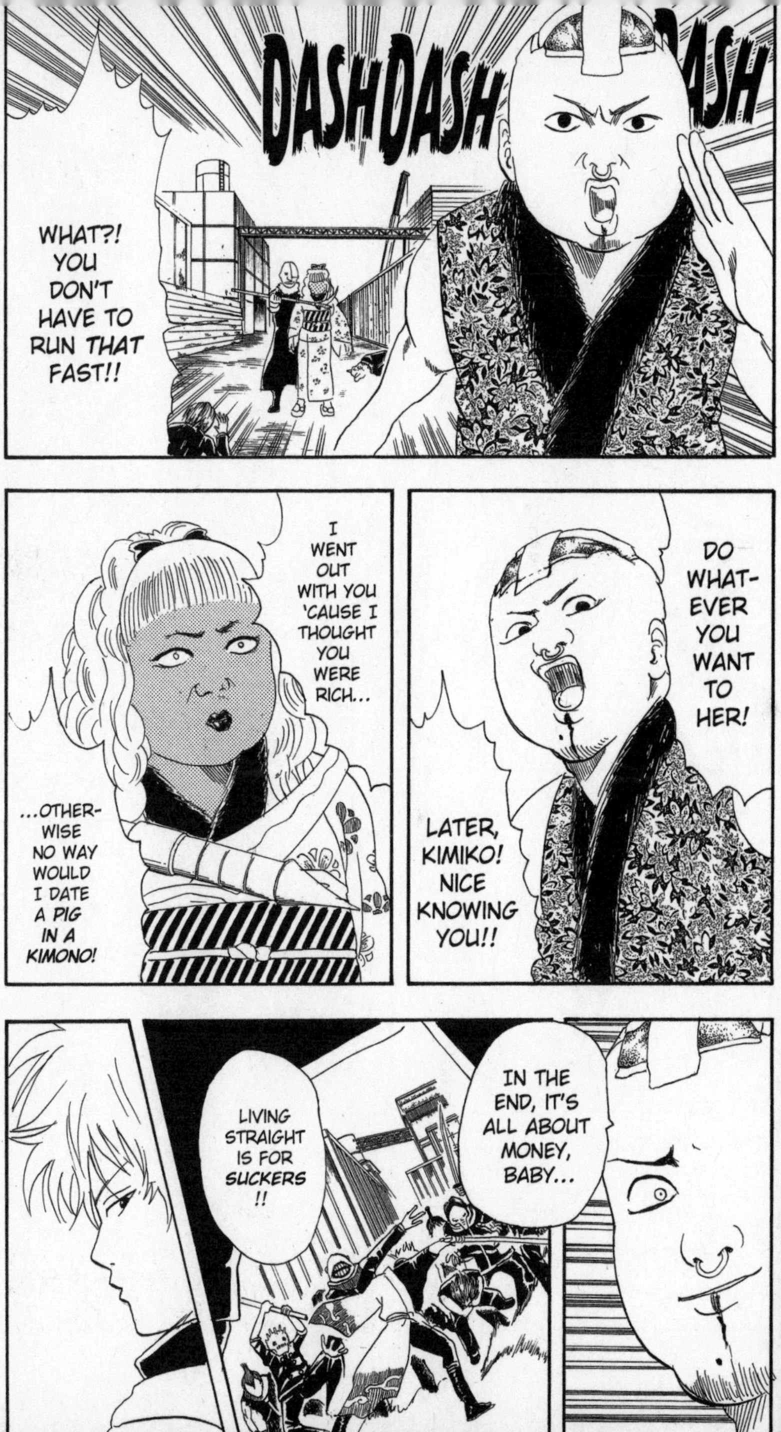
DASHDASHDASH
WHAT?! YOU DON'T HAVE TO RUN THAT FAST!!
DO WHATEVER YOU WANT TO HER!
LATER, KIMIKO! NICE KNOWING YOU!!
I WENT OUT WITH YOU 'CAUSE I THOUGHT YOU WERE RICH...
...OTHERWISE NO WAY WOULD I DATE A PIG IN A KIMONO!
IN THE END, IT'S ALL ABOUT MONEY, BABY...
LIVING STRAIGHT IS FOR SUCKERS!!

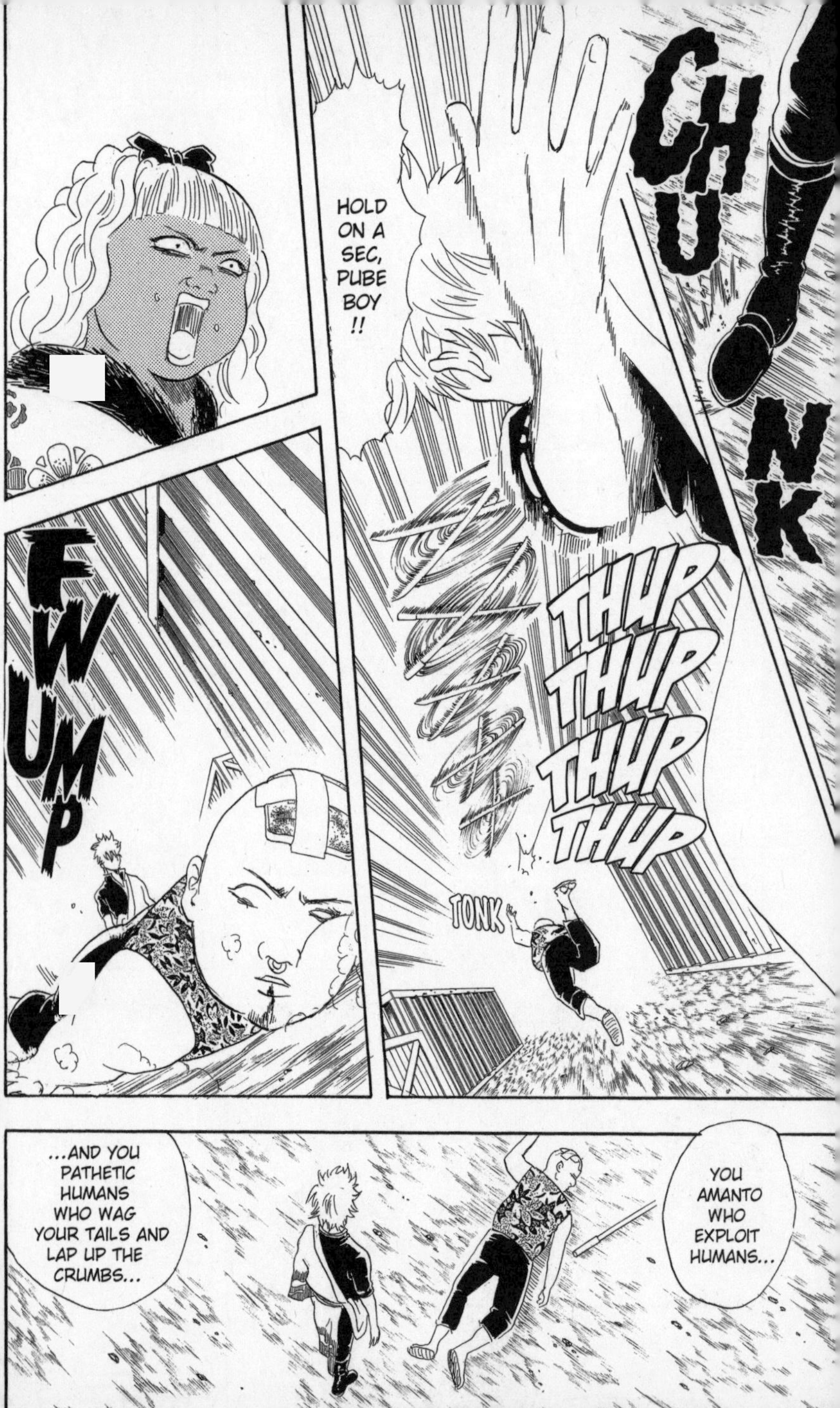
CHUNK
HOLD ON A SEC, PUBE BOY!!
THUP THUP THUP THUP
TONK
FWUMP
YOU AMANTO WHO EXPLOIT HUMANS...
...AND YOU PATHETIC HUMANS WHO WAG YOUR TAILS AND LAP UP THE CRUMBS...

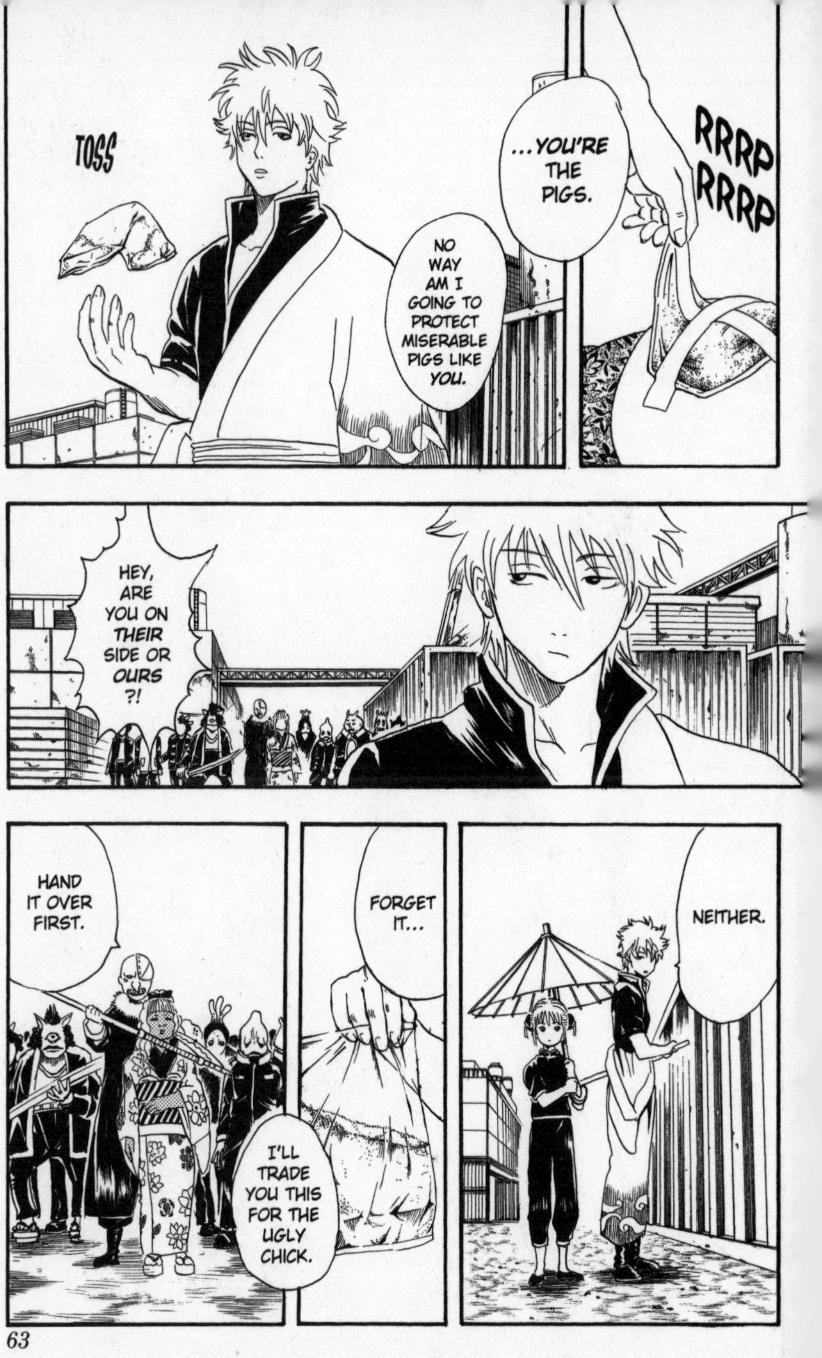
RRRP RRRP
...YOU'RE THE PIGS.
NO WAY AM I GOING TO PROTECT MISERABLE PIGS LIKE YOU.
TOSS
HEY, ARE YOU ON THEIR SIDE OR OURS?!
NEITHER.
FORGET IT...
I'LL TRADE YOU THIS FOR THE UGLY CHICK.
HAND IT OVER FIRST.

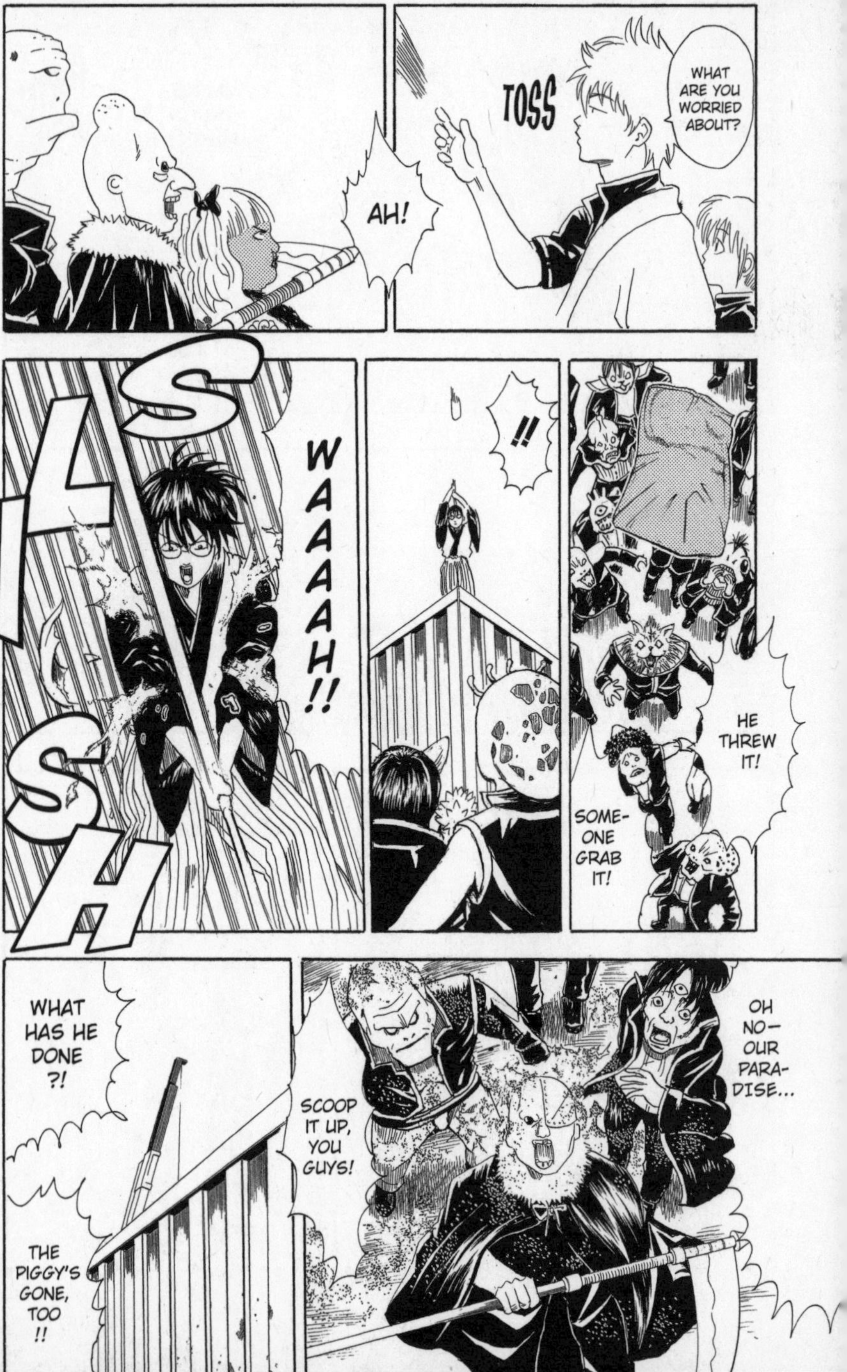
WHAT ARE YOU WORRIED ABOUT?
TOSS
AH!
HE THREW IT!
SOME-ONE GRAB IT!
!!
WAAAAAAH!!
SWISH
OH NO— OUR PARA-DISE...
SCOOP IT UP, YOU GUYS!
WHAT HAS HE DONE ?!
THE PIGGY'S GONE, TOO !!

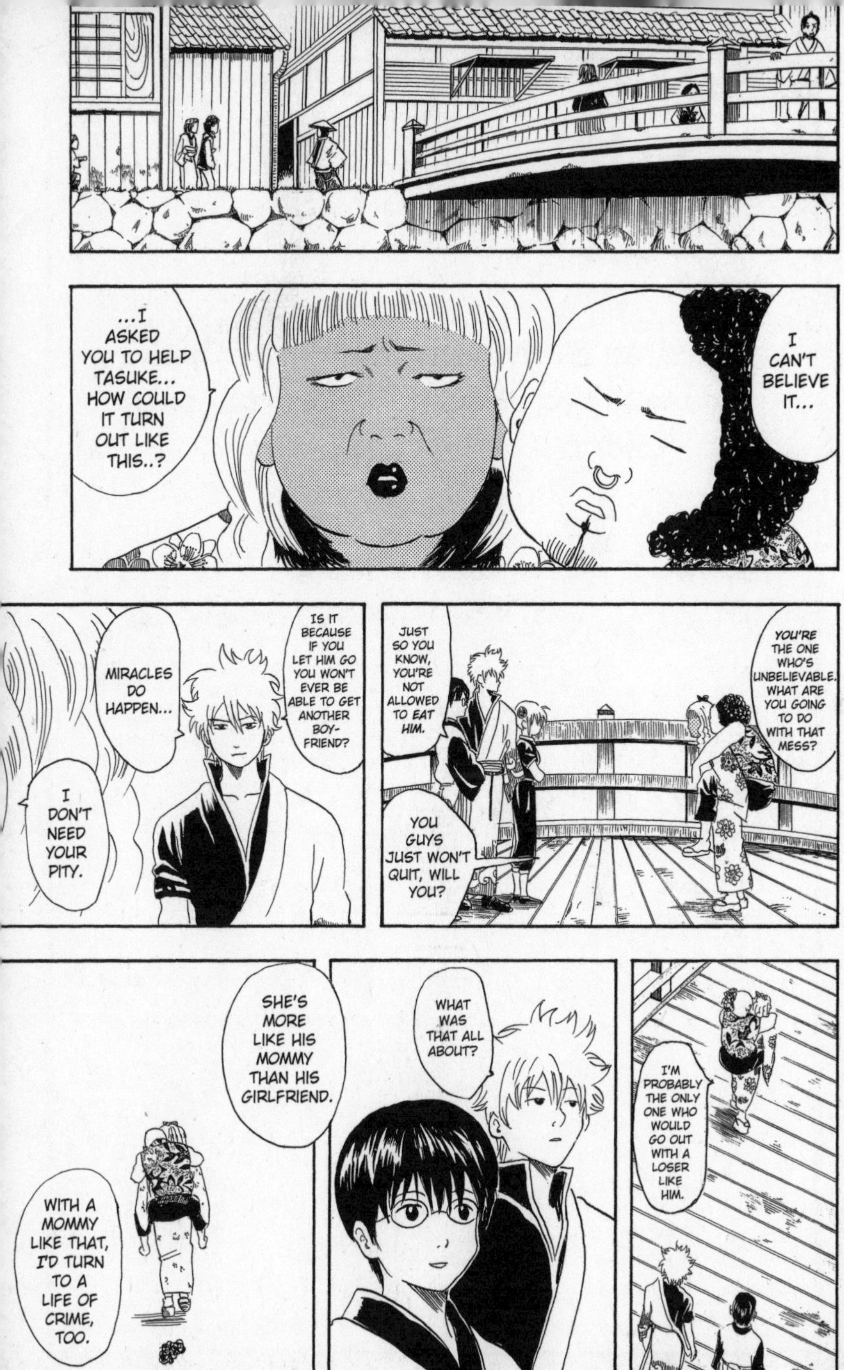
I CAN'T BELIEVE IT...
...I ASKED YOU TO HELP TASUKE... HOW COULD IT TURN OUT LIKE THIS..?
YOU'RE THE ONE WHO'S UNBELIEVABLE. WHAT ARE YOU GOING TO DO WITH THAT MESS?
JUST SO YOU KNOW, YOU'RE NOT ALLOWED TO EAT HIM.
YOU GUYS JUST WON'T QUIT, WILL YOU?
IS IT BECAUSE IF YOU LET HIM GO YOU WON'T EVER BE ABLE TO GET ANOTHER BOY-FRIEND?
MIRACLES DO HAPPEN...
I DON'T NEED YOUR PITY.
I'M PROBABLY THE ONLY ONE WHO WOULD GO OUT WITH A LOSER LIKE HIM.
WHAT WAS THAT ALL ABOUT?
SHE'S MORE LIKE HIS MOMMY THAN HIS GIRLFRIEND.
WITH A MOMMY LIKE THAT, I'D TURN TO A LIFE OF CRIME, TOO.

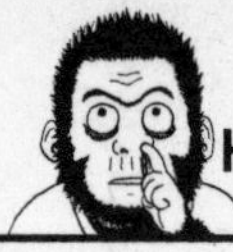

Sorachi's Q&A
Hanging with the Readers #2

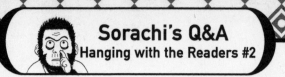

Question from Kanatsu-san of Osaka:
Please tell us about the backgrounds of the major characters.

I don't give much thought to them..
If you want their ages, roughly...

Gin	Twenties
Shinpachi	16
Kagura Around	13 or 14
Big Sister	18
Granny	60~65
Catherine	30~35
Hasegawa	35~40

More next time.

(Continued on page 90)

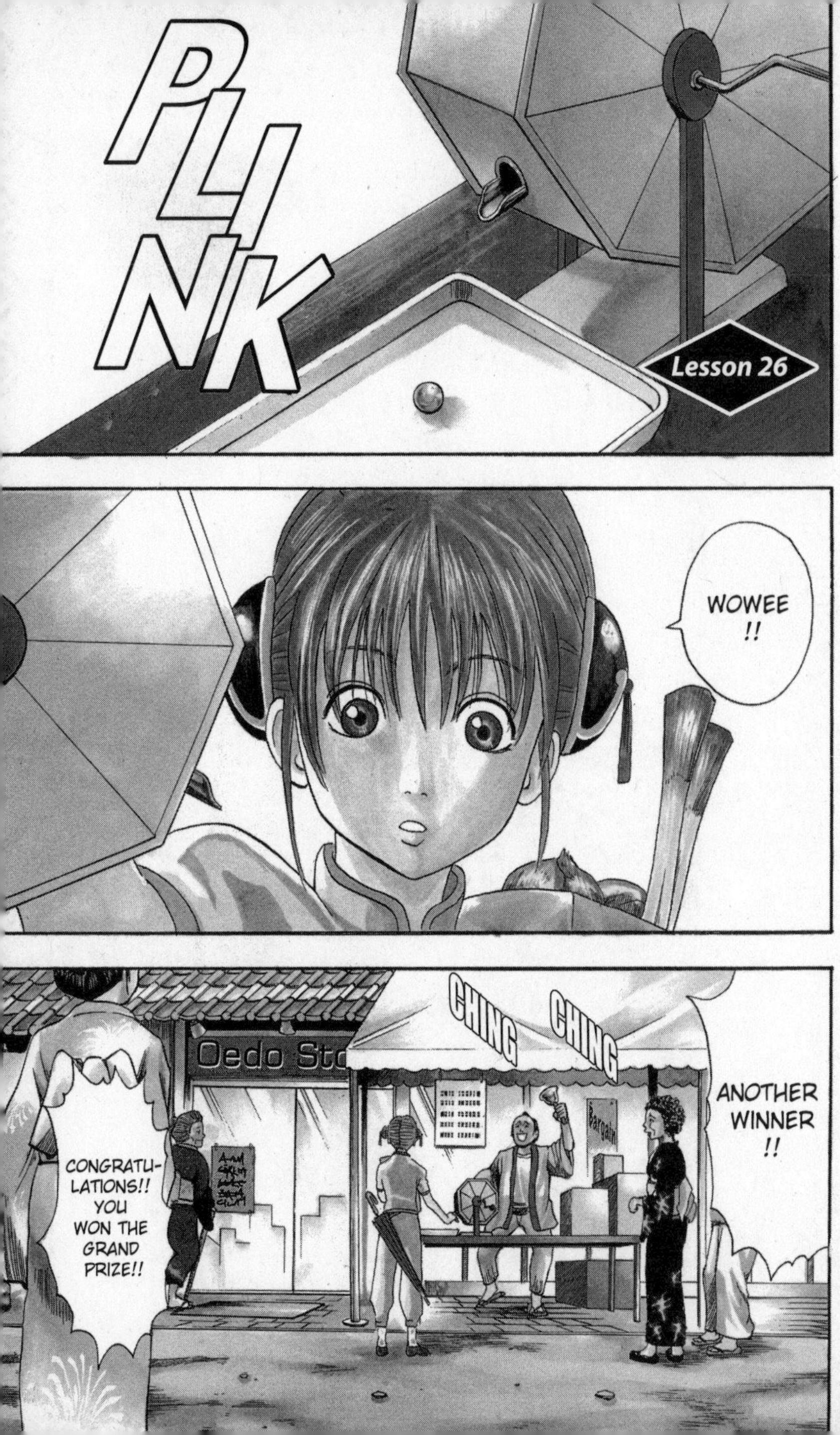
PLINK
Lesson 26
WOWEE!!
ANOTHER WINNER!!
CHING
CHING
Bargain
Oedo Sto
CONGRATULATIONS!! YOU WON THE GRAND PRIZE!!

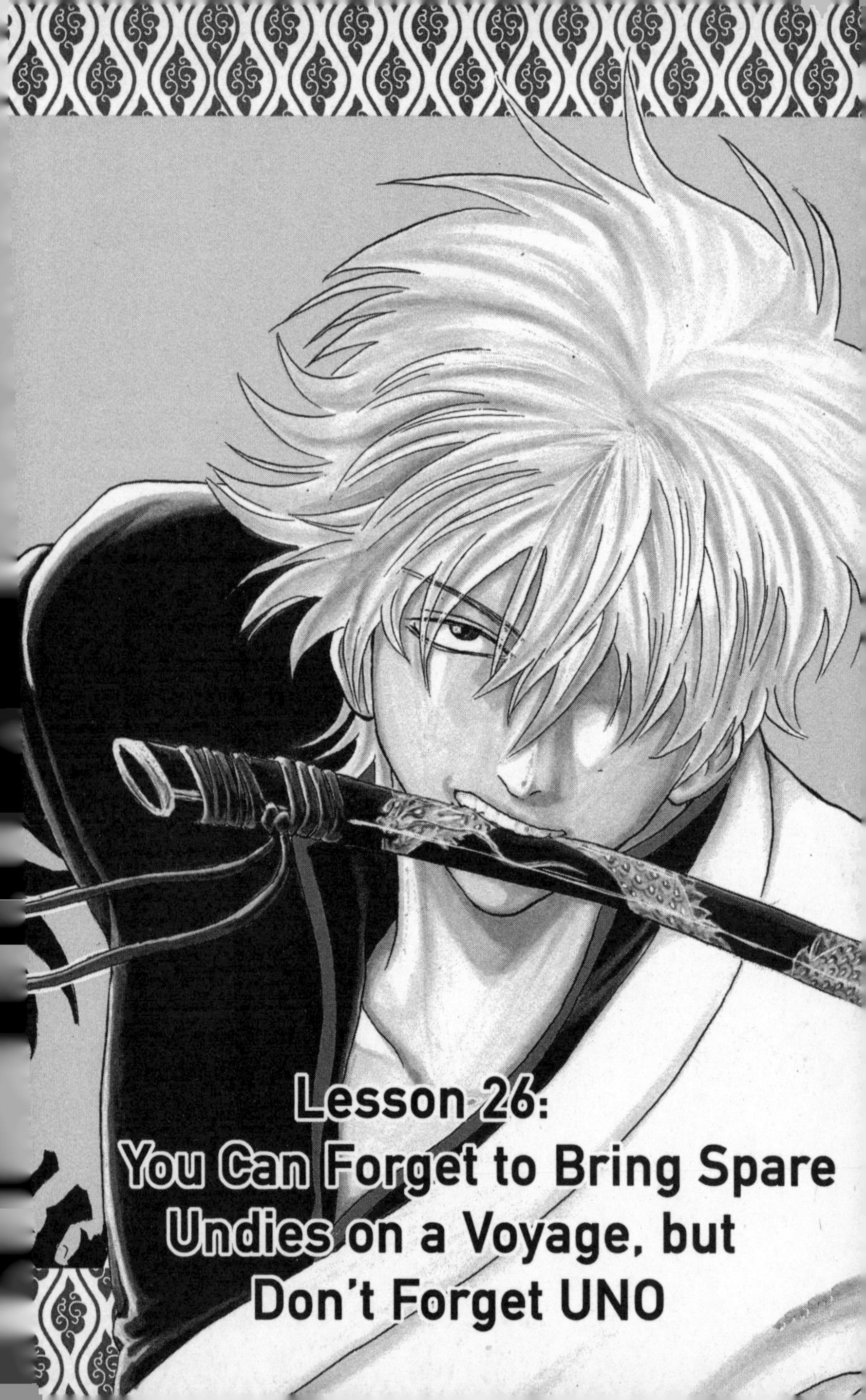
Lesson 26:
You Can Forget to Bring Spare Undies on a Voyage, but Don't Forget UNO

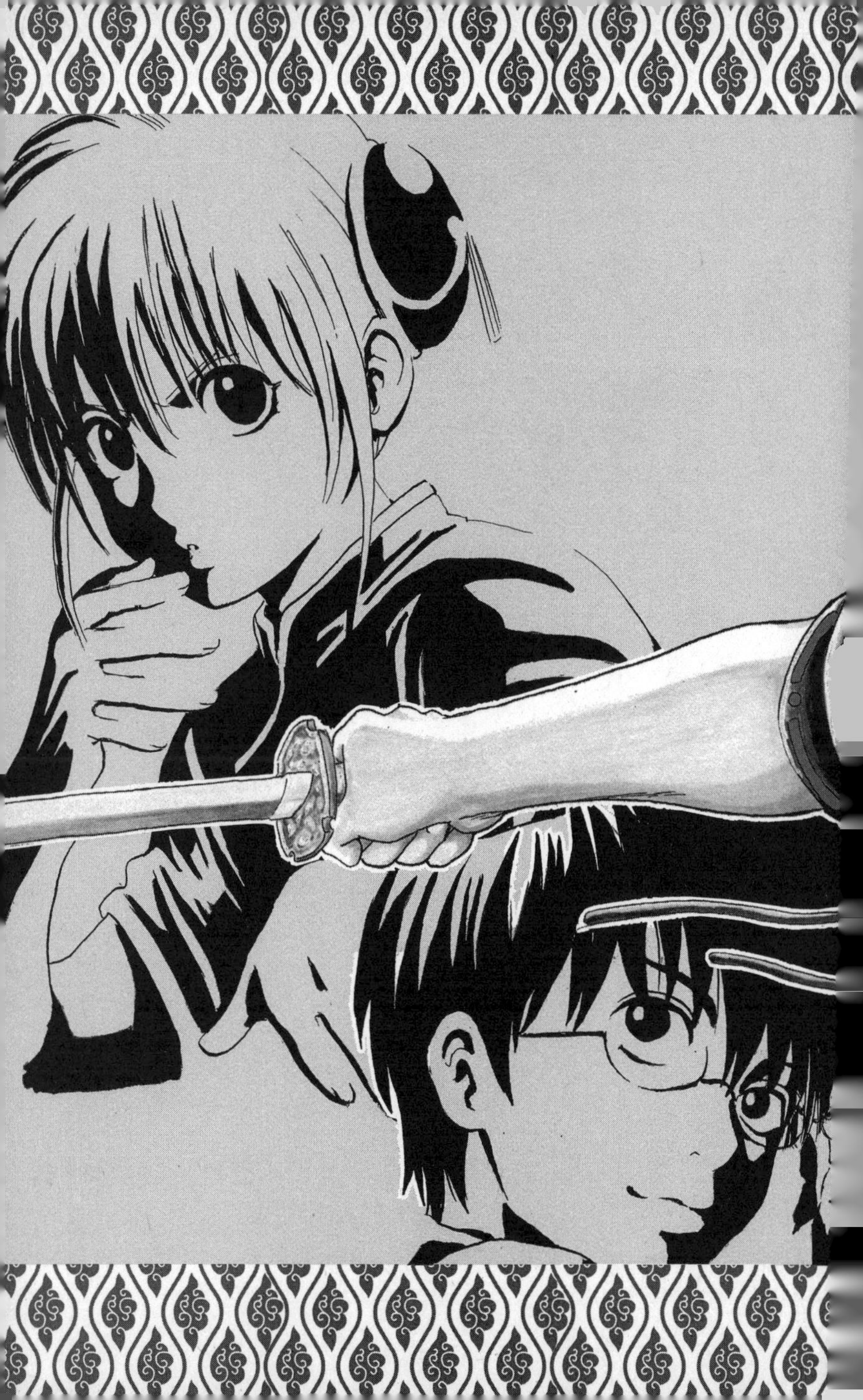

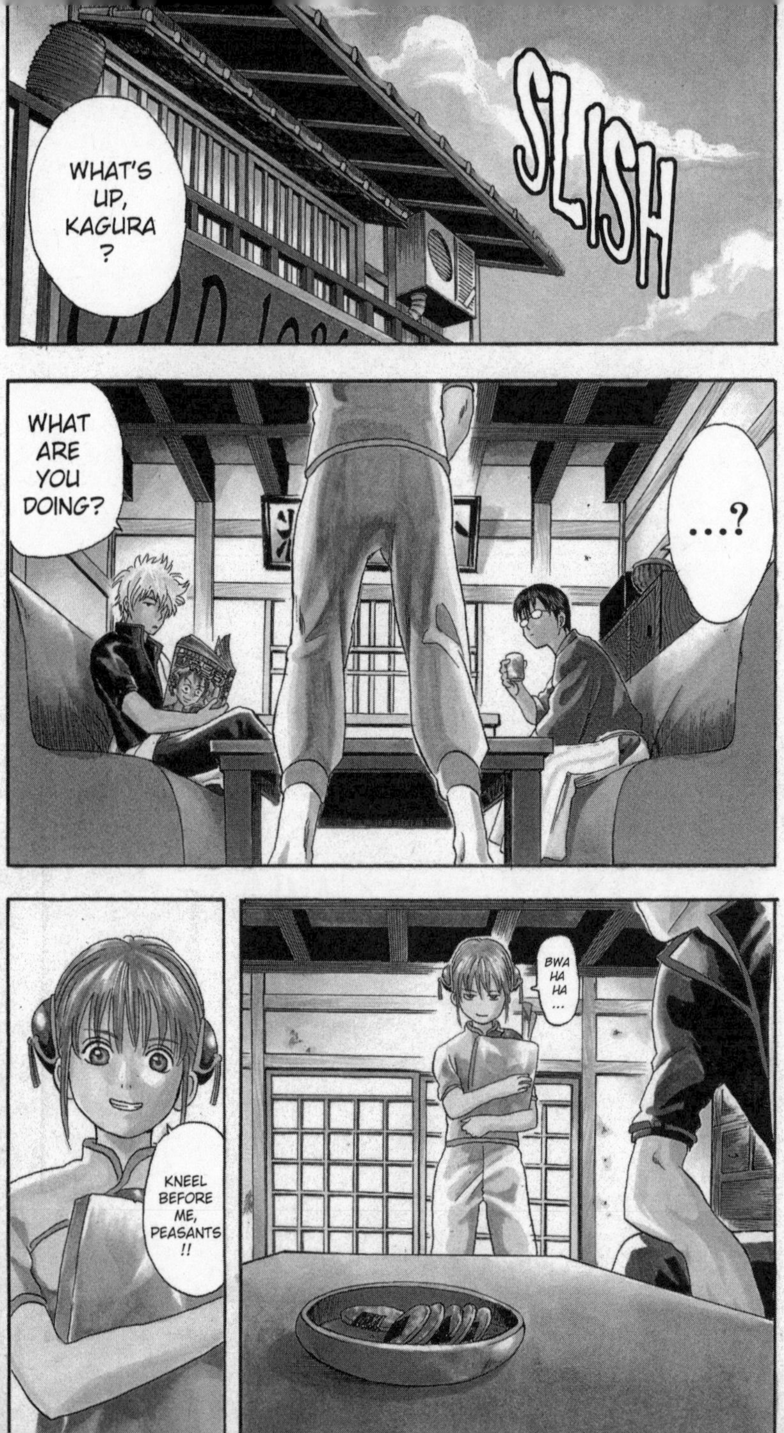
SLISH
WHAT'S UP, KAGURA?
...?
WHAT ARE YOU DOING?
BWA HA HA...
KNEEL BEFORE ME, PEASANTS!!

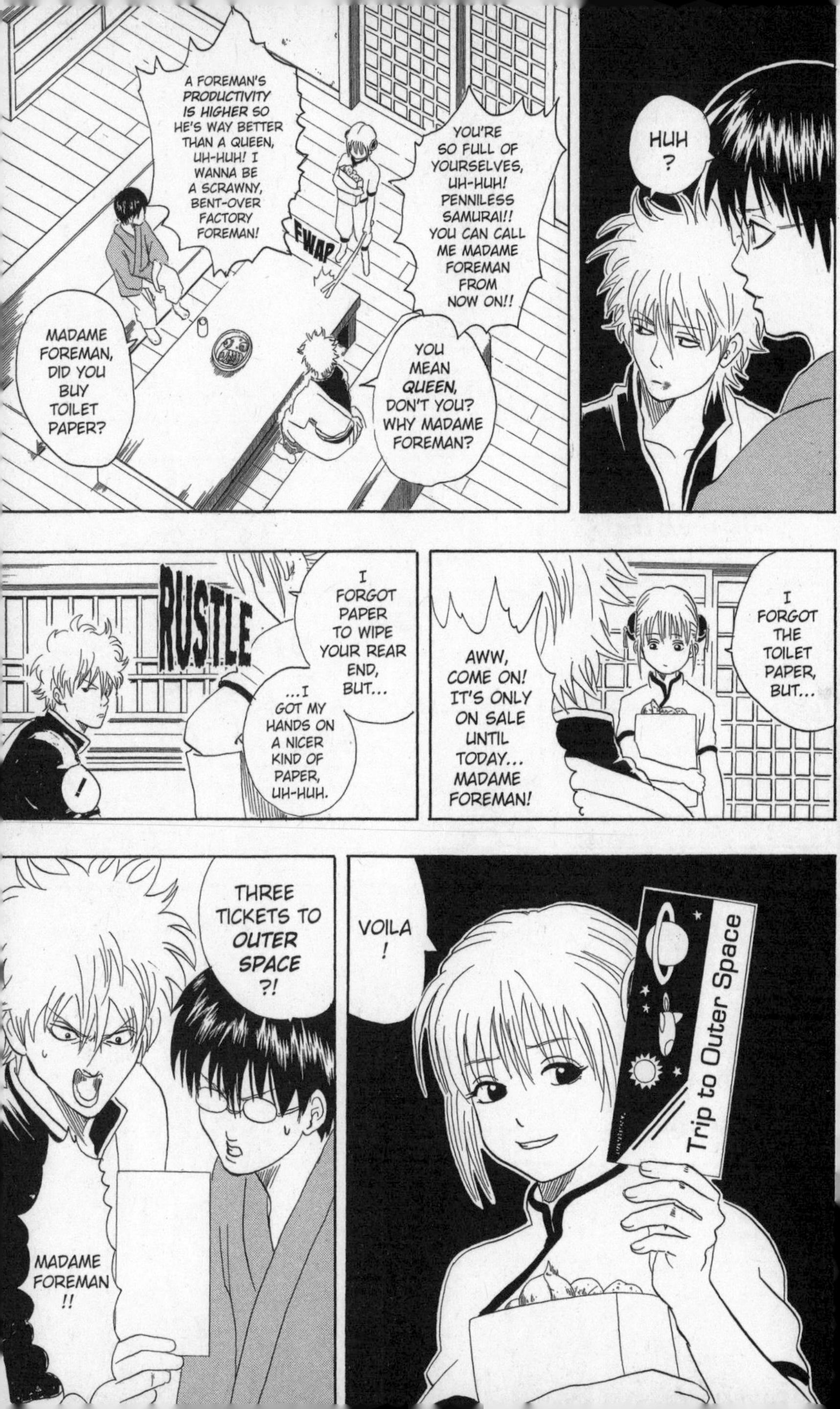
HUH?
YOU'RE SO FULL OF YOURSELVES, UH-HUH! PENNILESS SAMURAI!! YOU CAN CALL ME MADAME FOREMAN FROM NOW ON!!
A FOREMAN'S PRODUCTIVITY IS HIGHER SO HE'S WAY BETTER THAN A QUEEN, UH-HUH! I WANNA BE A SCRAWNY, BENT-OVER FACTORY FOREMAN!
FWAP
YOU MEAN QUEEN, DON'T YOU? WHY MADAME FOREMAN?
MADAME FOREMAN, DID YOU BUY TOILET PAPER?
I FORGOT THE TOILET PAPER, BUT...
AWW, COME ON! IT'S ONLY ON SALE UNTIL TODAY... MADAME FOREMAN!
I FORGOT PAPER TO WIPE YOUR REAR END, BUT...
RUSTLE
...I GOT MY HANDS ON A NICER KIND OF PAPER, UH-HUH.
!
VOILA!
Trip to Outer Space
THREE TICKETS TO OUTER SPACE ?!
MADAME FOREMAN !!

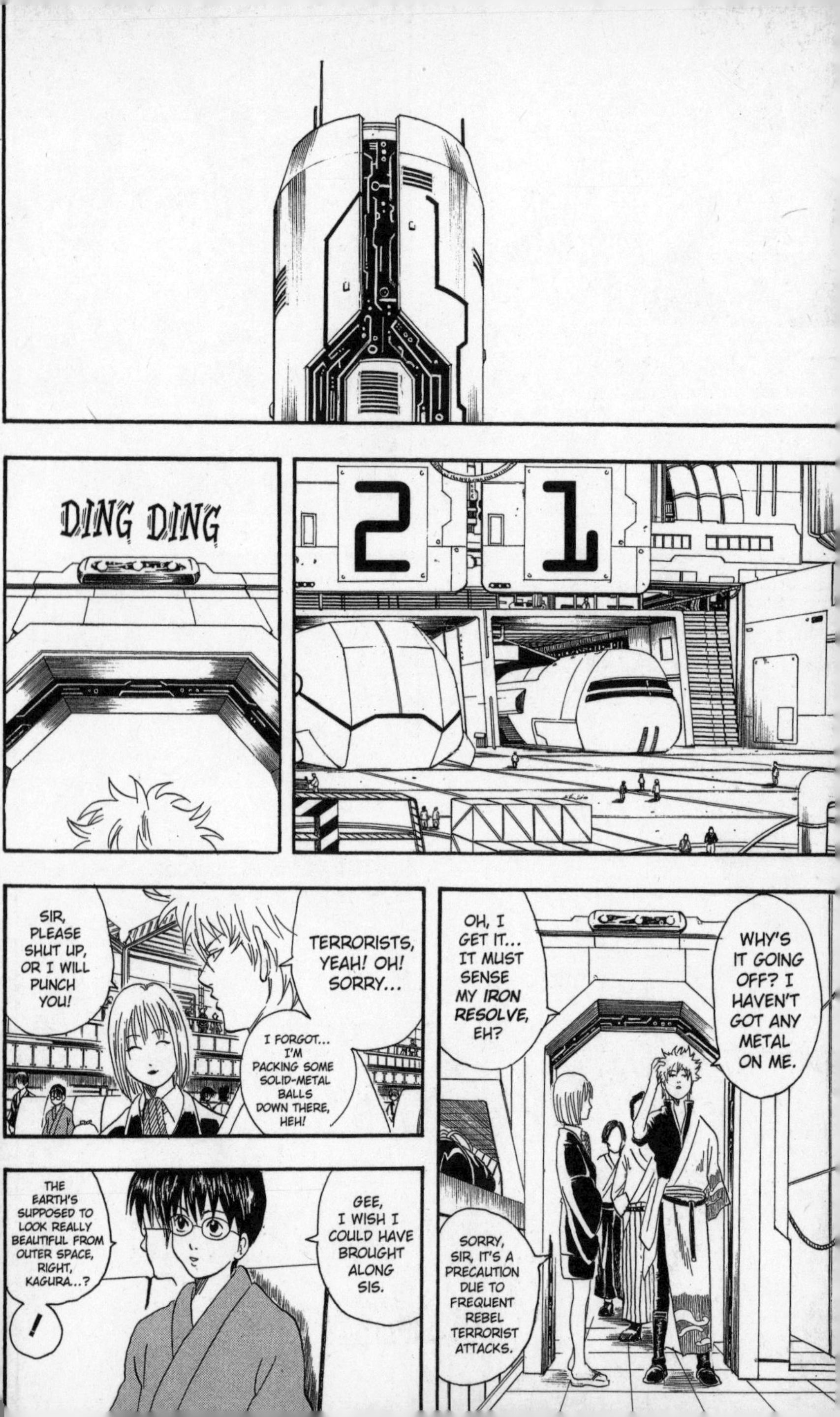

DING DING
WHY'S IT GOING OFF? I HAVEN'T GOT ANY METAL ON ME.
OH, I GET IT... IT MUST SENSE MY IRON RESOLVE, EH?
SORRY, SIR, IT'S A PRECAUTION DUE TO FREQUENT REBEL TERRORIST ATTACKS.
TERRORISTS, YEAH! OH! SORRY...
I FORGOT... I'M PACKING SOME SOLID-METAL BALLS DOWN THERE, HEH!
SIR, PLEASE SHUT UP, OR I WILL PUNCH YOU!
GEE, I WISH I COULD HAVE BROUGHT ALONG SIS.
THE EARTH'S SUPPOSED TO LOOK REALLY BEAUTIFUL FROM OUTER SPACE, RIGHT, KAGURA...?
!

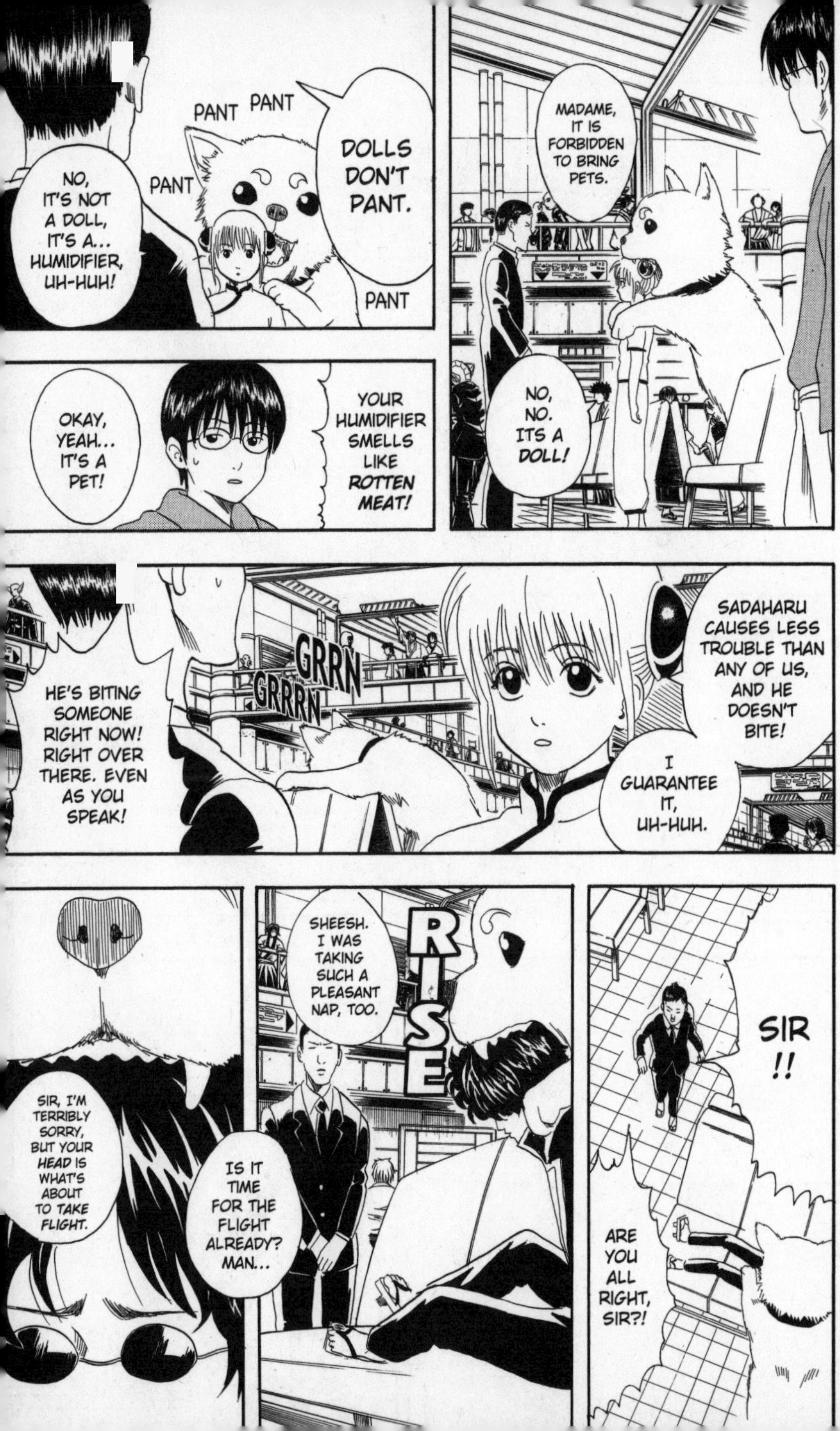
MADAME, IT IS FORBIDDEN TO BRING PETS.
NO, NO. ITS A DOLL!
PANT PANT
PANT
PANT
DOLLS DON'T PANT.
NO, IT'S NOT A DOLL, IT'S A... HUMIDIFIER, UH-HUH!
YOUR HUMIDIFIER SMELLS LIKE ROTTEN MEAT!
OKAY, YEAH... IT'S A PET!
SADAHARU CAUSES LESS TROUBLE THAN ANY OF US, AND HE DOESN'T BITE!
I GUARANTEE IT, UH-HUH.
GRRN
GRRRN
HE'S BITING SOMEONE RIGHT NOW! RIGHT OVER THERE. EVEN AS YOU SPEAK!
SIR !!
ARE YOU ALL RIGHT, SIR?!
RISE
SHEESH. I WAS TAKING SUCH A PLEASANT NAP, TOO.
IS IT TIME FOR THE FLIGHT ALREADY? MAN...
SIR, I'M TERRIBLY SORRY, BUT YOUR HEAD IS WHAT'S ABOUT TO TAKE FLIGHT.

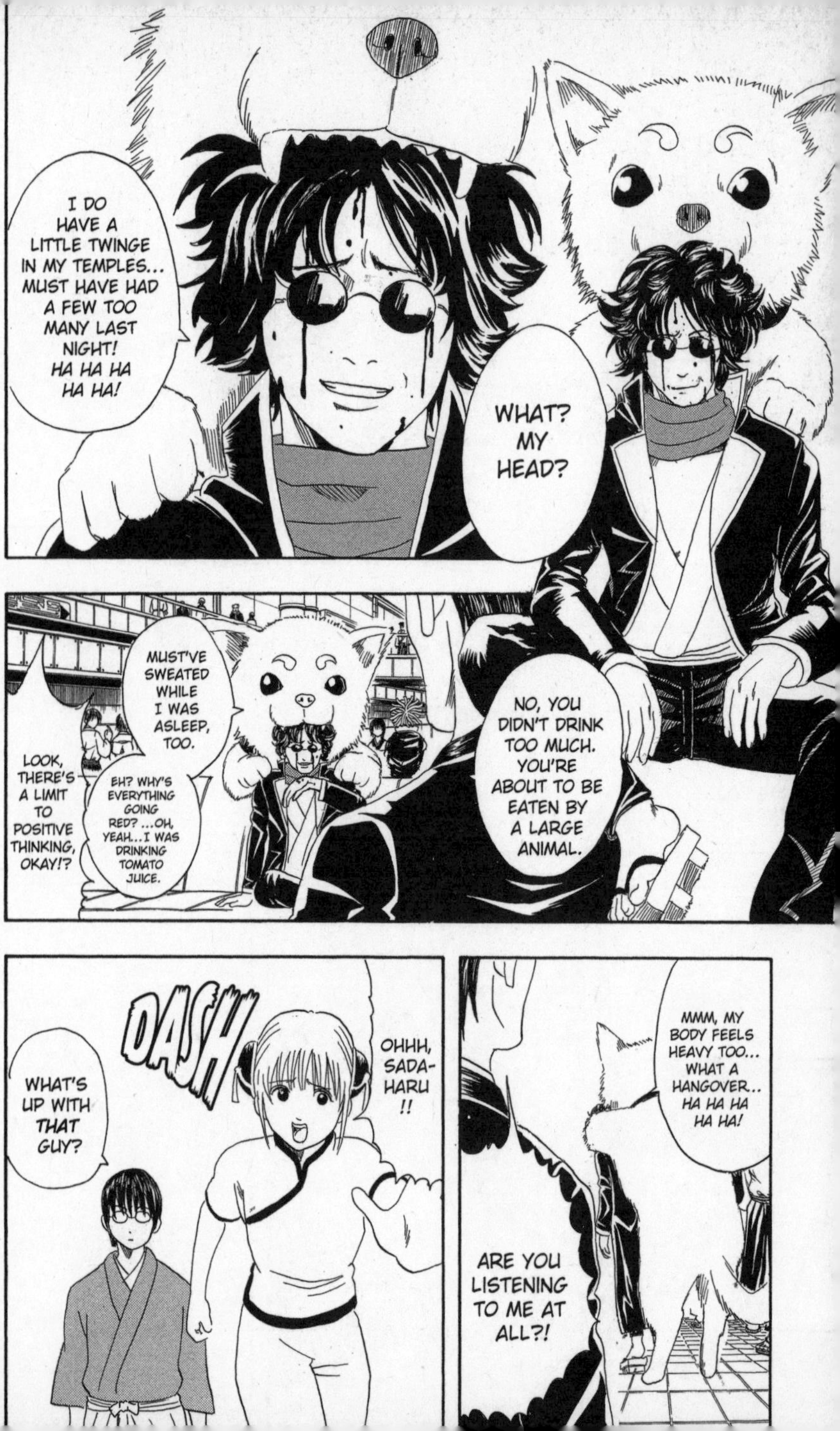
WHAT? MY HEAD?
I DO HAVE A LITTLE TWINGE IN MY TEMPLES... MUST HAVE HAD A FEW TOO MANY LAST NIGHT! HA HA HA HA HA!
NO, YOU DIDN'T DRINK TOO MUCH. YOU'RE ABOUT TO BE EATEN BY A LARGE ANIMAL.
MUST'VE SWEATED WHILE I WAS ASLEEP, TOO.
EH? WHY'S EVERYTHING GOING RED? ...OH, YEAH...I WAS DRINKING TOMATO JUICE.
LOOK, THERE'S A LIMIT TO POSITIVE THINKING, OKAY!?
MMM, MY BODY FEELS HEAVY TOO... WHAT A HANGOVER.. HA HA HA HA HA!
ARE YOU LISTENING TO ME AT ALL?!
OHHH, SADA-HARU!!
DASH
WHAT'S UP WITH THAT GUY?

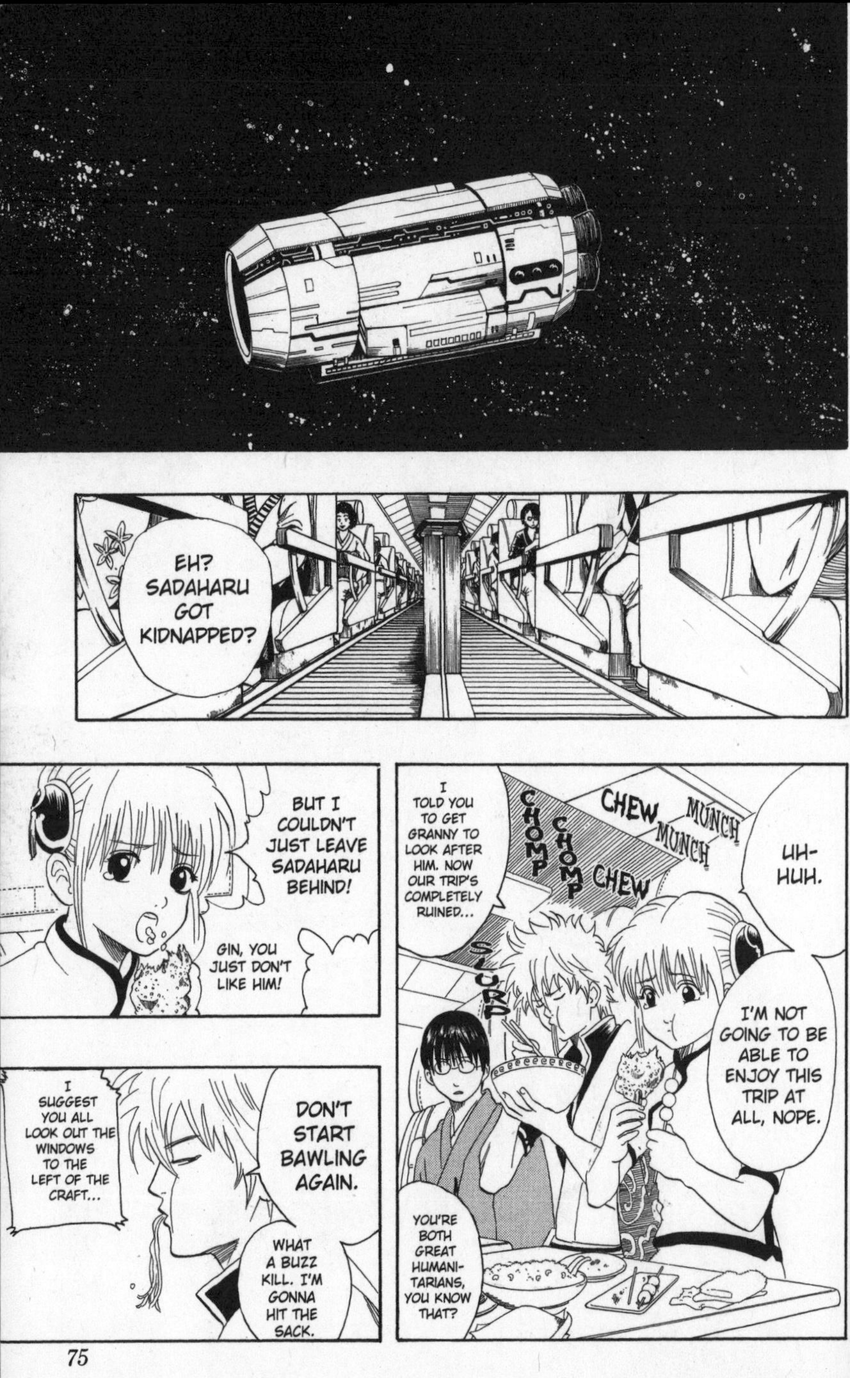
EH? SADAHARU GOT KIDNAPPED?
UH-HUH.
I TOLD YOU TO GET GRANNY TO LOOK AFTER HIM. NOW OUR TRIP'S COMPLETELY RUINED...
CHEW MUNCH MUNCH
CHOMP CHOMP CHEW
SLURP
I'M NOT GOING TO BE ABLE TO ENJOY THIS TRIP AT ALL, NOPE.
YOU'RE BOTH GREAT HUMANITARIANS, YOU KNOW THAT?
BUT I COULDN'T JUST LEAVE SADAHARU BEHIND!
GIN, YOU JUST DON'T LIKE HIM!
DON'T START BAWLING AGAIN.
WHAT A BUZZ KILL. I'M GONNA HIT THE SACK.
I SUGGEST YOU ALL LOOK OUT THE WINDOWS TO THE LEFT OF THE CRAFT...

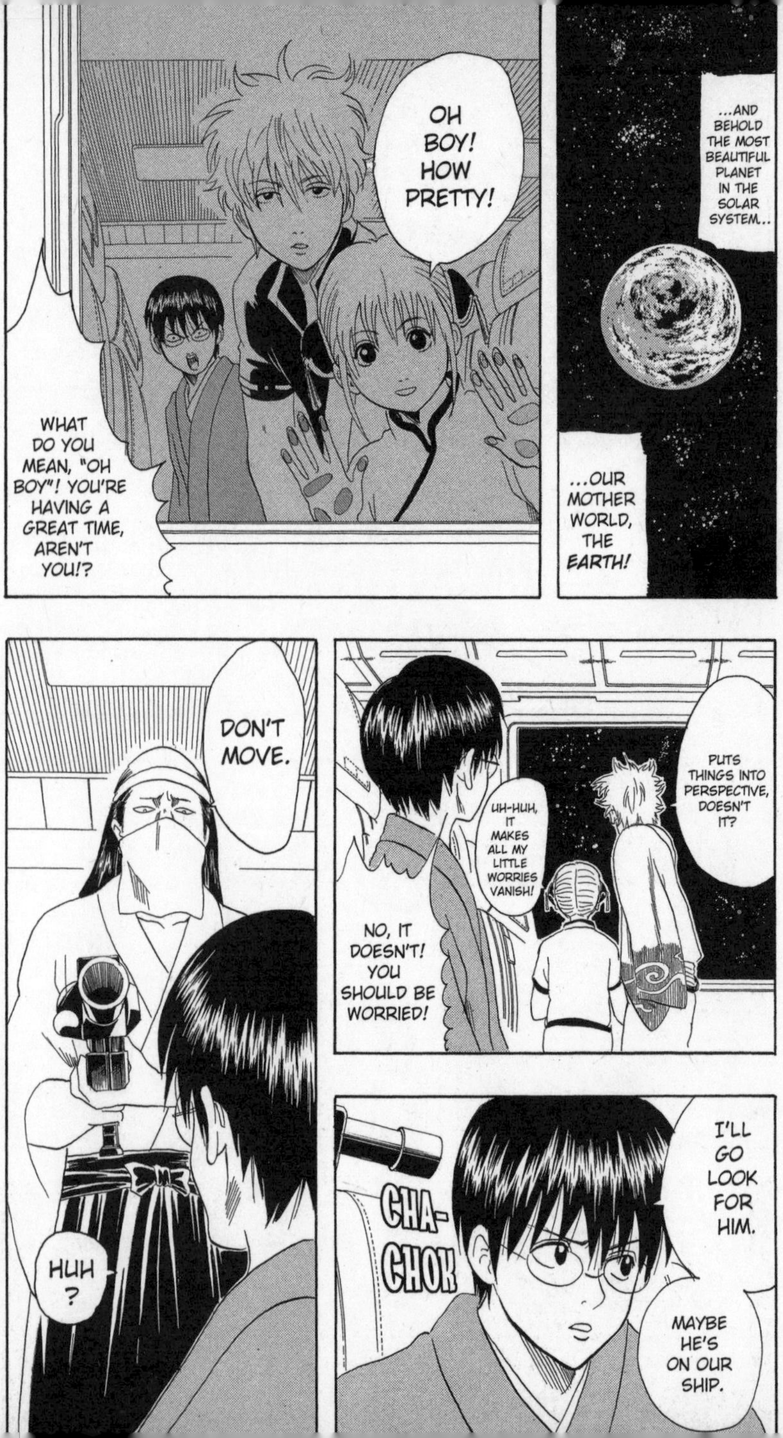
...AND BEHOLD THE MOST BEAUTIFUL PLANET IN THE SOLAR SYSTEM...
...OUR MOTHER WORLD, THE EARTH!
OH BOY! HOW PRETTY!
WHAT DO YOU MEAN, "OH BOY"! YOU'RE HAVING A GREAT TIME, AREN'T YOU!?
PUTS THINGS INTO PERSPECTIVE, DOESN'T IT?
UH-HUH, IT MAKES ALL MY LITTLE WORRIES VANISH!
NO, IT DOESN'T! YOU SHOULD BE WORRIED!
I'LL GO LOOK FOR HIM.
MAYBE HE'S ON OUR SHIP.
CHA-CHOK
DON'T MOVE.
HUH?

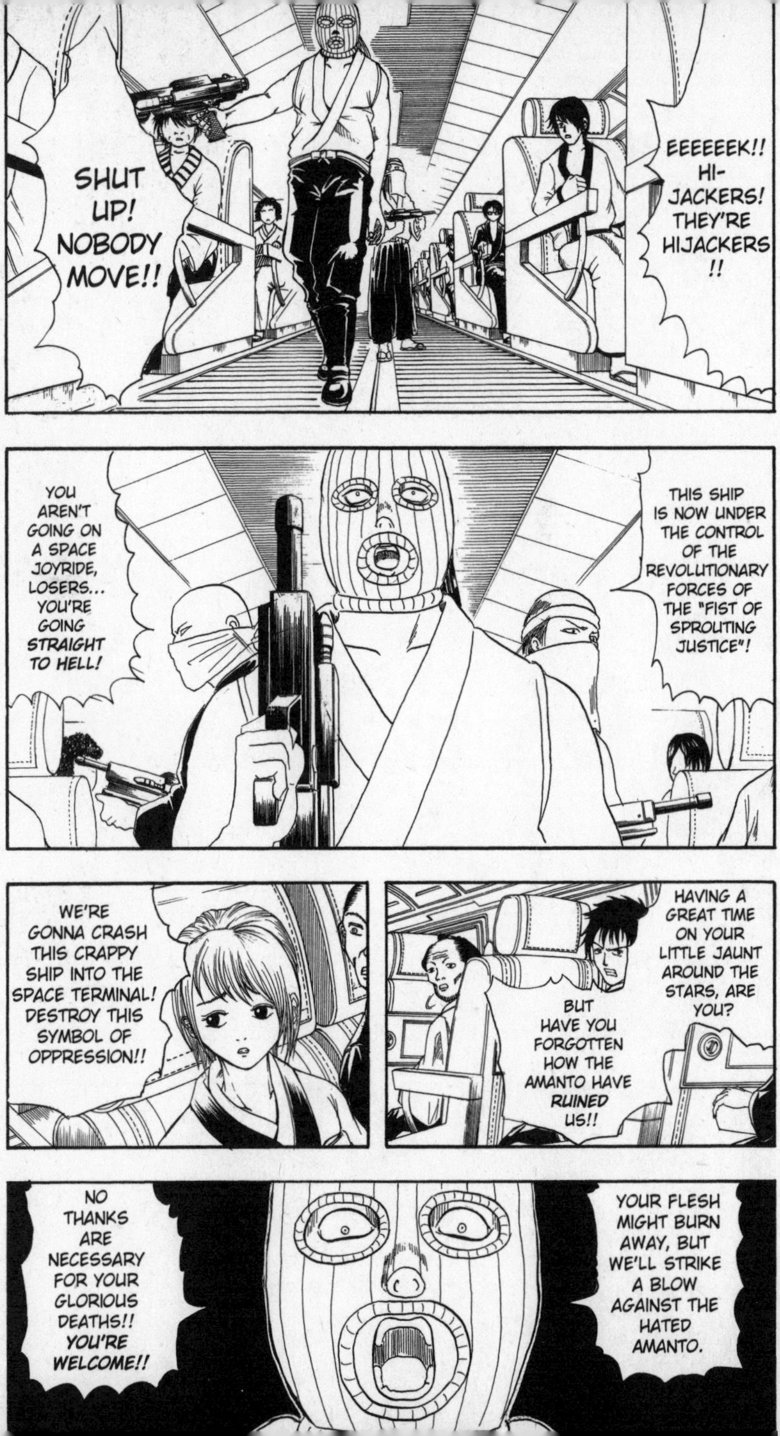
EEEEEEK!! HI-JACKERS! THEY'RE HIJACKERS !!
SHUT UP! NOBODY MOVE!!
THIS SHIP IS NOW UNDER THE CONTROL OF THE REVOLUTIONARY FORCES OF THE "FIST OF SPROUTING JUSTICE"!
YOU AREN'T GOING ON A SPACE JOYRIDE, LOSERS... YOU'RE GOING STRAIGHT TO HELL!
HAVING A GREAT TIME ON YOUR LITTLE JAUNT AROUND THE STARS, ARE YOU?
BUT HAVE YOU FORGOTTEN HOW THE AMANTO HAVE RUINED US!!
WE'RE GONNA CRASH THIS CRAPPY SHIP INTO THE SPACE TERMINAL! DESTROY THIS SYMBOL OF OPPRESSION!!
YOUR FLESH MIGHT BURN AWAY, BUT WE'LL STRIKE A BLOW AGAINST THE HATED AMANTO.
NO THANKS ARE NECESSARY FOR YOUR GLORIOUS DEATHS!! YOU'RE WELCOME!!

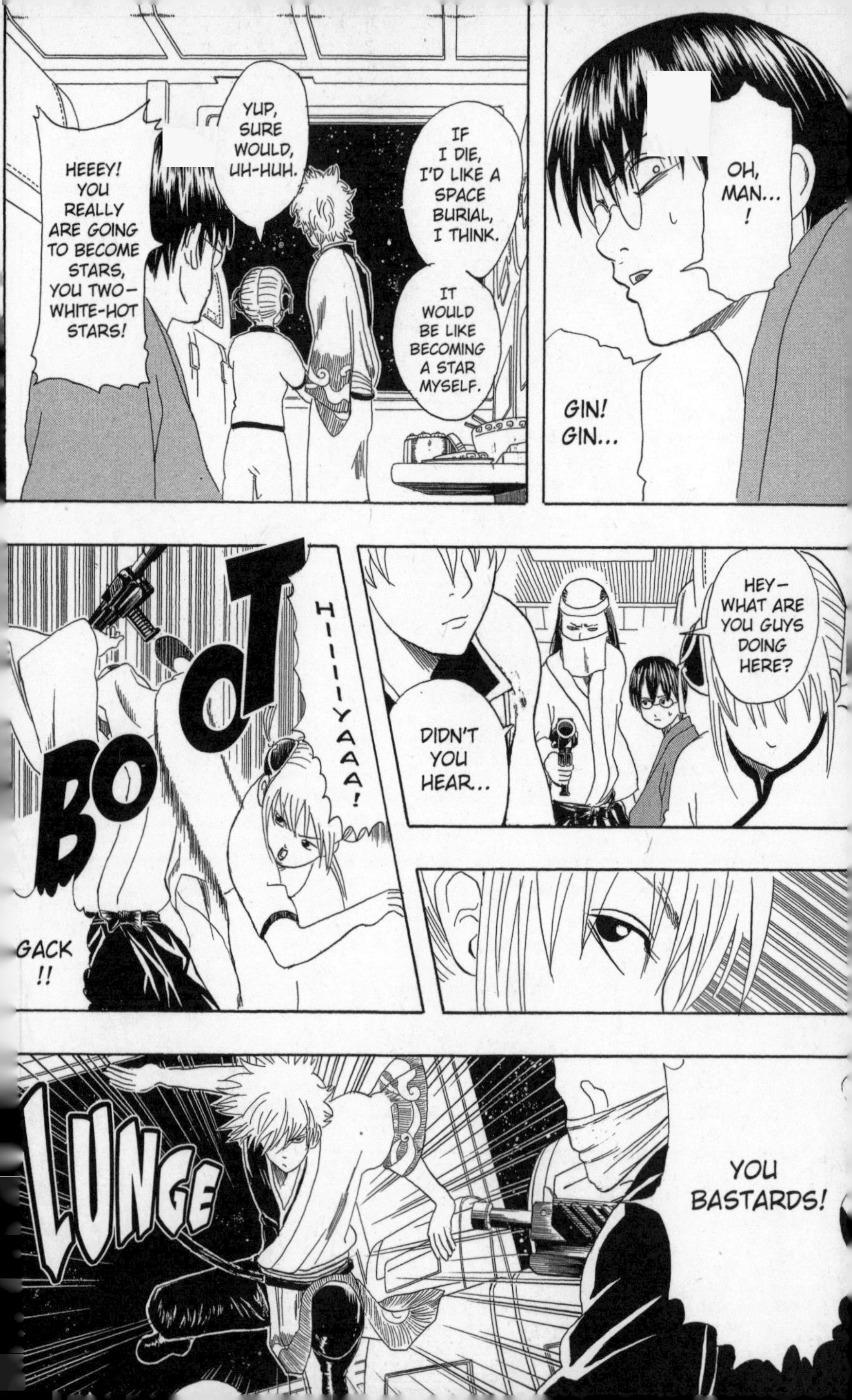
OH, MAN... !
GIN! GIN...
IF I DIE, I'D LIKE A SPACE BURIAL, I THINK.
IT WOULD BE LIKE BECOMING A STAR MYSELF.
YUP, SURE WOULD, UH-HUH.
HEEEY! YOU REALLY ARE GOING TO BECOME STARS, YOU TWO—WHITE-HOT STARS!
HEY—WHAT ARE YOU GUYS DOING HERE?
DIDN'T YOU HEAR...
HIIIIYAAAA!
BOOT
GACK !!
YOU BASTARDS!
LUNGE

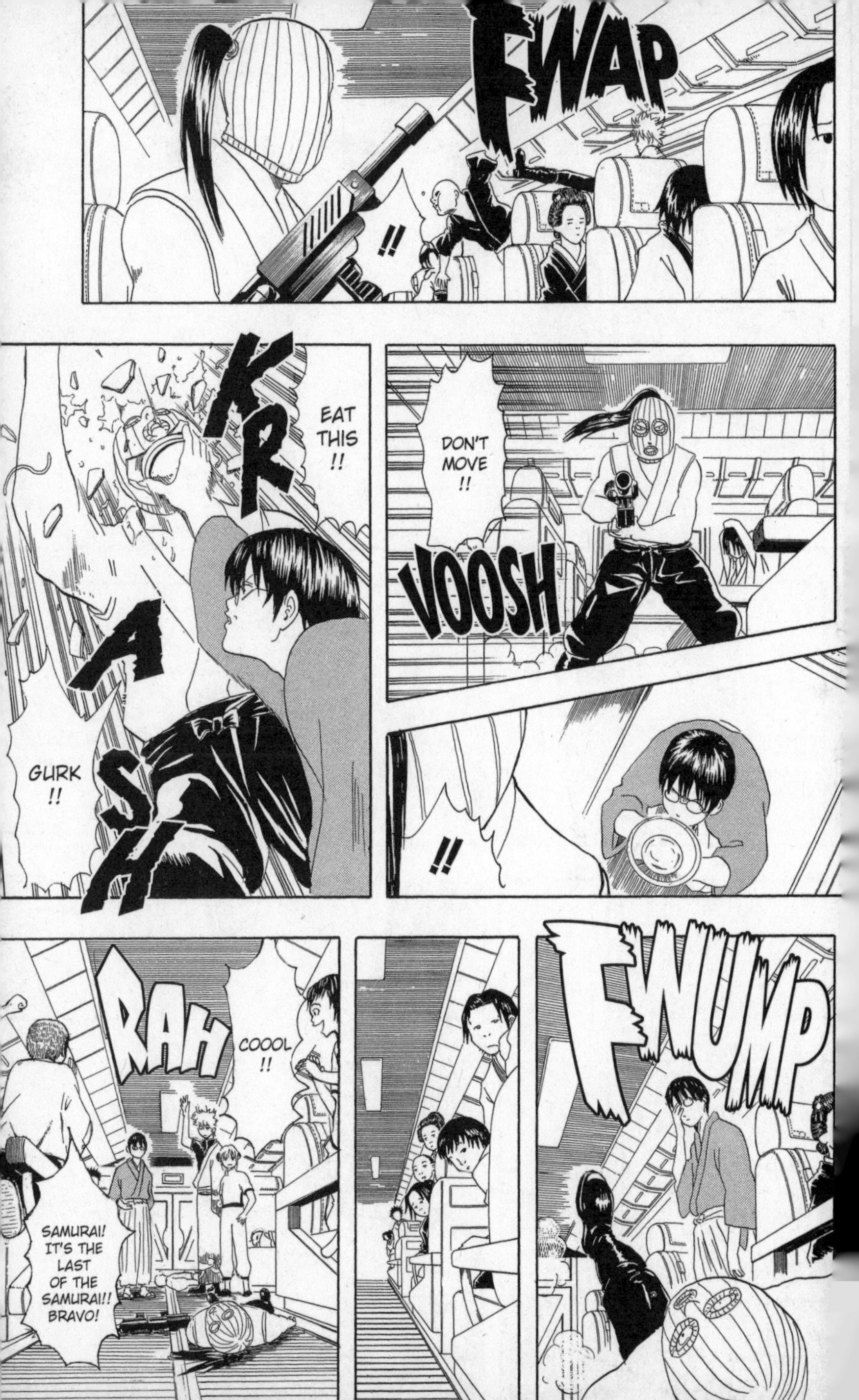
FWAP
!!
DON'T MOVE !!
VOOSH
!!
EAT THIS !!
KRASH
GURK !!
FWUMP
RAH
COOOL !!
SAMURAI! IT'S THE LAST OF THE SAMURAI!! BRAVO!

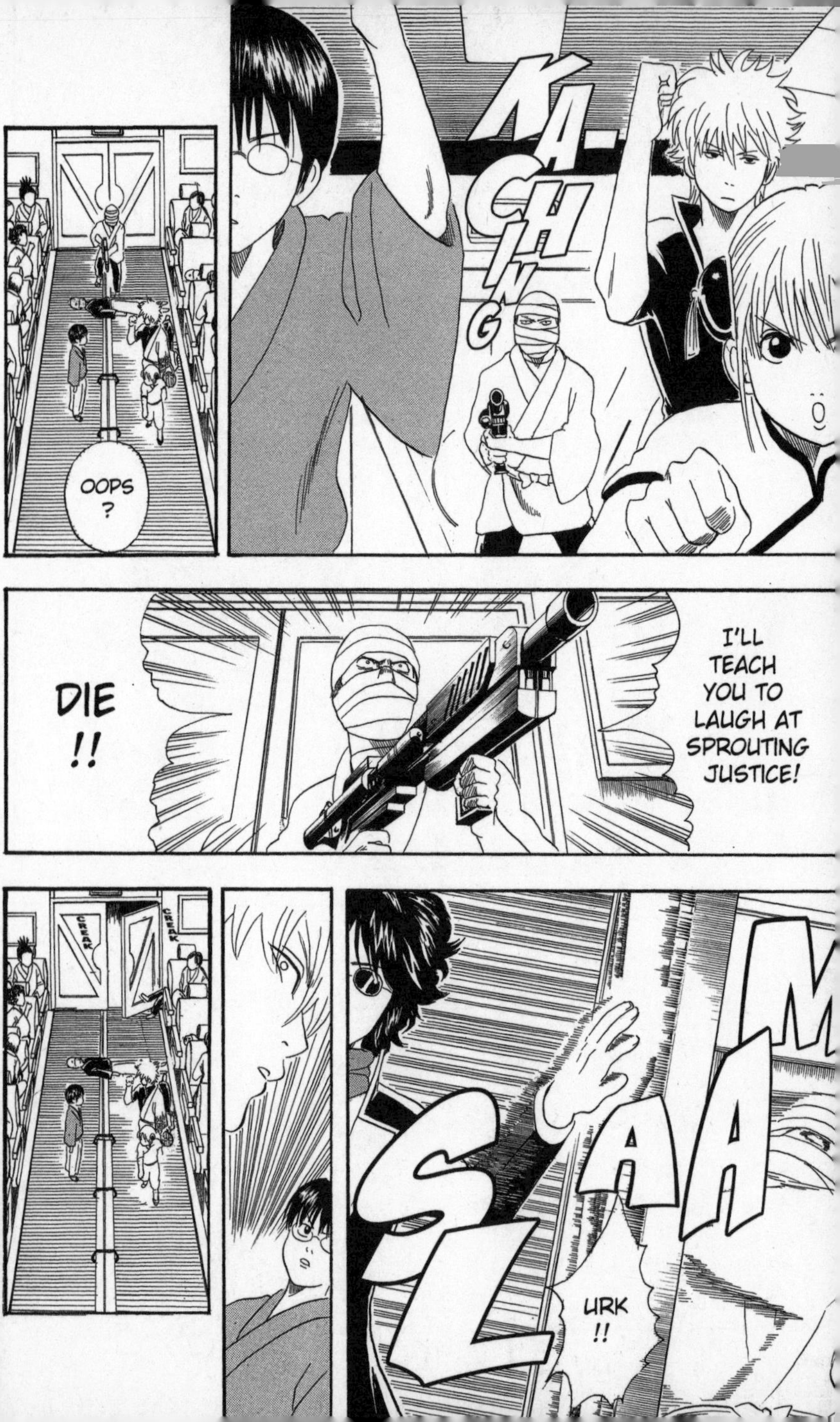
KA-CHING
OOPS?
I'LL TEACH YOU TO LAUGH AT SPROUTING JUSTICE!
DIE!!
SLAAM
URK!!
CREAK
CREAK

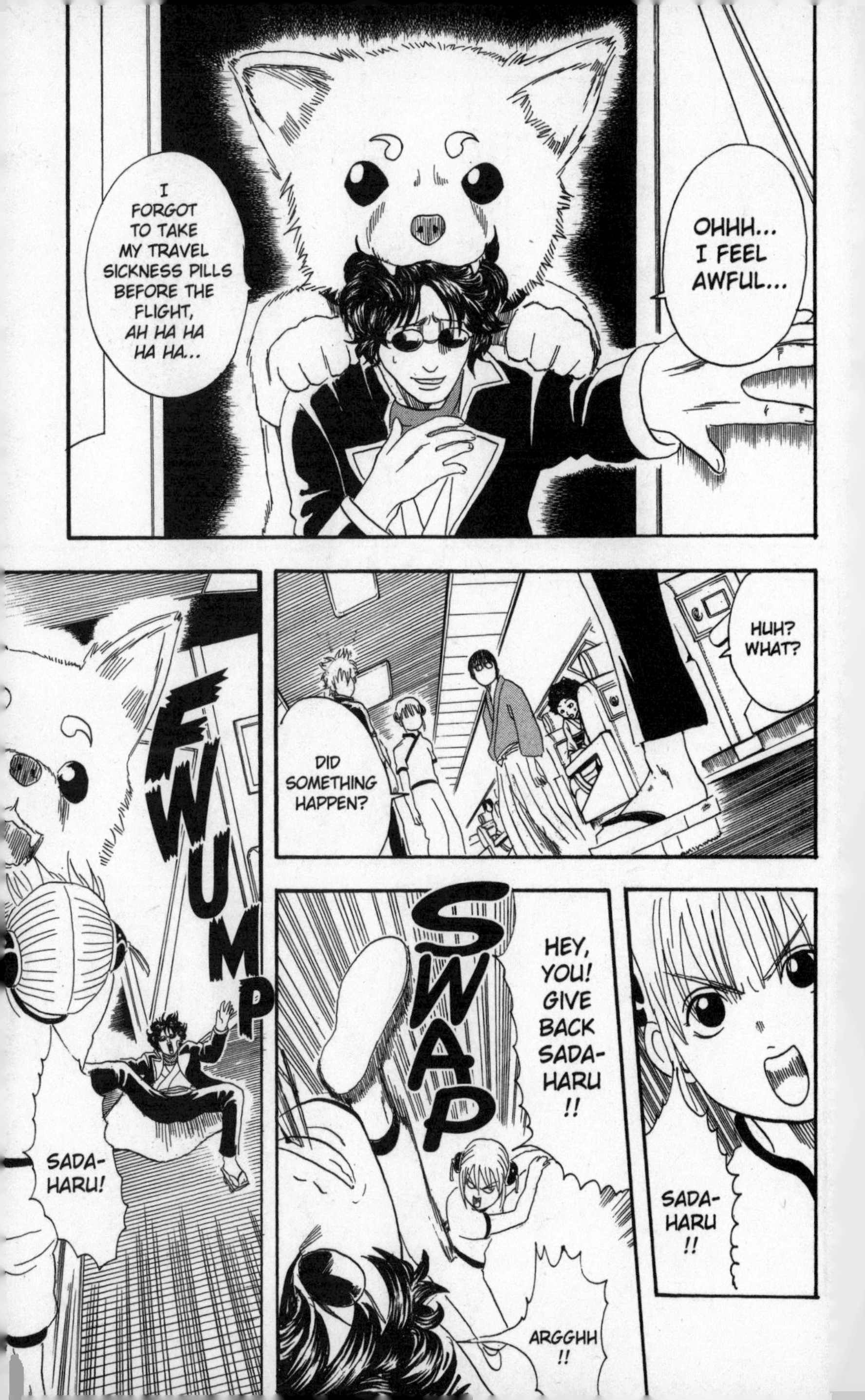
OHHH... I FEEL AWFUL...
I FORGOT TO TAKE MY TRAVEL SICKNESS PILLS BEFORE THE FLIGHT, AH HA HA HA HA...
HUH? WHAT?
DID SOMETHING HAPPEN?
SADA-HARU !!
HEY, YOU! GIVE BACK SADA-HARU !!
SWAP
ARGGHH !!
FWUMP
SADA-HARU!

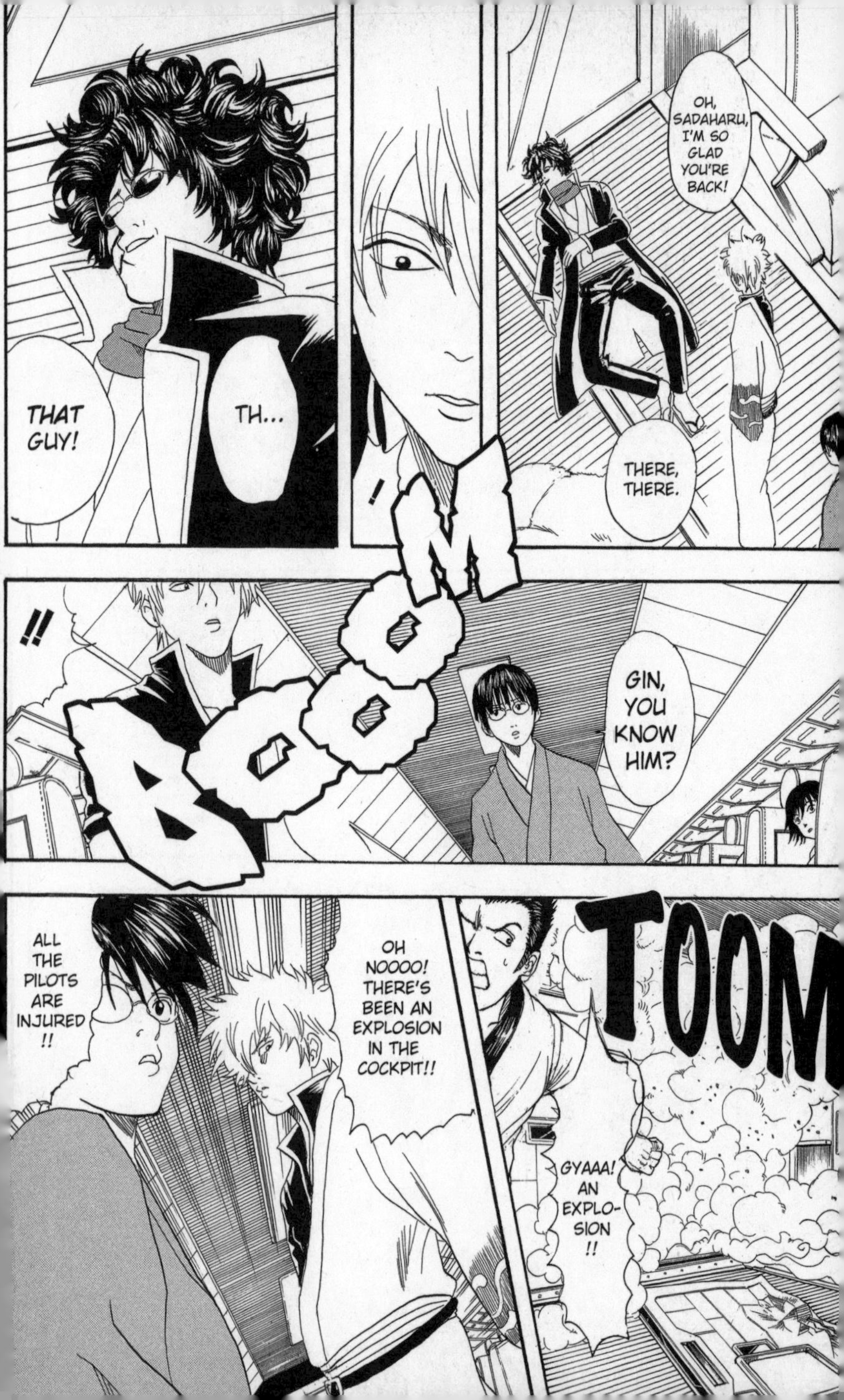
OH, SADAHARU, I'M SO GLAD YOU'RE BACK!
THERE, THERE.
!
TH...
THAT GUY!
GIN, YOU KNOW HIM?
BOOOM
!!
TOOM
GYAAA! AN EXPLOSION!!
OH NOOOO! THERE'S BEEN AN EXPLOSION IN THE COCKPIT!!
ALL THE PILOTS ARE INJURED!!

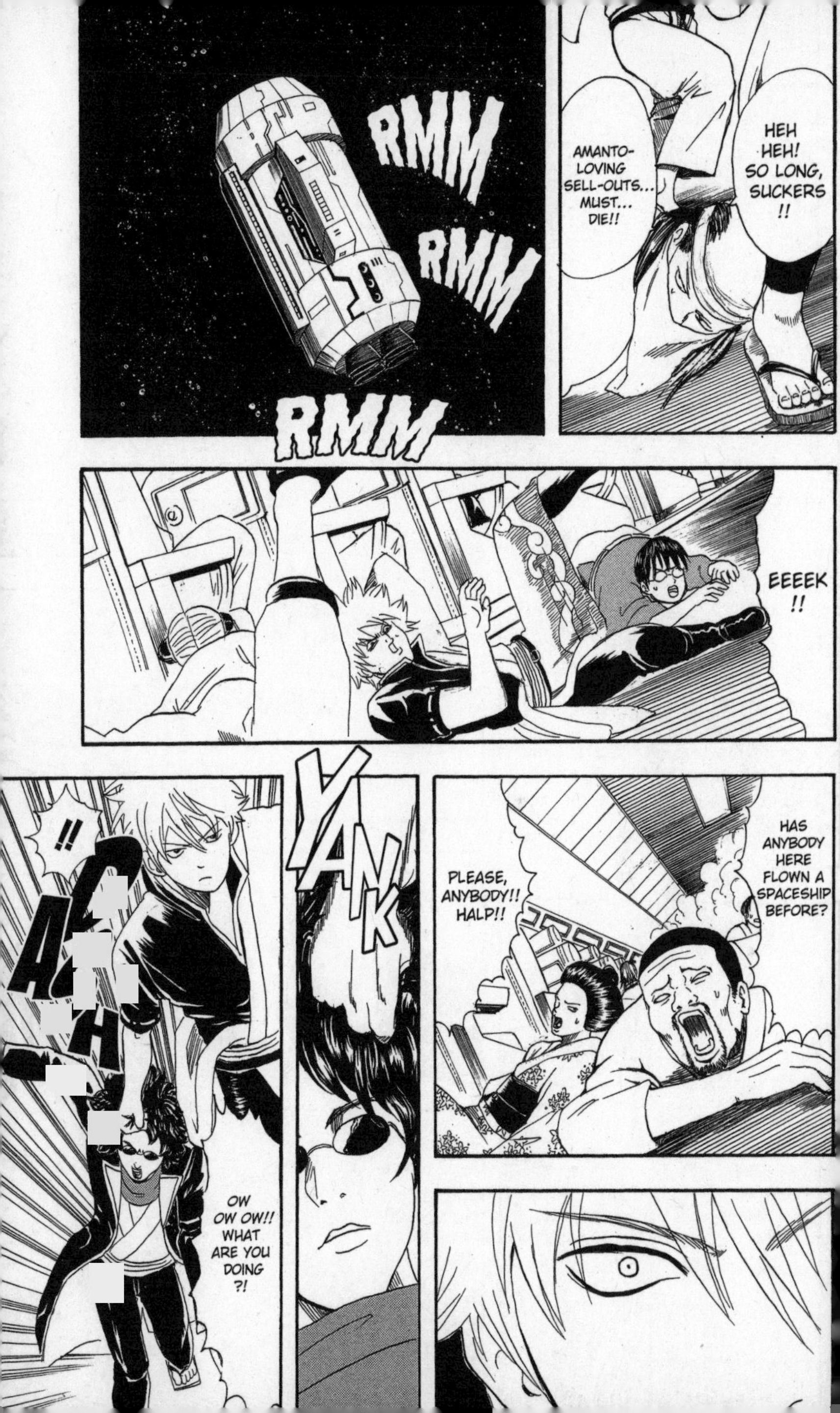
HEH HEH! SO LONG, SUCKERS!!
AMANTO-LOVING SELL-OUTS... MUST... DIE!!
RMM
RMM
RMM
EEEEK!!
HAS ANYBODY HERE FLOWN A SPACESHIP BEFORE?
PLEASE, ANYBODY!! HALP!!
YANK
!!
OW OW OW!! WHAT ARE YOU DOING?!

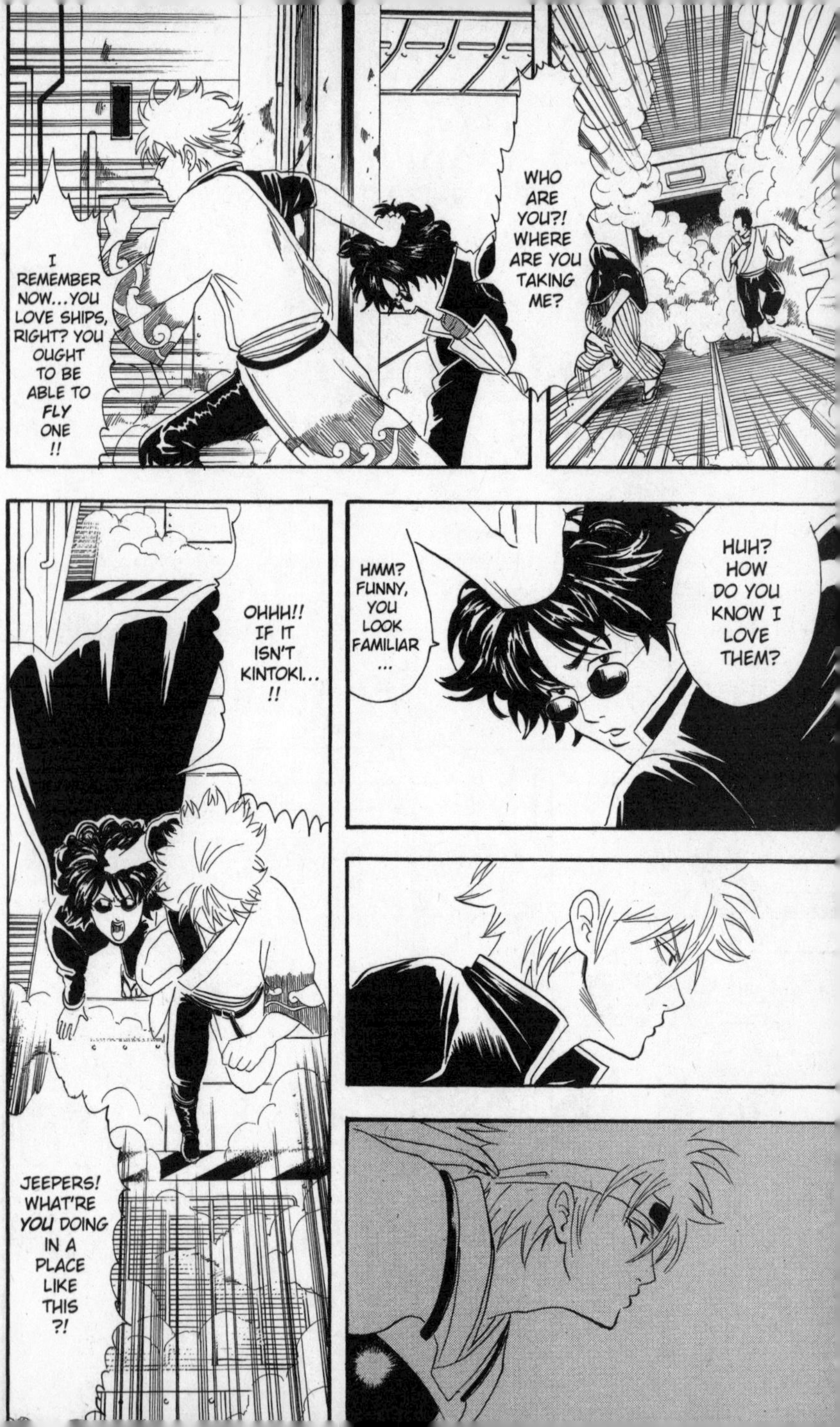
WHO ARE YOU?! WHERE ARE YOU TAKING ME?
I REMEMBER NOW...YOU LOVE SHIPS, RIGHT? YOU OUGHT TO BE ABLE TO FLY ONE !!
HUH? HOW DO YOU KNOW I LOVE THEM?
HMM? FUNNY, YOU LOOK FAMILIAR ...
OHHH!! IF IT ISN'T KINTOKI... !!
JEEPERS! WHAT'RE YOU DOING IN A PLACE LIKE THIS ?!

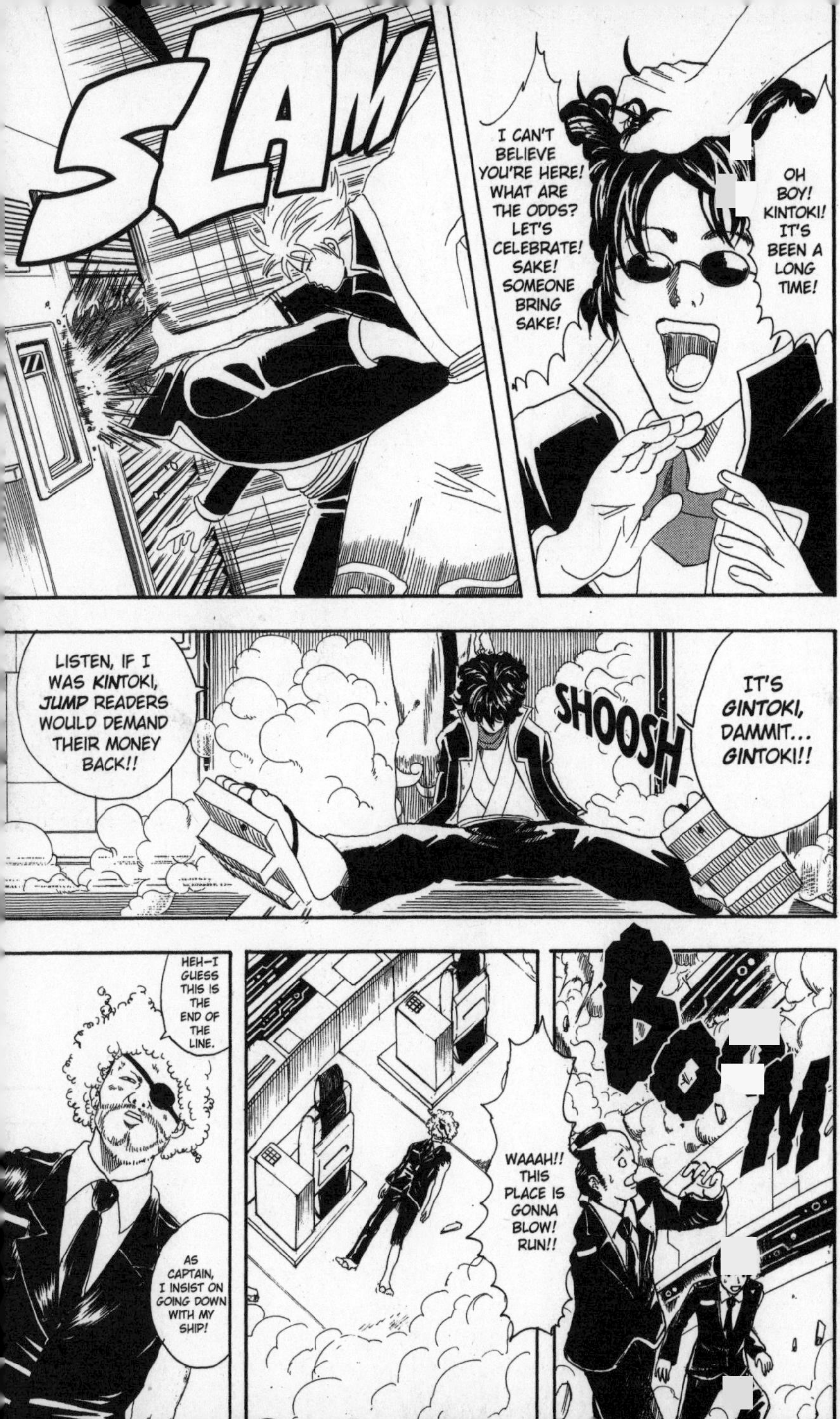
OH BOY! KINTOKI! IT'S BEEN A LONG TIME!
I CAN'T BELIEVE YOU'RE HERE! WHAT ARE THE ODDS? LET'S CELEBRATE! SAKE! SOMEONE BRING SAKE!
SLAM
IT'S GINTOKI, DAMMIT... GINTOKI!!
SHOOSH
LISTEN, IF I WAS KINTOKI, JUMP READERS WOULD DEMAND THEIR MONEY BACK!!
BOOM
WAAAH!! THIS PLACE IS GONNA BLOW! RUN!!
HEH—I GUESS THIS IS THE END OF THE LINE.
AS CAPTAIN, I INSIST ON GOING DOWN WITH MY SHIP!

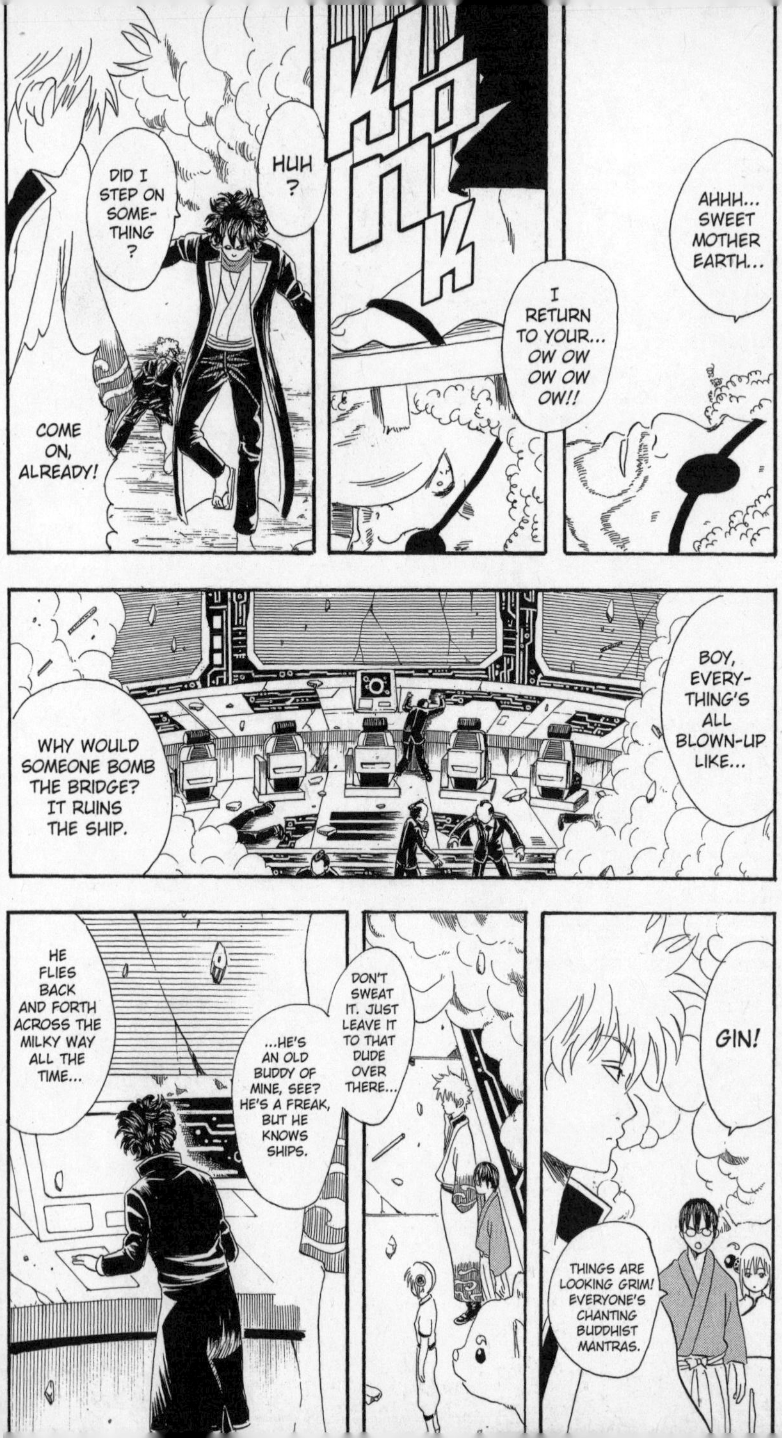
AHHH... SWEET MOTHER EARTH...
KLONK
I RETURN TO YOUR... OW OW OW OW OW!!
HUH?
DID I STEP ON SOMETHING?
COME ON, ALREADY!
BOY, EVERYTHING'S ALL BLOWN-UP LIKE...
WHY WOULD SOMEONE BOMB THE BRIDGE? IT RUINS THE SHIP.
GIN!
THINGS ARE LOOKING GRIM! EVERYONE'S CHANTING BUDDHIST MANTRAS.
DON'T SWEAT IT. JUST LEAVE IT TO THAT DUDE OVER THERE...
...HE'S AN OLD BUDDY OF MINE, SEE? HE'S A FREAK, BUT HE KNOWS SHIPS.
HE FLIES BACK AND FORTH ACROSS THE MILKY WAY ALL THE TIME...

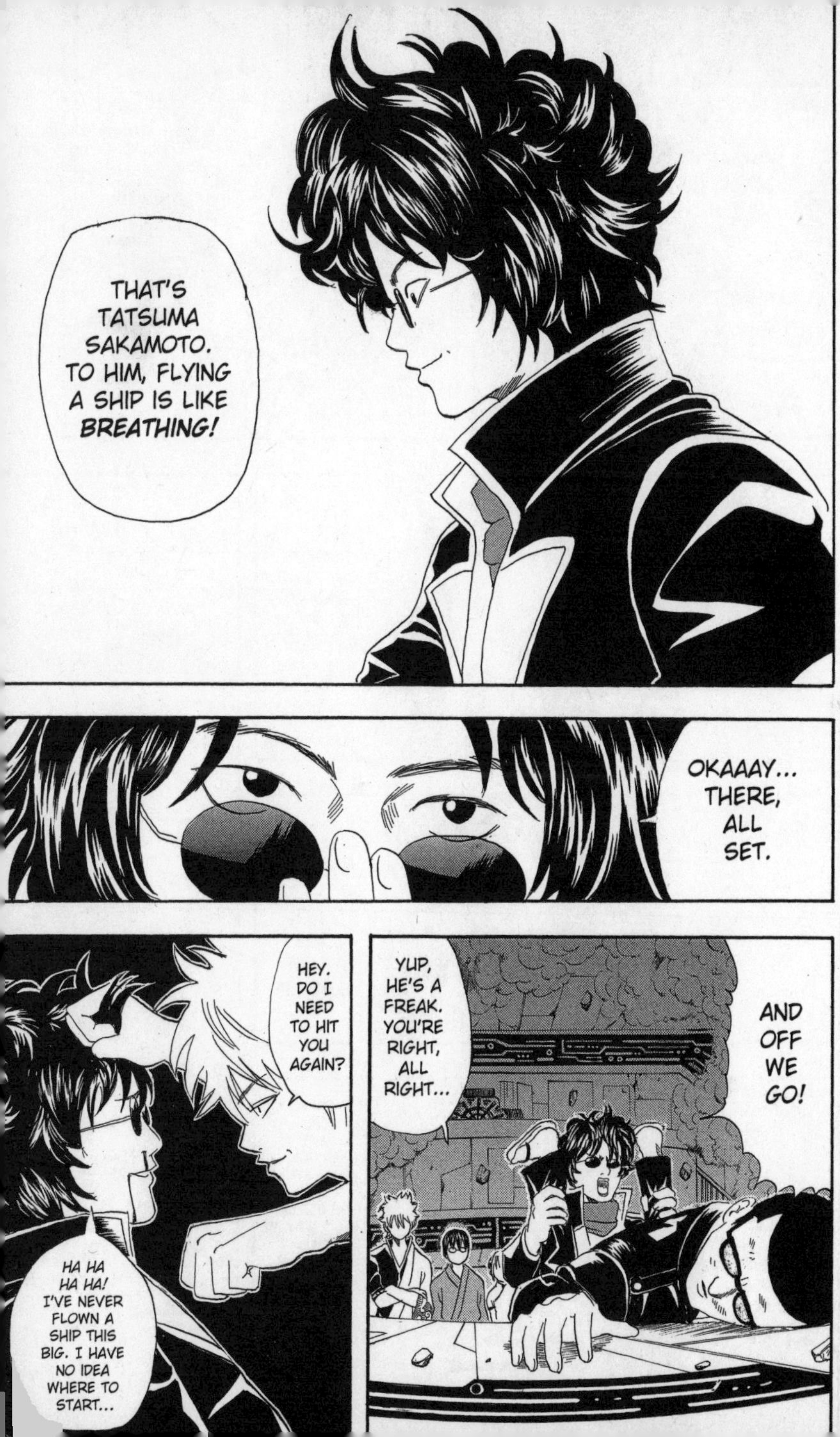
THAT'S TATSUMA SAKAMOTO. TO HIM, FLYING A SHIP IS LIKE BREATHING!
OKAAAY... THERE, ALL SET.
AND OFF WE GO!
YUP, HE'S A FREAK. YOU'RE RIGHT, ALL RIGHT...
HEY. DO I NEED TO HIT YOU AGAIN?
HA HA HA HA! I'VE NEVER FLOWN A SHIP THIS BIG. I HAVE NO IDEA WHERE TO START...

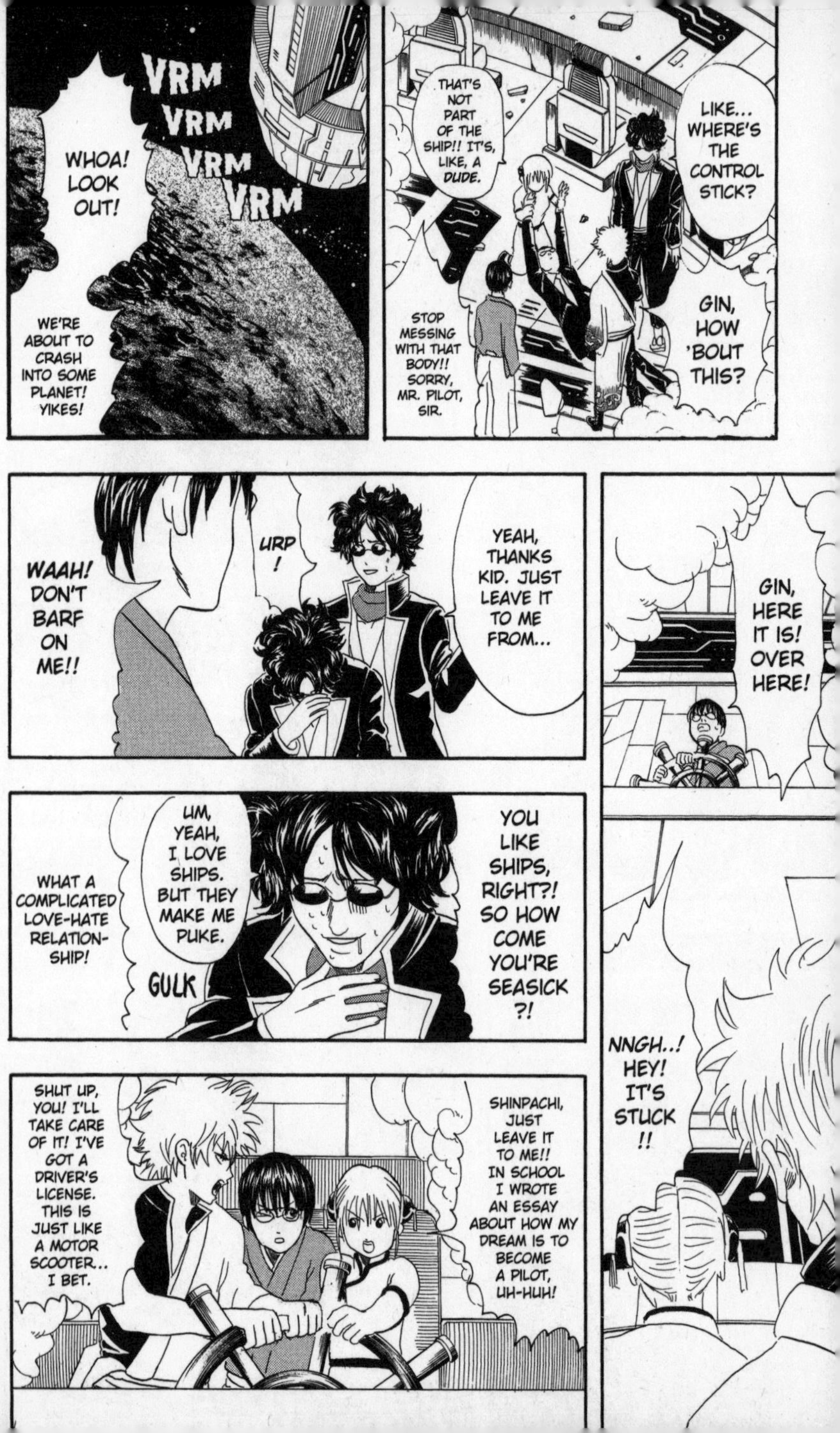
LIKE... WHERE'S THE CONTROL STICK?
THAT'S NOT PART OF THE SHIP!! IT'S, LIKE, A DUDE.
GIN, HOW 'BOUT THIS?
STOP MESSING WITH THAT BODY!! SORRY, MR. PILOT, SIR.
VRM VRM VRM VRM
WHOA! LOOK OUT!
WE'RE ABOUT TO CRASH INTO SOME PLANET! YIKES!
GIN, HERE IT IS! OVER HERE!
YEAH, THANKS KID. JUST LEAVE IT TO ME FROM...
URP!
WAAH! DON'T BARF ON ME!!
NNGH..! HEY! IT'S STUCK!!
YOU LIKE SHIPS, RIGHT?! SO HOW COME YOU'RE SEASICK?!
UM, YEAH, I LOVE SHIPS. BUT THEY MAKE ME PUKE.
WHAT A COMPLICATED LOVE-HATE RELATION-SHIP!
GULK
SHINPACHI, JUST LEAVE IT TO ME!! IN SCHOOL I WROTE AN ESSAY ABOUT HOW MY DREAM IS TO BECOME A PILOT, UH-HUH!
SHUT UP, YOU! I'LL TAKE CARE OF IT! I'VE GOT A DRIVER'S LICENSE. THIS IS JUST LIKE A MOTOR SCOOTER... I BET.

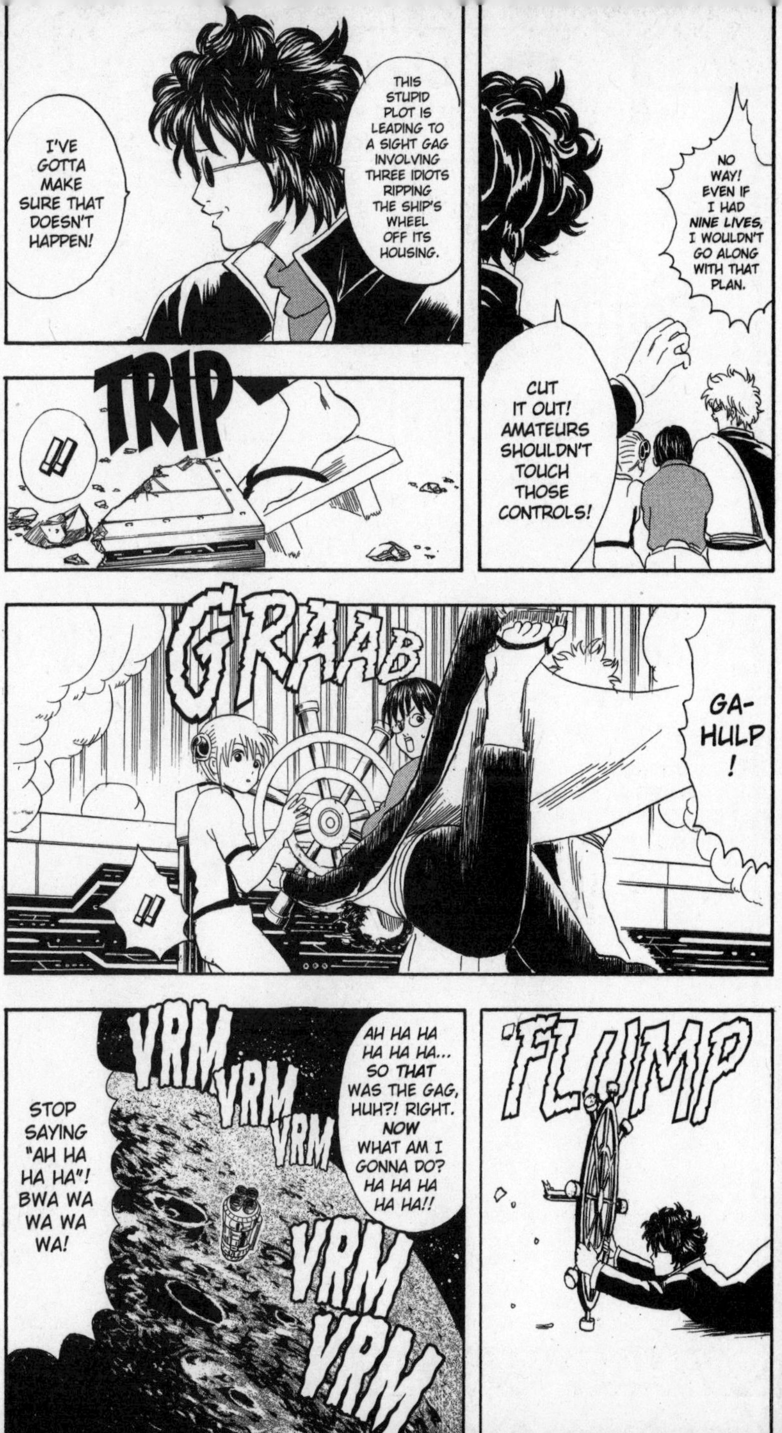
NO WAY! EVEN IF I HAD NINE LIVES, I WOULDN'T GO ALONG WITH THAT PLAN.
CUT IT OUT! AMATEURS SHOULDN'T TOUCH THOSE CONTROLS!
THIS STUPID PLOT IS LEADING TO A SIGHT GAG INVOLVING THREE IDIOTS RIPPING THE SHIP'S WHEEL OFF ITS HOUSING.
I'VE GOTTA MAKE SURE THAT DOESN'T HAPPEN!
TRIP
!!
GRAAB
GA-HULP!
!!
FLUMP
VRM VRM VRM
AH HA HA HA HA HA... SO THAT WAS THE GAG, HUH?! RIGHT. NOW WHAT AM I GONNA DO? HA HA HA HA HA!!
VRM VRM
STOP SAYING "AH HA HA HA"! BWA WA WA WA WA!

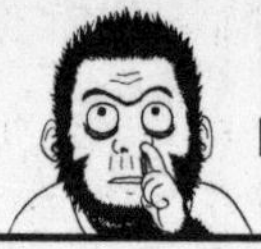

Sorachi's Q&A
Hanging with the Readers #2
(continued)

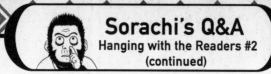

Continued from page 66

Katsura	Twenties
Sakamoto	"
Takasugi	"
Kondo	"
Hijikata	"
Okita	Late teens, even though he was drinking sake

Well I hope this satisfies you, jerk!

(Q&A #3 is on page 110)

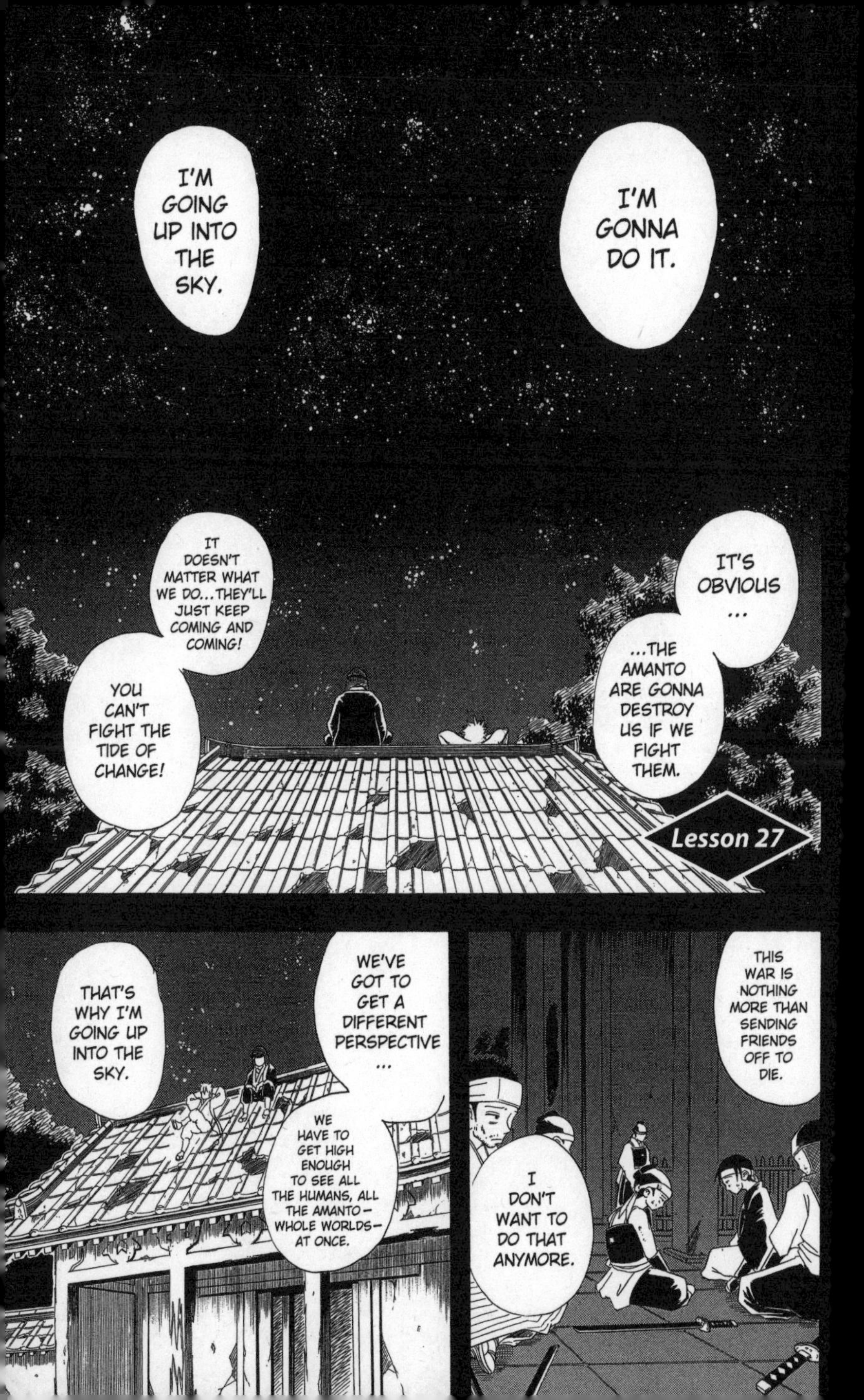
I'M GONNA DO IT.
I'M GOING UP INTO THE SKY.
IT'S OBVIOUS...
...THE AMANTO ARE GONNA DESTROY US IF WE FIGHT THEM.
IT DOESN'T MATTER WHAT WE DO...THEY'LL JUST KEEP COMING AND COMING!
YOU CAN'T FIGHT THE TIDE OF CHANGE!
Lesson 27
THIS WAR IS NOTHING MORE THAN SENDING FRIENDS OFF TO DIE.
I DON'T WANT TO DO THAT ANYMORE.
WE'VE GOT TO GET A DIFFERENT PERSPECTIVE...
WE HAVE TO GET HIGH ENOUGH TO SEE ALL THE HUMANS, ALL THE AMANTO—WHOLE WORLDS—AT ONCE.
THAT'S WHY I'M GOING UP INTO THE SKY.

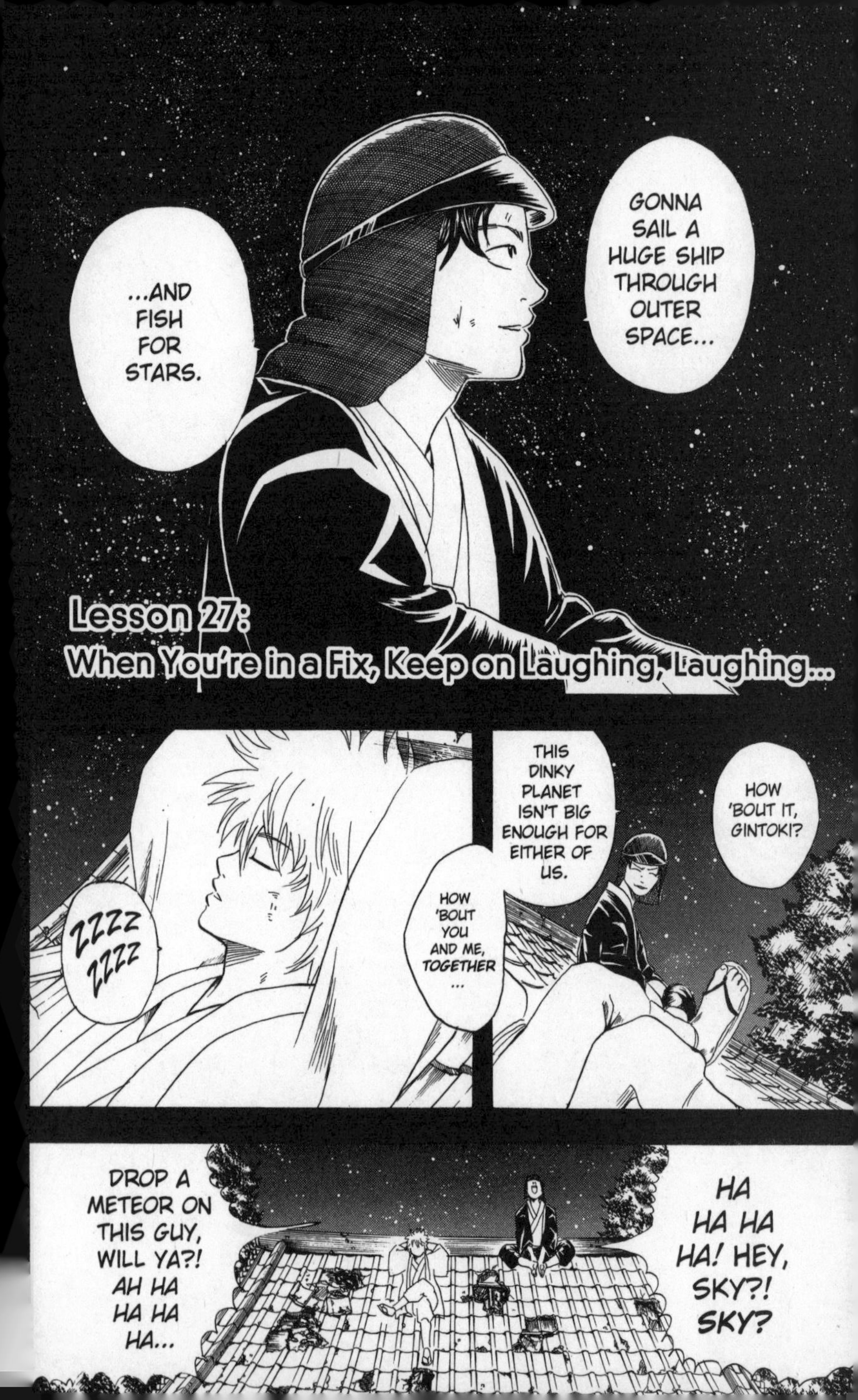
GONNA SAIL A HUGE SHIP THROUGH OUTER SPACE...
...AND FISH FOR STARS.
Lesson 27:
When You're in a Fix, Keep on Laughing, Laughing...
HOW 'BOUT IT, GINTOKI?
THIS DINKY PLANET ISN'T BIG ENOUGH FOR EITHER OF US.
HOW 'BOUT YOU AND ME, TOGETHER...
ZZZZ ZZZZ
HA HA HA HA! HEY, SKY?! SKY?
DROP A METEOR ON THIS GUY, WILL YA?! AH HA HA HA HA...

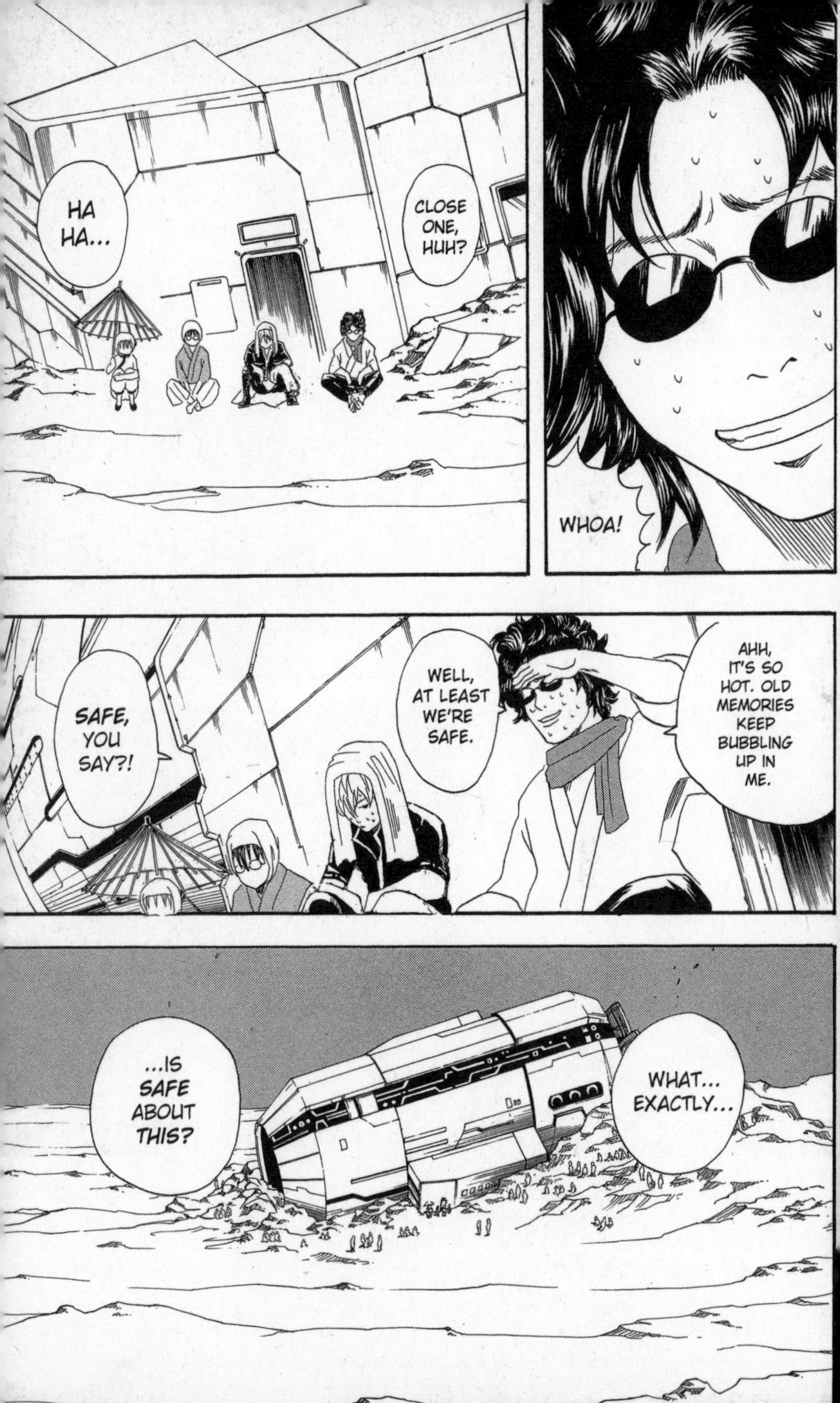
WHOA!
CLOSE ONE, HUH?
HA HA...
AHH, IT'S SO HOT. OLD MEMORIES KEEP BUBBLING UP IN ME.
WELL, AT LEAST WE'RE SAFE.
SAFE, YOU SAY?!
WHAT... EXACTLY...
...IS SAFE ABOUT THIS?

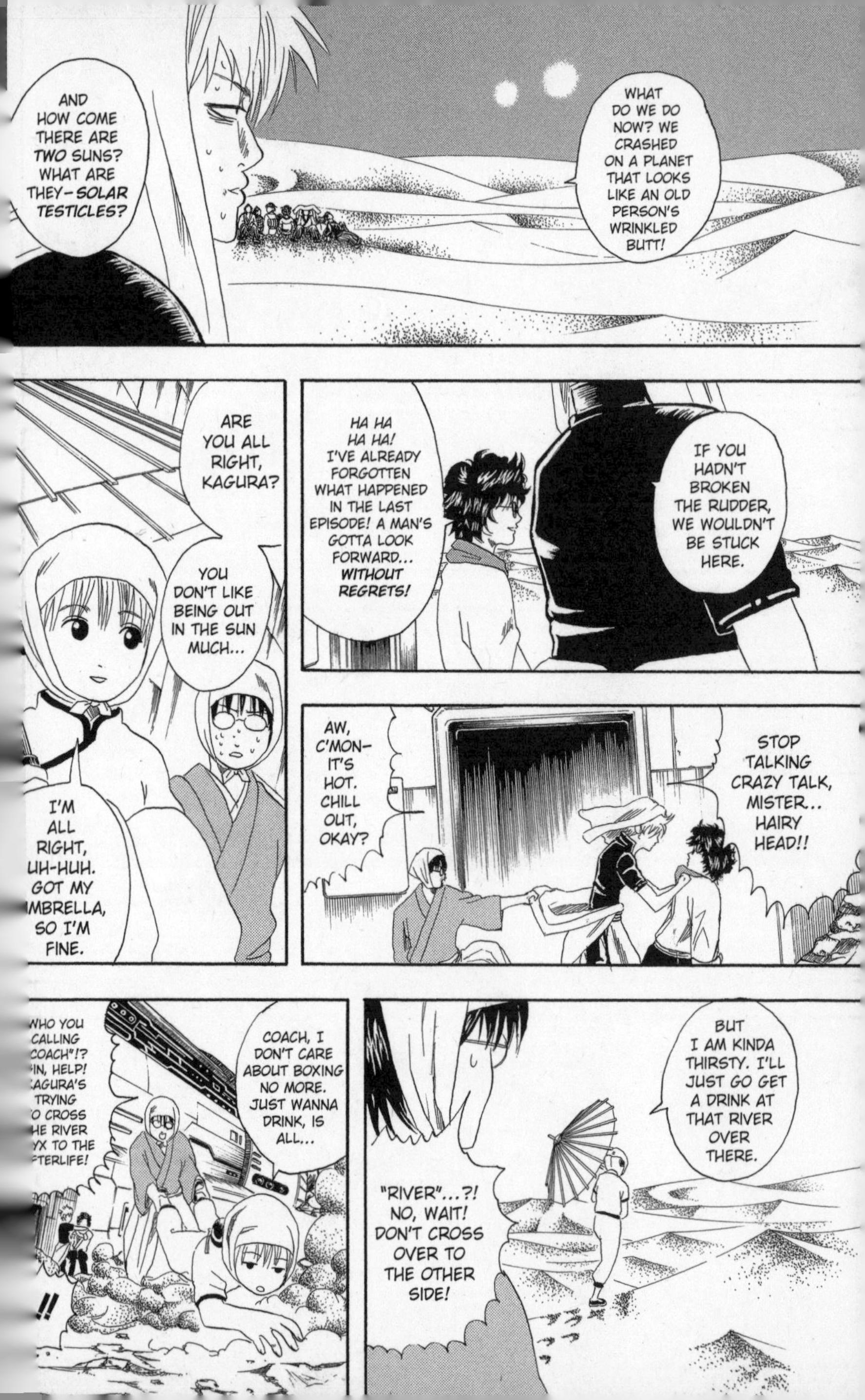
WHAT DO WE DO NOW? WE CRASHED ON A PLANET THAT LOOKS LIKE AN OLD PERSON'S WRINKLED BUTT!
AND HOW COME THERE ARE *TWO SUNS?* WHAT ARE THEY—*SOLAR TESTICLES?*
IF YOU HADN'T BROKEN THE RUDDER, WE WOULDN'T BE STUCK HERE.
HA HA HA HA! I'VE ALREADY FORGOTTEN WHAT HAPPENED IN THE LAST EPISODE! A MAN'S GOTTA LOOK FORWARD... **WITHOUT REGRETS!**
STOP TALKING CRAZY TALK, MISTER... HAIRY HEAD!!
AW, C'MON—IT'S HOT. CHILL OUT, OKAY?
ARE YOU ALL RIGHT, KAGURA?
YOU DON'T LIKE BEING OUT IN THE SUN MUCH...
I'M ALL RIGHT, UH-HUH. GOT MY MBRELLA, SO I'M FINE.
BUT I AM KINDA THIRSTY. I'LL JUST GO GET A DRINK AT THAT RIVER OVER THERE.
"RIVER"...?! NO, WAIT! DON'T CROSS OVER TO THE OTHER SIDE!
COACH, I DON'T CARE ABOUT BOXING NO MORE. JUST WANNA DRINK, IS ALL...
WHO YOU CALLING "COACH"!? FIN, HELP! AGURA'S TRYING O CROSS HE RIVER YX TO THE FTERLIFE!
!!

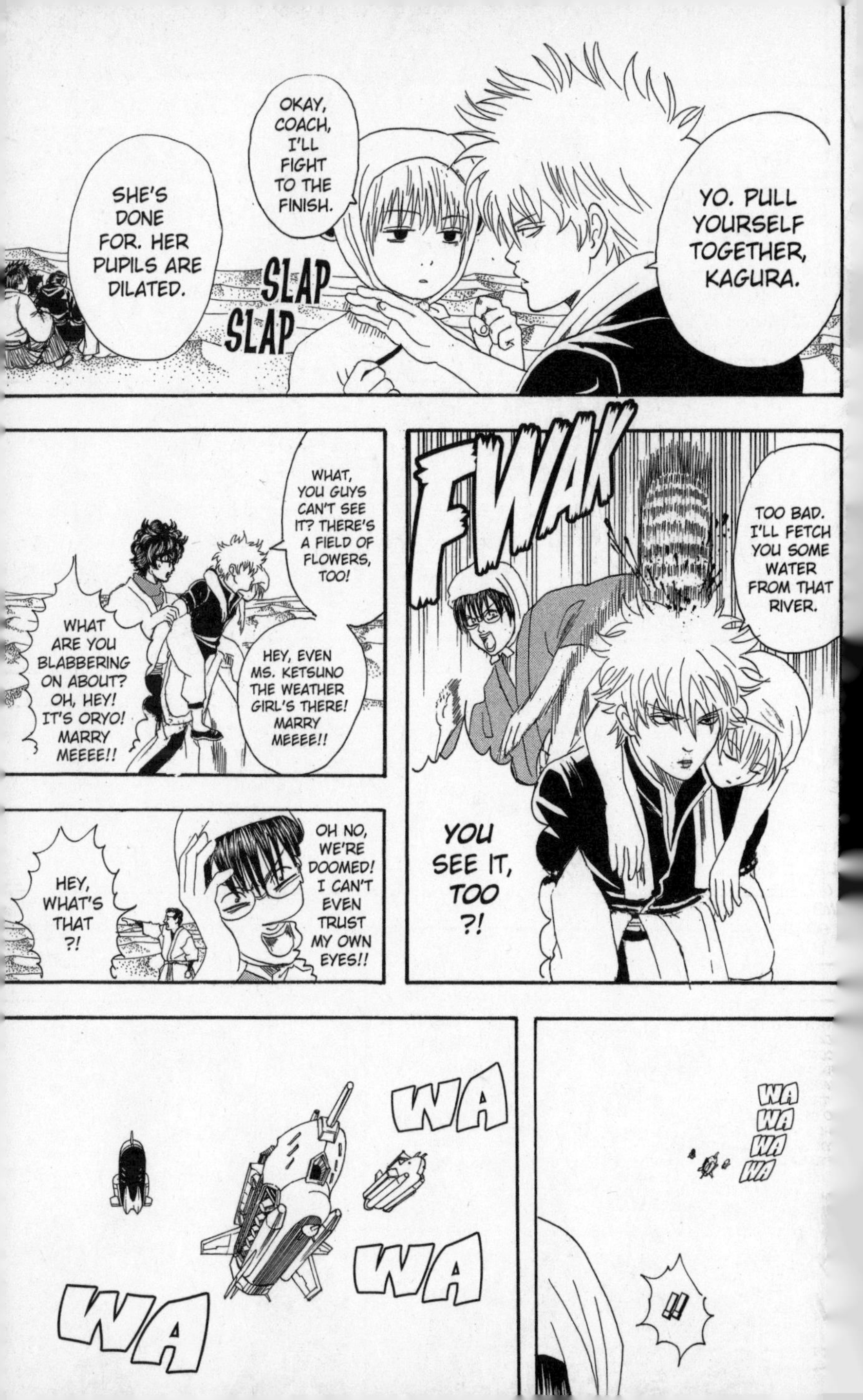
YO. PULL YOURSELF TOGETHER, KAGURA.
OKAY, COACH, I'LL FIGHT TO THE FINISH.
SLAP SLAP
SHE'S DONE FOR. HER PUPILS ARE DILATED.
TOO BAD. I'LL FETCH YOU SOME WATER FROM THAT RIVER.
FWAK
YOU SEE IT, TOO?!
WHAT, YOU GUYS CAN'T SEE IT? THERE'S A FIELD OF FLOWERS, TOO!
HEY, EVEN MS. KETSUNO THE WEATHER GIRL'S THERE! MARRY MEEEE!!
WHAT ARE YOU BLABBERING ON ABOUT? OH, HEY! IT'S ORYO! MARRY MEEEE!!
OH NO, WE'RE DOOMED! I CAN'T EVEN TRUST MY OWN EYES!!
HEY, WHAT'S THAT?!
WA WA WA WA
!!
WA
WA
WA

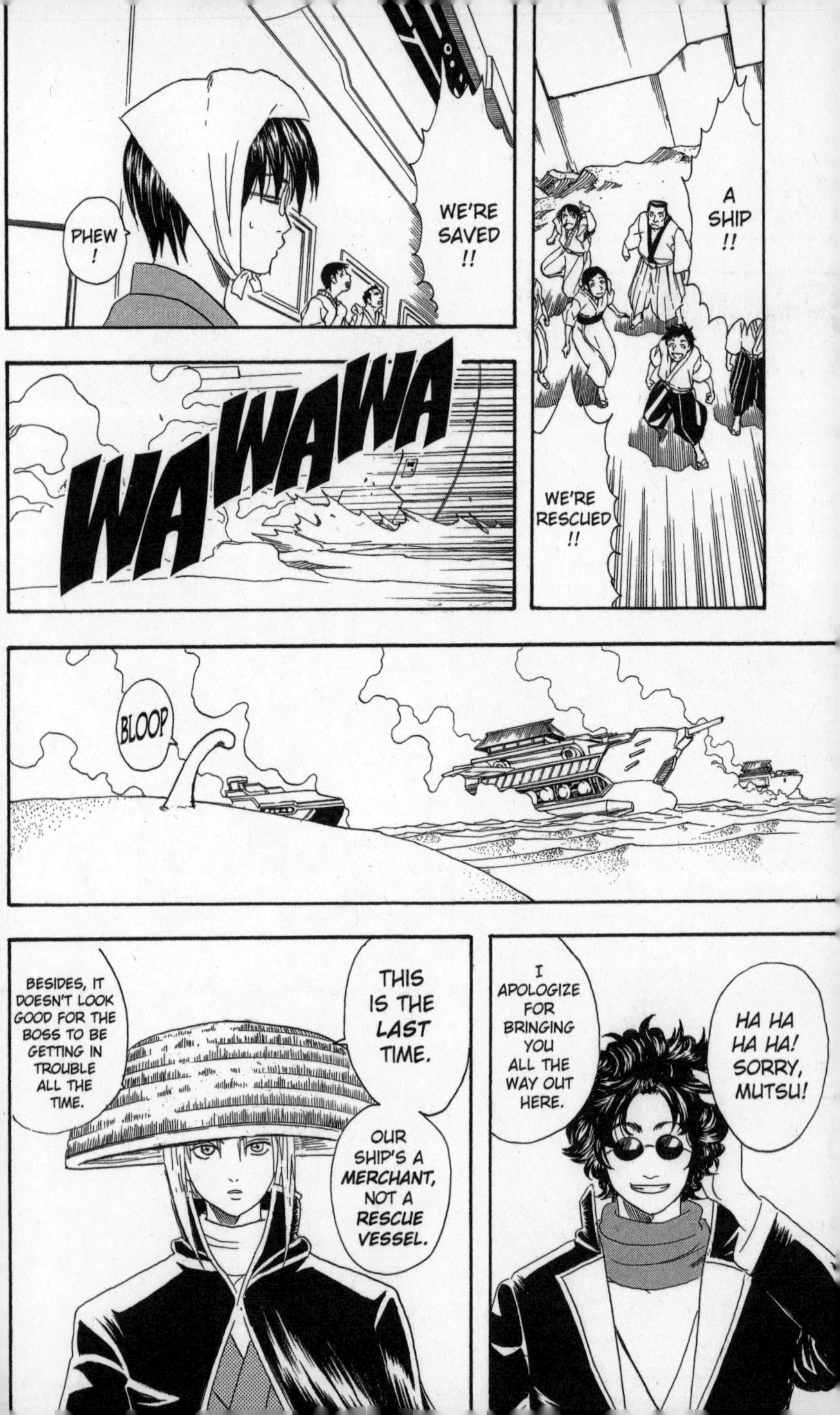
A SHIP!!
WE'RE RESCUED!!
WE'RE SAVED!!
PHEW!
WAWAWA
BLOOP
HA HA HA HA! SORRY, MUTSU!
I APOLOGIZE FOR BRINGING YOU ALL THE WAY OUT HERE.
THIS IS THE LAST TIME.
OUR SHIP'S A MERCHANT, NOT A RESCUE VESSEL.
BESIDES, IT DOESN'T LOOK GOOD FOR THE BOSS TO BE GETTING IN TROUBLE ALL THE TIME.

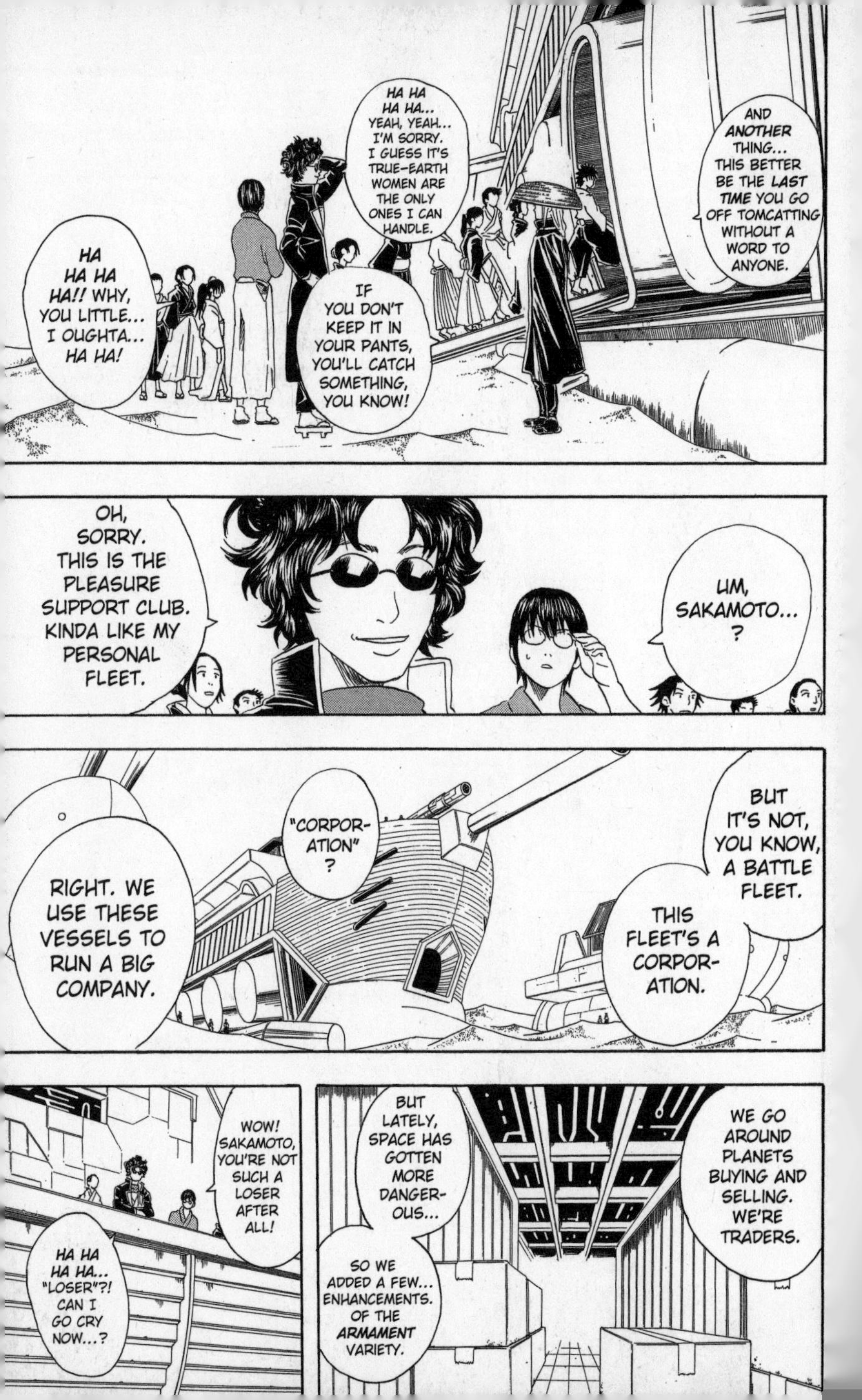
AND ANOTHER THING... THIS BETTER BE THE LAST TIME YOU GO OFF TOMCATTING WITHOUT A WORD TO ANYONE.
HA HA HA HA... YEAH, YEAH... I'M SORRY. I GUESS IT'S TRUE-EARTH WOMEN ARE THE ONLY ONES I CAN HANDLE.
IF YOU DON'T KEEP IT IN YOUR PANTS, YOU'LL CATCH SOMETHING, YOU KNOW!
HA HA HA HA!! WHY, YOU LITTLE... I OUGHTA... HA HA!
UM, SAKAMOTO...?
OH, SORRY. THIS IS THE PLEASURE SUPPORT CLUB. KINDA LIKE MY PERSONAL FLEET.
BUT IT'S NOT, YOU KNOW, A BATTLE FLEET.
THIS FLEET'S A CORPORATION.
"CORPORATION"?
RIGHT. WE USE THESE VESSELS TO RUN A BIG COMPANY.
WE GO AROUND PLANETS BUYING AND SELLING. WE'RE TRADERS.
BUT LATELY, SPACE HAS GOTTEN MORE DANGEROUS...
SO WE ADDED A FEW... ENHANCEMENTS. OF THE ARMAMENT VARIETY.
WOW! SAKAMOTO, YOU'RE NOT SUCH A LOSER AFTER ALL!
HA HA HA HA... "LOSER"?! CAN I GO CRY NOW...?

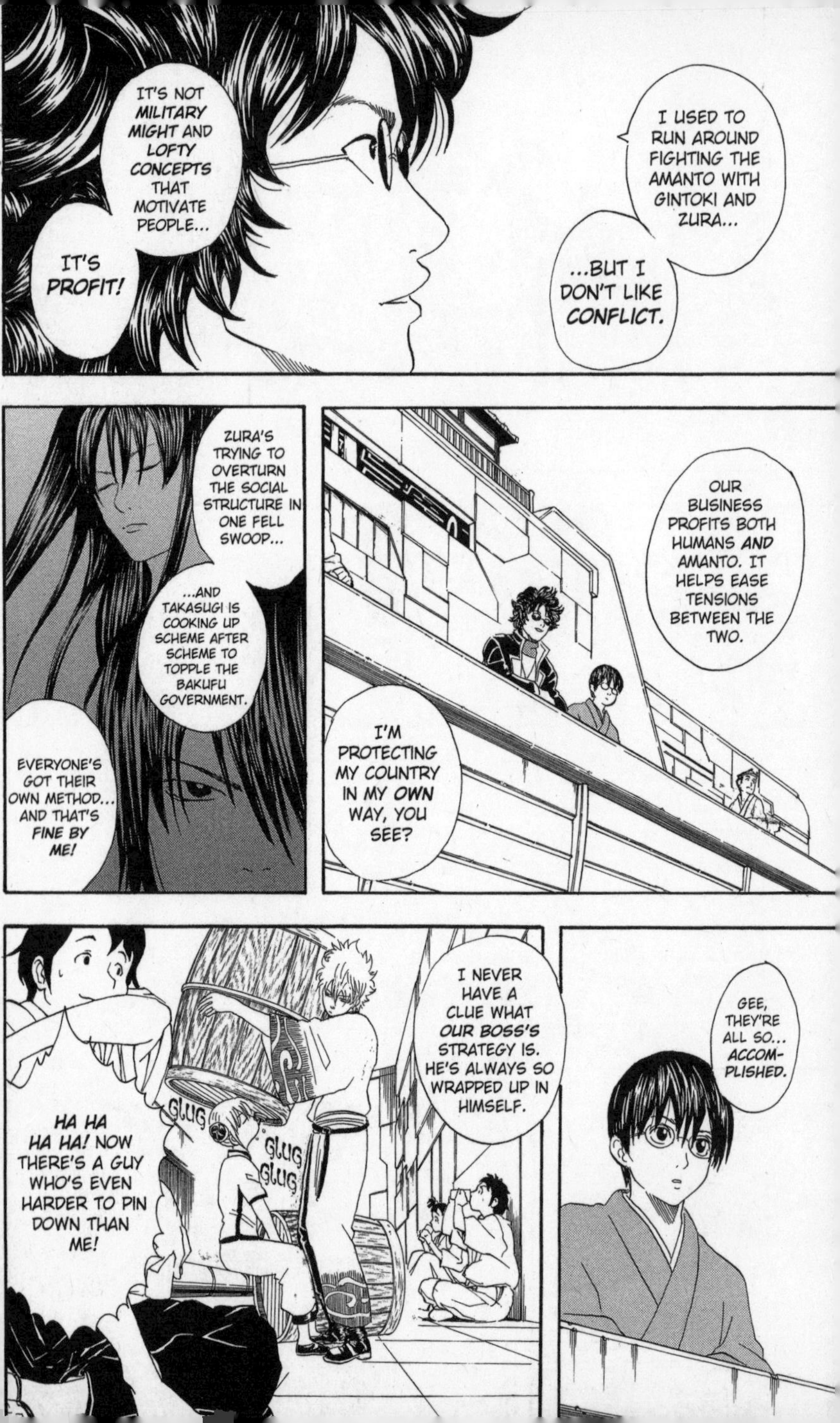
I USED TO RUN AROUND FIGHTING THE AMANTO WITH GINTOKI AND ZURA...
...BUT I DON'T LIKE CONFLICT.
IT'S NOT MILITARY MIGHT AND LOFTY CONCEPTS THAT MOTIVATE PEOPLE...
IT'S PROFIT!
OUR BUSINESS PROFITS BOTH HUMANS AND AMANTO. IT HELPS EASE TENSIONS BETWEEN THE TWO.
I'M PROTECTING MY COUNTRY IN MY OWN WAY, YOU SEE?
ZURA'S TRYING TO OVERTURN THE SOCIAL STRUCTURE IN ONE FELL SWOOP...
...AND TAKASUGI IS COOKING UP SCHEME AFTER SCHEME TO TOPPLE THE BAKUFU GOVERNMENT.
EVERYONE'S GOT THEIR OWN METHOD... AND THAT'S FINE BY ME!
GEE, THEY'RE ALL SO... ACCOMPLISHED.
I NEVER HAVE A CLUE WHAT OUR BOSS'S STRATEGY IS. HE'S ALWAYS SO WRAPPED UP IN HIMSELF.
GLUG
GLUG GLUG
HA HA HA HA! NOW THERE'S A GUY WHO'S EVEN HARDER TO PIN DOWN THAN ME!

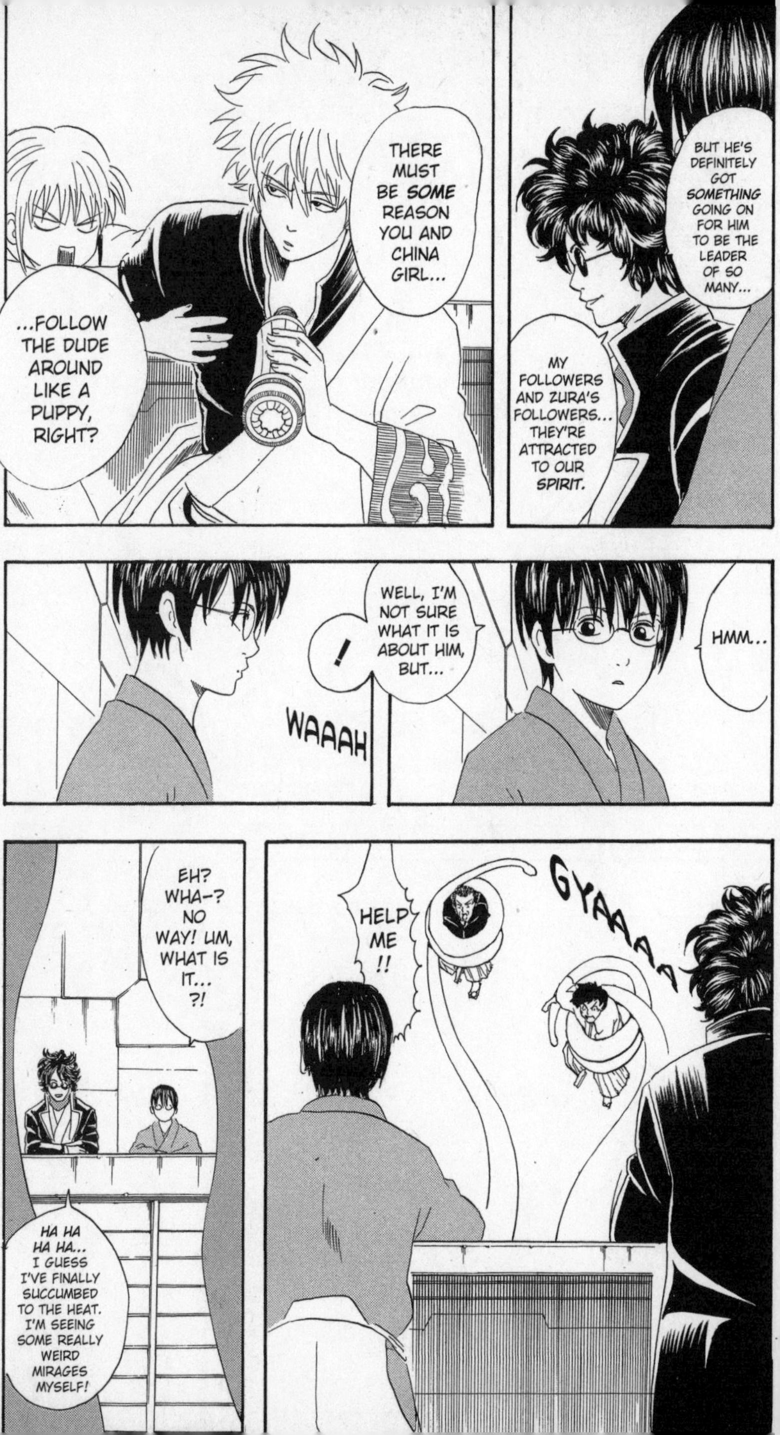
BUT HE'S DEFINITELY GOT SOMETHING GOING ON FOR HIM TO BE THE LEADER OF SO MANY...
MY FOLLOWERS AND ZURA'S FOLLOWERS... THEY'RE ATTRACTED TO OUR SPIRIT.
THERE MUST BE SOME REASON YOU AND CHINA GIRL...
...FOLLOW THE DUDE AROUND LIKE A PUPPY, RIGHT?
HMM...
WELL, I'M NOT SURE WHAT IT IS ABOUT HIM, BUT...
!
WAAAH
GYAAAAA
HELP ME!!
EH? WHA-? NO WAY! UM, WHAT IS IT...?!
HA HA HA HA... I GUESS I'VE FINALLY SUCCUMBED TO THE HEAT. I'M SEEING SOME REALLY WEIRD MIRAGES MYSELF!

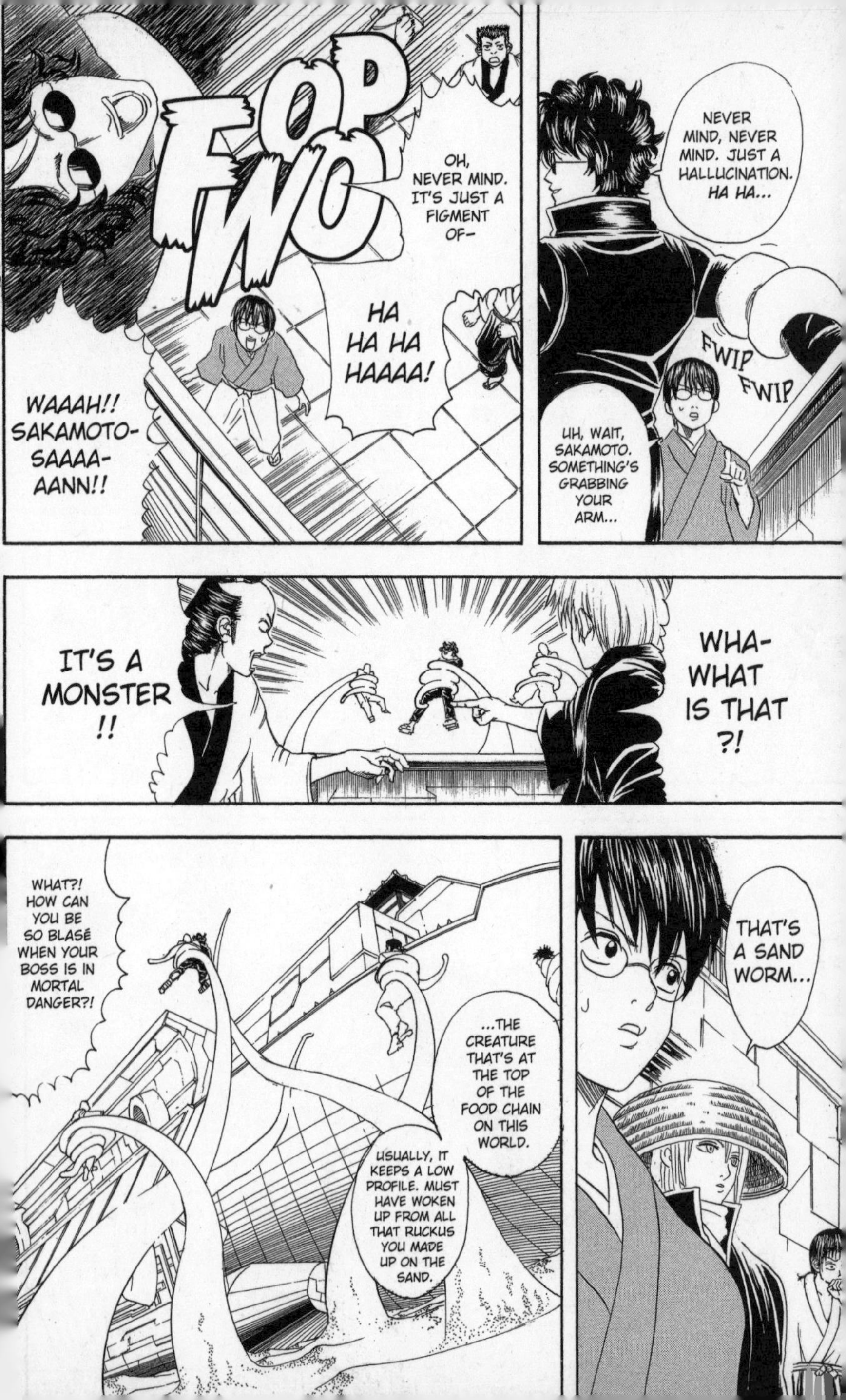
NEVER MIND, NEVER MIND. JUST A HALLUCINATION. HA HA...
FWIP FWIP
UH, WAIT, SAKAMOTO. SOMETHING'S GRABBING YOUR ARM...
OH, NEVER MIND. IT'S JUST A FIGMENT OF-
HA HA HA HAAAA!
WAAAH!! SAKAMOTO-SAAAA-AANN!!
WHA-WHAT IS THAT ?!
IT'S A MONSTER !!
THAT'S A SAND WORM...
...THE CREATURE THAT'S AT THE TOP OF THE FOOD CHAIN ON THIS WORLD.
USUALLY, IT KEEPS A LOW PROFILE. MUST HAVE WOKEN UP FROM ALL THAT RUCKUS YOU MADE UP ON THE SAND.
WHAT?! HOW CAN YOU BE SO BLASÉ WHEN YOUR BOSS IS IN MORTAL DANGER?!

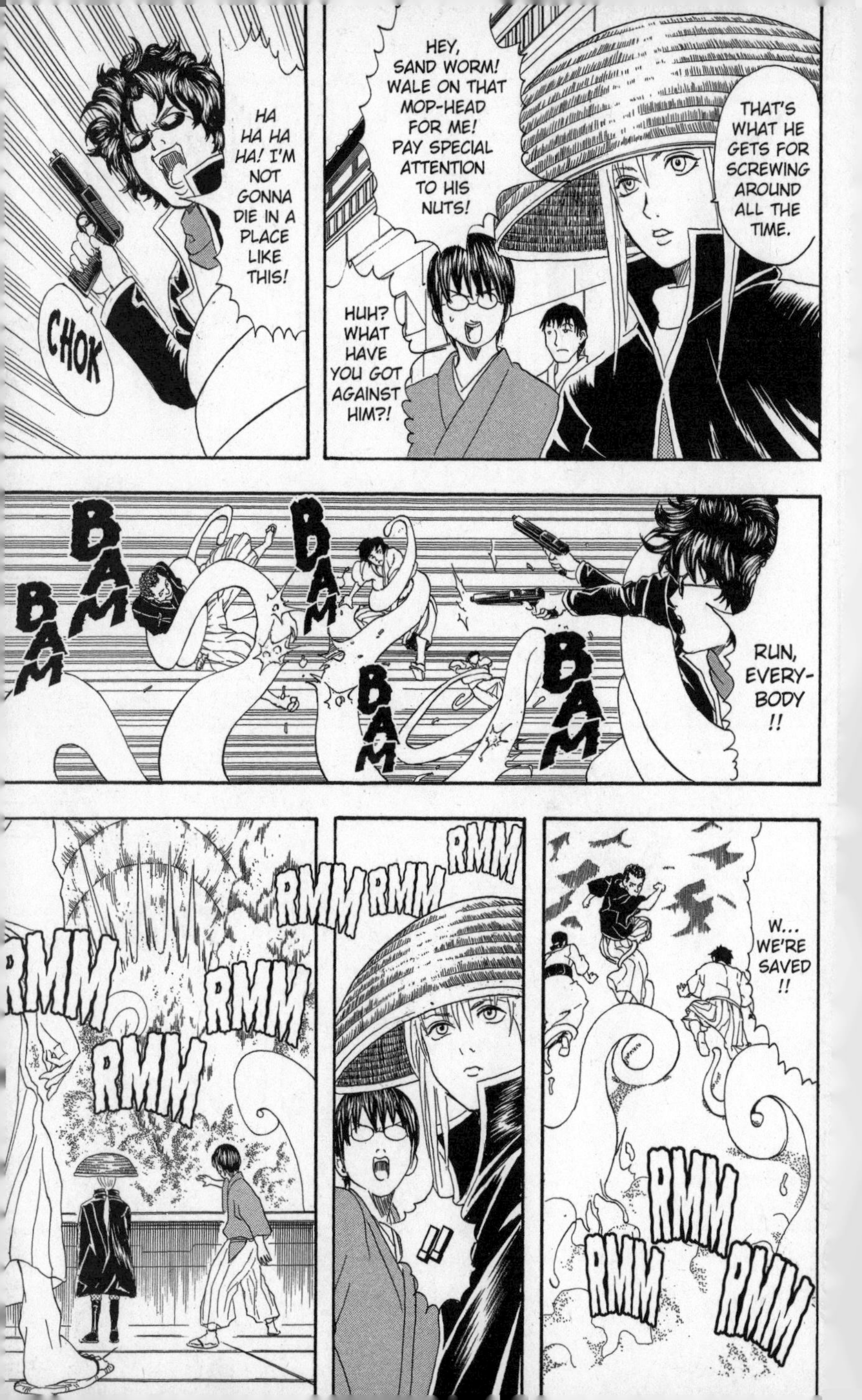
HEY, SAND WORM! WALE ON THAT MOP-HEAD FOR ME! PAY SPECIAL ATTENTION TO HIS NUTS!
HUH? WHAT HAVE YOU GOT AGAINST HIM?!
THAT'S WHAT HE GETS FOR SCREWING AROUND ALL THE TIME.
HA HA HA HA! I'M NOT GONNA DIE IN A PLACE LIKE THIS!
CHOK
RUN, EVERYBODY!!
BAM
BAM
BAM
BAM
BAM
W... WE'RE SAVED!!
RMM
RMM
RMM
RMM
RMM RMM
!!
RMM
RMM
RMM

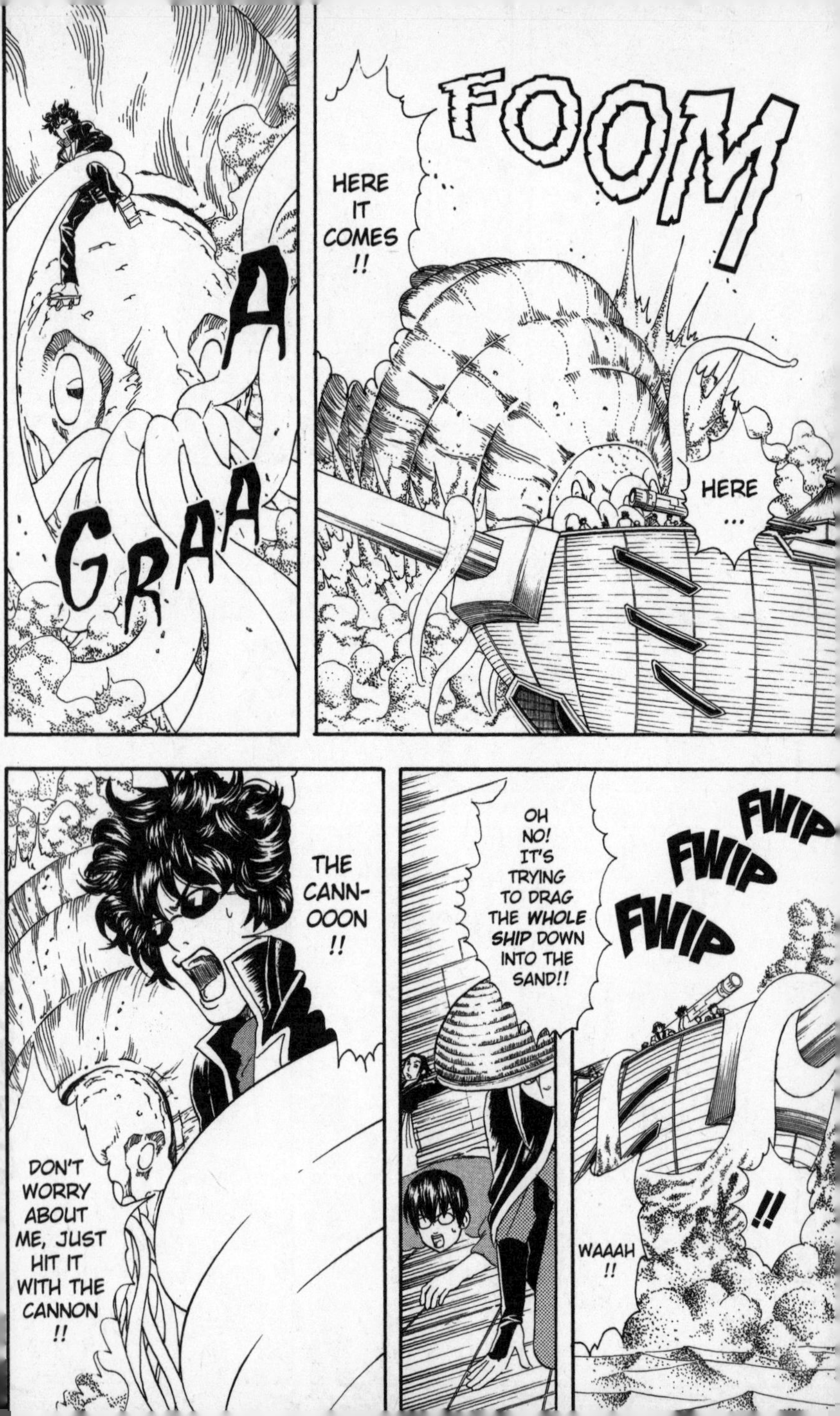
FOOM
HERE...
HERE IT COMES!!
GRAAA
FWIP
FWIP
FWIP
OH NO! IT'S TRYING TO DRAG THE WHOLE SHIP DOWN INTO THE SAND!!
!!
WAAAH!!
THE CANN-OOON!!
DON'T WORRY ABOUT ME, JUST HIT IT WITH THE CANNON!!

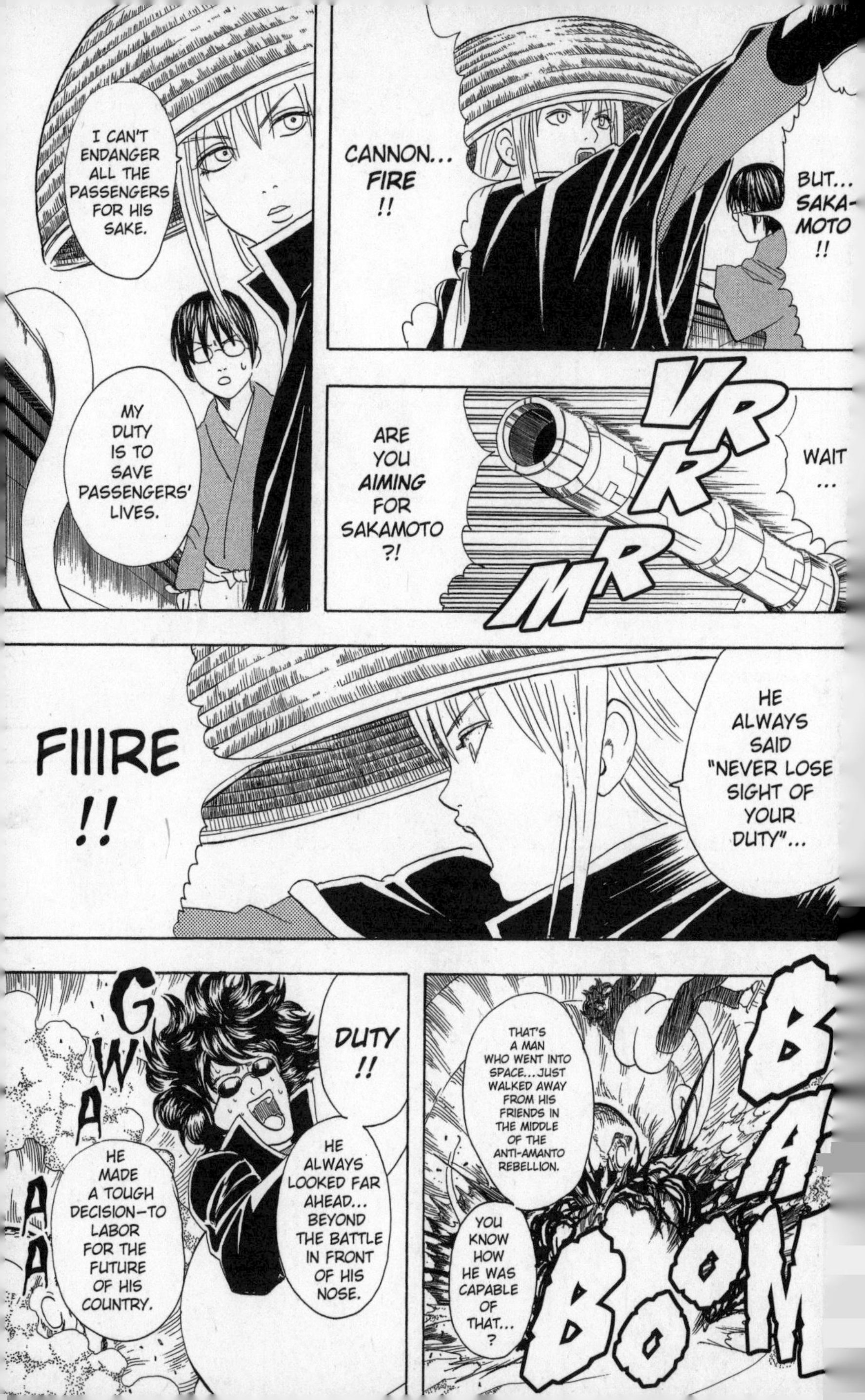
BUT... SAKAMOTO !!
CANNON... FIRE !!
WAIT ...
VRRMR
ARE YOU AIMING FOR SAKAMOTO ?!
I CAN'T ENDANGER ALL THE PASSENGERS FOR HIS SAKE.
MY DUTY IS TO SAVE PASSENGERS' LIVES.
HE ALWAYS SAID "NEVER LOSE SIGHT OF YOUR DUTY"...
FIIIRE !!
BAA
BOOM
THAT'S A MAN WHO WENT INTO SPACE... JUST WALKED AWAY FROM HIS FRIENDS IN THE MIDDLE OF THE ANTI-AMANTO REBELLION.
YOU KNOW HOW HE WAS CAPABLE OF THAT... ?
DUTY !!
HE ALWAYS LOOKED FAR AHEAD... BEYOND THE BATTLE IN FRONT OF HIS NOSE.
GWAAA
HE MADE A TOUGH DECISION—TO LABOR FOR THE FUTURE OF HIS COUNTRY.

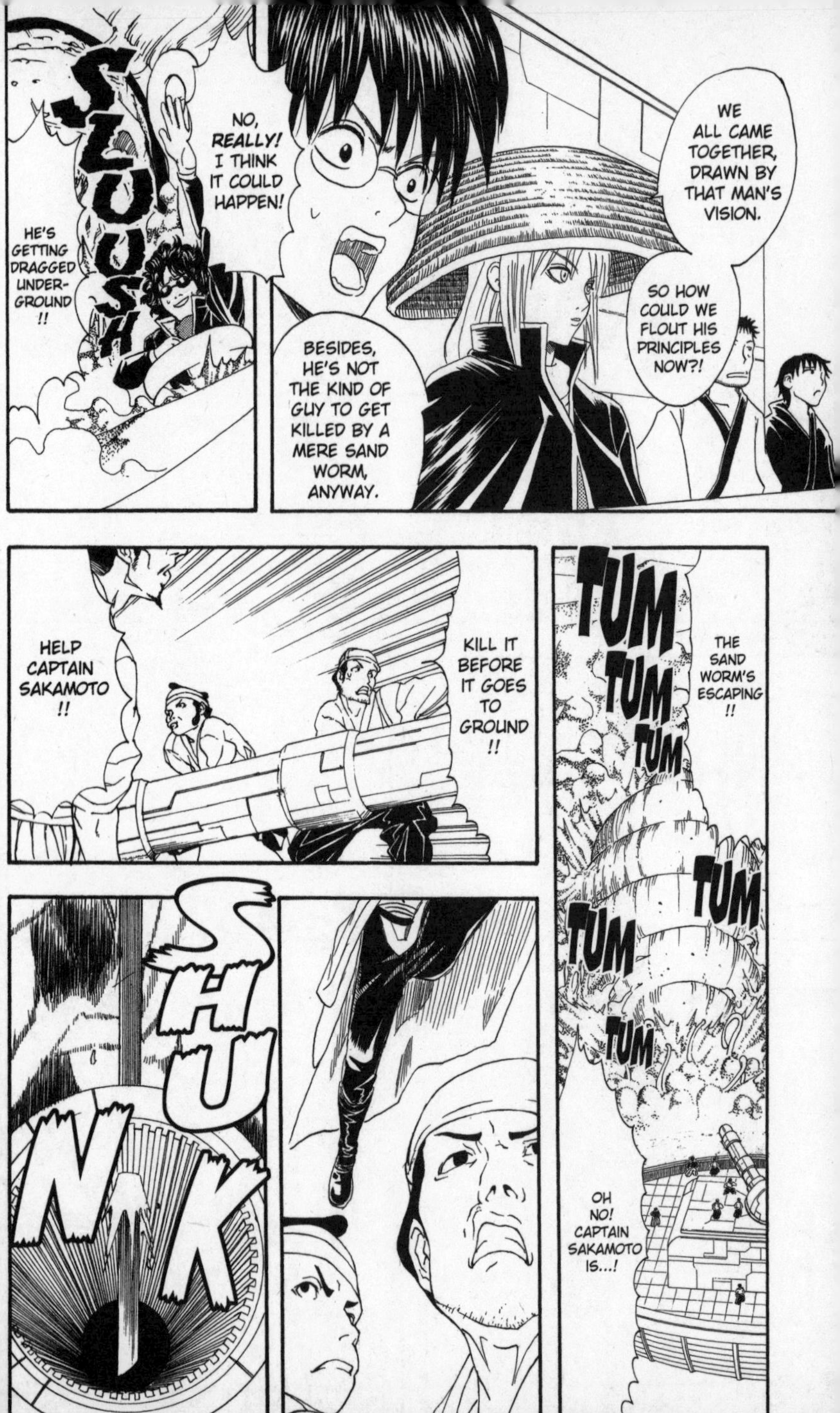
WE ALL CAME TOGETHER, DRAWN BY THAT MAN'S VISION.
SO HOW COULD WE FLOUT HIS PRINCIPLES NOW?!
BESIDES, HE'S NOT THE KIND OF GUY TO GET KILLED BY A MERE SAND WORM, ANYWAY.
NO, REALLY! I THINK IT COULD HAPPEN!
SLUSH
HE'S GETTING DRAGGED UNDER-GROUND !!
TUM TUM TUM
THE SAND WORM'S ESCAPING !!
TUM
TUM
TUM
OH NO! CAPTAIN SAKAMOTO IS...!
KILL IT BEFORE IT GOES TO GROUND !!
HELP CAPTAIN SAKAMOTO !!
SHUNK

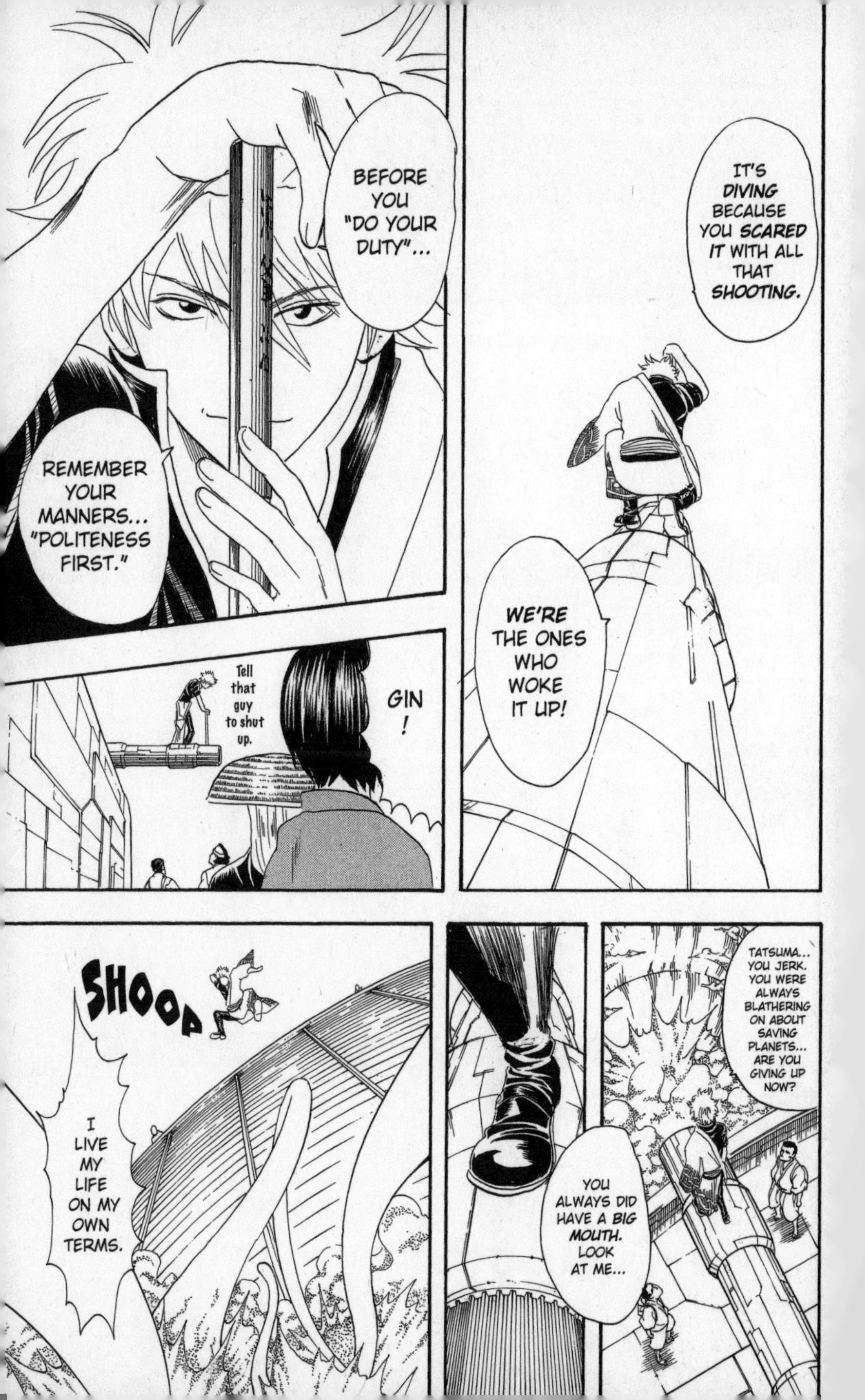
IT'S DIVING BECAUSE YOU SCARED IT WITH ALL THAT SHOOTING.
WE'RE THE ONES WHO WOKE IT UP!
BEFORE YOU "DO YOUR DUTY"...
REMEMBER YOUR MANNERS... "POLITENESS FIRST."
GIN!
Tell that guy to shut up.
TATSUMA... YOU JERK. YOU WERE ALWAYS BLATHERING ON ABOUT SAVING PLANETS... ARE YOU GIVING UP NOW?
YOU ALWAYS DID HAVE A BIG MOUTH. LOOK AT ME...
SHOOP
I LIVE MY LIFE ON MY OWN TERMS.

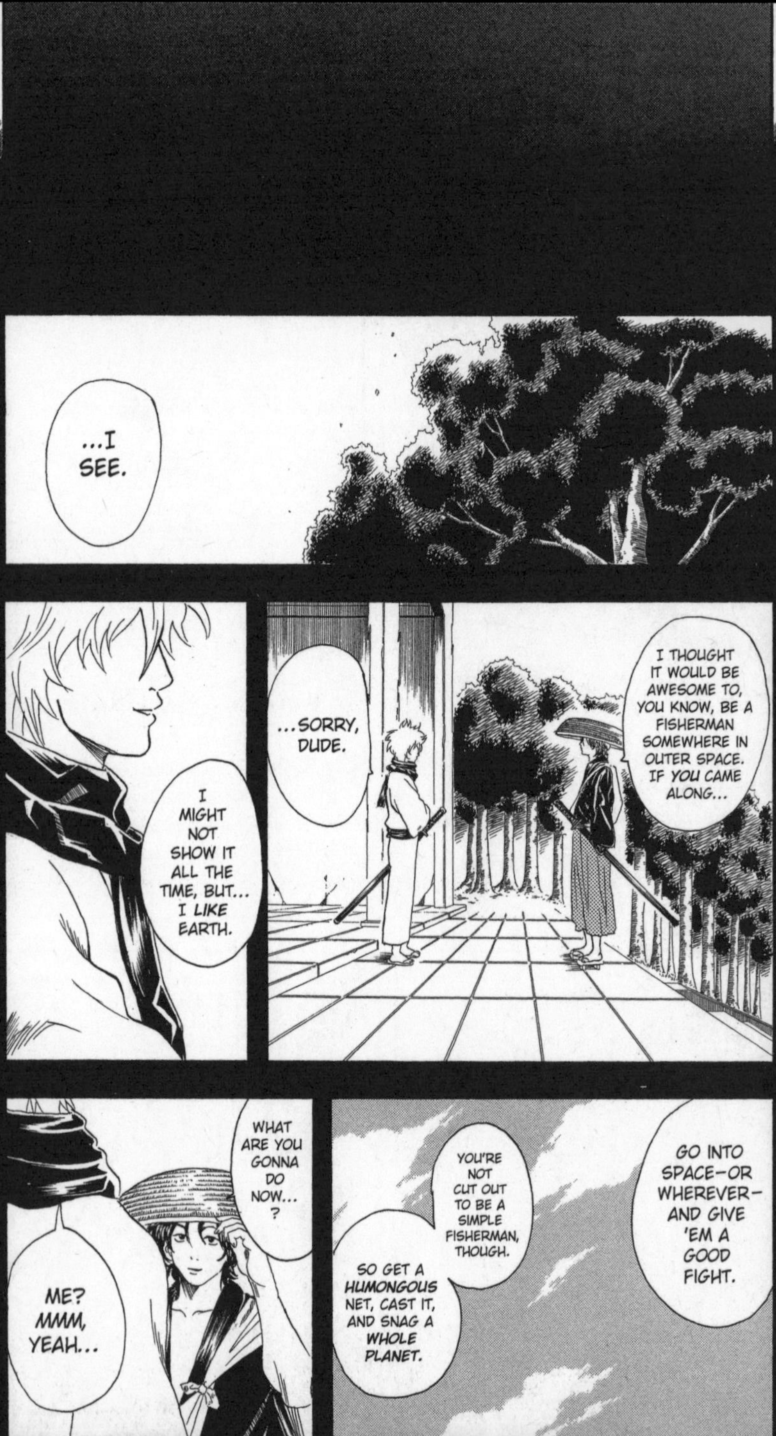
...I SEE.
I THOUGHT IT WOULD BE AWESOME TO, YOU KNOW, BE A FISHERMAN SOMEWHERE IN OUTER SPACE. IF *YOU* CAME ALONG...
...SORRY, DUDE.
I MIGHT NOT SHOW IT ALL THE TIME, BUT... I *LIKE* EARTH.
GO INTO SPACE—OR WHEREVER—AND GIVE 'EM A GOOD FIGHT.
YOU'RE NOT CUT OUT TO BE A SIMPLE FISHERMAN, THOUGH.
SO GET A *HUMONGOUS* NET, CAST IT, AND SNAG A *WHOLE PLANET.*
WHAT ARE YOU GONNA DO NOW...?
ME? *MMM,* YEAH...

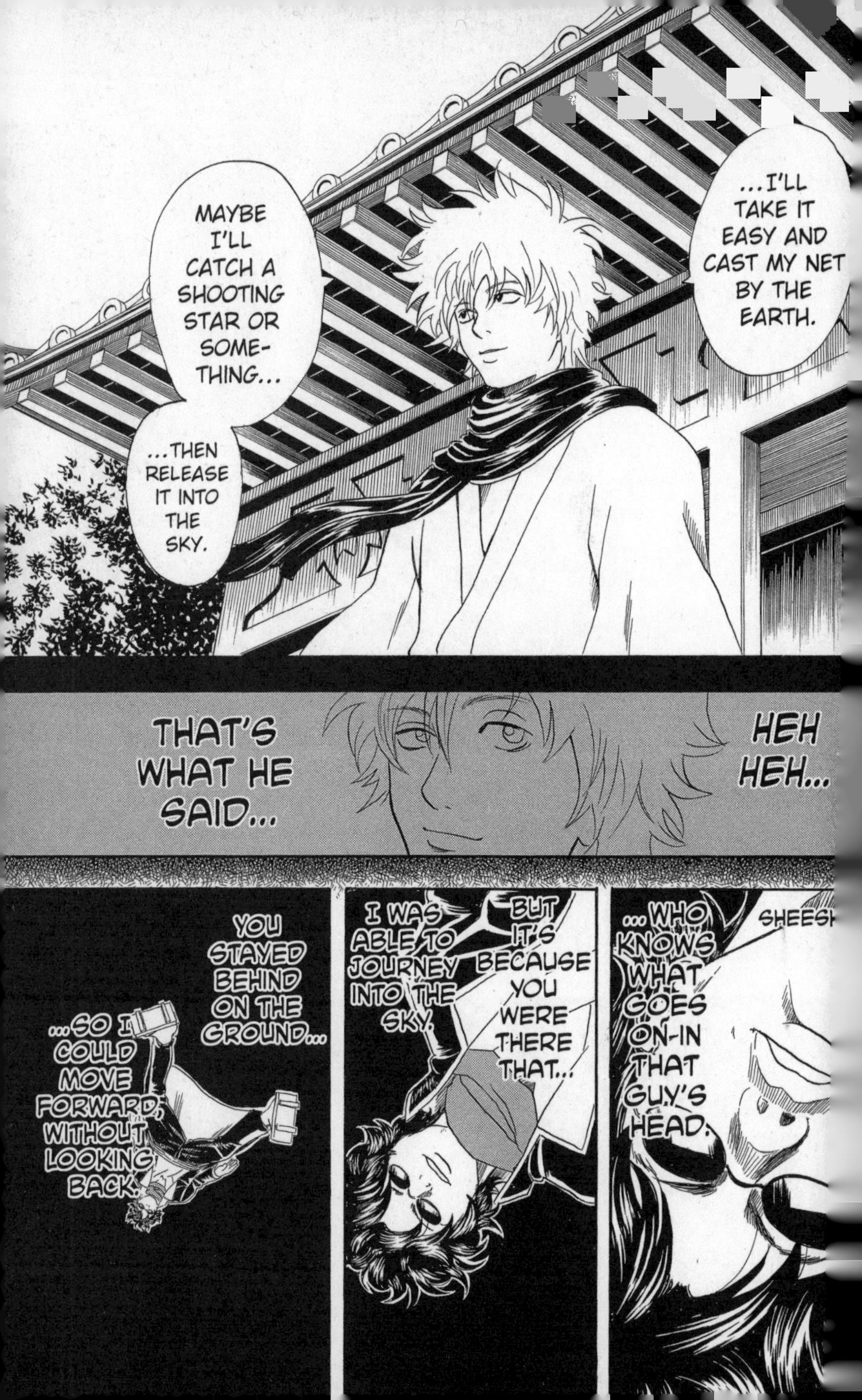
...I'LL TAKE IT EASY AND CAST MY NET BY THE EARTH.
MAYBE I'LL CATCH A SHOOTING STAR OR SOME-THING...
...THEN RELEASE IT INTO THE SKY.
HEH HEH...
THAT'S WHAT HE SAID...
SHEESH
...WHO KNOWS WHAT GOES ON IN THAT GUY'S HEAD.
BUT IT'S BECAUSE YOU WERE THERE THAT...
I WAS ABLE TO JOURNEY INTO THE SKY.
YOU STAYED BEHIND ON THE GROUND...
...SO I COULD MOVE FORWARD, WITHOUT LOOKING BACK.

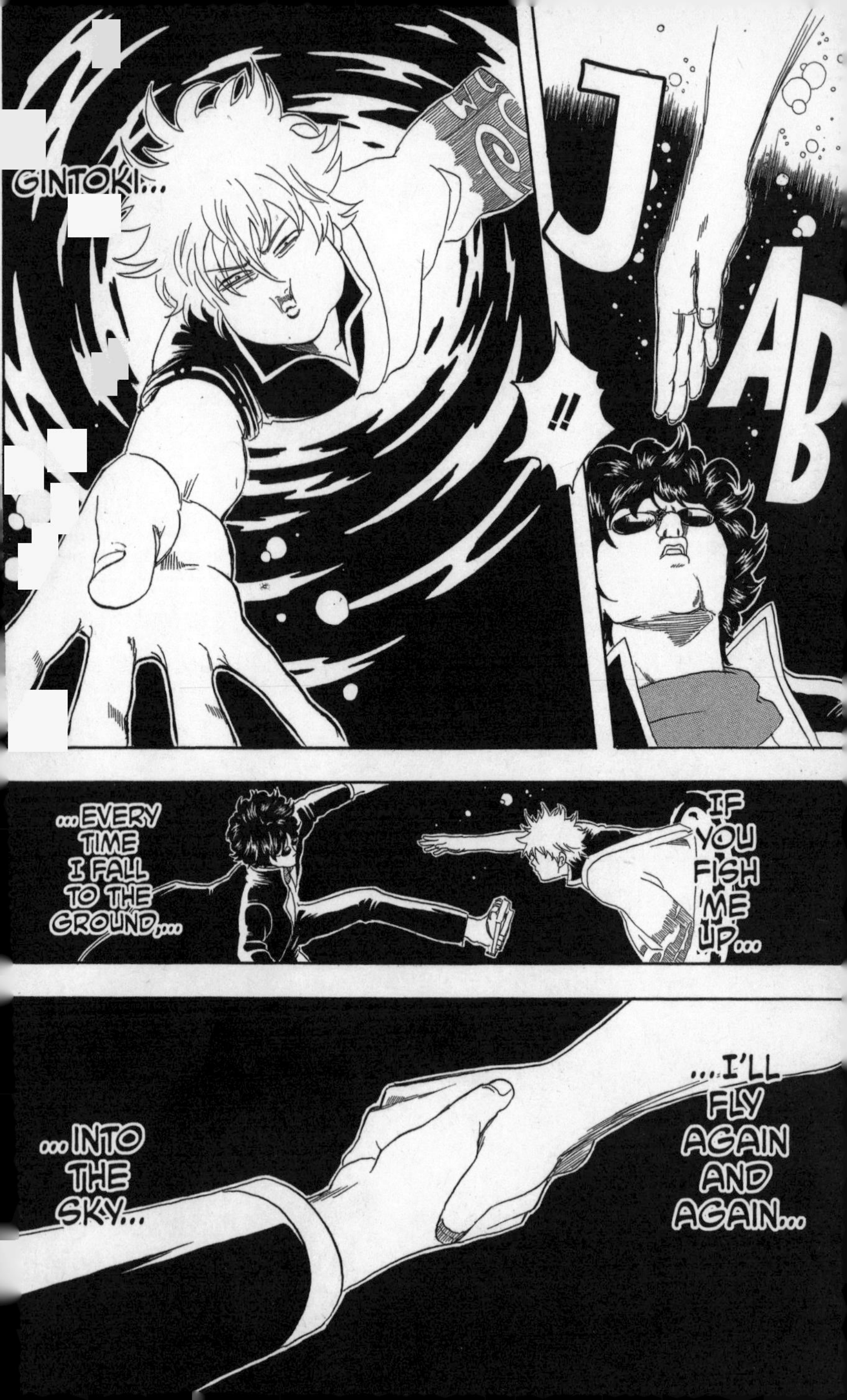
JAB
!!
GINTOKI...
IF YOU FISH ME UP...
...EVERY TIME I FALL TO THE GROUND,...
...I'LL FLY AGAIN AND AGAIN...
...INTO THE SKY...

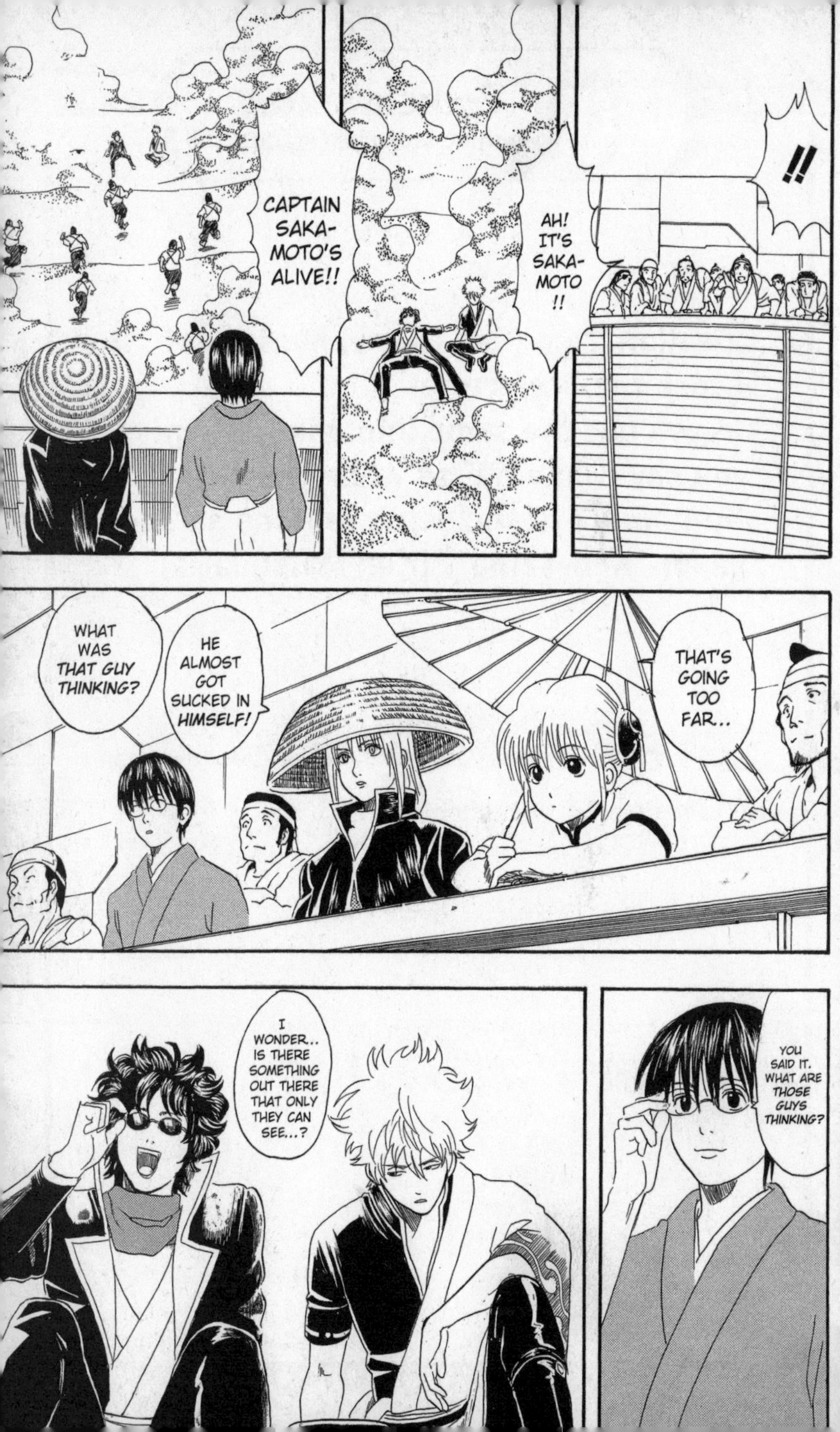
!!
AH! IT'S SAKAMOTO!!
CAPTAIN SAKAMOTO'S ALIVE!!
THAT'S GOING TOO FAR...
HE ALMOST GOT SUCKED IN HIMSELF!
WHAT WAS THAT GUY THINKING?
YOU SAID IT. WHAT ARE THOSE GUYS THINKING?
I WONDER... IS THERE SOMETHING OUT THERE THAT ONLY THEY CAN SEE...?

Sorachi's Q&A
Hanging with the Readers #3

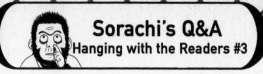

Question from (Pen Name) Marirou of Hiroshima Prefecture:
Do you use the same intonation when you say "Gintama" as when you say "Kintama"? [testicles] Or is it the same as for "Ken-sama"? [Ken Matsudaira]

It's the same as "Yoon Son-Ha." [A Korean actress]

(Q&A #4 is on page 130)

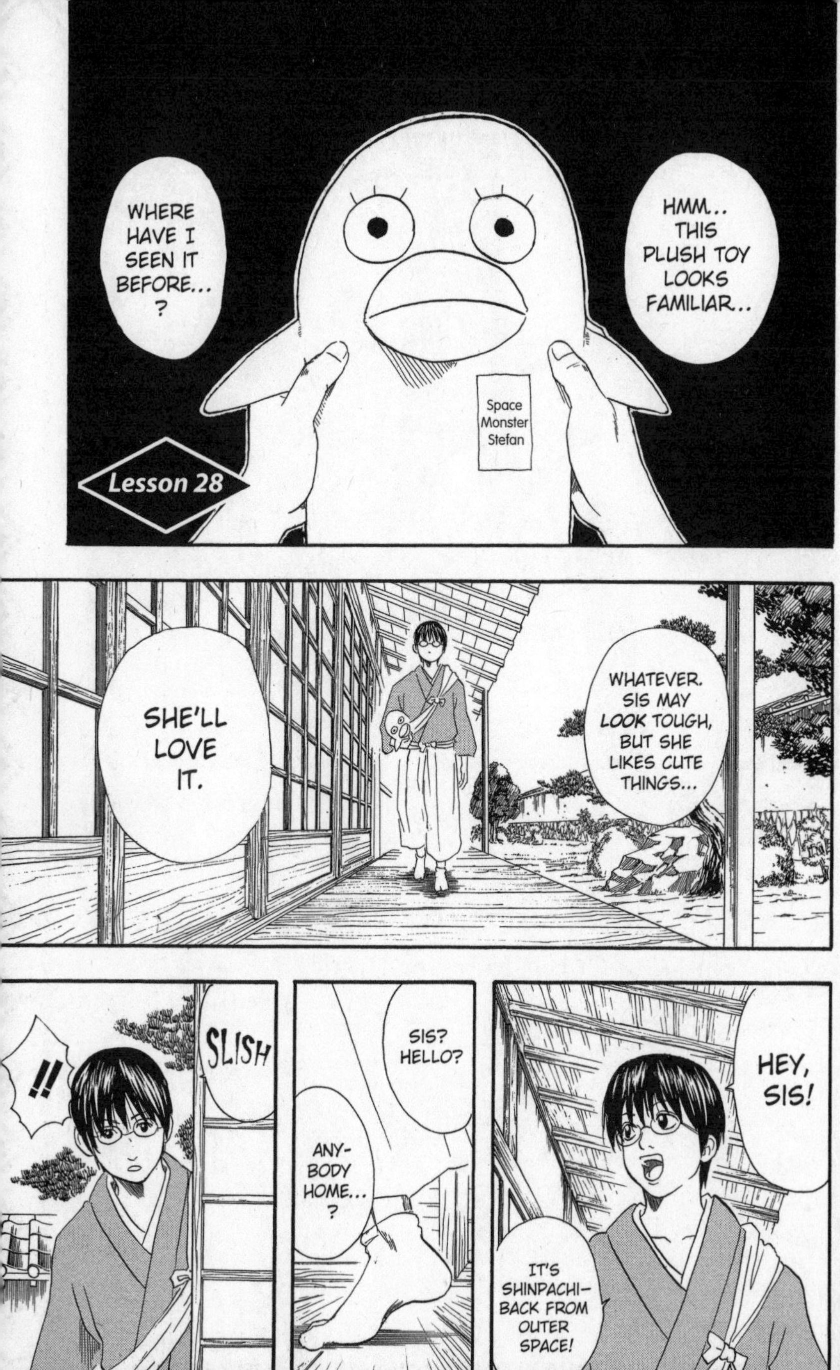
Lesson 28
HMM... THIS PLUSH TOY LOOKS FAMILIAR...
WHERE HAVE I SEEN IT BEFORE...?
Space Monster Stefan
WHATEVER. SIS MAY LOOK TOUGH, BUT SHE LIKES CUTE THINGS...
SHE'LL LOVE IT.
HEY, SIS!
IT'S SHINPACHI—BACK FROM OUTER SPACE!
SIS? HELLO?
ANYBODY HOME...?
SLISH
!!

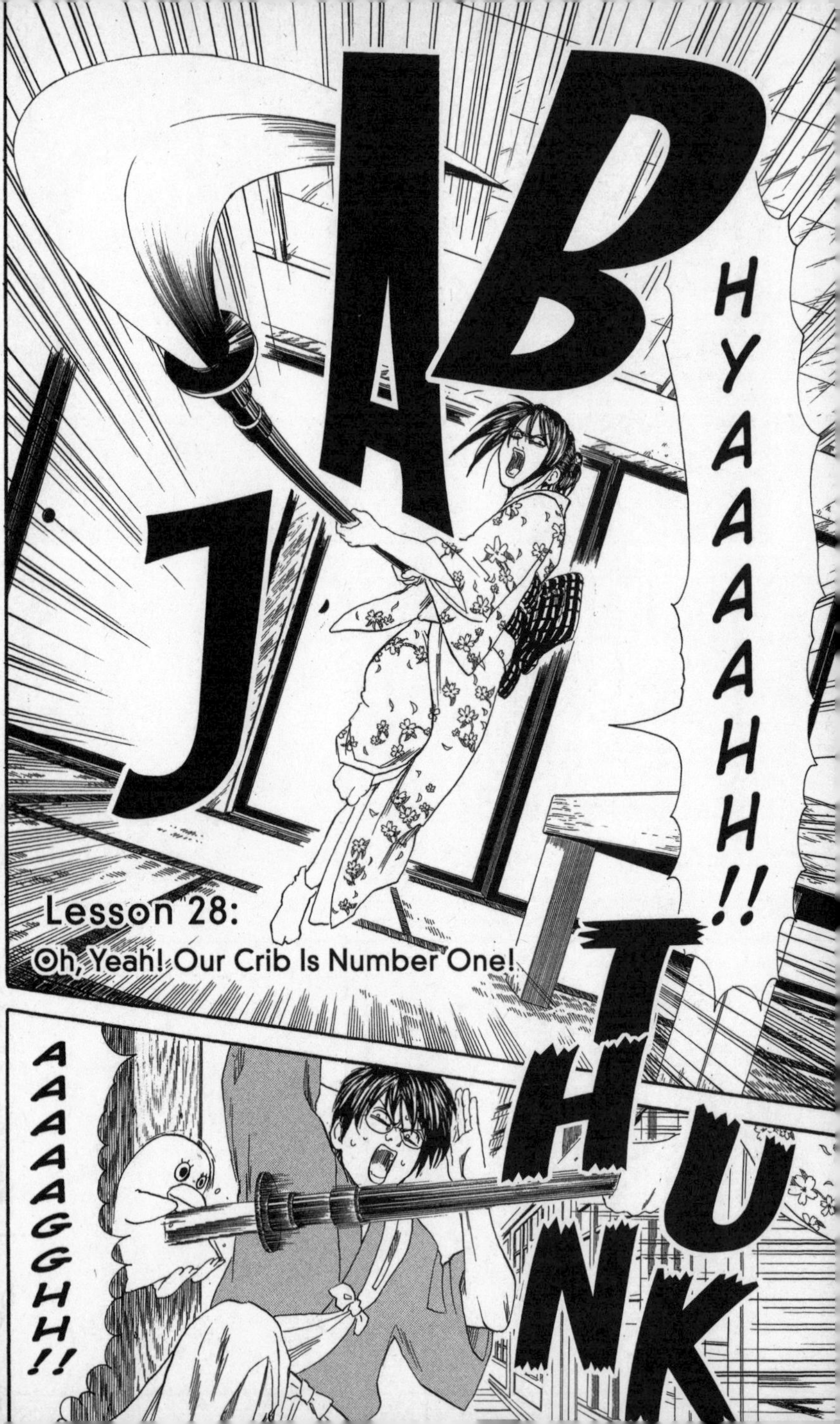
HYAAAAHH!!
JAB
Lesson 28:
Oh, Yeah! Our Crib Is Number One!
THUNK
AAAAAGGHH!!

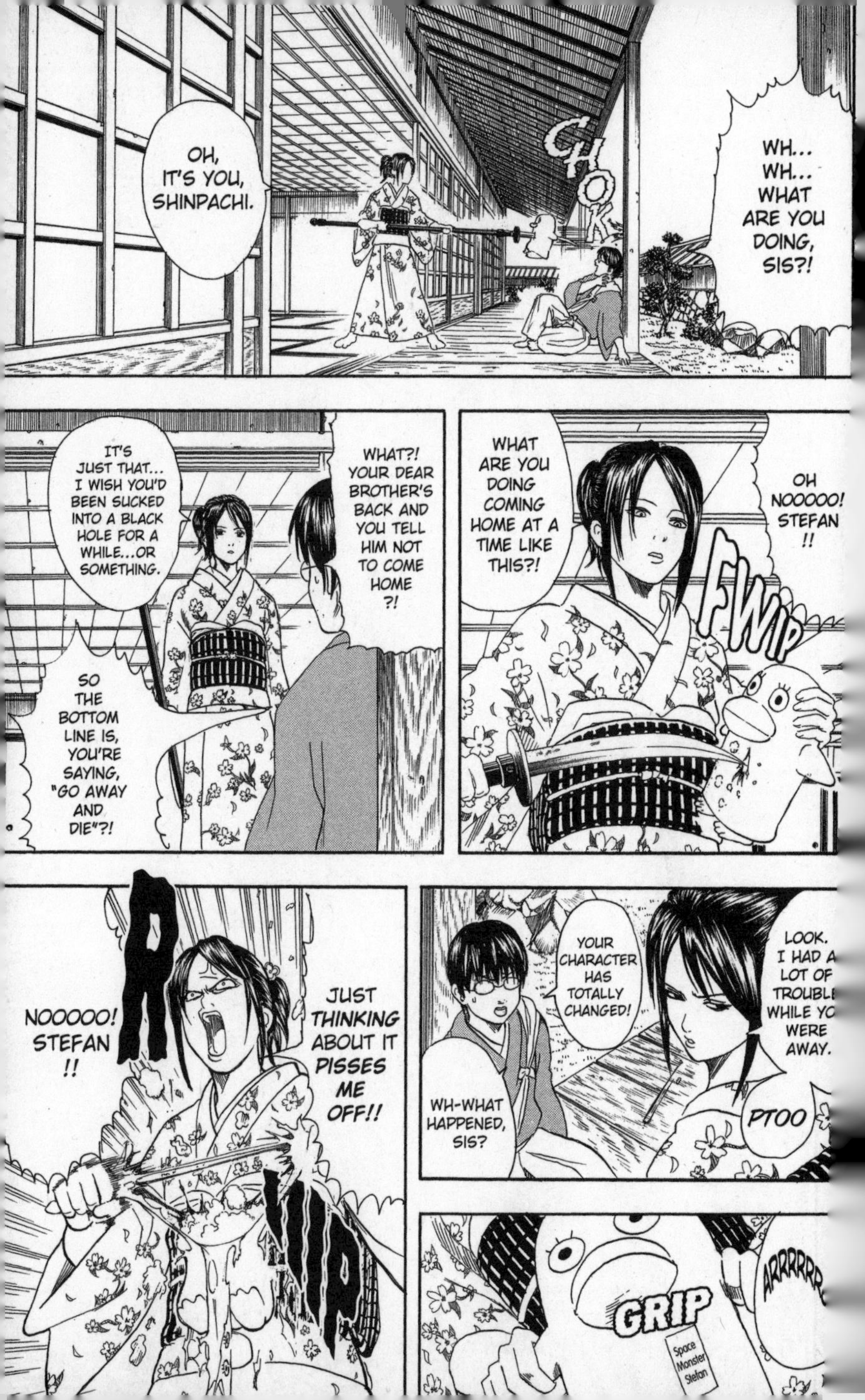
WH... WH... WHAT ARE YOU DOING, SIS?!
CHOK
OH, IT'S YOU, SHINPACHI.
OH NOOOOO! STEFAN !!
FWIP
WHAT ARE YOU DOING COMING HOME AT A TIME LIKE THIS?!
WHAT?! YOUR DEAR BROTHER'S BACK AND YOU TELL HIM NOT TO COME HOME ?!
IT'S JUST THAT... I WISH YOU'D BEEN SUCKED INTO A BLACK HOLE FOR A WHILE...OR SOMETHING.
SO THE BOTTOM LINE IS, YOU'RE SAYING, "GO AWAY AND DIE"?!
LOOK. I HAD A LOT OF TROUBLE WHILE YO WERE AWAY.
YOUR CHARACTER HAS TOTALLY CHANGED!
PTOO
WH-WHAT HAPPENED, SIS?
ARRRRRR
GRIP
Space Monster Stefan
JUST THINKING ABOUT IT PISSES ME OFF!!
NOOOOO! STEFAN !!
RIP

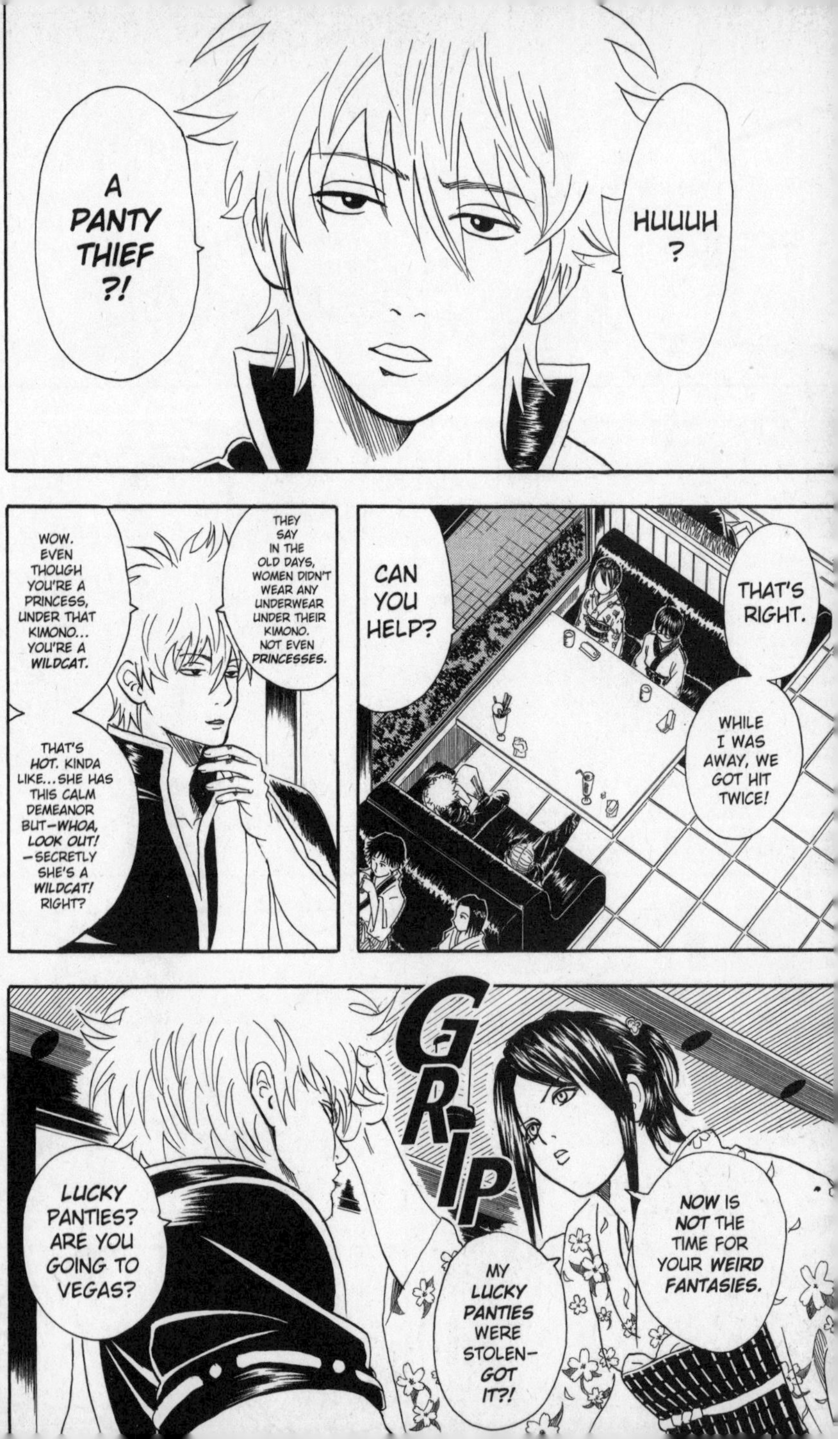
HUUUH ?
A PANTY THIEF ?!
THAT'S RIGHT.
WHILE I WAS AWAY, WE GOT HIT TWICE!
CAN YOU HELP?
THEY SAY IN THE OLD DAYS, WOMEN DIDN'T WEAR ANY UNDERWEAR UNDER THEIR KIMONO. NOT EVEN PRINCESSES.
WOW. EVEN THOUGH YOU'RE A PRINCESS, UNDER THAT KIMONO... YOU'RE A WILDCAT.
THAT'S HOT. KINDA LIKE...SHE HAS THIS CALM DEMEANOR BUT—WHOA, LOOK OUT! —SECRETLY SHE'S A WILDCAT! RIGHT?
NOW IS NOT THE TIME FOR YOUR WEIRD FANTASIES.
MY LUCKY PANTIES WERE STOLEN—GOT IT?!
GRIP
LUCKY PANTIES? ARE YOU GOING TO VEGAS?

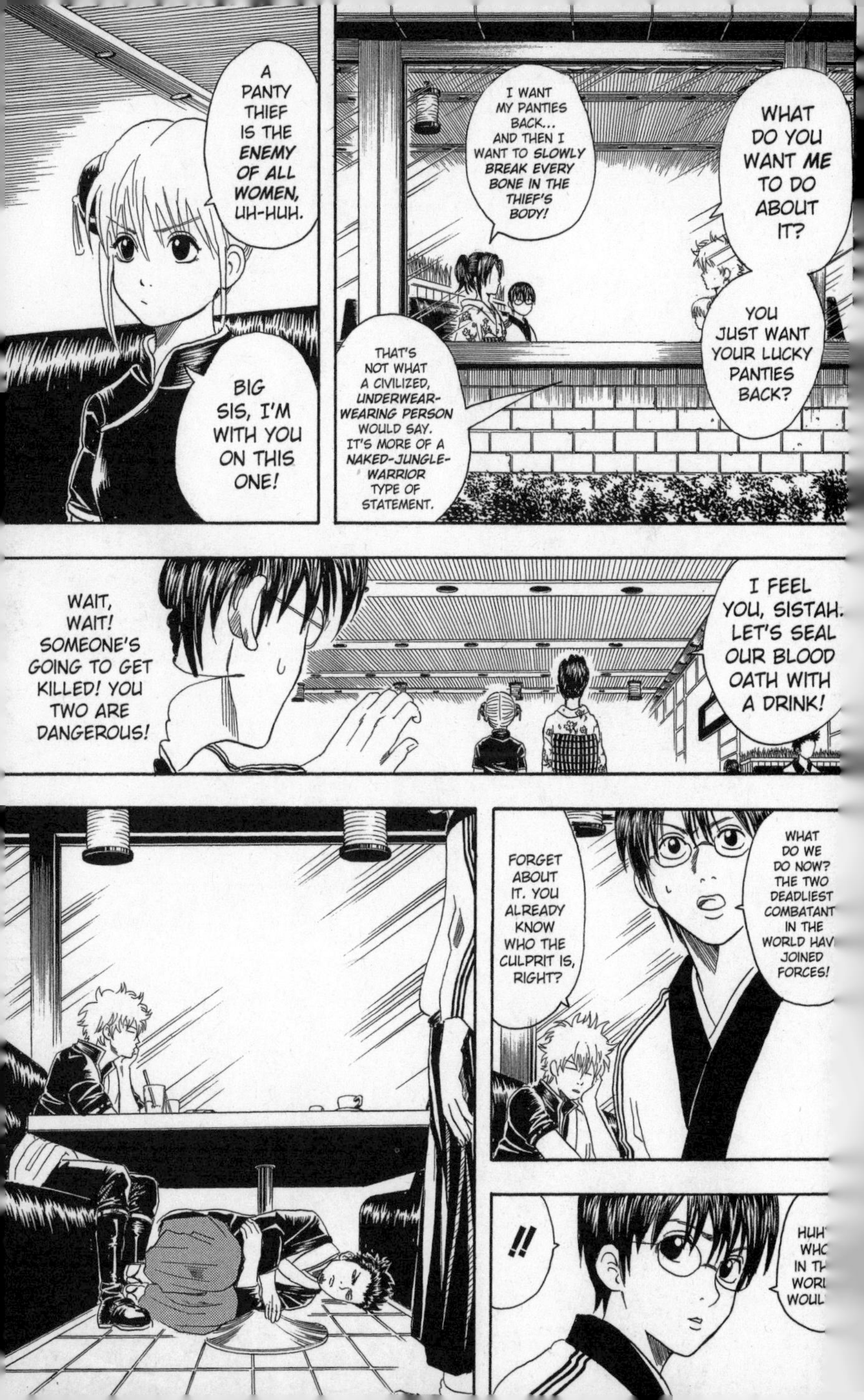
WHAT DO YOU WANT ME TO DO ABOUT IT?
YOU JUST WANT YOUR LUCKY PANTIES BACK?
I WANT MY PANTIES BACK... AND THEN I WANT TO SLOWLY BREAK EVERY BONE IN THE THIEF'S BODY!
THAT'S NOT WHAT A CIVILIZED, UNDERWEAR-WEARING PERSON WOULD SAY. IT'S MORE OF A NAKED-JUNGLE-WARRIOR TYPE OF STATEMENT.
A PANTY THIEF IS THE ENEMY OF ALL WOMEN, UH-HUH.
BIG SIS, I'M WITH YOU ON THIS ONE!
I FEEL YOU, SISTAH. LET'S SEAL OUR BLOOD OATH WITH A DRINK!
WAIT, WAIT! SOMEONE'S GOING TO GET KILLED! YOU TWO ARE DANGEROUS!
WHAT DO WE DO NOW? THE TWO DEADLIEST COMBATANT IN THE WORLD HAV JOINED FORCES!
FORGET ABOUT IT. YOU ALREADY KNOW WHO THE CULPRIT IS, RIGHT?
HUH WHO IN TH WORL WOUL
!!

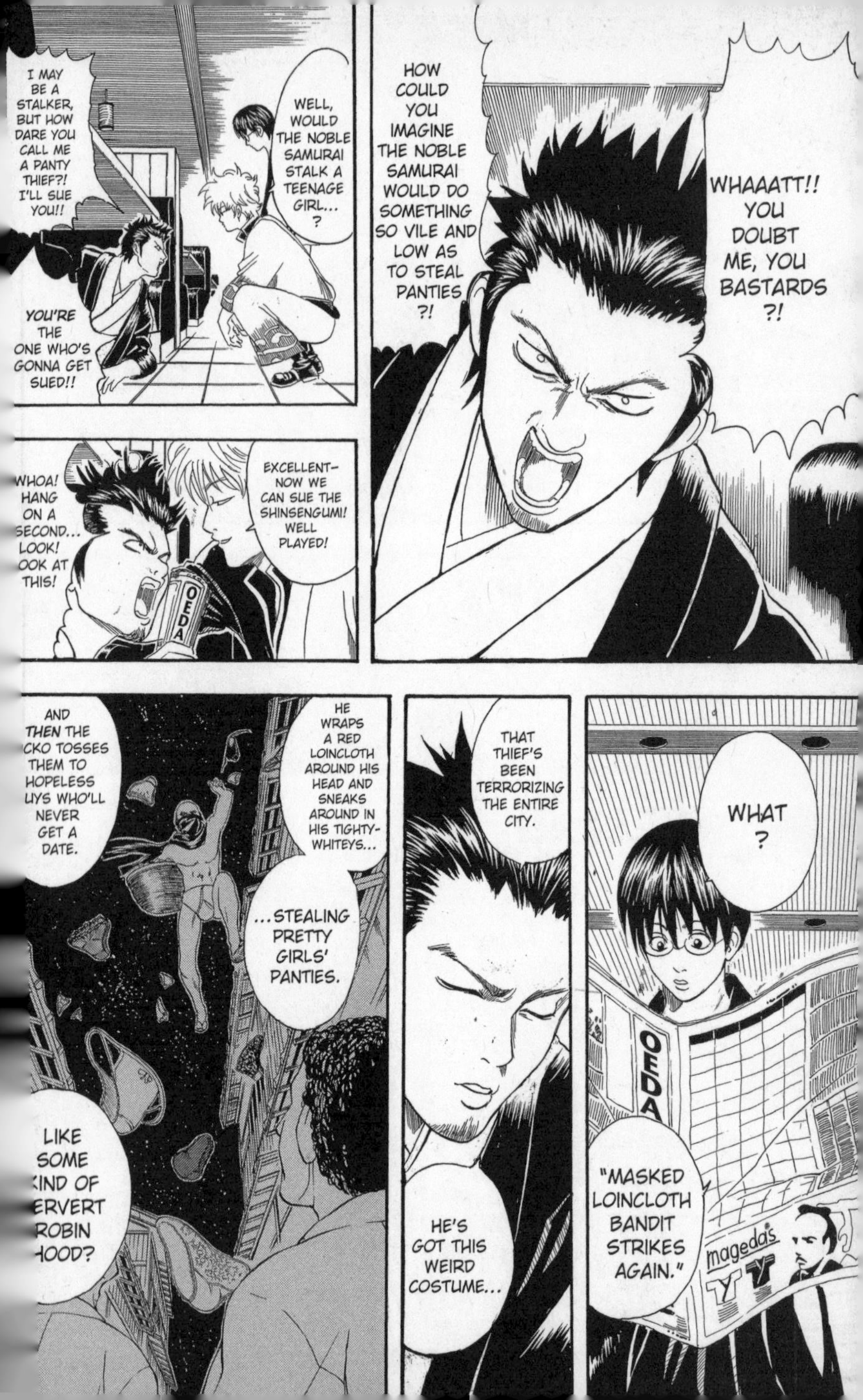
WHAAATT!! YOU DOUBT ME, YOU BASTARDS?!
HOW COULD YOU IMAGINE THE NOBLE SAMURAI WOULD DO SOMETHING SO VILE AND LOW AS TO STEAL PANTIES?!
WELL, WOULD THE NOBLE SAMURAI STALK A TEENAGE GIRL...?
I MAY BE A STALKER, BUT HOW DARE YOU CALL ME A PANTY THIEF?! I'LL SUE YOU!!
YOU'RE THE ONE WHO'S GONNA GET SUED!!
EXCELLENT— NOW WE CAN SUE THE SHINSENGUMI! WELL PLAYED!
WHOA! HANG ON A SECOND... LOOK! OOK AT THIS!
OEDA
WHAT?
OEDA
"MASKED LOINCLOTH BANDIT STRIKES AGAIN."
mageda's
THAT THIEF'S BEEN TERRORIZING THE ENTIRE CITY.
HE'S GOT THIS WEIRD COSTUME...
HE WRAPS A RED LOINCLOTH AROUND HIS HEAD AND SNEAKS AROUND IN HIS TIGHTY-WHITEYS...
...STEALING PRETTY GIRLS' PANTIES.
AND THEN THE CKO TOSSES THEM TO HOPELESS UYS WHO'LL NEVER GET A DATE.
LIKE SOME KIND OF ERVERT ROBIN HOOD?

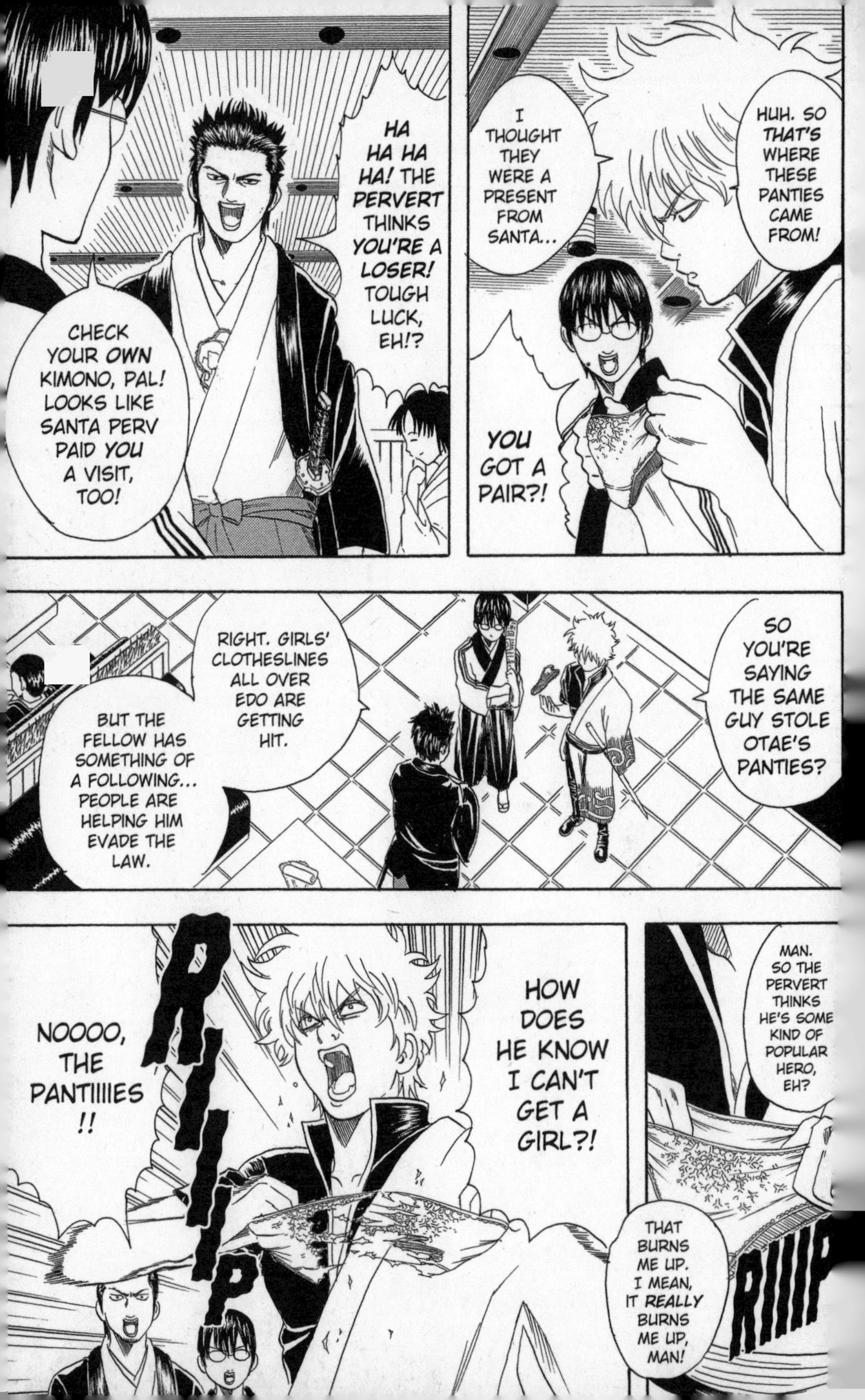
HUH. SO THAT'S WHERE THESE PANTIES CAME FROM!
I THOUGHT THEY WERE A PRESENT FROM SANTA...
YOU GOT A PAIR?!
HA HA HA HA! THE PERVERT THINKS YOU'RE A LOSER! TOUGH LUCK, EH!?
CHECK YOUR OWN KIMONO, PAL! LOOKS LIKE SANTA PERV PAID YOU A VISIT, TOO!
SO YOU'RE SAYING THE SAME GUY STOLE OTAE'S PANTIES?
RIGHT. GIRLS' CLOTHESLINES ALL OVER EDO ARE GETTING HIT.
BUT THE FELLOW HAS SOMETHING OF A FOLLOWING... PEOPLE ARE HELPING HIM EVADE THE LAW.
MAN. SO THE PERVERT THINKS HE'S SOME KIND OF POPULAR HERO, EH?
THAT BURNS ME UP. I MEAN, IT REALLY BURNS ME UP, MAN!
RIIIP
HOW DOES HE KNOW I CAN'T GET A GIRL?!
NOOOO, THE PANTIIIIES!!
RIP

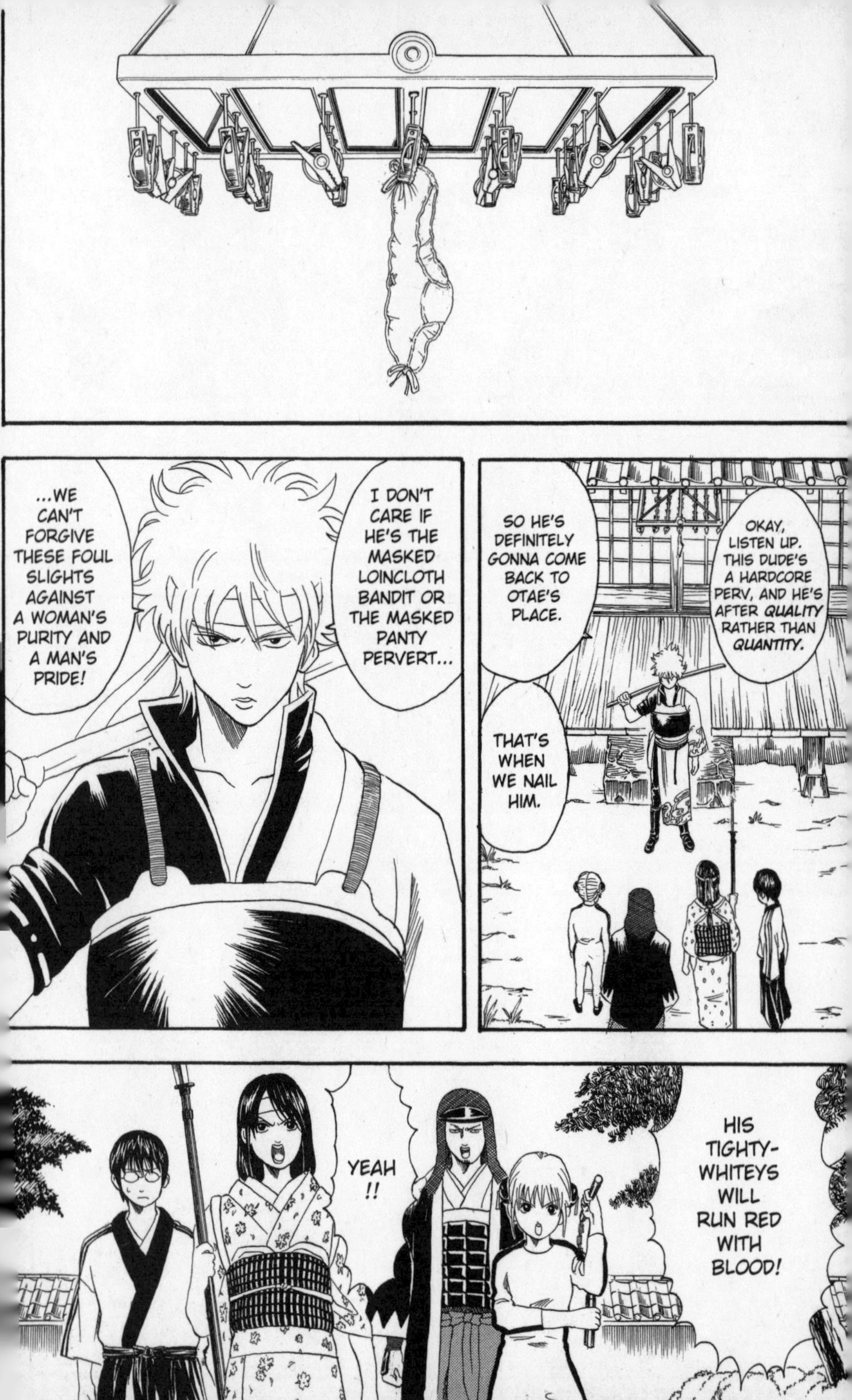
OKAY, LISTEN UP. THIS DUDE'S A HARDCORE PERV, AND HE'S AFTER *QUALITY* RATHER THAN *QUANTITY*.
SO HE'S DEFINITELY GONNA COME BACK TO OTAE'S PLACE.
THAT'S WHEN WE NAIL HIM.
I DON'T CARE IF HE'S THE MASKED LOINCLOTH BANDIT OR THE MASKED PANTY PERVERT...
...WE CAN'T FORGIVE THESE FOUL SLIGHTS AGAINST A WOMAN'S PURITY AND A MAN'S PRIDE!
HIS TIGHTY-WHITEYS WILL RUN RED WITH BLOOD!
YEAH !!

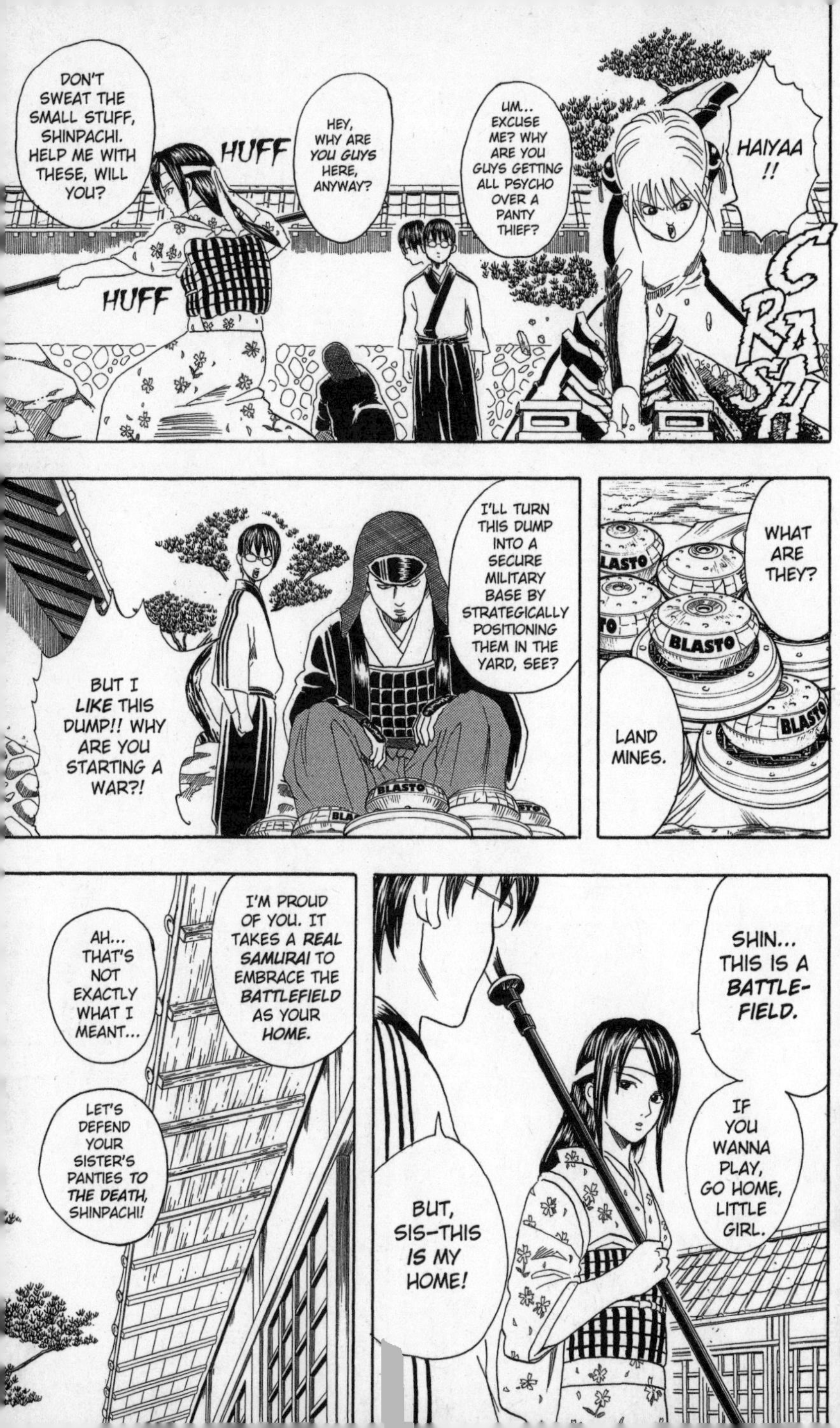
HAIYAA!!
CRASH
UM... EXCUSE ME? WHY ARE YOU GUYS GETTING ALL PSYCHO OVER A PANTY THIEF?
HEY, WHY ARE YOU GUYS HERE, ANYWAY?
HUFF
DON'T SWEAT THE SMALL STUFF, SHINPACHI. HELP ME WITH THESE, WILL YOU?
HUFF
BLASTO
WHAT ARE THEY?
LAND MINES.
I'LL TURN THIS DUMP INTO A SECURE MILITARY BASE BY STRATEGICALLY POSITIONING THEM IN THE YARD, SEE?
BUT I LIKE THIS DUMP!! WHY ARE YOU STARTING A WAR?!
BLASTO
SHIN... THIS IS A BATTLEFIELD.
IF YOU WANNA PLAY, GO HOME, LITTLE GIRL.
BUT, SIS—THIS IS MY HOME!
I'M PROUD OF YOU. IT TAKES A REAL SAMURAI TO EMBRACE THE BATTLEFIELD AS YOUR HOME.
AH... THAT'S NOT EXACTLY WHAT I MEANT...
LET'S DEFEND YOUR SISTER'S PANTIES TO THE DEATH, SHINPACHI!

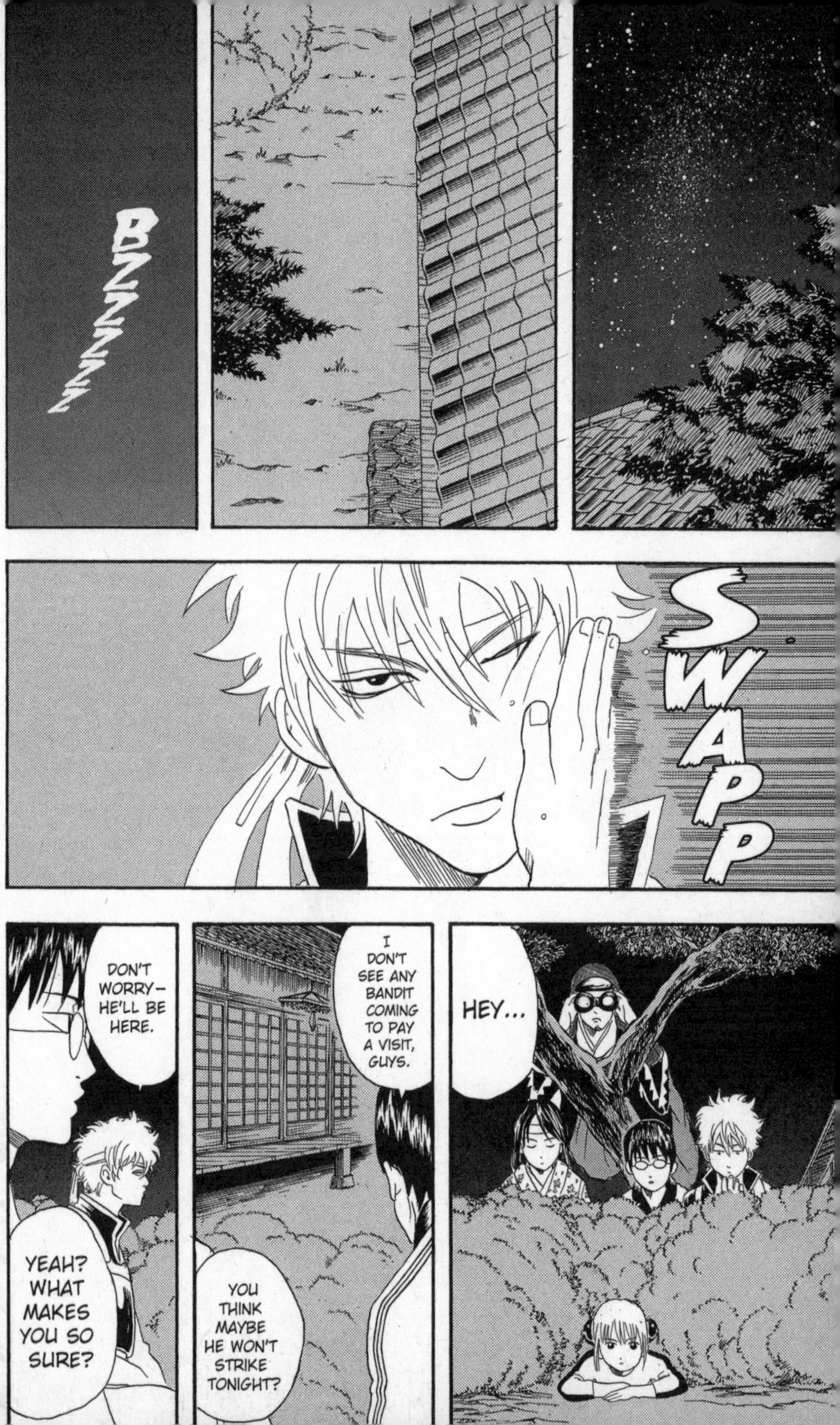
BZZZZZZ
SWAPP
HEY...
I DON'T SEE ANY BANDIT COMING TO PAY A VISIT, GUYS.
YOU THINK MAYBE HE WON'T STRIKE TONIGHT?
DON'T WORRY— HE'LL BE HERE.
YEAH? WHAT MAKES YOU SO SURE?

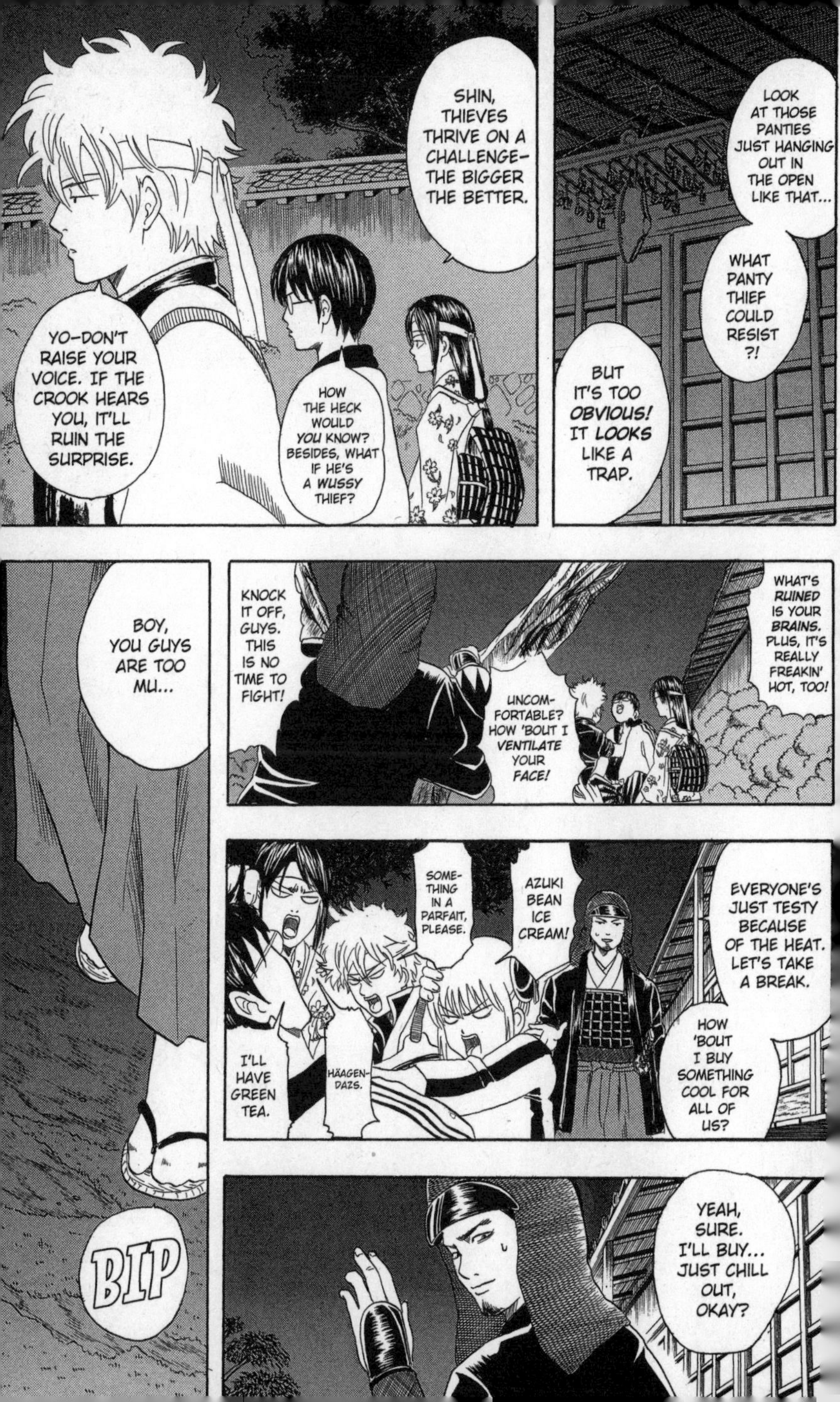

LOOK AT THOSE PANTIES JUST HANGING OUT IN THE OPEN LIKE THAT...
WHAT PANTY THIEF COULD RESIST ?!
BUT IT'S TOO *OBVIOUS!* IT *LOOKS* LIKE A TRAP.
SHIN, THIEVES THRIVE ON A CHALLENGE–THE BIGGER THE BETTER.
YO–DON'T RAISE YOUR VOICE. IF THE CROOK HEARS YOU, IT'LL RUIN THE SURPRISE.
HOW THE HECK WOULD *YOU* KNOW? BESIDES, WHAT IF HE'S A *WUSSY* THIEF?
WHAT'S *RUINED* IS YOUR *BRAINS.* PLUS, IT'S REALLY FREAKIN' HOT, TOO!
UNCOMFORTABLE? HOW 'BOUT I *VENTILATE* YOUR *FACE!*
KNOCK IT OFF, GUYS. THIS IS NO TIME TO FIGHT!
EVERYONE'S JUST TESTY BECAUSE OF THE HEAT. LET'S TAKE A BREAK.
HOW 'BOUT I BUY SOMETHING COOL FOR ALL OF US?
AZUKI BEAN ICE CREAM!
SOMETHING IN A PARFAIT, PLEASE.
HÄAGEN-DAZS.
I'LL HAVE GREEN TEA.
YEAH, SURE. I'LL BUY... JUST CHILL OUT, OKAY?
BOY, YOU GUYS ARE TOO MU...
BIP

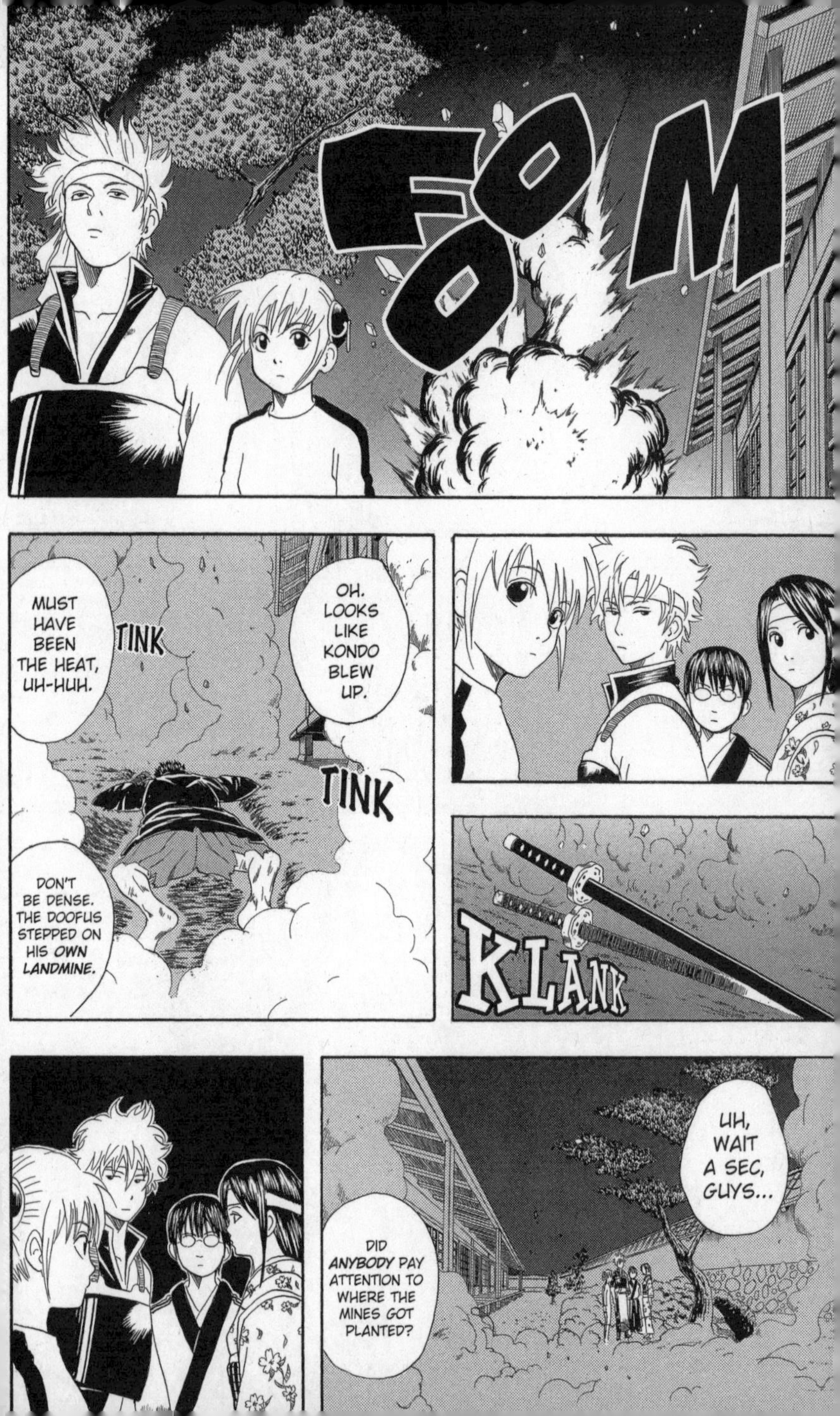
FOOM
KLANK
OH. LOOKS LIKE KONDO BLEW UP.
TINK
MUST HAVE BEEN THE HEAT, UH-HUH.
TINK
DON'T BE DENSE. THE DOOFUS STEPPED ON HIS *OWN* *LANDMINE*.
UH, WAIT A SEC, GUYS...
DID *ANYBODY* PAY ATTENTION TO WHERE THE MINES GOT PLANTED?

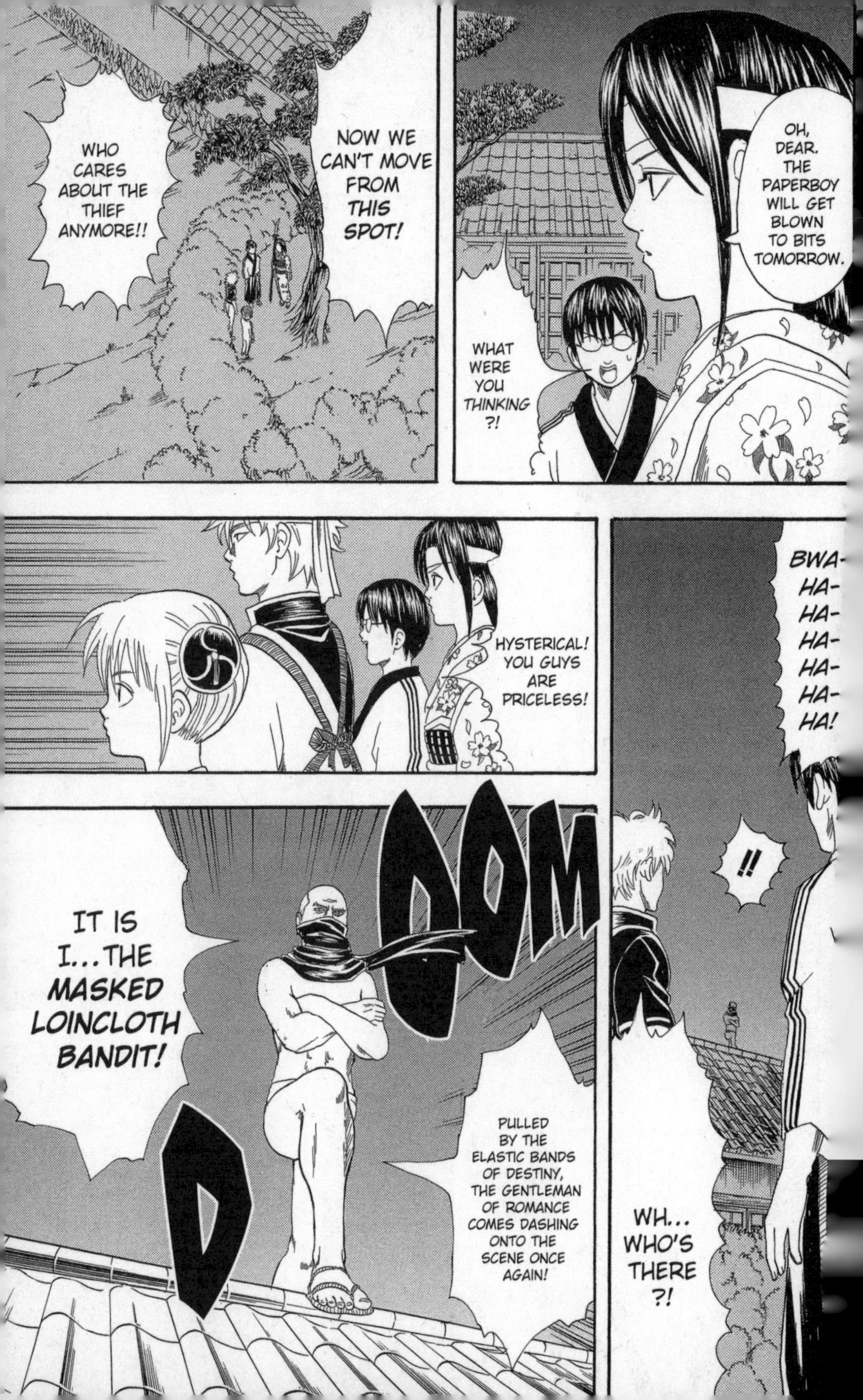
OH, DEAR. THE PAPERBOY WILL GET BLOWN TO BITS TOMORROW.
WHAT WERE YOU THINKING?!
NOW WE CAN'T MOVE FROM THIS SPOT!
WHO CARES ABOUT THE THIEF ANYMORE!!
BWA-HA-HA-HA-HA-HA-HA!
HYSTERICAL! YOU GUYS ARE PRICELESS!
!!
WH... WHO'S THERE?!
DOM
D
PULLED BY THE ELASTIC BANDS OF DESTINY, THE GENTLEMAN OF ROMANCE COMES DASHING ONTO THE SCENE ONCE AGAIN!
IT IS I... THE MASKED LOINCLOTH BANDIT!

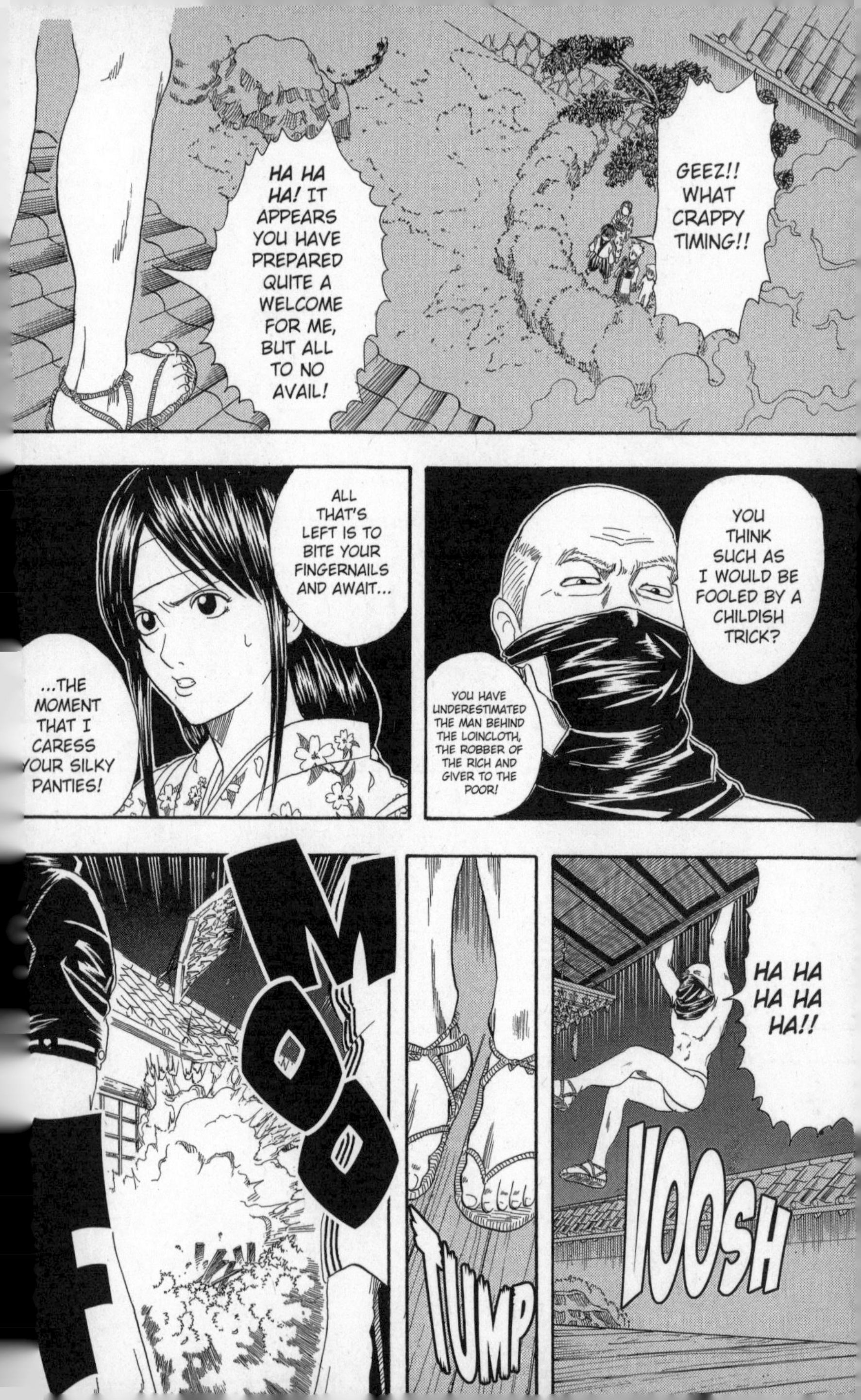
GEEZ!! WHAT CRAPPY TIMING!!
HA HA HA! IT APPEARS YOU HAVE PREPARED QUITE A WELCOME FOR ME, BUT ALL TO NO AVAIL!
YOU THINK SUCH AS I WOULD BE FOOLED BY A CHILDISH TRICK?
YOU HAVE UNDERESTIMATED THE MAN BEHIND THE LOINCLOTH, THE ROBBER OF THE RICH AND GIVER TO THE POOR!
ALL THAT'S LEFT IS TO BITE YOUR FINGERNAILS AND AWAIT...
...THE MOMENT THAT I CARESS YOUR SILKY PANTIES!
HA HA HA HA HA!!
WOOSH
TUMP

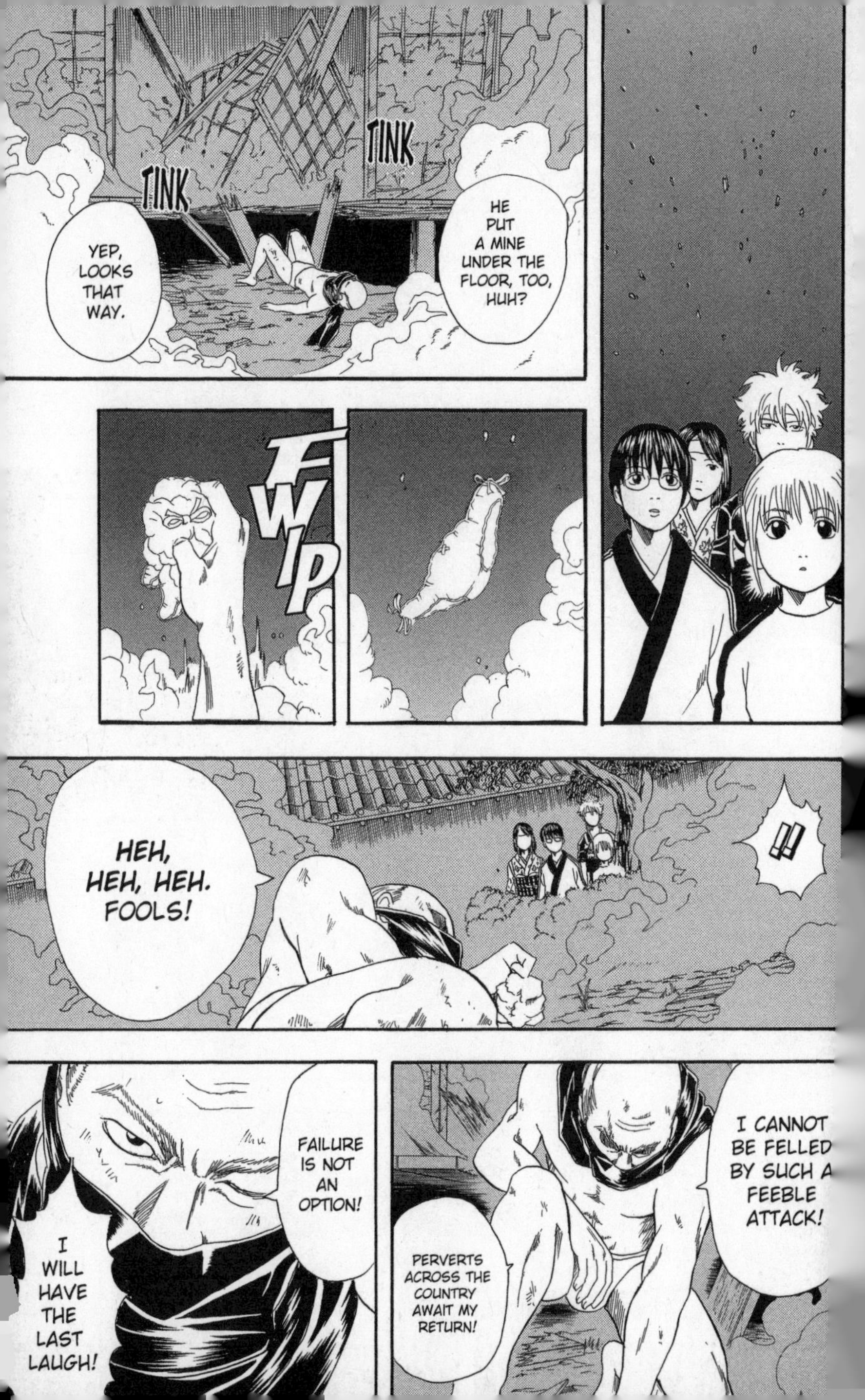
TINK
TINK
HE PUT A MINE UNDER THE FLOOR, TOO, HUH?
YEP, LOOKS THAT WAY.
FWIP
!!
HEH, HEH, HEH. FOOLS!
I CANNOT BE FELLED BY SUCH A FEEBLE ATTACK!
PERVERTS ACROSS THE COUNTRY AWAIT MY RETURN!
FAILURE IS NOT AN OPTION!
I WILL HAVE THE LAST LAUGH!

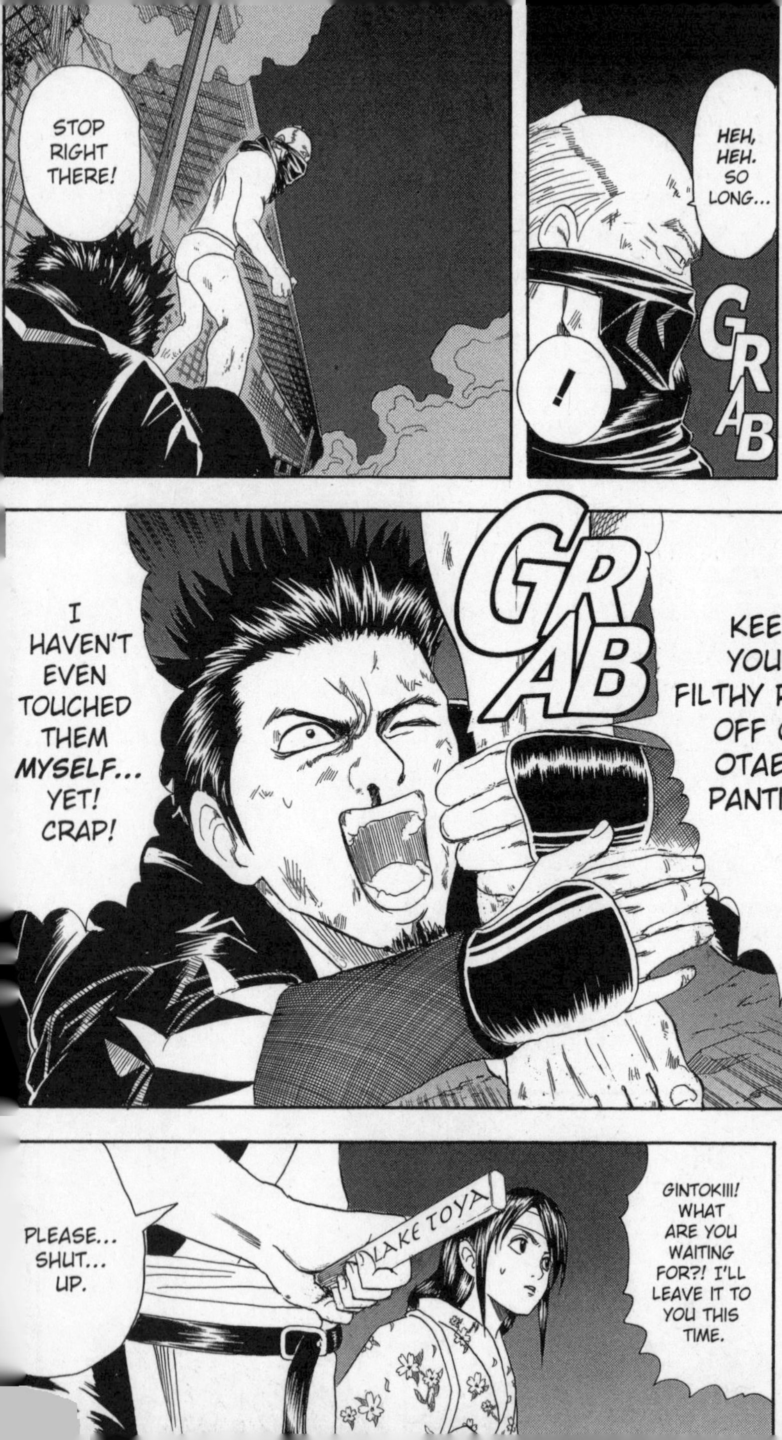
HEH, HEH. SO LONG...
!
GRAB
STOP RIGHT THERE!
GRAB
KEEP YOUR FILTHY PAWS OFF OF OTAE'S PANTIES!
I HAVEN'T EVEN TOUCHED THEM MYSELF... YET! CRAP!
GINTOKIII! WHAT ARE YOU WAITING FOR?! I'LL LEAVE IT TO YOU THIS TIME.
LAKE TOYA
PLEASE... SHUT... UP.

READ THIS WAY

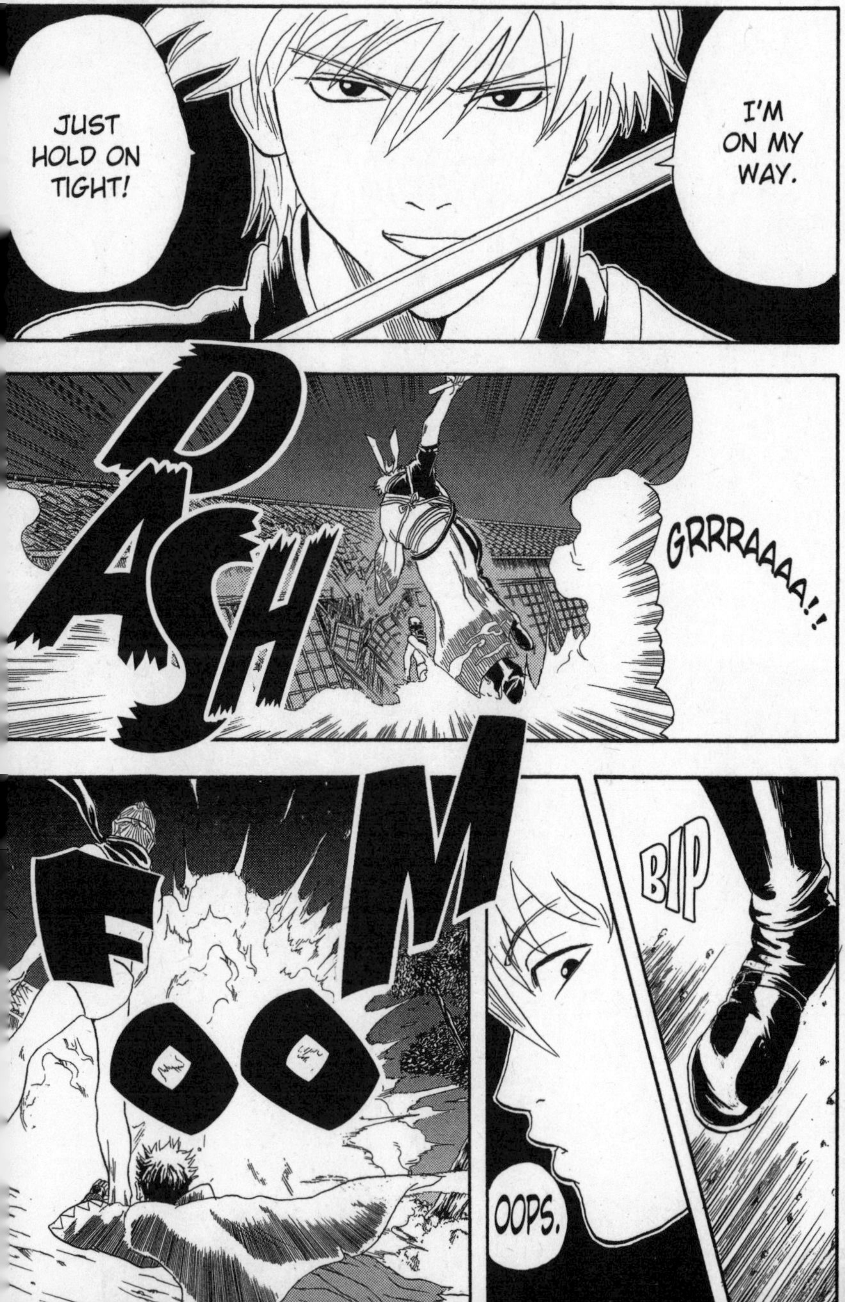

I'M ON MY WAY.
JUST HOLD ON TIGHT!
GRRRAAAAA!!
DASH
BIP
OOPS.
FOOM

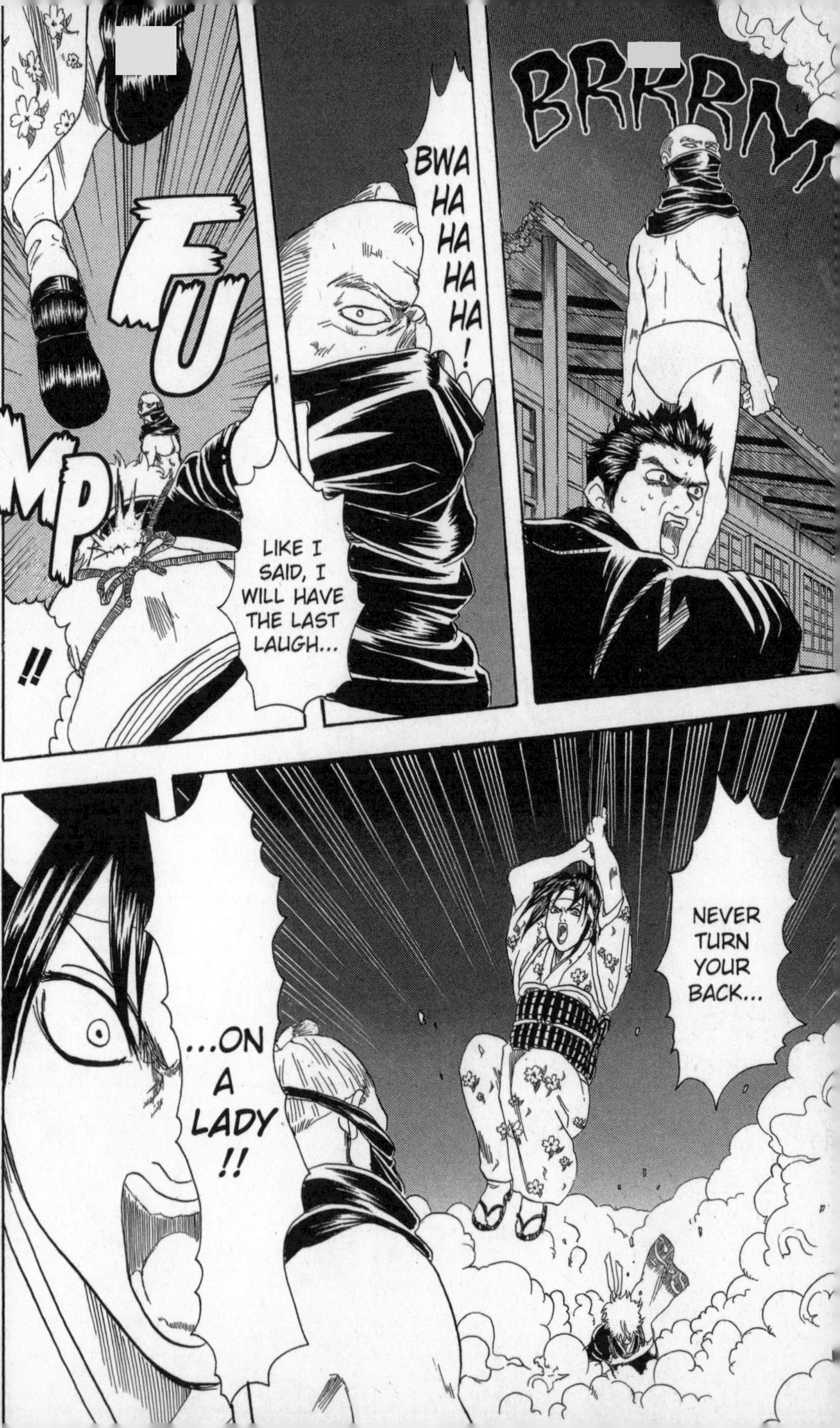
BRRRM
BWA HA HA HA HA!
LIKE I SAID, I WILL HAVE THE LAST LAUGH...
FUMP
!!
NEVER TURN YOUR BACK...
...ON A LADY!!

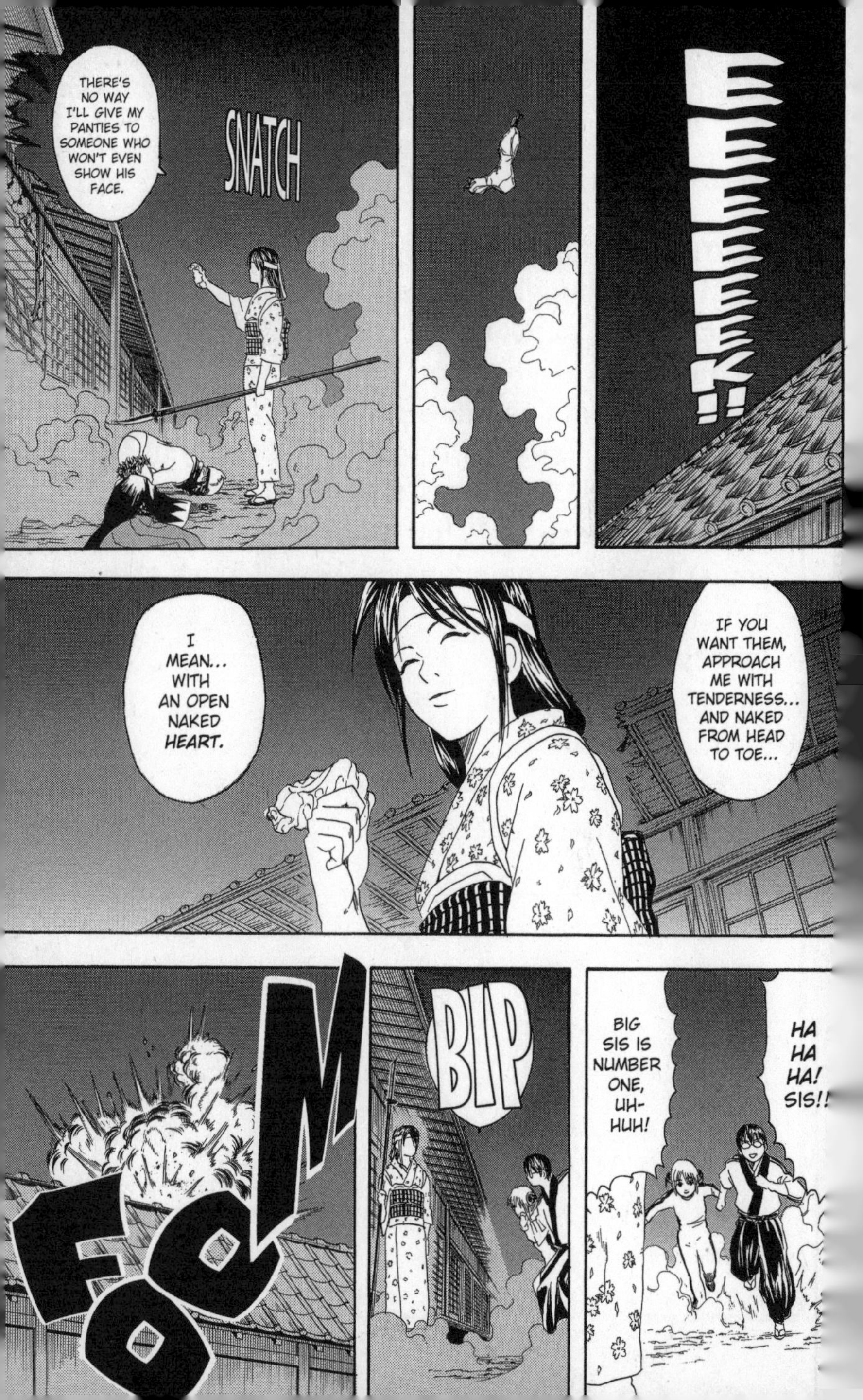
EEEEEEEK!!
SNATCH
THERE'S NO WAY I'LL GIVE MY PANTIES TO SOMEONE WHO WON'T EVEN SHOW HIS FACE.
IF YOU WANT THEM, APPROACH ME WITH TENDERNESS... AND NAKED FROM HEAD TO TOE...
I MEAN... WITH AN OPEN NAKED HEART.
HA HA HA! SIS!!
BIG SIS IS NUMBER ONE, UH-HUH!
BLIP
FOOM

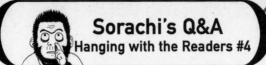

Sorachi's Q&A
Hanging with the Readers #4

Question from Kashiwatani of Tokyo:
What keeps bugging me is, you know, Cat's Punch, which appears in Lesson 24, right? Its members are Kurikan, Hattori, (ex-member) Catherine, and one more person, the guy who looks like Ji, Jagged Claw. What I'd really like to know is all of their full names and bios, but if thinking those up is too much of a pain, could you at least tell me his name? See, I love Cat's Punch. Just make up any name for him and I'll be happy. Please!

Um...... Kashiwatani.

(Continues with #5 on page 150)

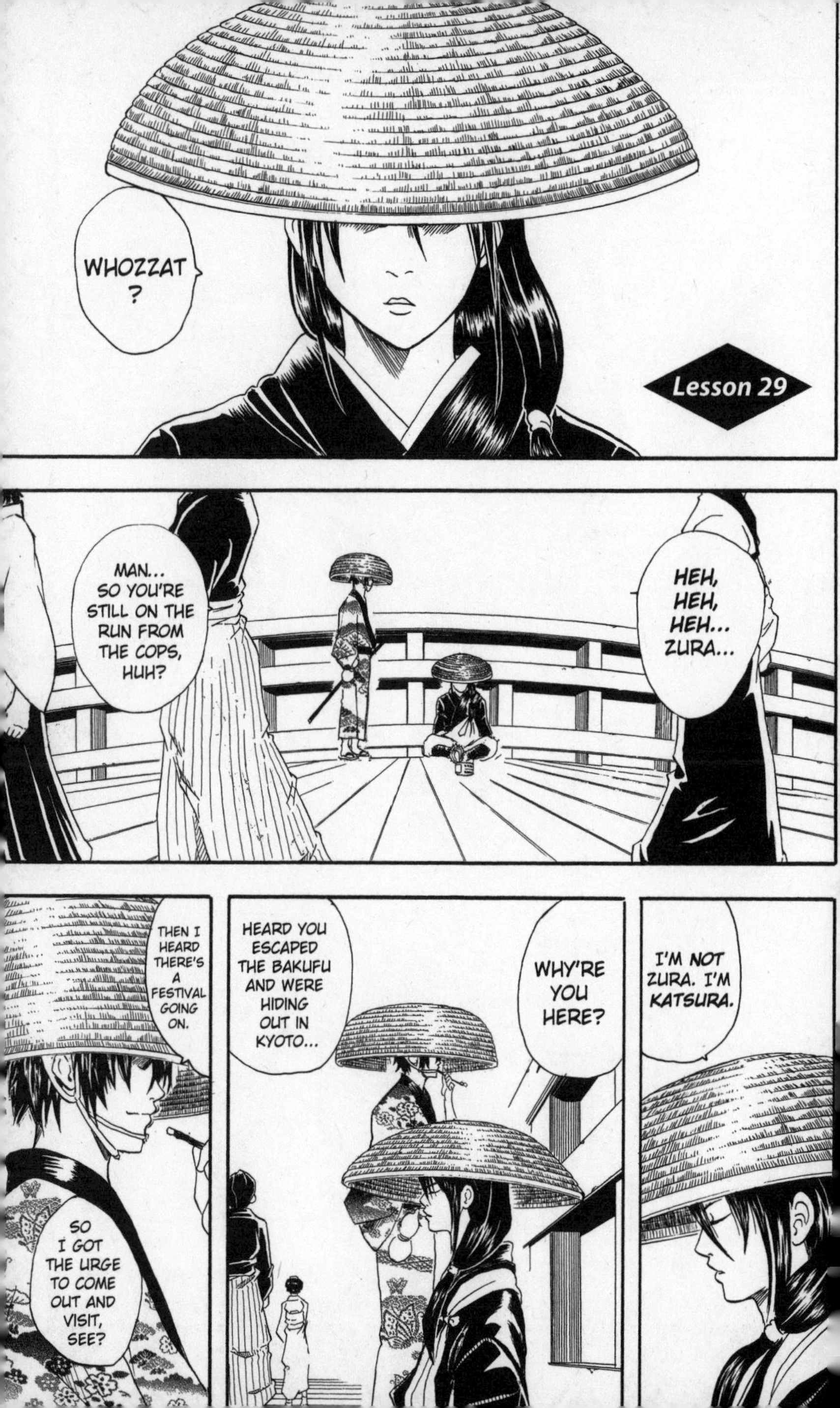
WHOZZAT?
Lesson 29
HEH, HEH, HEH... ZURA...
MAN... SO YOU'RE STILL ON THE RUN FROM THE COPS, HUH?
I'M NOT ZURA. I'M KATSURA.
WHY'RE YOU HERE?
HEARD YOU ESCAPED THE BAKUFU AND WERE HIDING OUT IN KYOTO...
THEN I HEARD THERE'S A FESTIVAL GOING ON.
SO I GOT THE URGE TO COME OUT AND VISIT, SEE?

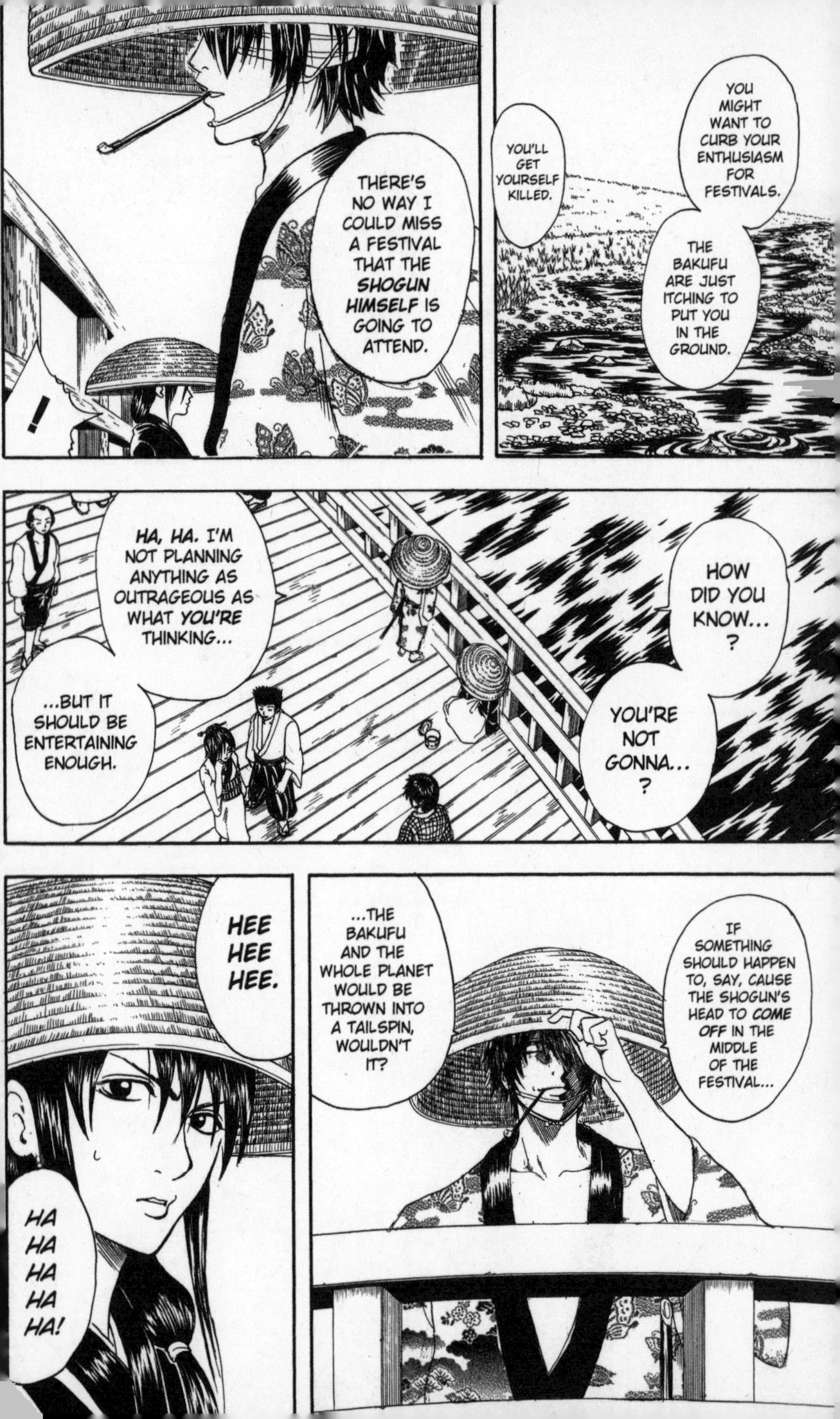
YOU MIGHT WANT TO CURB YOUR ENTHUSIASM FOR FESTIVALS.
THE BAKUFU ARE JUST ITCHING TO PUT YOU IN THE GROUND.
YOU'LL GET YOURSELF KILLED.
THERE'S NO WAY I COULD MISS A FESTIVAL THAT THE *SHOGUN HIMSELF* IS GOING TO ATTEND.
!
HOW DID YOU KNOW...?
YOU'RE NOT GONNA...?
HA, HA. I'M NOT PLANNING ANYTHING AS OUTRAGEOUS AS WHAT *YOU'RE* THINKING...
...BUT IT SHOULD BE ENTERTAINING ENOUGH.
IF SOMETHING SHOULD HAPPEN TO, SAY, CAUSE THE SHOGUN'S HEAD TO *COME OFF* IN THE MIDDLE OF THE FESTIVAL...
...THE BAKUFU AND THE WHOLE PLANET WOULD BE THROWN INTO A TAILSPIN, WOULDN'T IT?
HEE HEE HEE.
HA HA HA HA HA!

Lesson 29

You Really Think You Can Study for Exams While Listening to Music?! Turn It off Already!

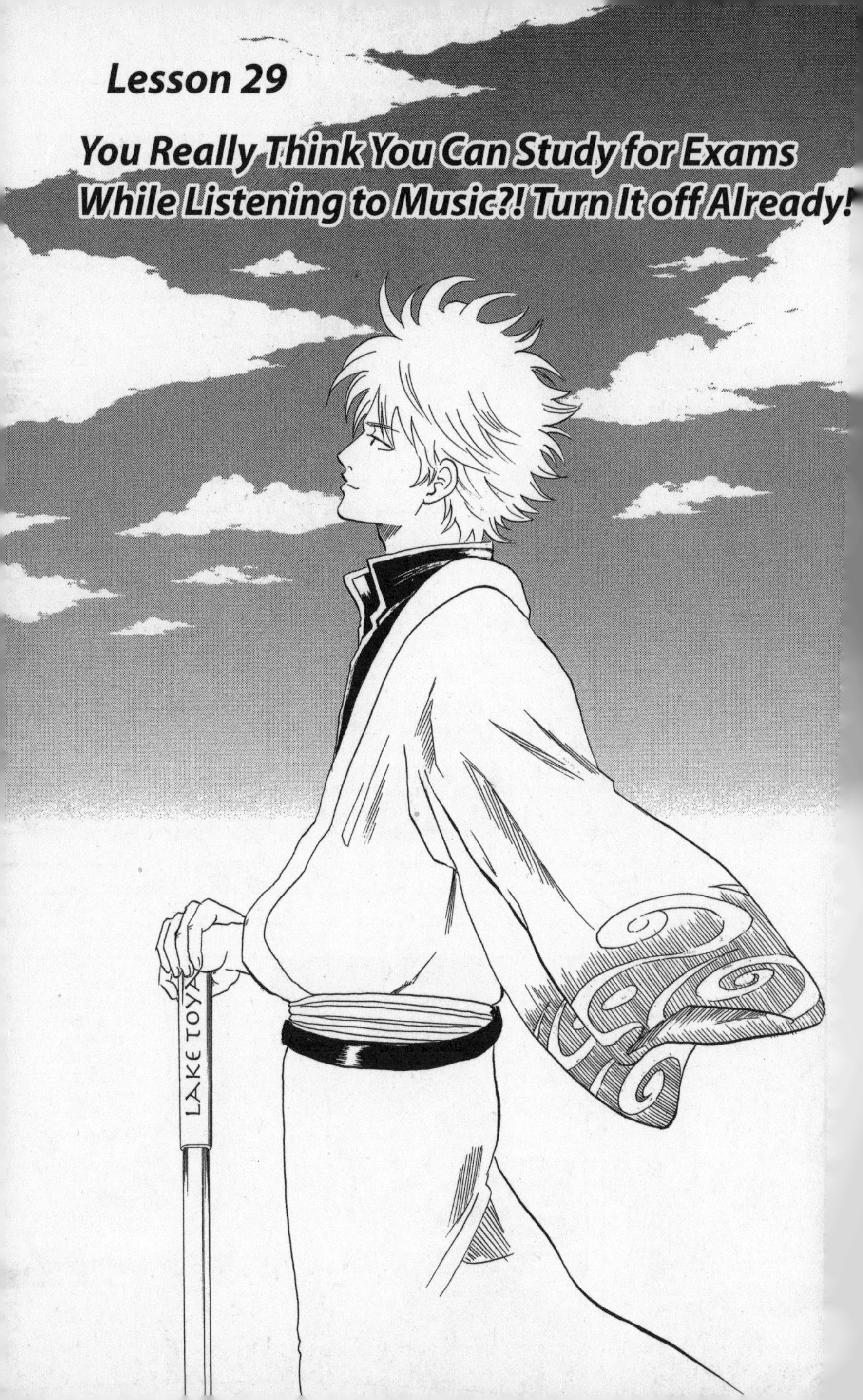
LAKE TOYA

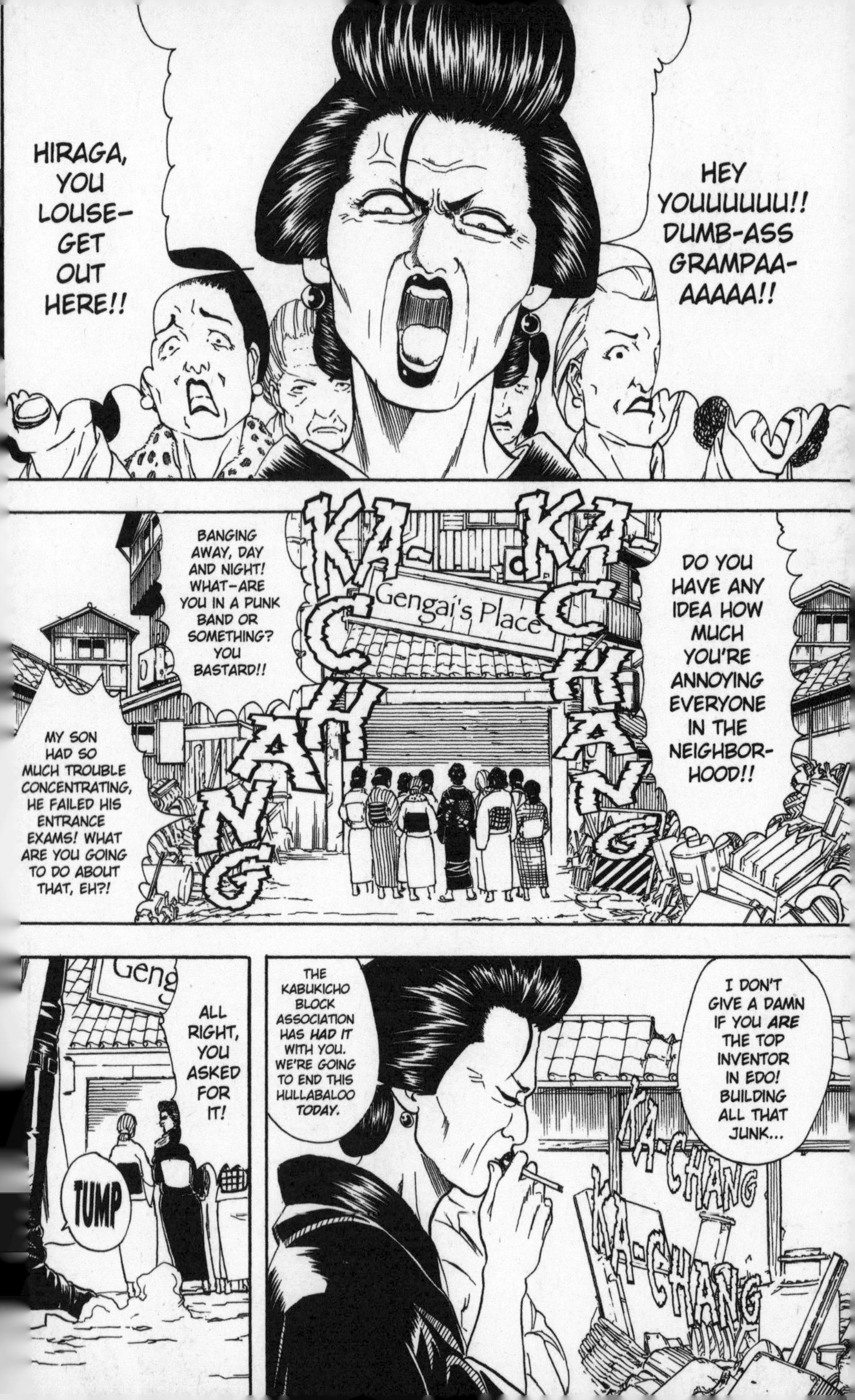
HEY YOUUUUUU!! DUMB-ASS GRAMPAA-AAAAA!!
HIRAGA, YOU LOUSE—GET OUT HERE!!
DO YOU HAVE ANY IDEA HOW MUCH YOU'RE ANNOYING EVERYONE IN THE NEIGHBOR-HOOD!!
KA-CHANG
Gengai's Place
BANGING AWAY, DAY AND NIGHT! WHAT—ARE YOU IN A PUNK BAND OR SOMETHING? YOU BASTARD!!
KA-CHANG
MY SON HAD SO MUCH TROUBLE CONCENTRATING, HE FAILED HIS ENTRANCE EXAMS! WHAT ARE YOU GOING TO DO ABOUT THAT, EH?!
I DON'T GIVE A DAMN IF YOU *ARE* THE TOP INVENTOR IN EDO! BUILDING ALL THAT JUNK...
KA-CHANG
KA-CHANG
KA-CHANG
THE KABUKICHO BLOCK ASSOCIATION HAS *HAD* IT WITH YOU. WE'RE GOING TO END THIS HULLABALOO TODAY.
ALL RIGHT, YOU ASKED FOR IT!
Geng
TUMP

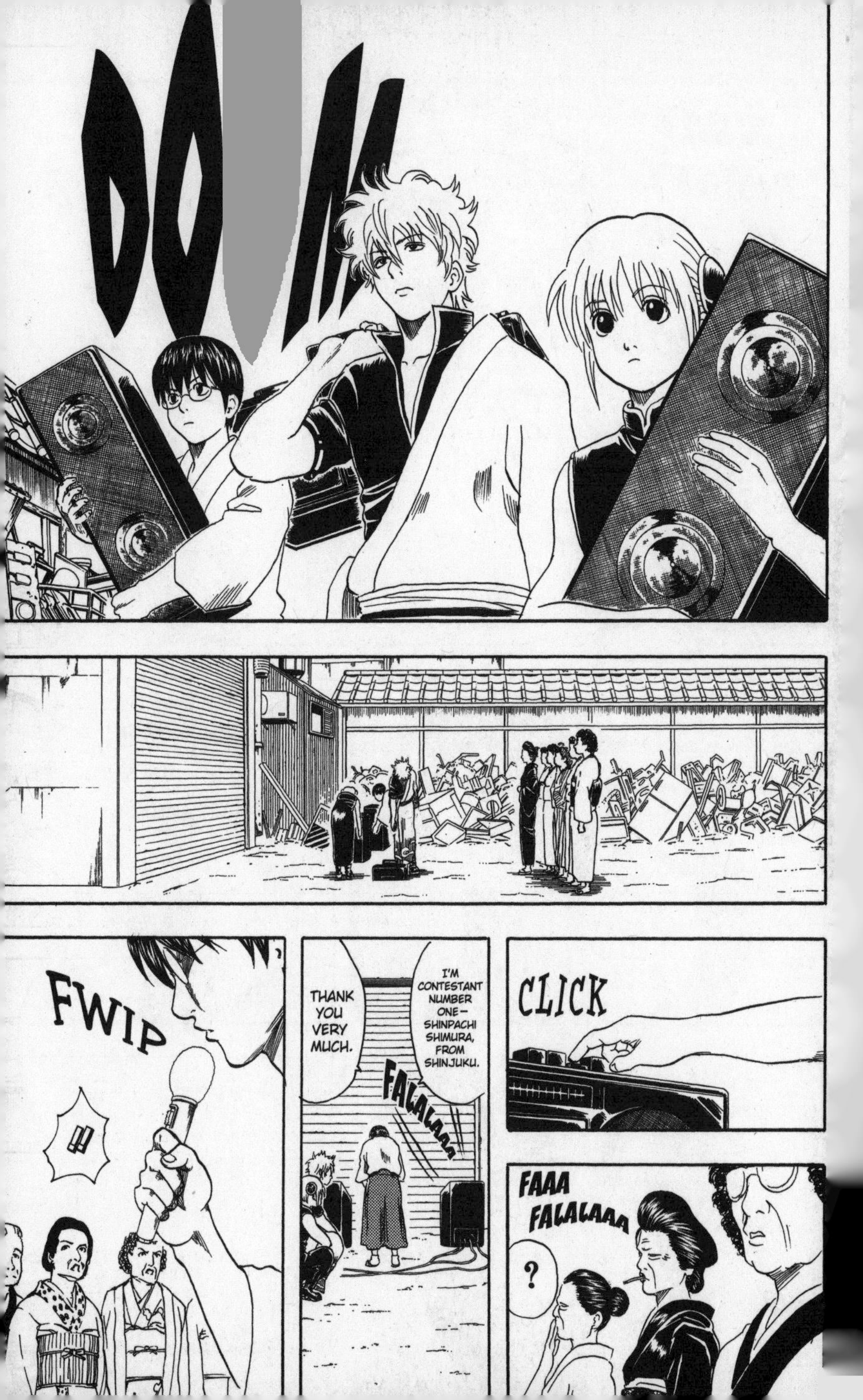
DOM
CLICK
FAAA
FALALAAA
?
I'M CONTESTANT NUMBER ONE— SHINPACHI SHIMURA, FROM SHINJUKU.
THANK YOU VERY MUCH.
FALALAAA
FWIP
!!

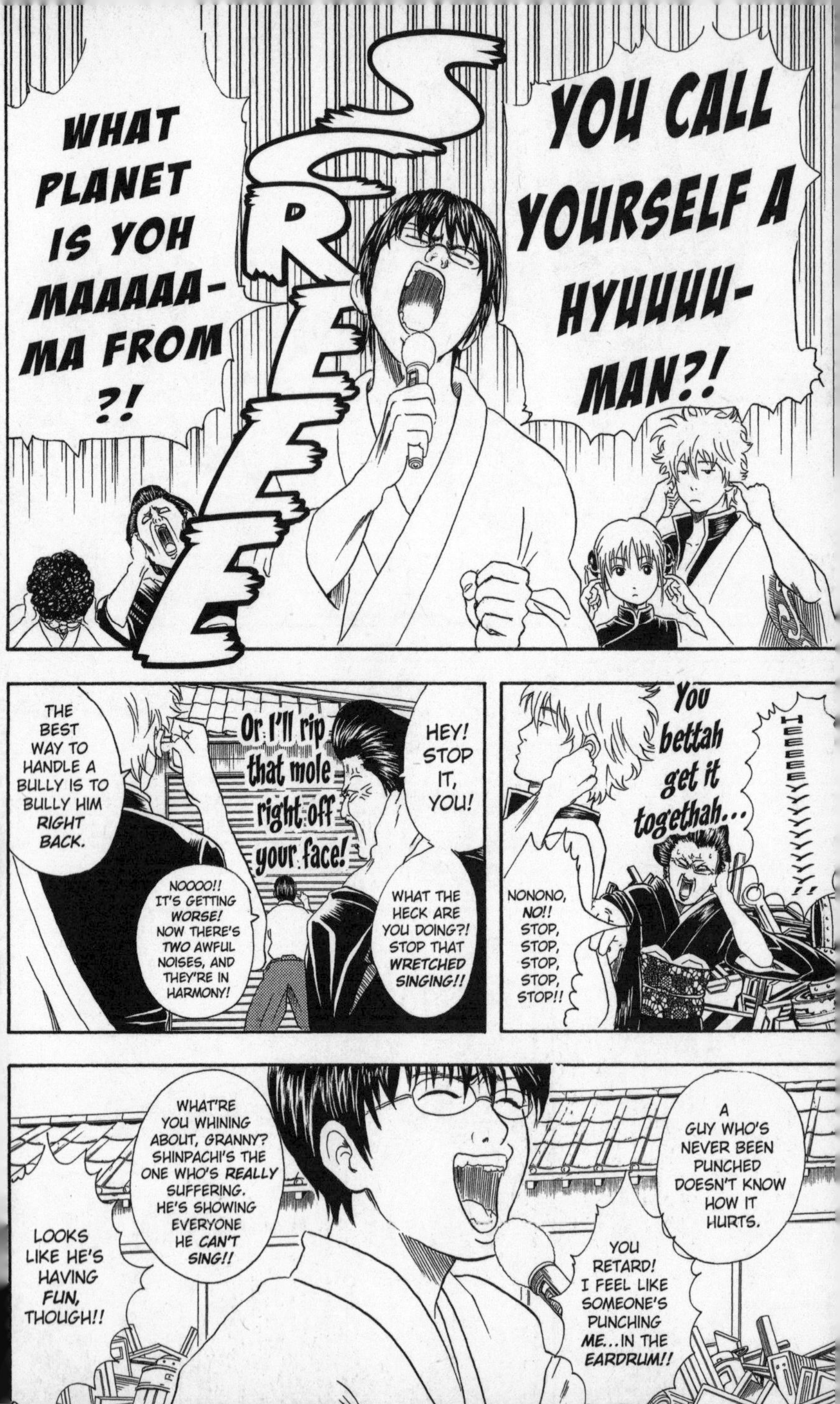
YOU CALL YOURSELF A HYUUUU-MAN?!
WHAT PLANET IS YOH MAAAAA-MA FROM ?!
REEEEE
You bettah get it togethah...
HEEEEEYYYYYYYYY!!
NONONO, NO!! STOP, STOP, STOP, STOP, STOP!!
HEY! STOP IT, YOU!
Or I'll rip that mole right off your face!
THE BEST WAY TO HANDLE A BULLY IS TO BULLY HIM RIGHT BACK.
WHAT THE HECK ARE YOU DOING?! STOP THAT WRETCHED SINGING!!
NOOOO!! IT'S GETTING WORSE! NOW THERE'S TWO AWFUL NOISES, AND THEY'RE IN HARMONY!
A GUY WHO'S NEVER BEEN PUNCHED DOESN'T KNOW HOW IT HURTS.
YOU RETARD! I FEEL LIKE SOMEONE'S PUNCHING ME...IN THE EARDRUM!!
WHAT'RE YOU WHINING ABOUT, GRANNY? SHINPACHI'S THE ONE WHO'S REALLY SUFFERING. HE'S SHOWING EVERYONE HE CAN'T SING!!
LOOKS LIKE HE'S HAVING FUN, THOUGH!!

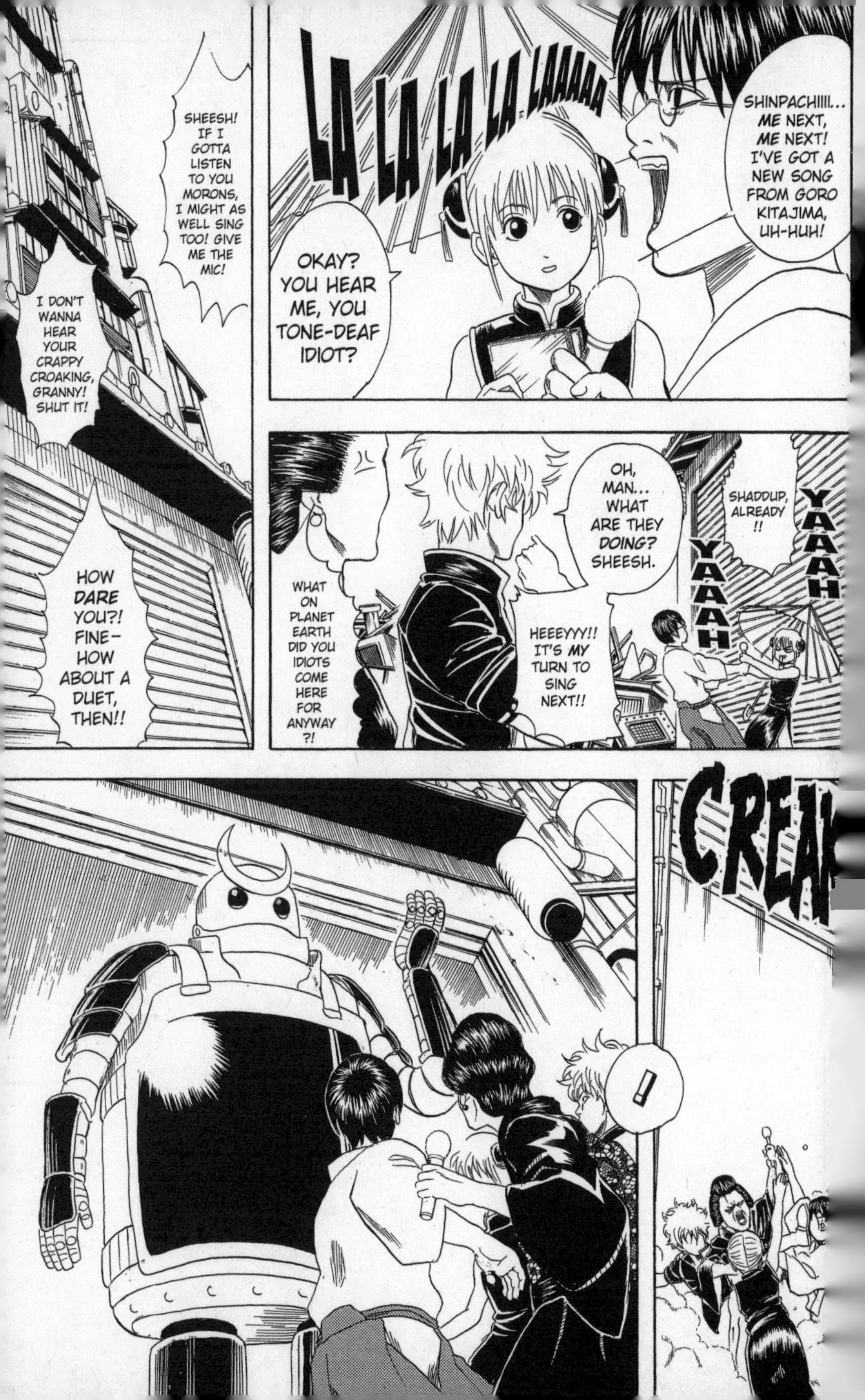
SHINPACHIIII... ME NEXT, ME NEXT! I'VE GOT A NEW SONG FROM GORO KITAJIMA, UH-HUH!
LA LA LA LA LAAAAA
OKAY? YOU HEAR ME, YOU TONE-DEAF IDIOT?
SHADDUP, ALREADY!!
YAAAH
YAAAH
OH, MAN... WHAT ARE THEY DOING? SHEESH.
HEEEYYY!! IT'S MY TURN TO SING NEXT!!
WHAT ON PLANET EARTH DID YOU IDIOTS COME HERE FOR ANYWAY?!
SHEESH! IF I GOTTA LISTEN TO YOU MORONS, I MIGHT AS WELL SING TOO! GIVE ME THE MIC!
I DON'T WANNA HEAR YOUR CRAPPY CROAKING, GRANNY! SHUT IT!
HOW DARE YOU?! FINE—HOW ABOUT A DUET, THEN!!
CREAK
!

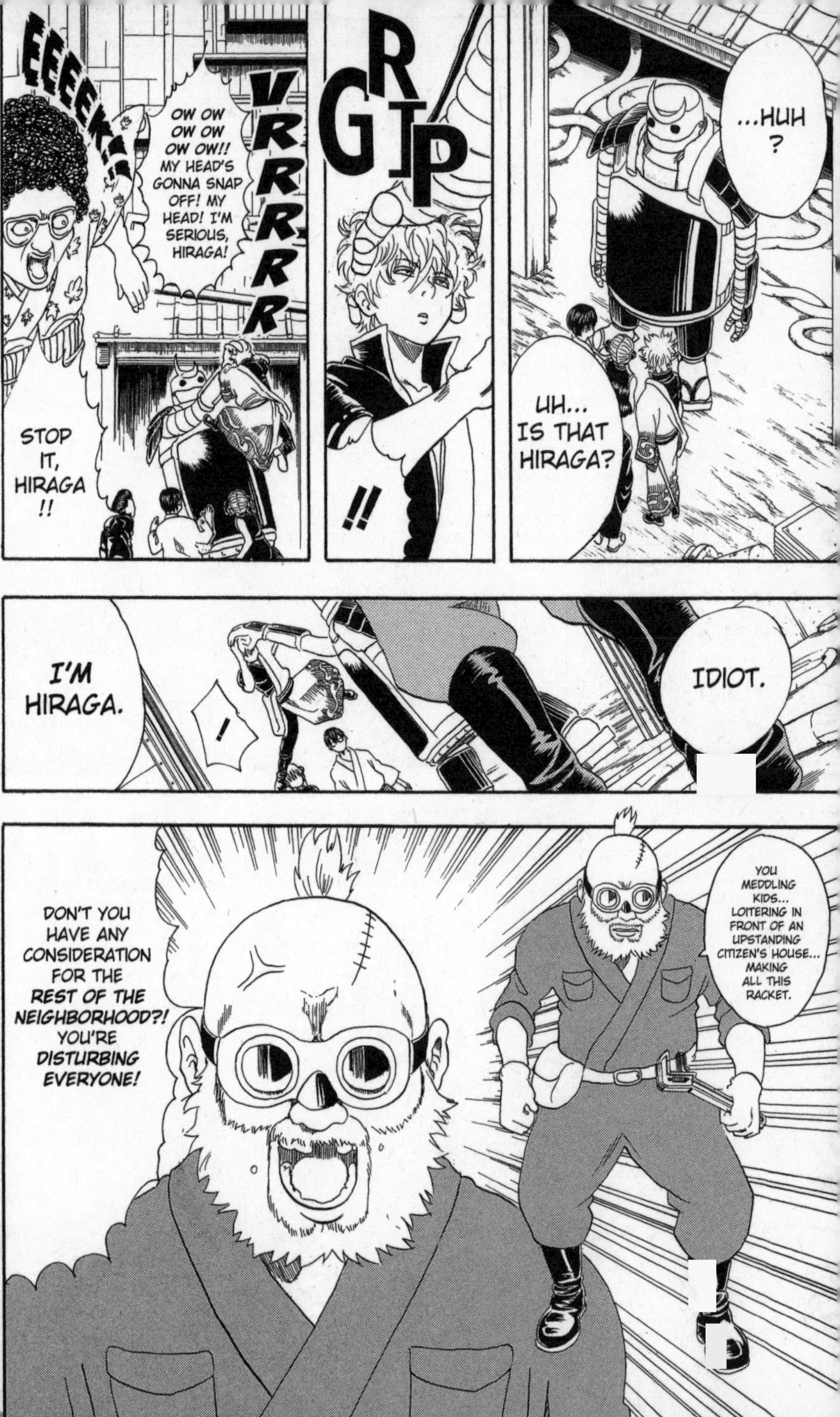

...HUH?
UH... IS THAT HIRAGA?
GRIP
!!
VRRRRRR
EEEEEK!!
OW OW OW OW OW OW!! MY HEAD'S GONNA SNAP OFF! MY HEAD! I'M SERIOUS, HIRAGA!
STOP IT, HIRAGA!!
IDIOT.
!
I'M HIRAGA.
YOU MEDDLING KIDS... LOITERING IN FRONT OF AN UPSTANDING CITIZEN'S HOUSE... MAKING ALL THIS RACKET.
DON'T YOU HAVE ANY CONSIDERATION FOR THE REST OF THE NEIGHBORHOOD?! YOU'RE DISTURBING EVERYONE!

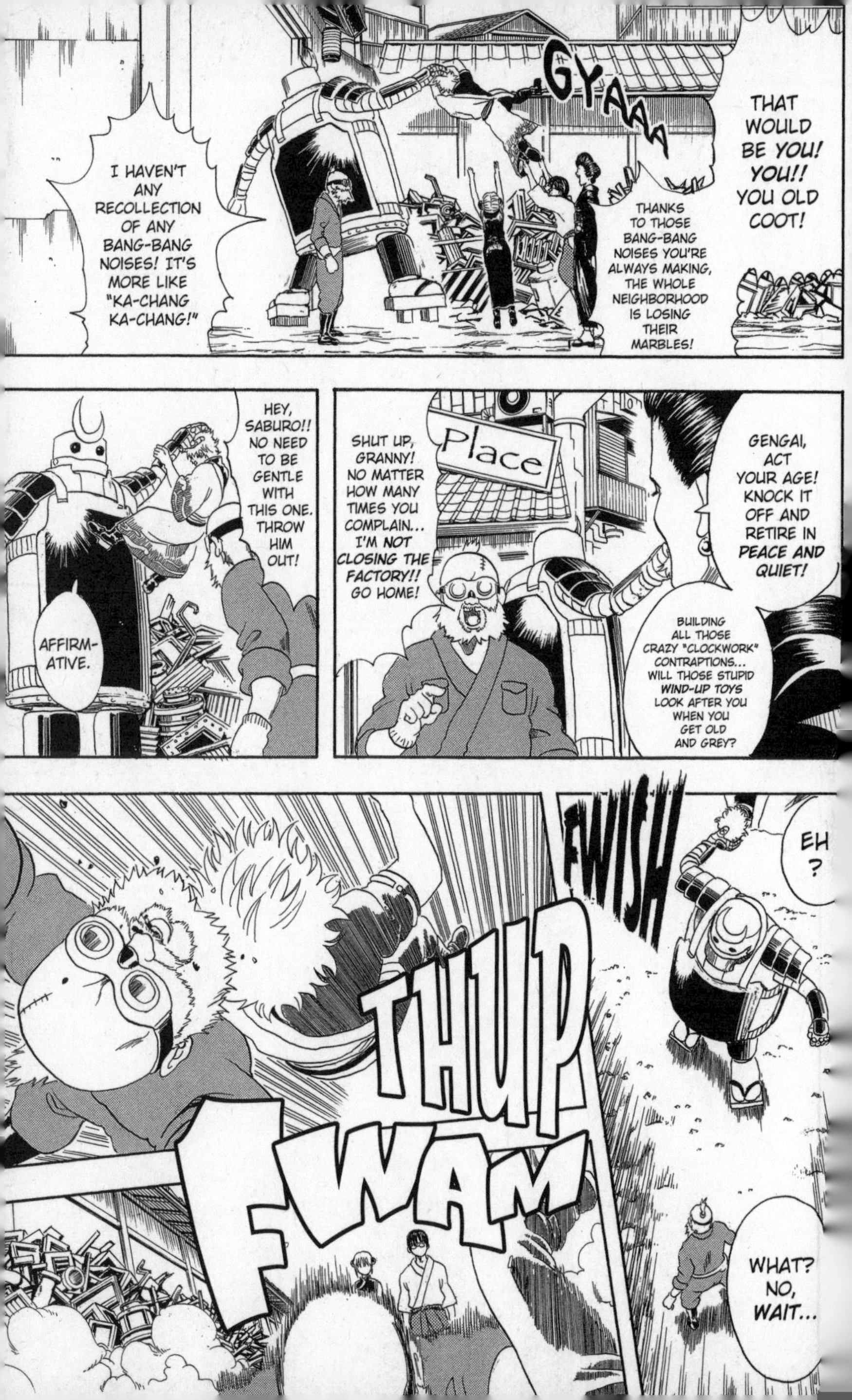
THAT WOULD BE YOU! YOU!! YOU OLD COOT!
GYAAA
THANKS TO THOSE BANG-BANG NOISES YOU'RE ALWAYS MAKING, THE WHOLE NEIGHBORHOOD IS LOSING THEIR MARBLES!
I HAVEN'T ANY RECOLLECTION OF ANY BANG-BANG NOISES! IT'S MORE LIKE "KA-CHANG KA-CHANG!"
GENGAI, ACT YOUR AGE! KNOCK IT OFF AND RETIRE IN PEACE AND QUIET!
BUILDING ALL THOSE CRAZY "CLOCKWORK" CONTRAPTIONS... WILL THOSE STUPID WIND-UP TOYS LOOK AFTER YOU WHEN YOU GET OLD AND GREY?
Place
SHUT UP, GRANNY! NO MATTER HOW MANY TIMES YOU COMPLAIN... I'M NOT CLOSING THE FACTORY!! GO HOME!
HEY, SABURO!! NO NEED TO BE GENTLE WITH THIS ONE. THROW HIM OUT!
AFFIRM-ATIVE.
EH ?
FWISH
THUP
FWAM
WHAT? NO, WAIT...

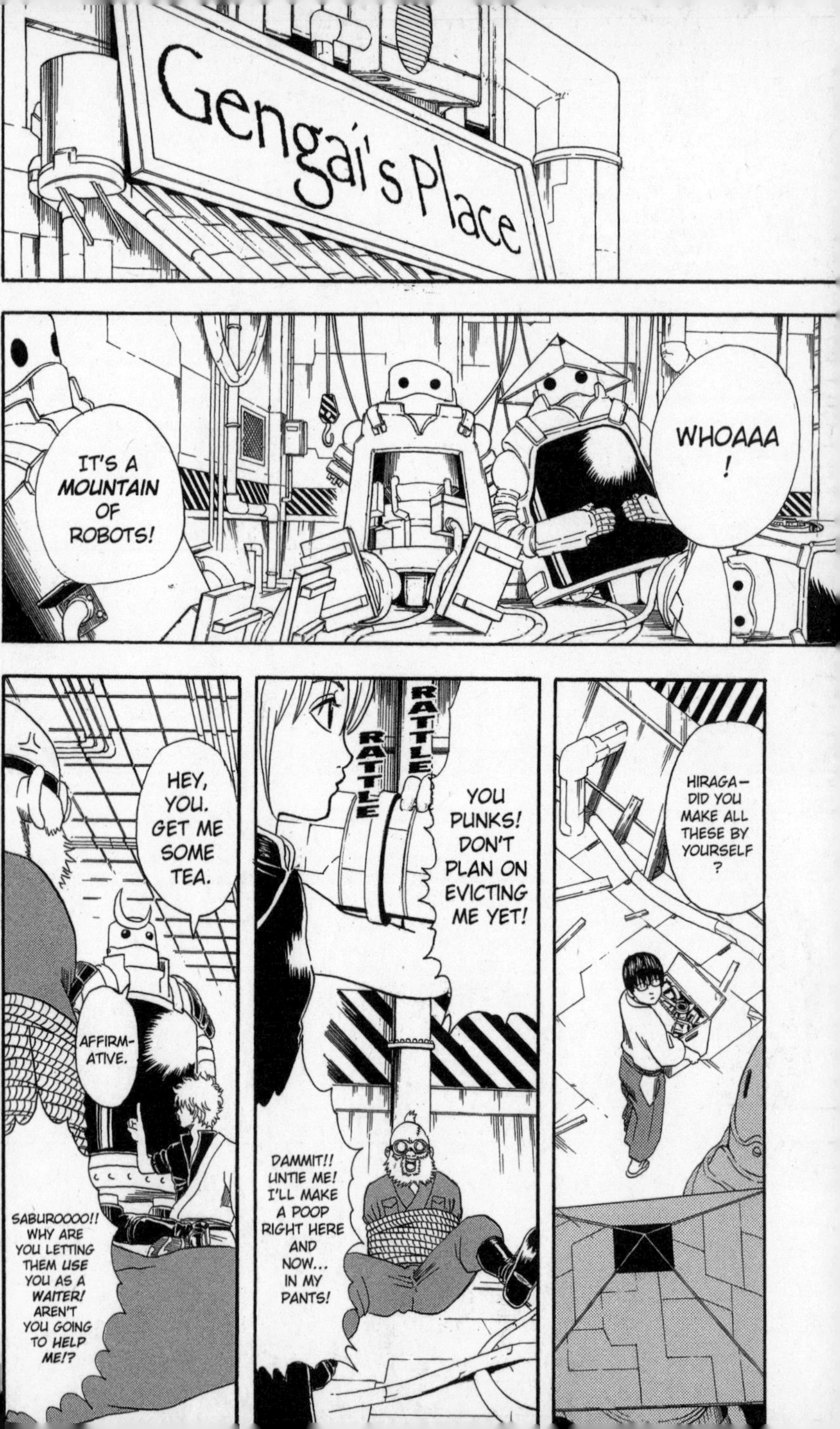
Gengai's Place
WHOAAA!
IT'S A MOUNTAIN OF ROBOTS!
HIRAGA— DID YOU MAKE ALL THESE BY YOURSELF?
RATTLE RATTLE
YOU PUNKS! DON'T PLAN ON EVICTING ME YET!
DAMMIT!! UNTIE ME! I'LL MAKE A POOP RIGHT HERE AND NOW... IN MY PANTS!
HEY, YOU. GET ME SOME TEA.
AFFIRM-ATIVE.
SABUROOOO!! WHY ARE YOU LETTING THEM USE YOU AS A WAITER! AREN'T YOU GOING TO HELP ME!?

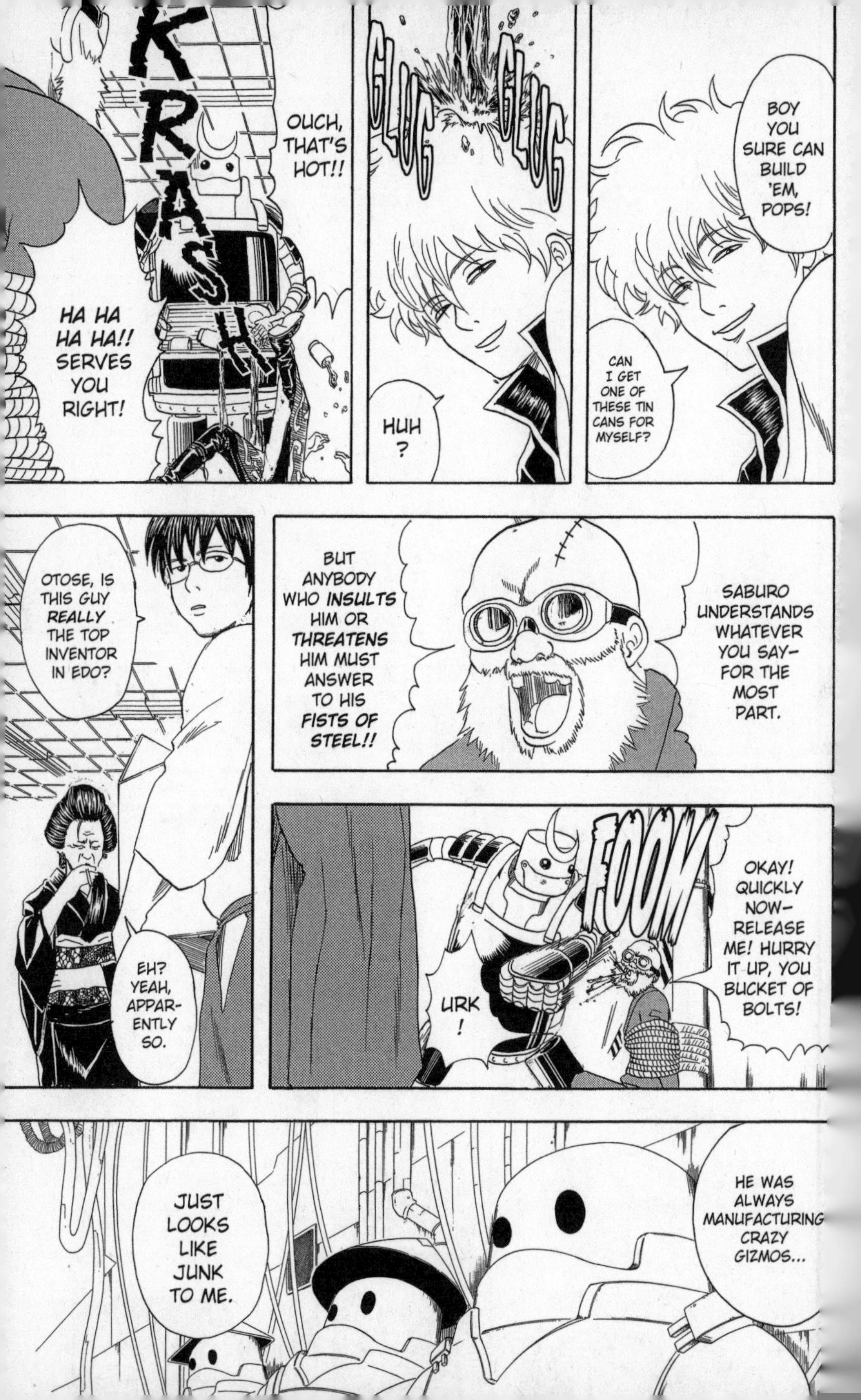
BOY YOU SURE CAN BUILD 'EM, POPS!
CAN I GET ONE OF THESE TIN CANS FOR MYSELF?
GLUG GLUG
HUH?
OUCH, THAT'S HOT!!
KRASH
HA HA HA HA!! SERVES YOU RIGHT!
SABURO UNDERSTANDS WHATEVER YOU SAY—FOR THE MOST PART.
BUT ANYBODY WHO INSULTS HIM OR THREATENS HIM MUST ANSWER TO HIS FISTS OF STEEL!!
OKAY! QUICKLY NOW—RELEASE ME! HURRY IT UP, YOU BUCKET OF BOLTS!
FOOM
URK!
OTOSE, IS THIS GUY REALLY THE TOP INVENTOR IN EDO?
EH? YEAH, APPAR-ENTLY SO.
HE WAS ALWAYS MANUFACTURING CRAZY GIZMOS...
JUST LOOKS LIKE JUNK TO ME.

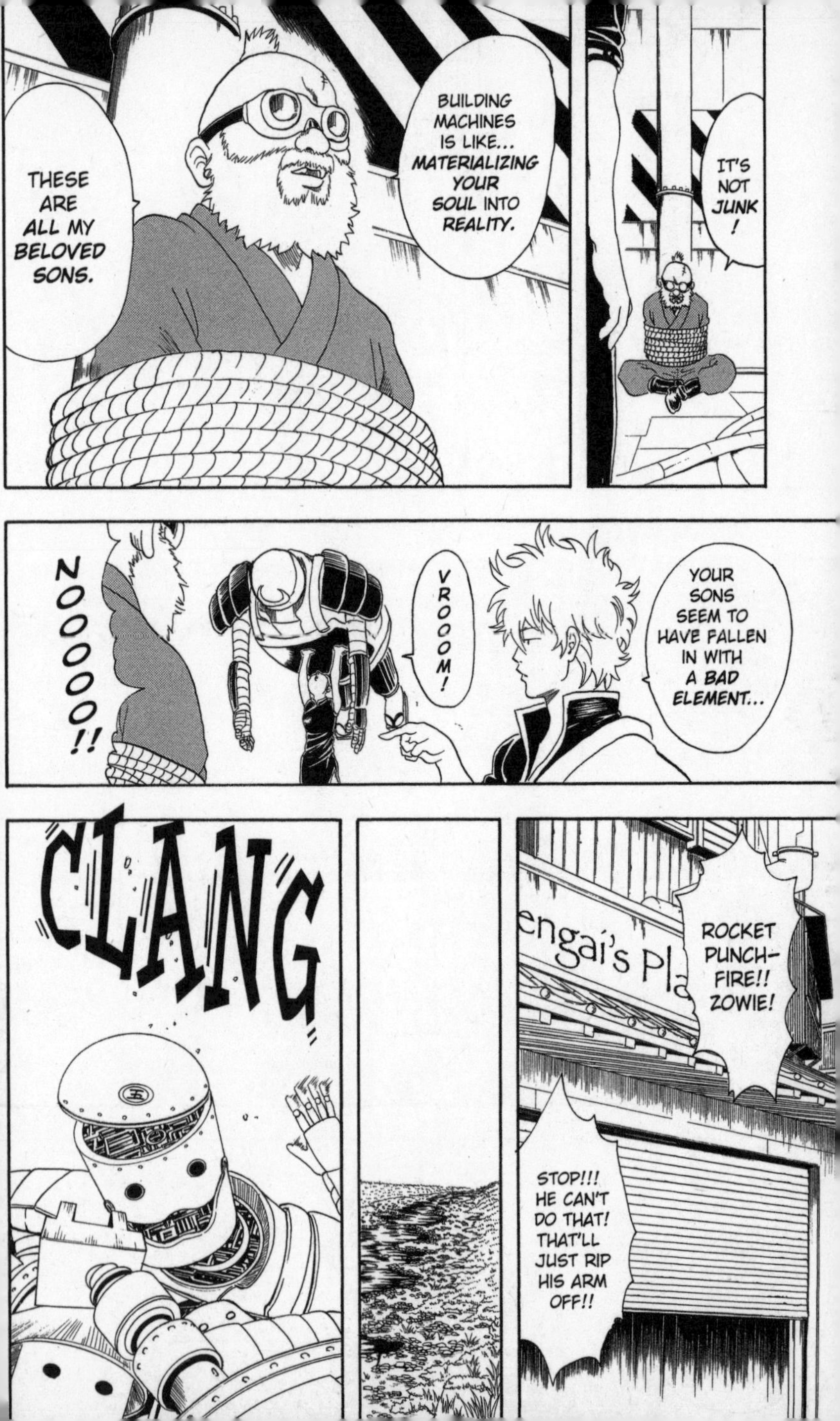
IT'S NOT JUNK!
BUILDING MACHINES IS LIKE... MATERIALIZING YOUR SOUL INTO REALITY.
THESE ARE ALL MY BELOVED SONS.
YOUR SONS SEEM TO HAVE FALLEN IN WITH A BAD ELEMENT...
VROOOOM!
NOOOOOO!!
engai's Pla
ROCKET PUNCH-FIRE!! ZOWIE!
STOP!!! HE CAN'T DO THAT! THAT'LL JUST RIP HIS ARM OFF!!
CLANG

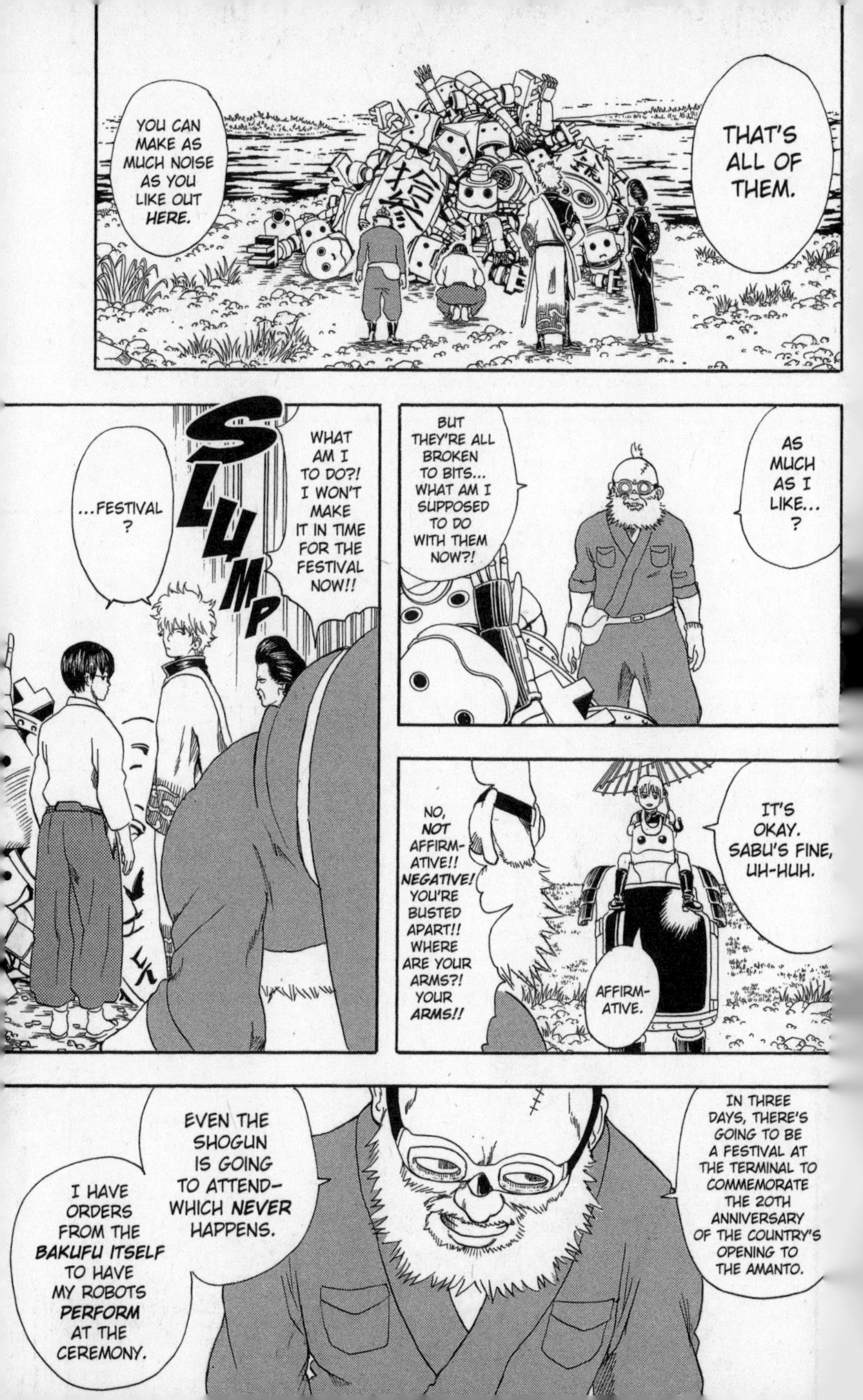
THAT'S ALL OF THEM.
YOU CAN MAKE AS MUCH NOISE AS YOU LIKE OUT HERE.
AS MUCH AS I LIKE...?
BUT THEY'RE ALL BROKEN TO BITS... WHAT AM I SUPPOSED TO DO WITH THEM NOW?!
IT'S OKAY. SABU'S FINE, UH-HUH.
AFFIRMATIVE.
NO, NOT AFFIRMATIVE!! NEGATIVE! YOU'RE BUSTED APART!! WHERE ARE YOUR ARMS?! YOUR ARMS!!
WHAT AM I TO DO?! I WON'T MAKE IT IN TIME FOR THE FESTIVAL NOW!!
SLUMP
...FESTIVAL?
IN THREE DAYS, THERE'S GOING TO BE A FESTIVAL AT THE TERMINAL TO COMMEMORATE THE 20TH ANNIVERSARY OF THE COUNTRY'S OPENING TO THE AMANTO.
EVEN THE SHOGUN IS GOING TO ATTEND-WHICH NEVER HAPPENS.
I HAVE ORDERS FROM THE BAKUFU ITSELF TO HAVE MY ROBOTS PERFORM AT THE CEREMONY.

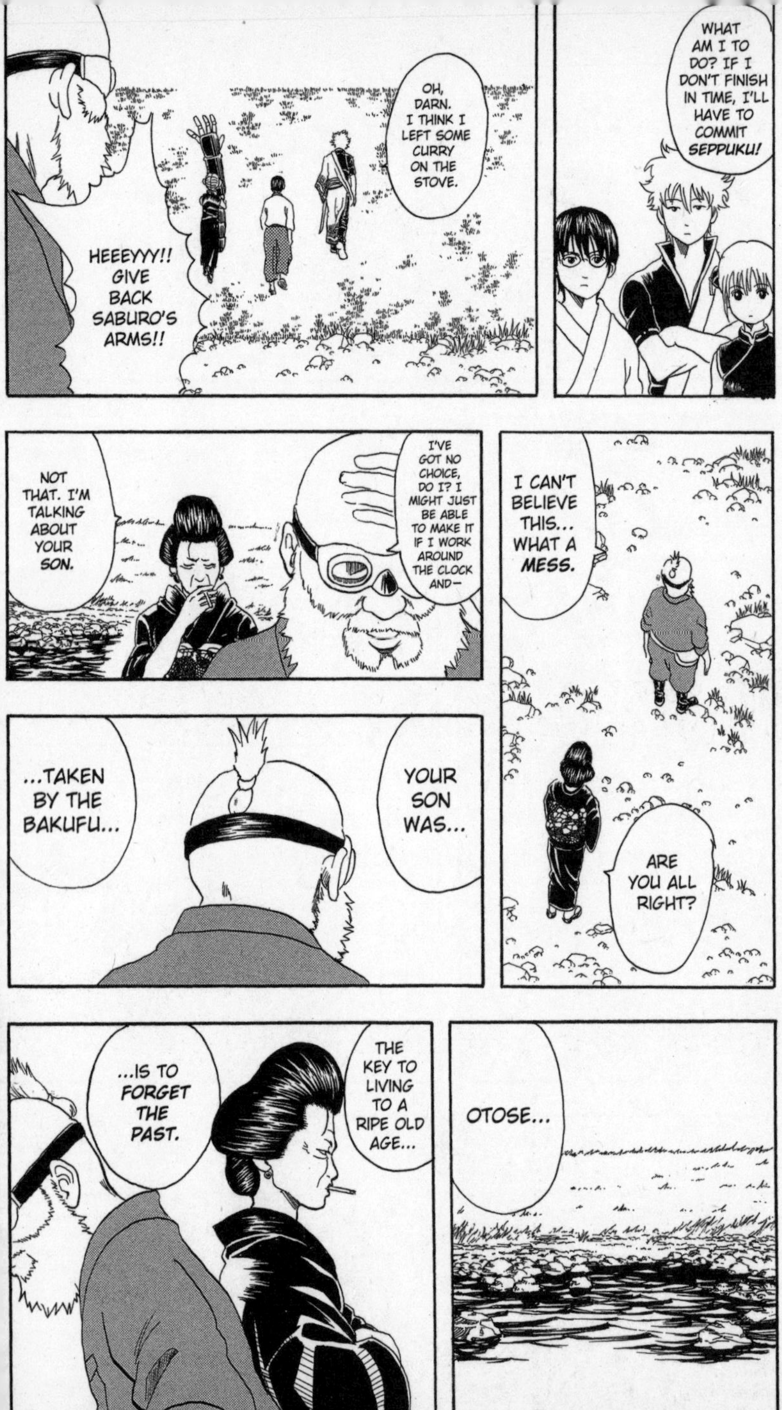
WHAT AM I TO DO? IF I DON'T FINISH IN TIME, I'LL HAVE TO COMMIT SEPPUKU!
OH, DARN. I THINK I LEFT SOME CURRY ON THE STOVE.
HEEEYYY!! GIVE BACK SABURO'S ARMS!!
I CAN'T BELIEVE THIS... WHAT A MESS.
ARE YOU ALL RIGHT?
I'VE GOT NO CHOICE, DO I? I MIGHT JUST BE ABLE TO MAKE IT IF I WORK AROUND THE CLOCK AND—
NOT THAT. I'M TALKING ABOUT YOUR SON.
YOUR SON WAS...
...TAKEN BY THE BAKUFU...
OTOSE...
THE KEY TO LIVING TO A RIPE OLD AGE...
...IS TO FORGET THE PAST.

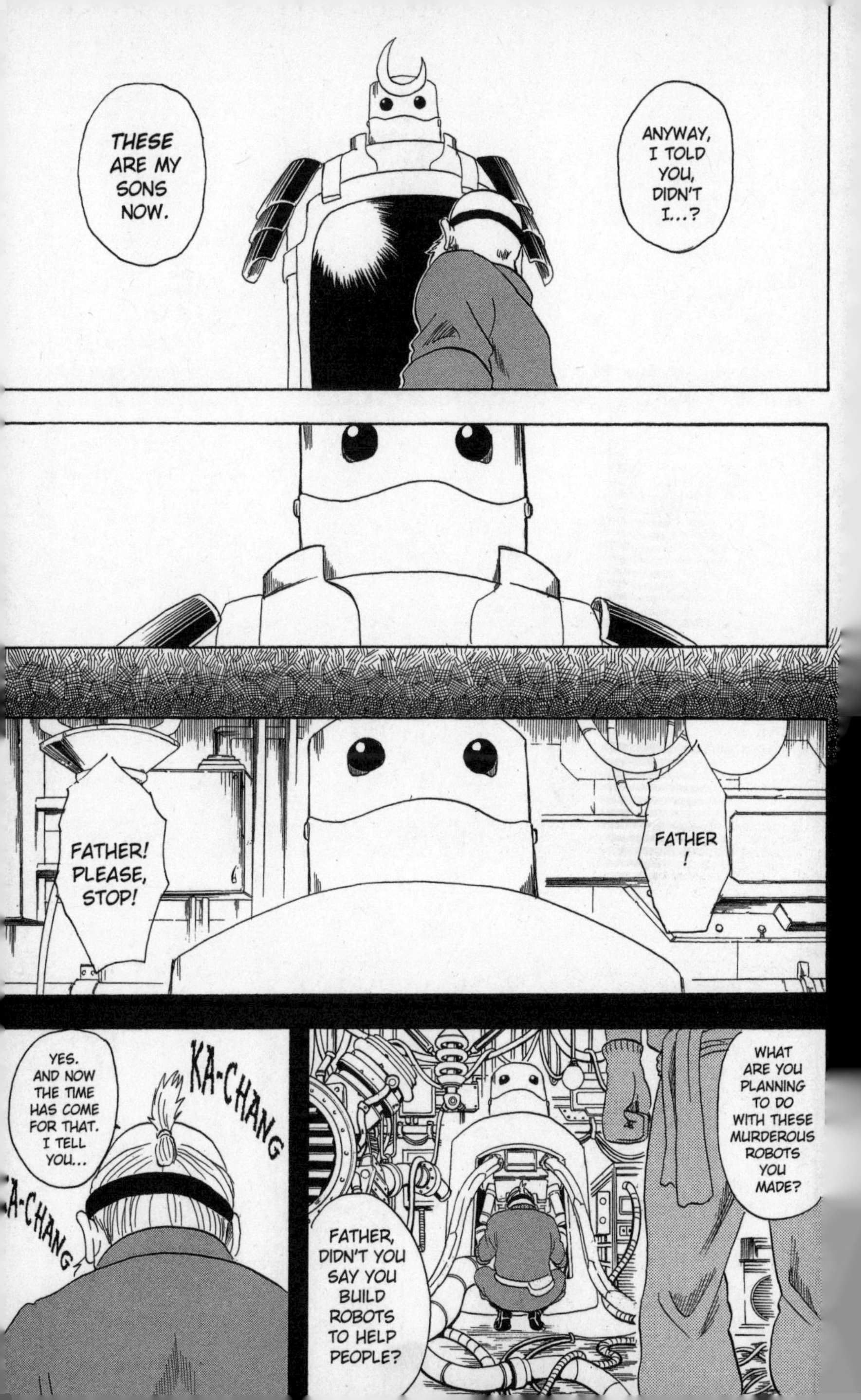
ANYWAY, I TOLD YOU, DIDN'T I...?
THESE ARE MY SONS NOW.
FATHER!
FATHER! PLEASE, STOP!
WHAT ARE YOU PLANNING TO DO WITH THESE MURDEROUS ROBOTS YOU MADE?
FATHER, DIDN'T YOU SAY YOU BUILD ROBOTS TO HELP PEOPLE?
KA-CHANG
YES. AND NOW THE TIME HAS COME FOR THAT. I TELL YOU...
A-CHANG

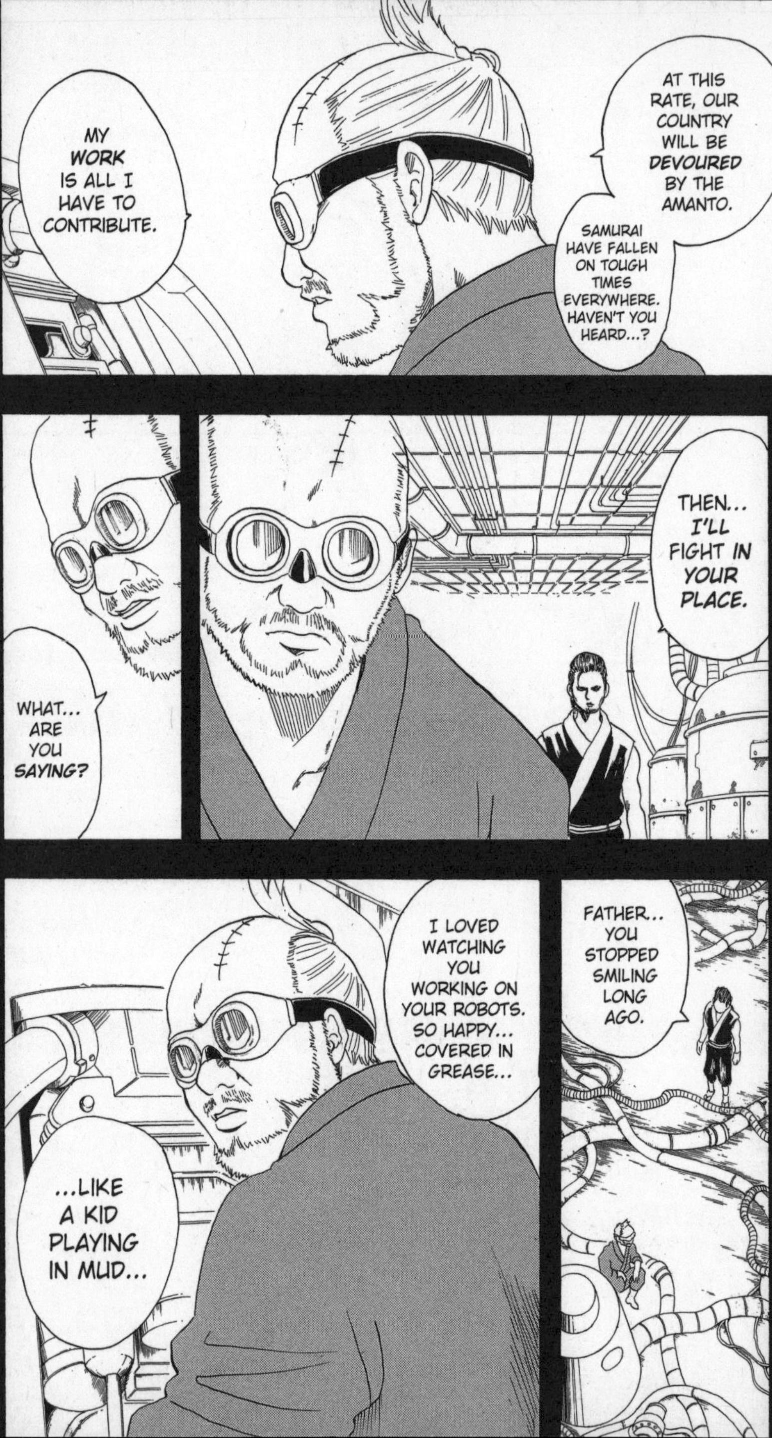
AT THIS RATE, OUR COUNTRY WILL BE DEVOURED BY THE AMANTO.
SAMURAI HAVE FALLEN ON TOUGH TIMES EVERYWHERE. HAVEN'T YOU HEARD...?
MY WORK IS ALL I HAVE TO CONTRIBUTE.
THEN... I'LL FIGHT IN YOUR PLACE.
WHAT... ARE YOU SAYING?
FATHER... YOU STOPPED SMILING LONG AGO.
I LOVED WATCHING YOU WORKING ON YOUR ROBOTS. SO HAPPY... COVERED IN GREASE...
...LIKE A KID PLAYING IN MUD...

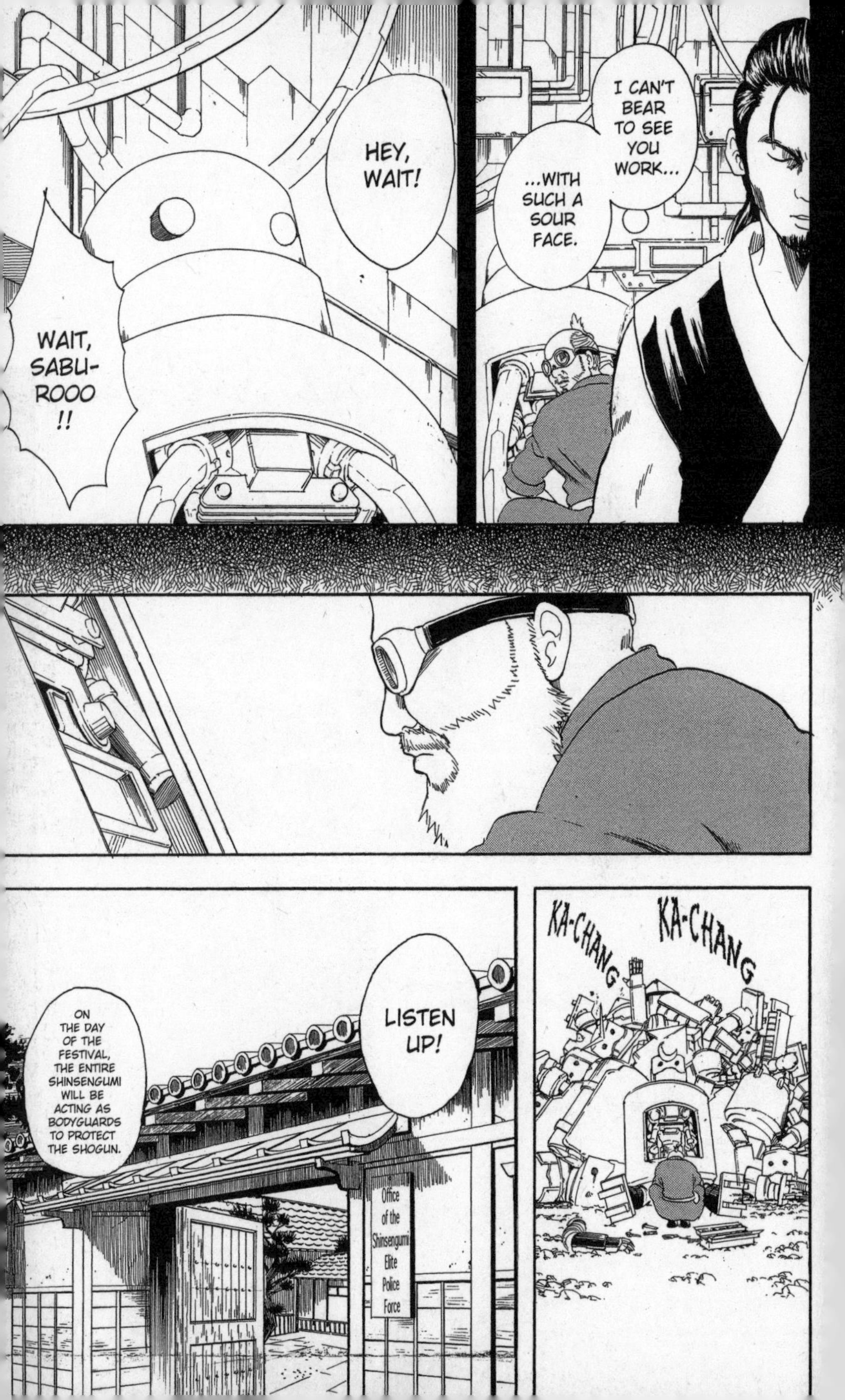

I CAN'T BEAR TO SEE YOU WORK...
...WITH SUCH A SOUR FACE.
HEY, WAIT!
WAIT, SABU-ROOO!!
KA-CHANG
KA-CHANG
LISTEN UP!
ON THE DAY OF THE FESTIVAL, THE ENTIRE SHINSENGUMI WILL BE ACTING AS BODYGUARDS TO PROTECT THE SHOGUN.
Office of the Shinsengumi Elite Police Force

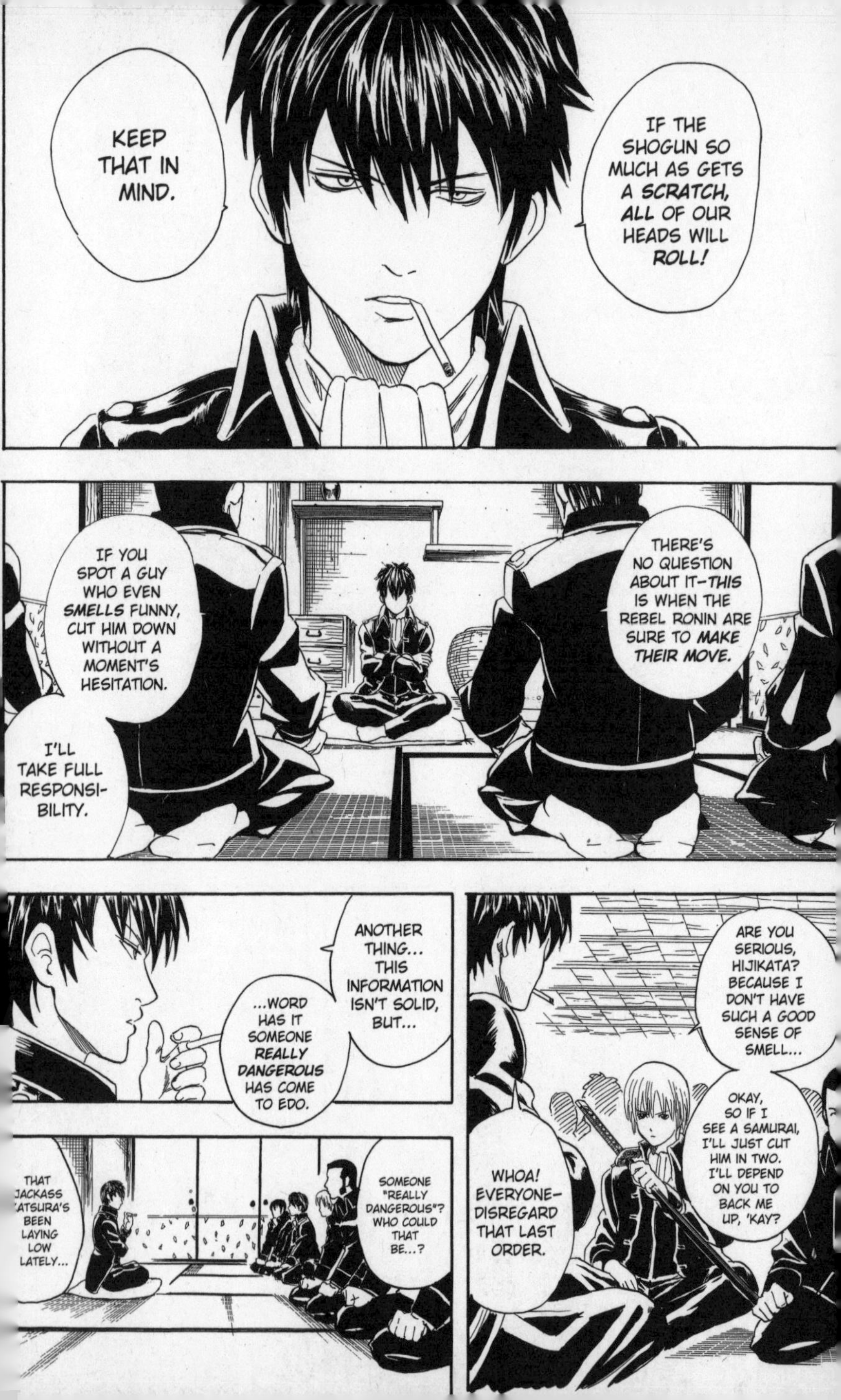
IF THE SHOGUN SO MUCH AS GETS A **SCRATCH**, **ALL** OF OUR HEADS WILL **ROLL!**
KEEP THAT IN MIND.
THERE'S NO QUESTION ABOUT IT—**THIS** IS WHEN THE REBEL RONIN ARE SURE TO **MAKE THEIR MOVE.**
IF YOU SPOT A GUY WHO EVEN **SMELLS** FUNNY, CUT HIM DOWN WITHOUT A MOMENT'S HESITATION.
I'LL TAKE FULL RESPONSI-BILITY.
ARE YOU SERIOUS, HIJIKATA? BECAUSE I DON'T HAVE SUCH A GOOD SENSE OF SMELL...
OKAY, SO IF I SEE A SAMURAI, I'LL JUST CUT HIM IN TWO. I'LL DEPEND ON YOU TO BACK ME UP, 'KAY?
WHOA! EVERYONE—DISREGARD THAT LAST ORDER.
ANOTHER THING... THIS INFORMATION ISN'T SOLID, BUT...
...WORD HAS IT SOMEONE **REALLY DANGEROUS** HAS COME TO EDO.
SOMEONE "REALLY DANGEROUS"? WHO COULD THAT BE...?
THAT JACKASS KATSURA'S BEEN LAYING LOW LATELY...

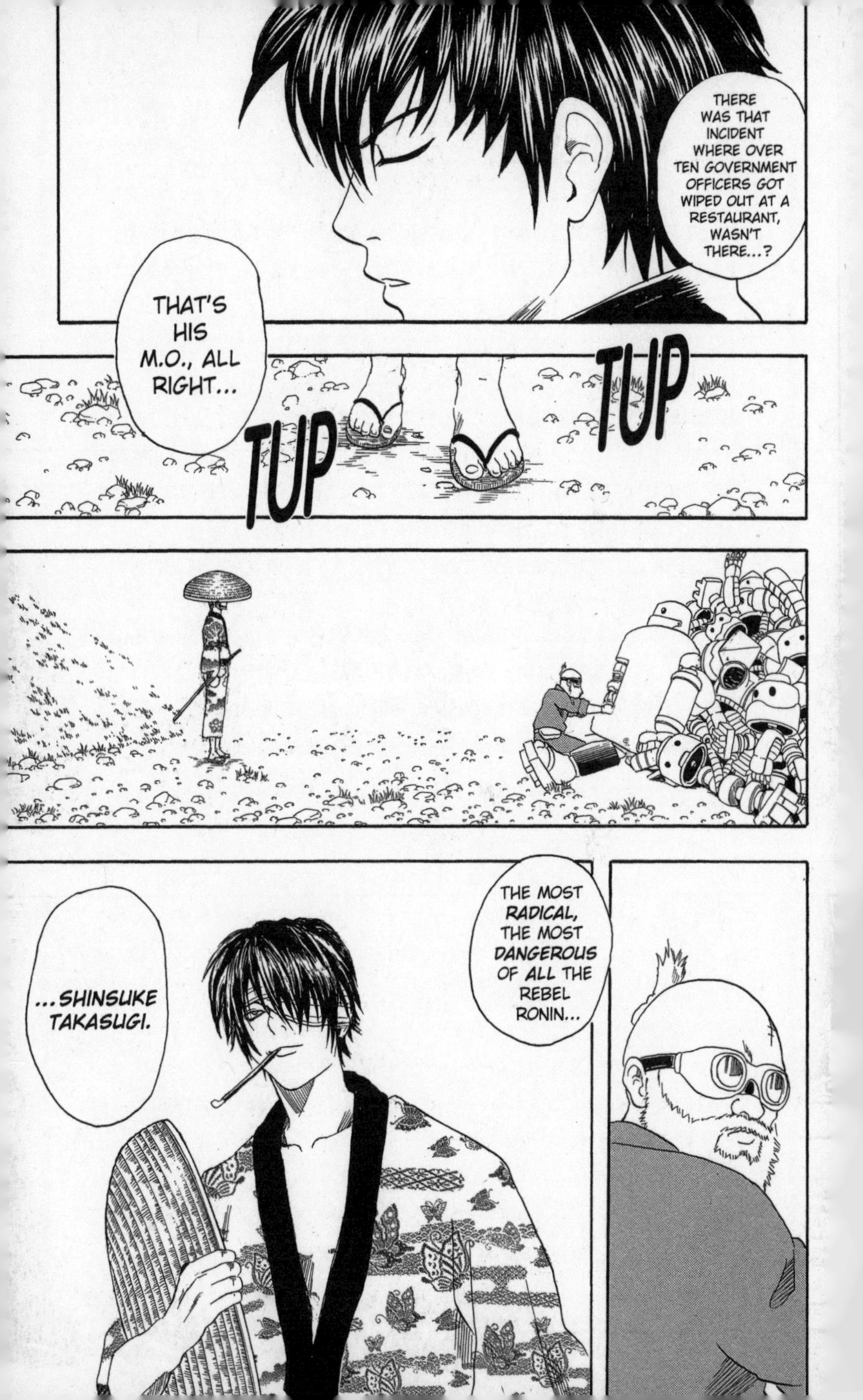
THERE WAS THAT INCIDENT WHERE OVER TEN GOVERNMENT OFFICERS GOT WIPED OUT AT A RESTAURANT, WASN'T THERE...?
THAT'S HIS M.O., ALL RIGHT...
TUP
TUP
THE MOST RADICAL, THE MOST DANGEROUS OF ALL THE REBEL RONIN...
...SHINSUKE TAKASUGI.

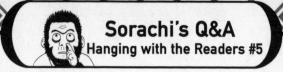

Sorachi's Q&A
Hanging with the Readers #5

Question from Pen Name "A Wife Who Wants to Play Badminton with Yamazaki-san" from Gunma Prefecture:
Hey, Sorachi-sensei!! I'm a 40-year-old housewife who's a fan of *Gin Tama*, and I'm really upset. Look at the omake supplement page for Volume 3. What the heck is that? Why don't you post a profile for some of the characters? I can't figure you out. My question is, how come Yamazaki of the Shinsengumi is always playing "minton" alone? That's all I have to say…
— The 40-year-old, number-one fan of Yamazaki's badminton.
P.S. If you publish this, can I get something for free? Probably not, huh? Well, just in case, I'll give you my address and phone number.

Madame,
Explaining a gag deals it a fatal blow! You can't laugh at it then! You say you want something in return if this gets published? Who would give something to yoouuuuuuu!? Get your husband to buy it, your husbaaaaand!! And then you say, "I'll give you my address and phone number." What's that about?! You're all prepared to receive something, aren't you!? Well, I said what I said, Madame, but I hope you will keep on reading Gin Tama. Buy a copy for the other wives in the neighborhood, too.

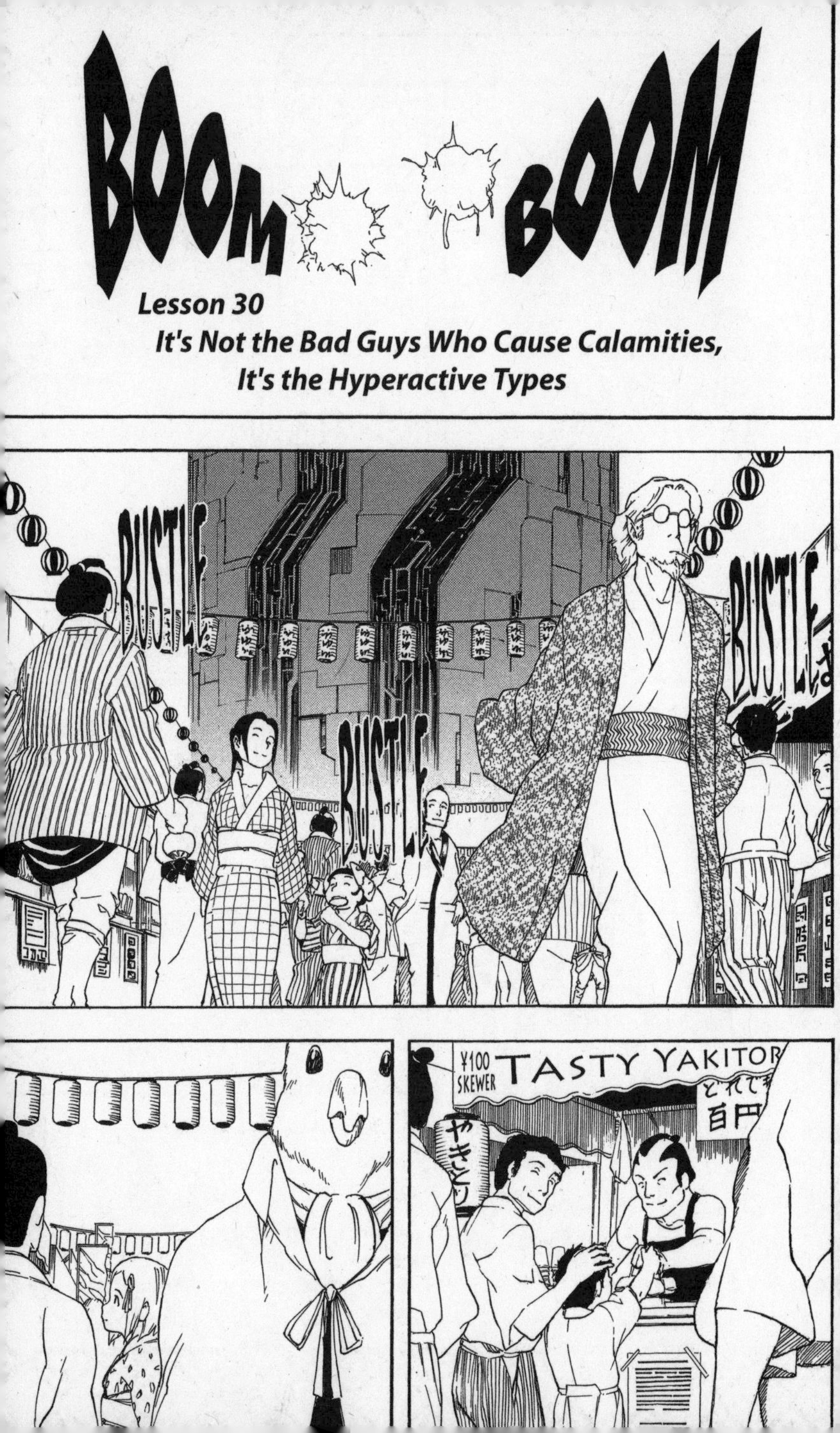
BOOM BOOM
Lesson 30
It's Not the Bad Guys Who Cause Calamities,
It's the Hyperactive Types
BUSTLE
BUSTLE
BUSTLE
BUSTLE
¥100
SKEWER
TASTY YAKITOR
百円
やきとり

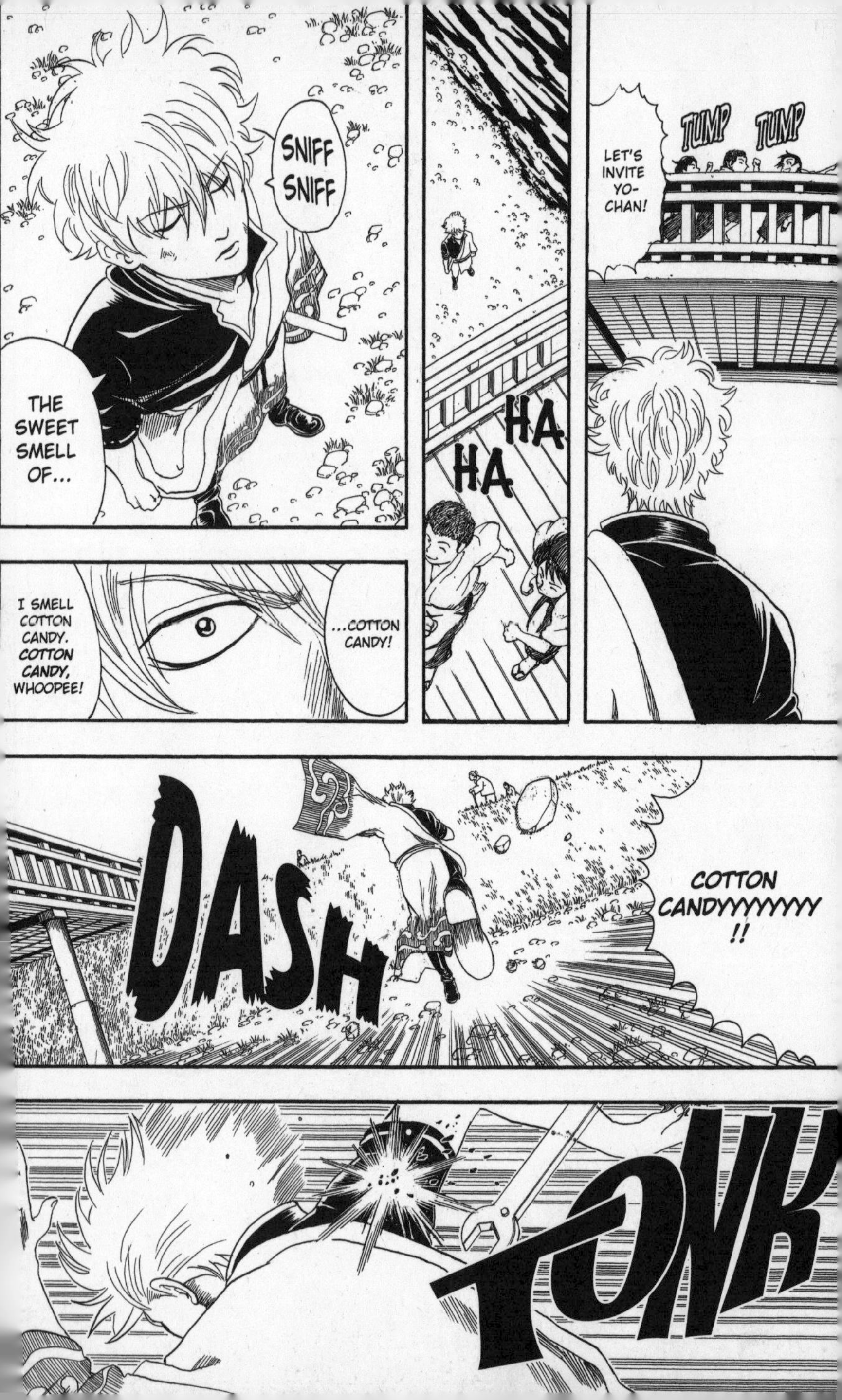
TUMP TUMP
LET'S INVITE YO-CHAN!
HA HA
SNIFF SNIFF
THE SWEET SMELL OF...
...COTTON CANDY!
I SMELL COTTON CANDY. COTTON CANDY, WHOOPEE!
COTTON CANDYYYYYYYY!!
DASH
TONK

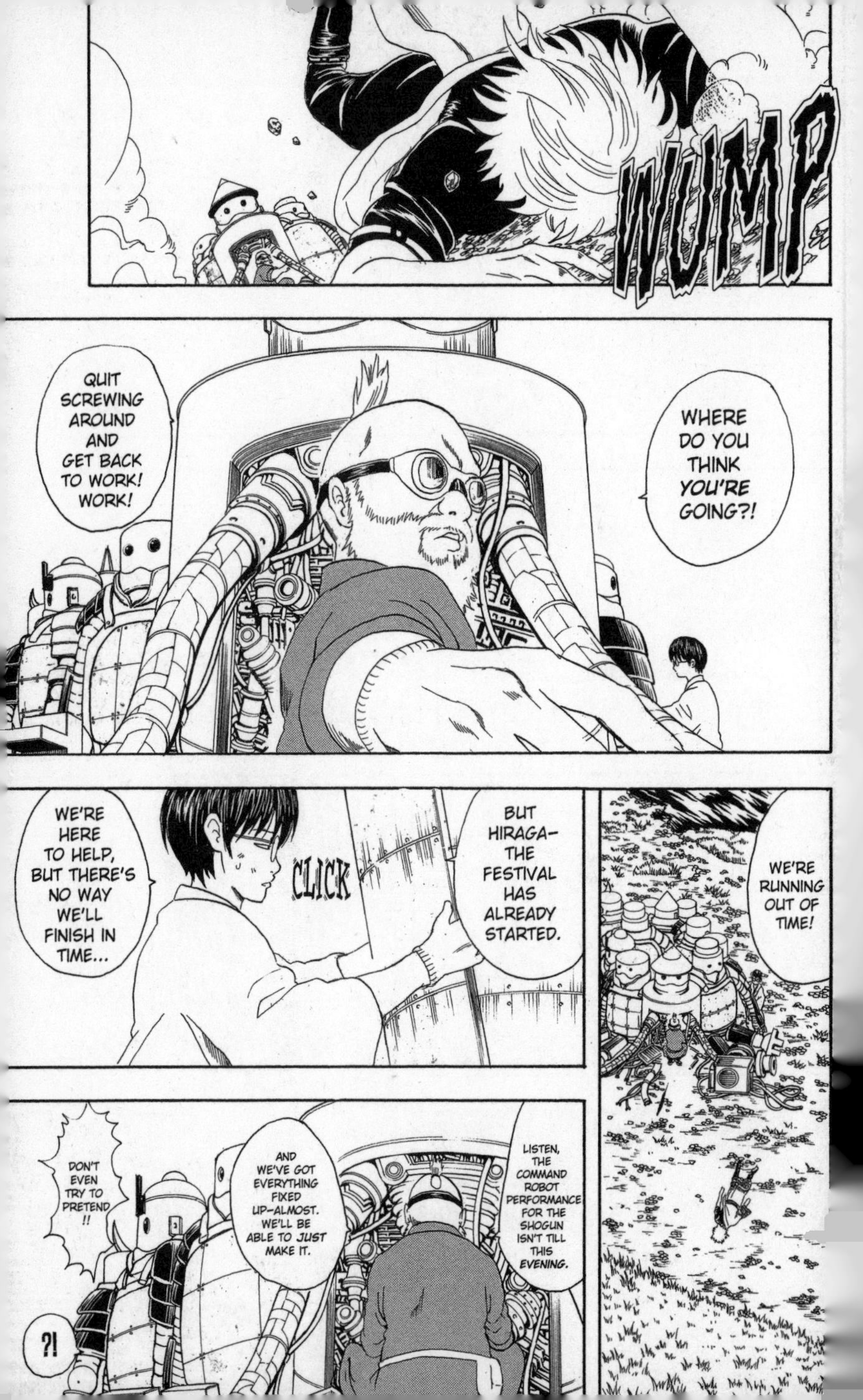
WUMP
WHERE DO YOU THINK YOU'RE GOING?!
QUIT SCREWING AROUND AND GET BACK TO WORK! WORK!
WE'RE RUNNING OUT OF TIME!
BUT HIRAGA—THE FESTIVAL HAS ALREADY STARTED.
CLICK
WE'RE HERE TO HELP, BUT THERE'S NO WAY WE'LL FINISH IN TIME...
LISTEN, THE COMMAND ROBOT PERFORMANCE FOR THE SHOGUN ISN'T TILL THIS EVENING.
AND WE'VE GOT EVERYTHING FIXED UP—ALMOST. WE'LL BE ABLE TO JUST MAKE IT.
DON'T EVEN TRY TO PRETEND!!
?!

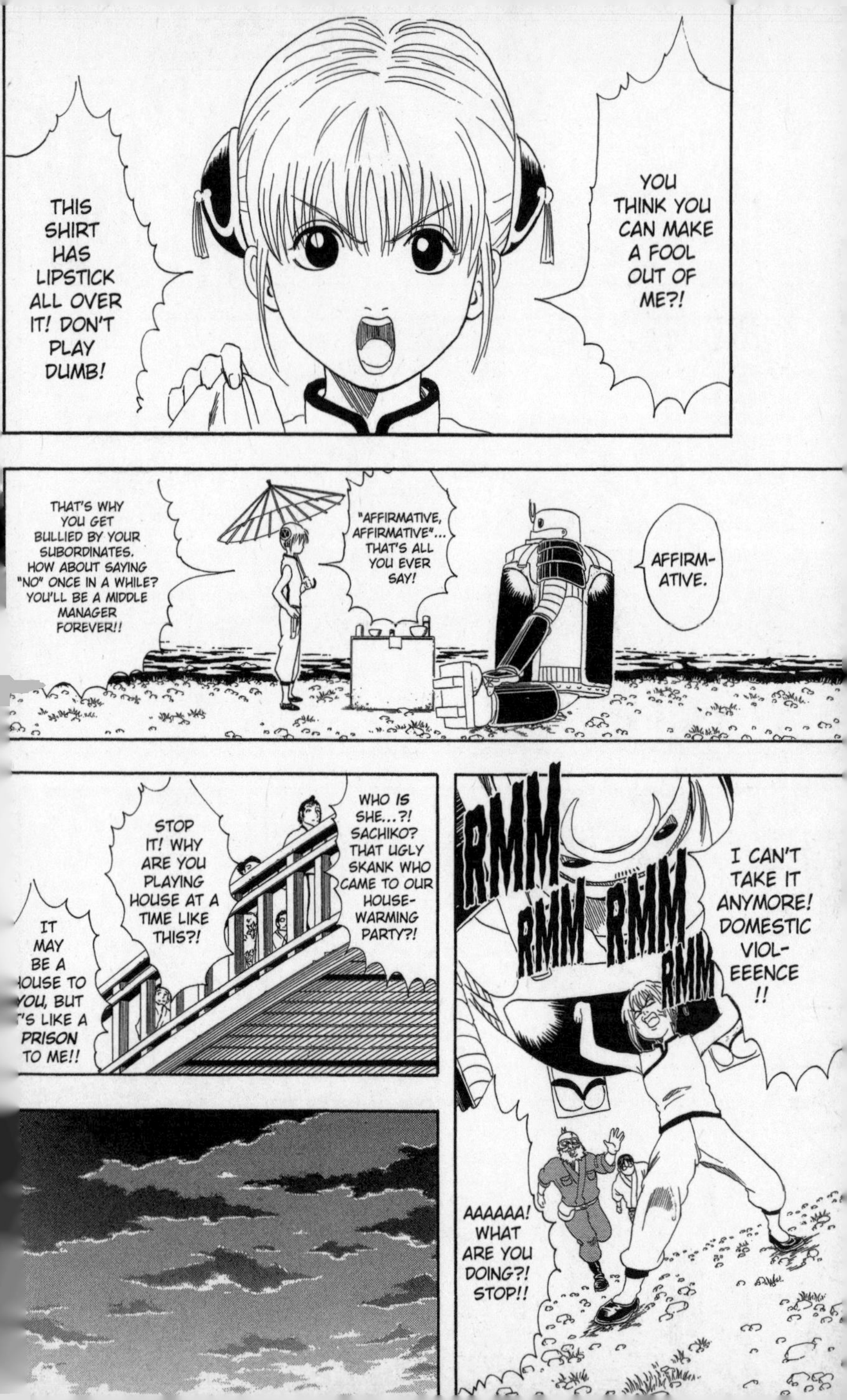
YOU THINK YOU CAN MAKE A FOOL OUT OF ME?!
THIS SHIRT HAS LIPSTICK ALL OVER IT! DON'T PLAY DUMB!
AFFIRM-ATIVE.
"AFFIRMATIVE, AFFIRMATIVE"... THAT'S ALL YOU EVER SAY!
THAT'S WHY YOU GET BULLIED BY YOUR SUBORDINATES. HOW ABOUT SAYING "NO" ONCE IN A WHILE? YOU'LL BE A MIDDLE MANAGER FOREVER!!
RMM
RMM RMM RMM
I CAN'T TAKE IT ANYMORE! DOMESTIC VIOL-EEENCE!!
AAAAAA! WHAT ARE YOU DOING?! STOP!!
WHO IS SHE...?! SACHIKO? THAT UGLY SKANK WHO CAME TO OUR HOUSE-WARMING PARTY?!
STOP IT! WHY ARE YOU PLAYING HOUSE AT A TIME LIKE THIS?!
IT MAY BE A HOUSE TO YOU, BUT T'S LIKE A PRISON TO ME!!

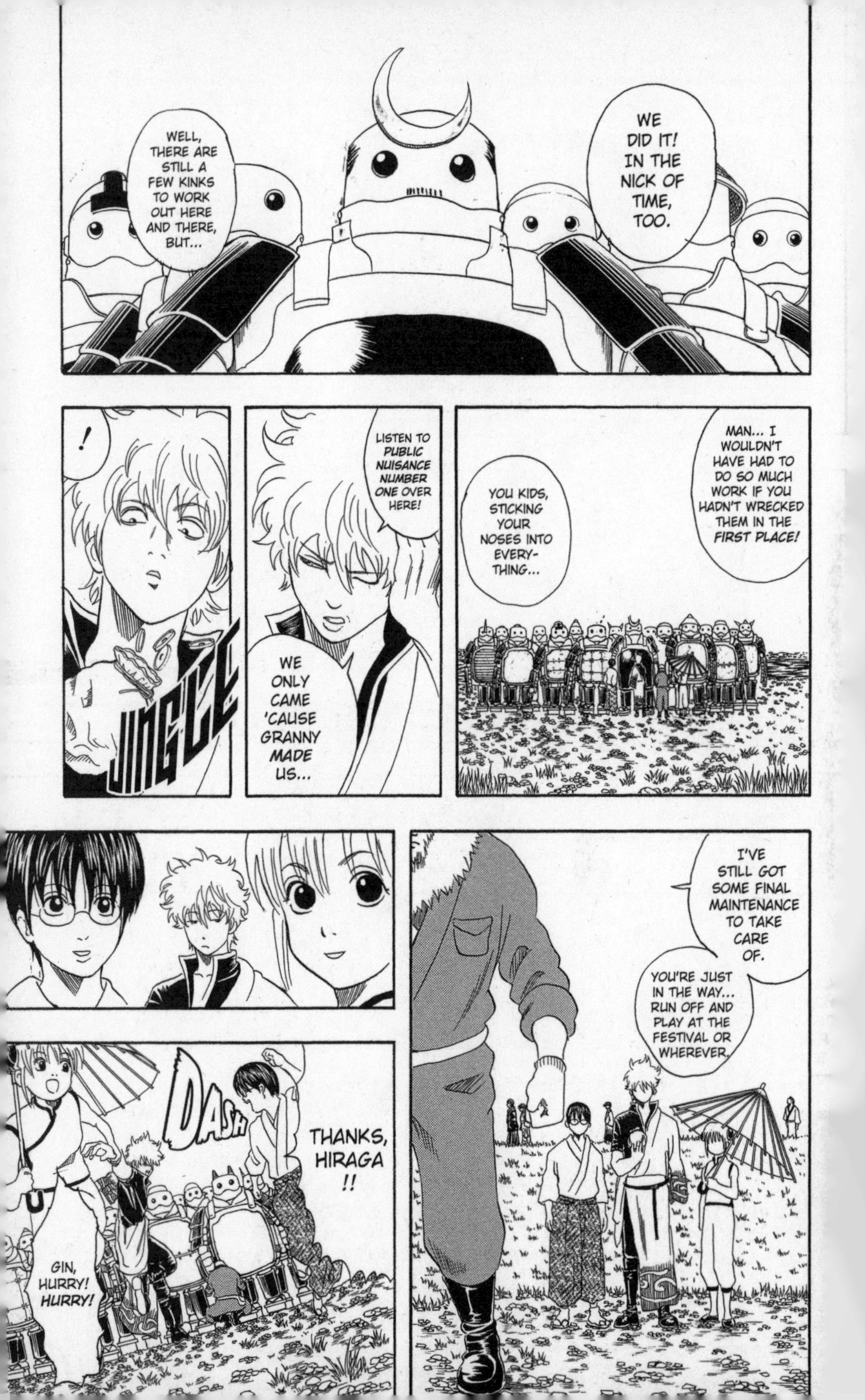
WE DID IT! IN THE NICK OF TIME, TOO.
WELL, THERE ARE STILL A FEW KINKS TO WORK OUT HERE AND THERE, BUT...
MAN... I WOULDN'T HAVE HAD TO DO SO MUCH WORK IF YOU HADN'T WRECKED THEM IN THE *FIRST PLACE!*
YOU KIDS, STICKING YOUR NOSES INTO EVERY-THING...
LISTEN TO *PUBLIC NUISANCE NUMBER ONE* OVER HERE!
WE ONLY CAME 'CAUSE GRANNY *MADE* US...
!
JINGLE
I'VE STILL GOT SOME FINAL MAINTENANCE TO TAKE CARE OF.
YOU'RE JUST IN THE WAY... RUN OFF AND PLAY AT THE FESTIVAL OR WHEREVER.
THANKS, HIRAGA !!
DASH
GIN, HURRY! *HURRY!*

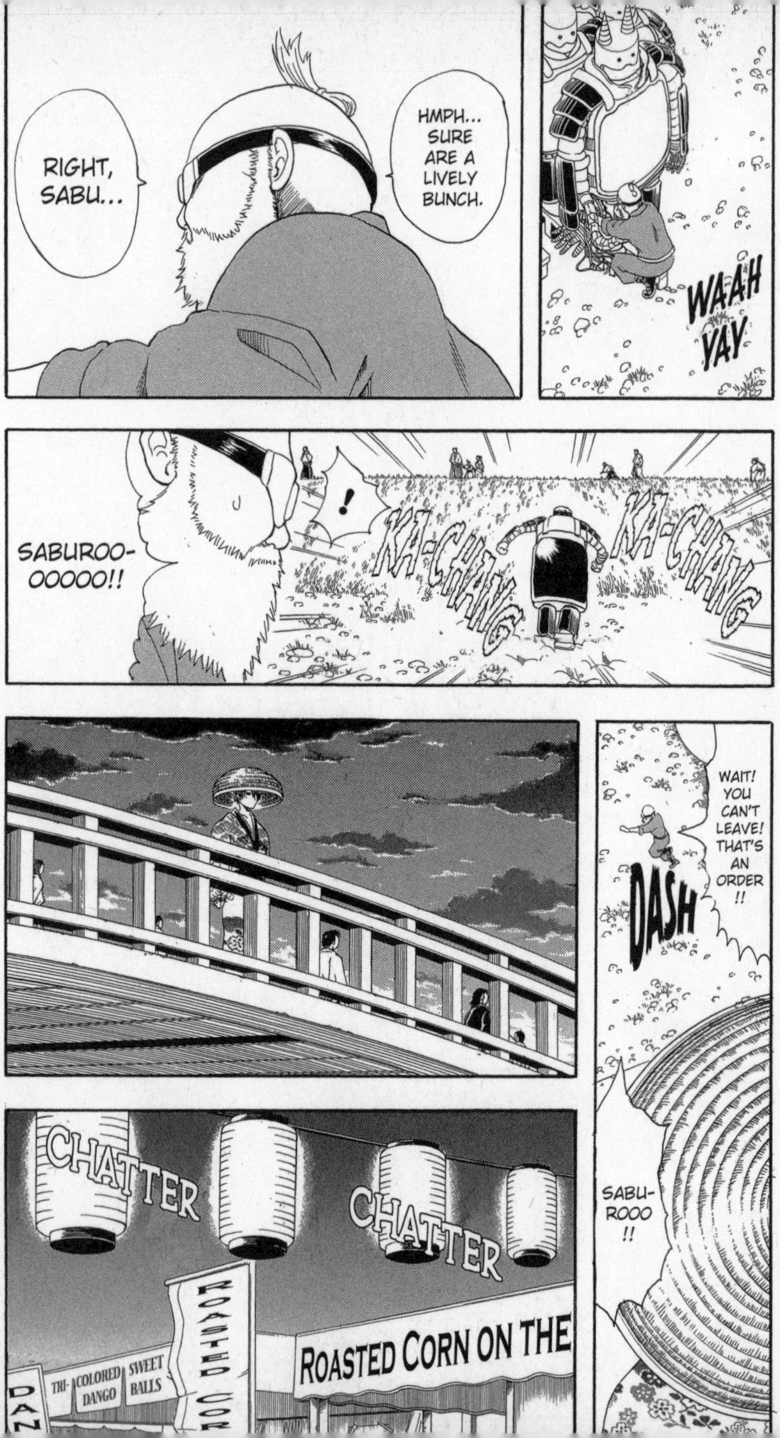
WAAH YAY
HMPH... SURE ARE A LIVELY BUNCH.
RIGHT, SABU...
KA-CHANG
!
KA-CHANG
SABUROO-OOOOO!!
WAIT! YOU CAN'T LEAVE! THAT'S AN ORDER!!
DASH
SABU-ROOO!!
CHATTER
CHATTER
ROASTED CORN ON THE
ROASTED COR
TRI-COLORED DANGO SWEET BALLS
DAN

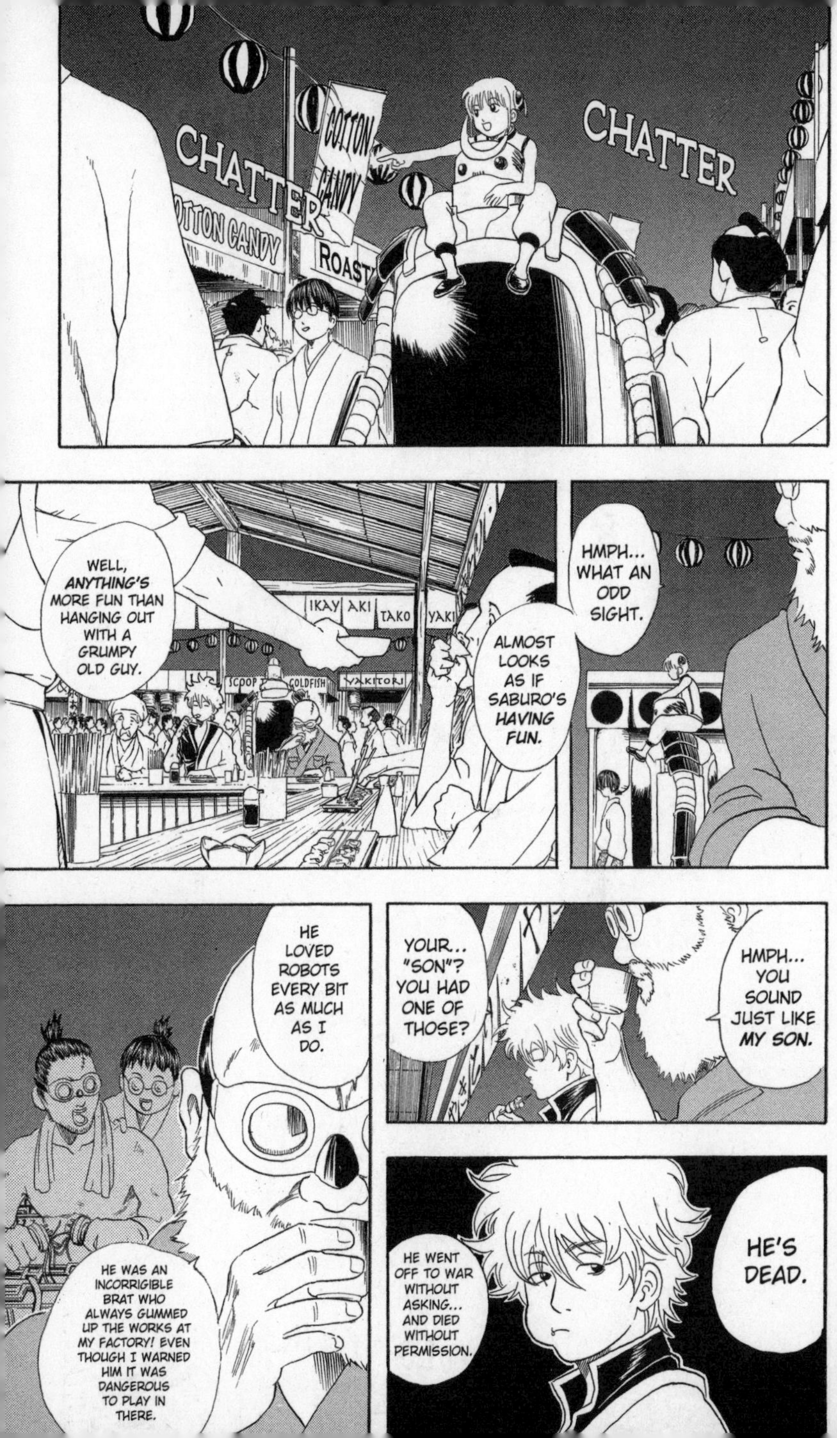
CHATTER
COTTON CANDY
CHATTER
OTTON CANDY
ROAST
HMPH... WHAT AN ODD SIGHT.
ALMOST LOOKS AS IF SABURO'S HAVING FUN.
WELL, *ANYTHING'S* MORE FUN THAN HANGING OUT WITH A GRUMPY OLD GUY.
IKAY AKI TAKO YAKI
SCOOP GOLDFISH
YAKITORI
HMPH... YOU SOUND JUST LIKE *MY SON.*
YOUR... "SON"? YOU HAD ONE OF THOSE?
HE'S DEAD.
HE WENT OFF TO WAR WITHOUT ASKING... AND DIED WITHOUT PERMISSION.
HE LOVED ROBOTS EVERY BIT AS MUCH AS I DO.
HE WAS AN INCORRIGIBLE BRAT WHO ALWAYS GUMMED UP THE WORKS AT MY FACTORY! EVEN THOUGH I WARNED HIM IT WAS DANGEROUS TO PLAY IN THERE.

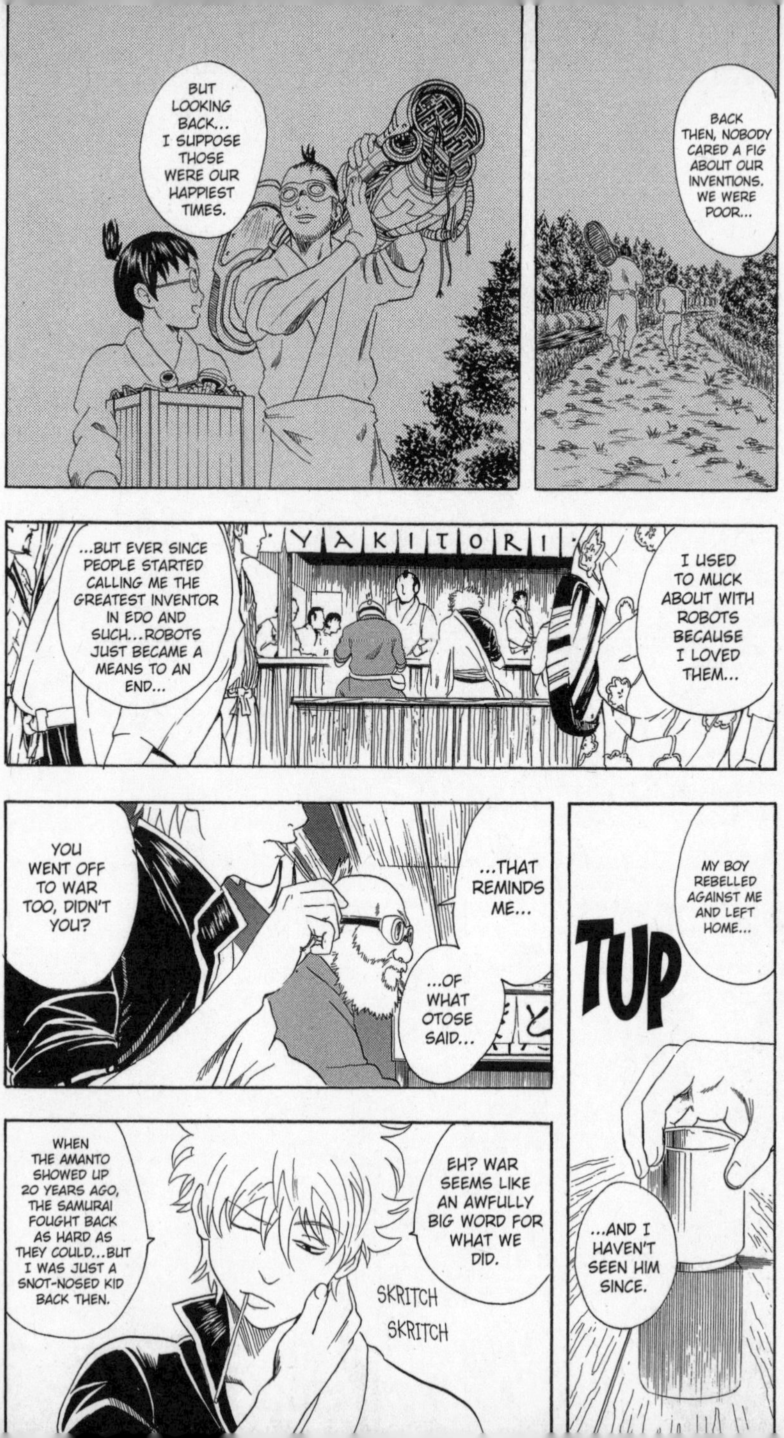
BACK THEN, NOBODY CARED A FIG ABOUT OUR INVENTIONS. WE WERE POOR...
BUT LOOKING BACK... I SUPPOSE THOSE WERE OUR HAPPIEST TIMES.
I USED TO MUCK ABOUT WITH ROBOTS BECAUSE I LOVED THEM...
YAKITORI
...BUT EVER SINCE PEOPLE STARTED CALLING ME THE GREATEST INVENTOR IN EDO AND SUCH...ROBOTS JUST BECAME A MEANS TO AN END...
MY BOY REBELLED AGAINST ME AND LEFT HOME...
TUP
...AND I HAVEN'T SEEN HIM SINCE.
...THAT REMINDS ME...
...OF WHAT OTOSE SAID...
YOU WENT OFF TO WAR TOO, DIDN'T YOU?
EH? WAR SEEMS LIKE AN AWFULLY BIG WORD FOR WHAT WE DID.
SKRITCH
SKRITCH
WHEN THE AMANTO SHOWED UP 20 YEARS AGO, THE SAMURAI FOUGHT BACK AS HARD AS THEY COULD...BUT I WAS JUST A SNOT-NOSED KID BACK THEN.

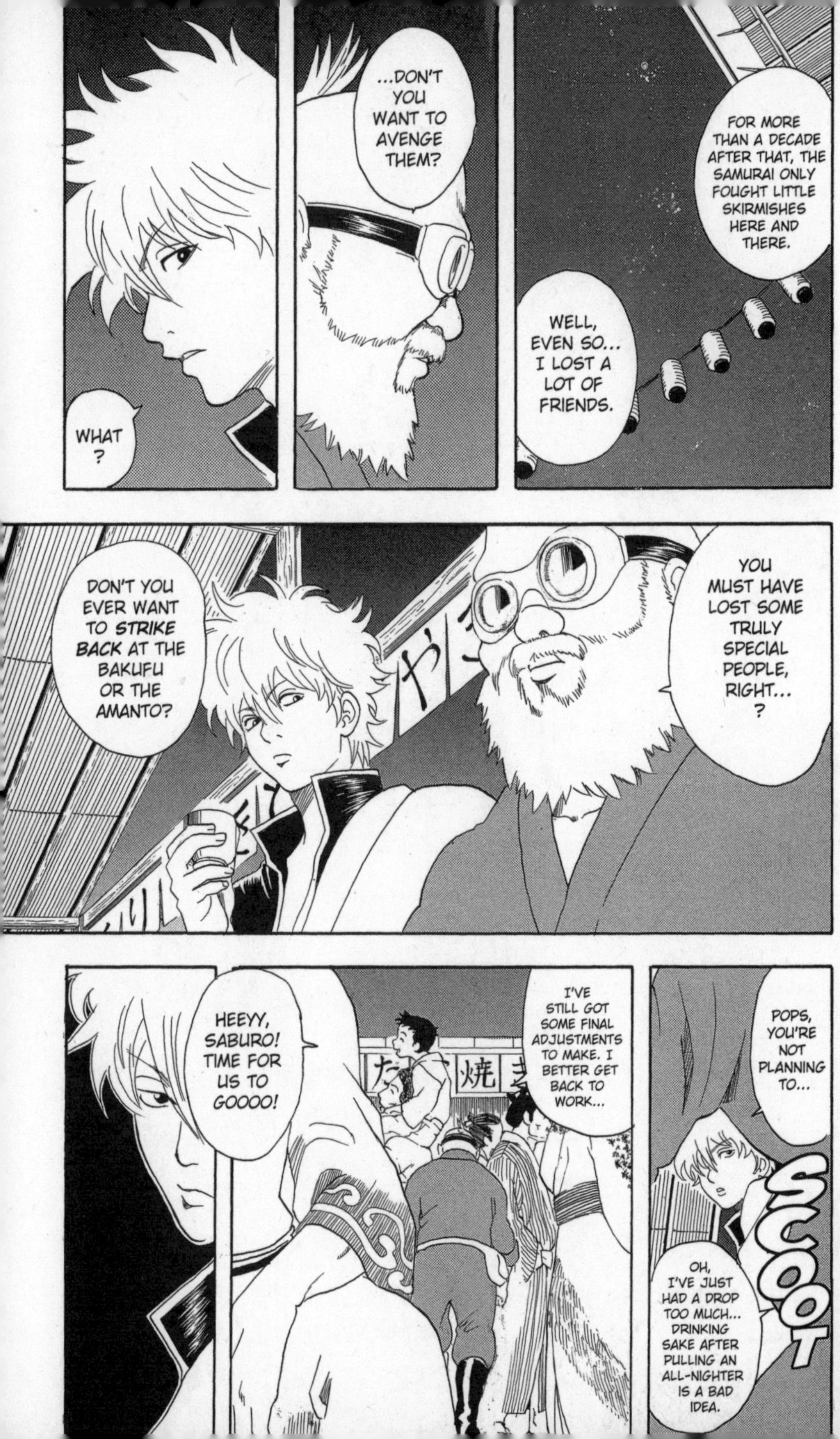
FOR MORE THAN A DECADE AFTER THAT, THE SAMURAI ONLY FOUGHT LITTLE SKIRMISHES HERE AND THERE.
WELL, EVEN SO... I LOST A LOT OF FRIENDS.
...DON'T YOU WANT TO AVENGE THEM?
WHAT?
YOU MUST HAVE LOST SOME TRULY SPECIAL PEOPLE, RIGHT...?
DON'T YOU EVER WANT TO STRIKE BACK AT THE BAKUFU OR THE AMANTO?
POPS, YOU'RE NOT PLANNING TO...
SCOOT
OH, I'VE JUST HAD A DROP TOO MUCH... DRINKING SAKE AFTER PULLING AN ALL-NIGHTER IS A BAD IDEA.
I'VE STILL GOT SOME FINAL ADJUSTMENTS TO MAKE. I BETTER GET BACK TO WORK...
HEEYY, SABURO! TIME FOR US TO GOOOO!

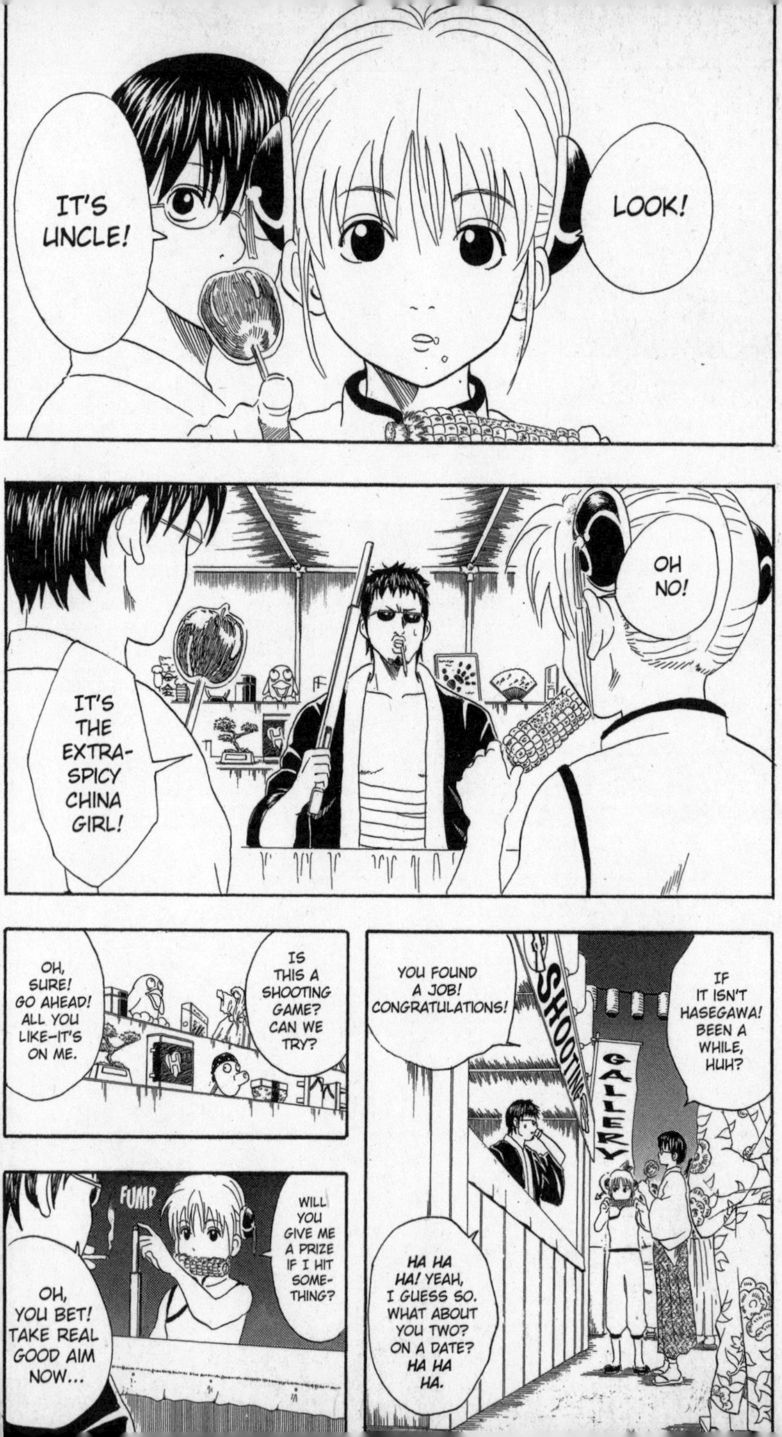
LOOK!
IT'S UNCLE!
OH NO!
IT'S THE EXTRA-SPICY CHINA GIRL!
IF IT ISN'T HASEGAWA! BEEN A WHILE, HUH?
YOU FOUND A JOB! CONGRATULATIONS!
SHOOTING GALLERY
HA HA HA! YEAH, I GUESS SO. WHAT ABOUT YOU TWO? ON A DATE? HA HA HA.
IS THIS A SHOOTING GAME? CAN WE TRY?
OH, SURE! GO AHEAD! ALL YOU LIKE—IT'S ON ME.
FUMP
WILL YOU GIVE ME A PRIZE IF I HIT SOMETHING?
OH, YOU BET! TAKE REAL GOOD AIM NOW...

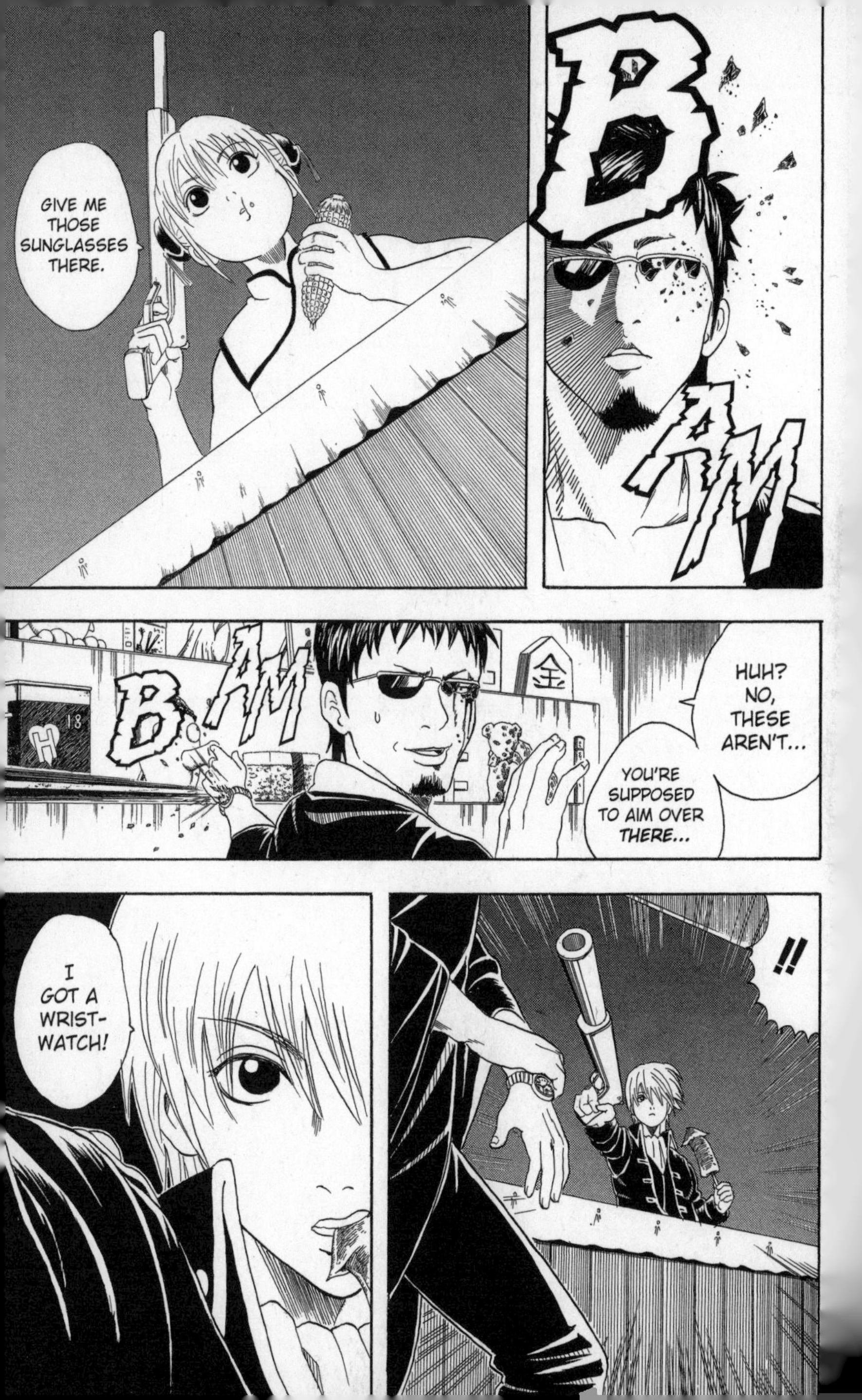
BAM
GIVE ME THOSE SUNGLASSES THERE.
HUH? NO, THESE AREN'T...
YOU'RE SUPPOSED TO AIM OVER THERE...
BAM
!!
I GOT A WRIST-WATCH!

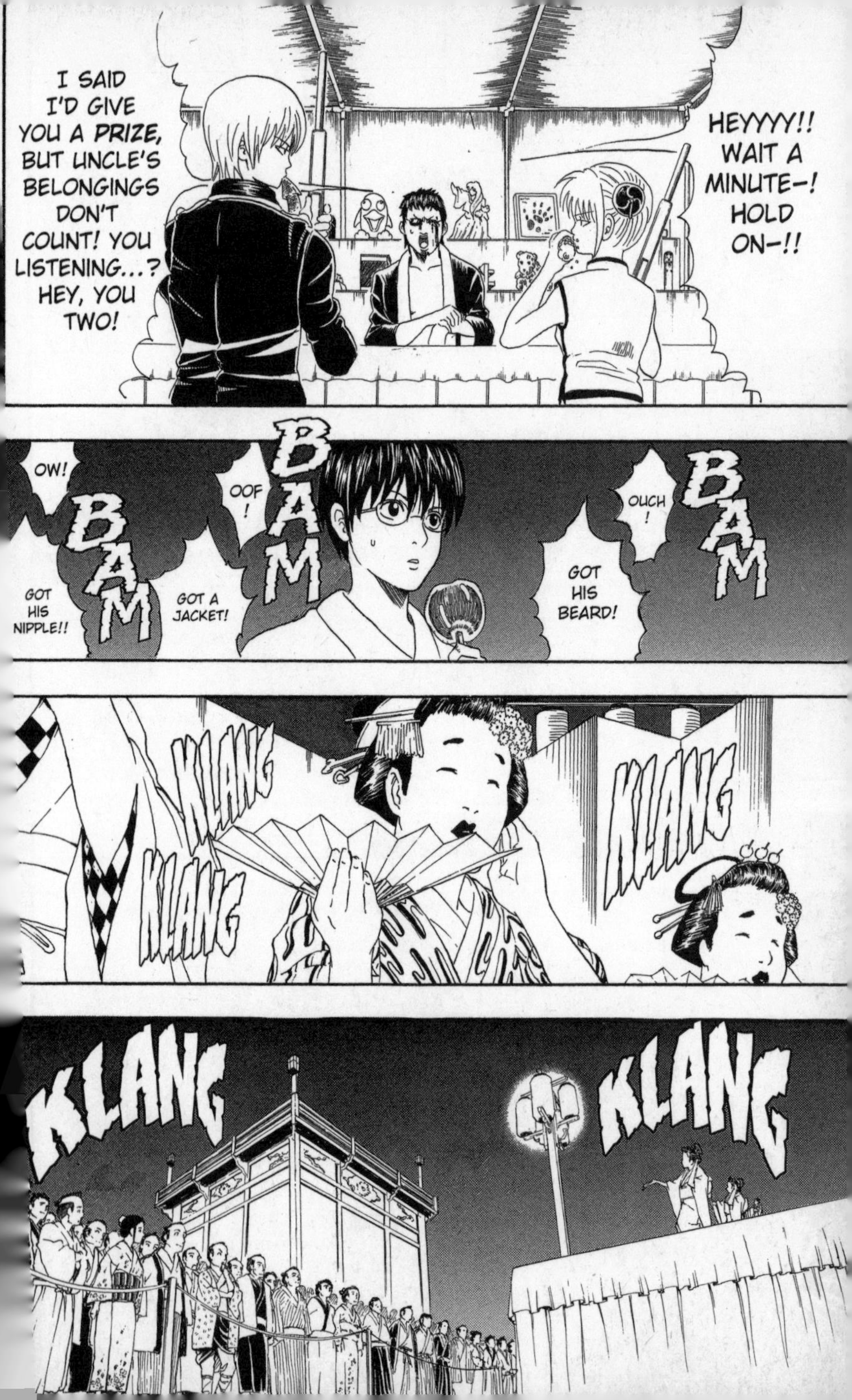

HEYYYY!! WAIT A MINUTE-! HOLD ON-!!
I SAID I'D GIVE YOU A PRIZE, BUT UNCLE'S BELONGINGS DON'T COUNT! YOU LISTENING...? HEY, YOU TWO!
BAM
OUCH!
GOT HIS BEARD!
BAM
OOF!
GOT A JACKET!
OW!
BAM
GOT HIS NIPPLE!!
KLANG
KLANG
KLANG
KLANG
KLANG

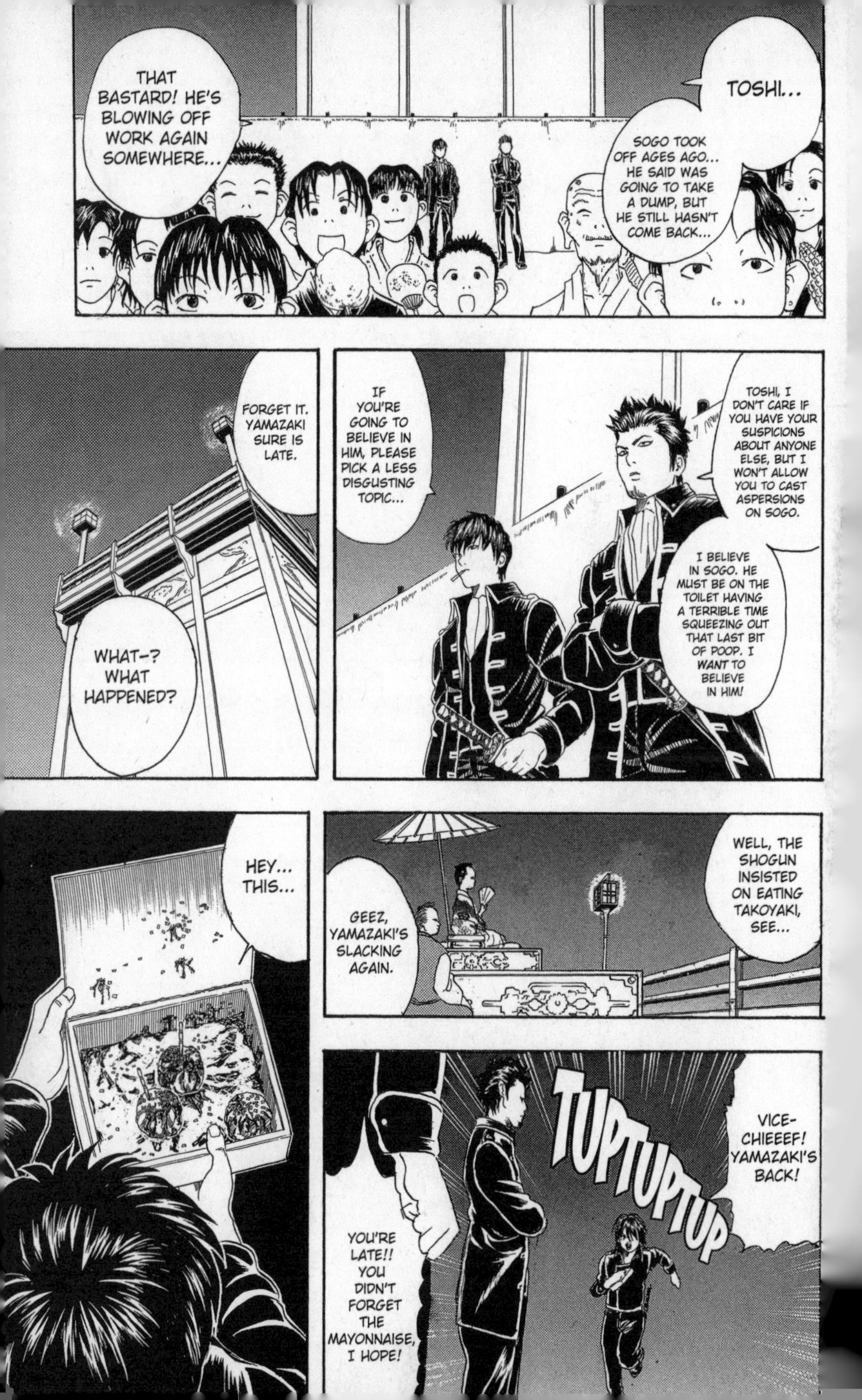
TOSHI...
SOGO TOOK OFF AGES AGO... HE SAID WAS GOING TO TAKE A DUMP, BUT HE STILL HASN'T COME BACK...
THAT BASTARD! HE'S BLOWING OFF WORK AGAIN SOMEWHERE...
TOSHI, I DON'T CARE IF YOU HAVE YOUR SUSPICIONS ABOUT ANYONE ELSE, BUT I WON'T ALLOW YOU TO CAST ASPERSIONS ON SOGO.
I BELIEVE IN SOGO. HE MUST BE ON THE TOILET HAVING A TERRIBLE TIME SQUEEZING OUT THAT LAST BIT OF POOP. I WANT TO BELIEVE IN HIM!
IF YOU'RE GOING TO BELIEVE IN HIM, PLEASE PICK A LESS DISGUSTING TOPIC...
FORGET IT. YAMAZAKI SURE IS LATE.
WHAT-? WHAT HAPPENED?
WELL, THE SHOGUN INSISTED ON EATING TAKOYAKI, SEE...
GEEZ, YAMAZAKI'S SLACKING AGAIN.
TUPTUPTUP
VICE-CHIEEEF! YAMAZAKI'S BACK!
YOU'RE LATE!! YOU DIDN'T FORGET THE MAYONNAISE, I HOPE!
HEY... THIS...

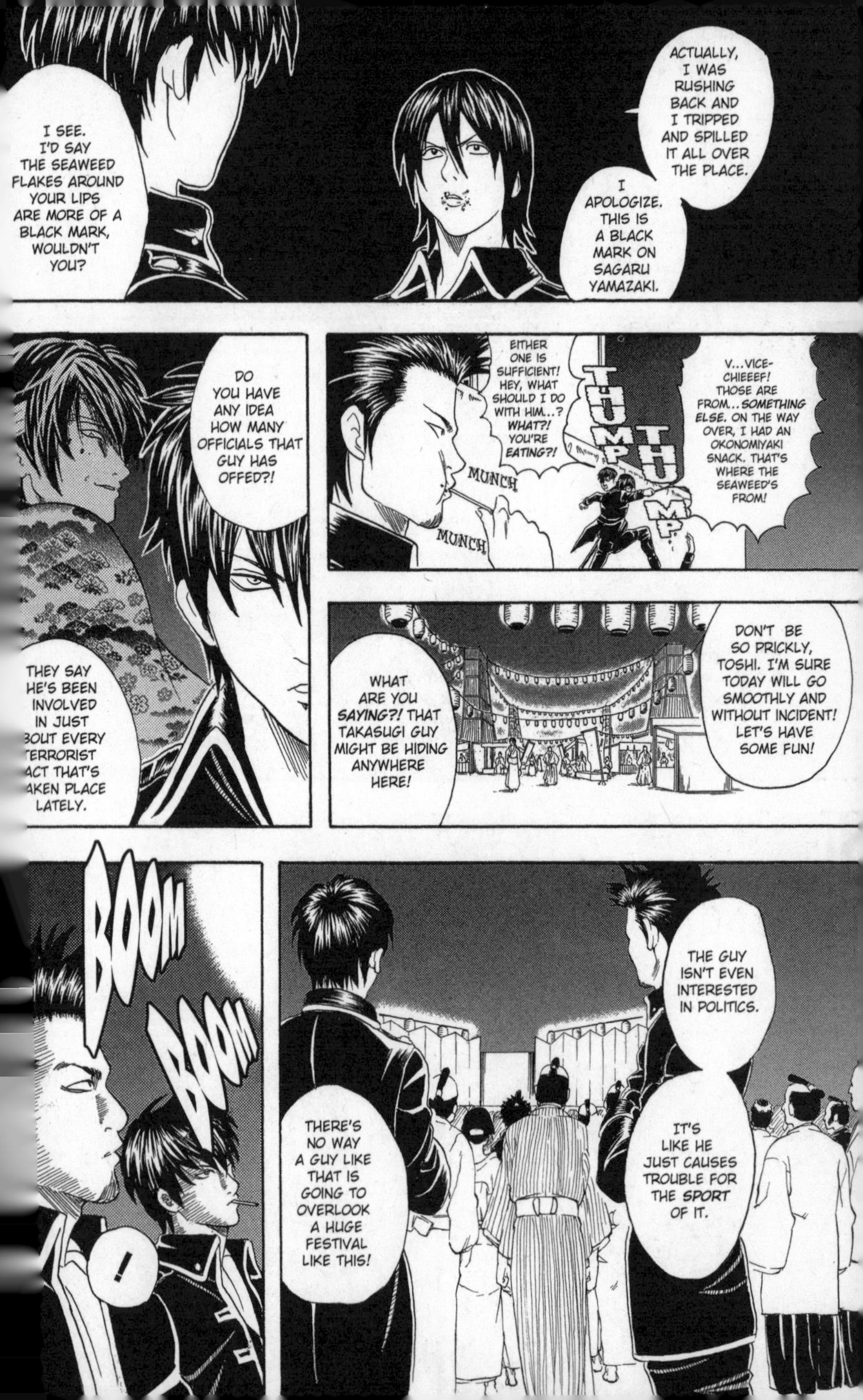
ACTUALLY, I WAS RUSHING BACK AND I TRIPPED AND SPILLED IT ALL OVER THE PLACE.
I APOLOGIZE. THIS IS A BLACK MARK ON SAGARU YAMAZAKI.
I SEE. I'D SAY THE SEAWEED FLAKES AROUND YOUR LIPS ARE MORE OF A BLACK MARK, WOULDN'T YOU?
V...VICE-CHIEEEF! THOSE ARE FROM... *SOMETHING ELSE.* ON THE WAY OVER, I HAD AN OKONOMIYAKI SNACK. THAT'S WHERE THE SEAWEED'S FROM!
THUMP
THUMP
EITHER ONE IS SUFFICIENT! HEY, WHAT SHOULD I DO WITH HIM...? *WHAT?!* YOU'RE *EATING?!*
MUNCH
MUNCH
DON'T BE SO PRICKLY, TOSHI. I'M SURE TODAY WILL GO SMOOTHLY AND WITHOUT INCIDENT! LET'S HAVE SOME FUN!
WHAT ARE YOU *SAYING?!* THAT TAKASUGI GUY MIGHT BE HIDING ANYWHERE HERE!
DO YOU HAVE ANY IDEA HOW MANY OFFICIALS THAT GUY HAS OFFED?!
THEY SAY HE'S BEEN INVOLVED IN JUST BOUT EVERY TERRORIST ACT THAT'S AKEN PLACE LATELY.
THE GUY ISN'T EVEN INTERESTED IN POLITICS.
IT'S LIKE HE JUST CAUSES TROUBLE FOR THE *SPORT* OF IT.
THERE'S NO WAY A GUY LIKE THAT IS GOING TO OVERLOOK A HUGE FESTIVAL LIKE THIS!
BOOM
BOOM
!

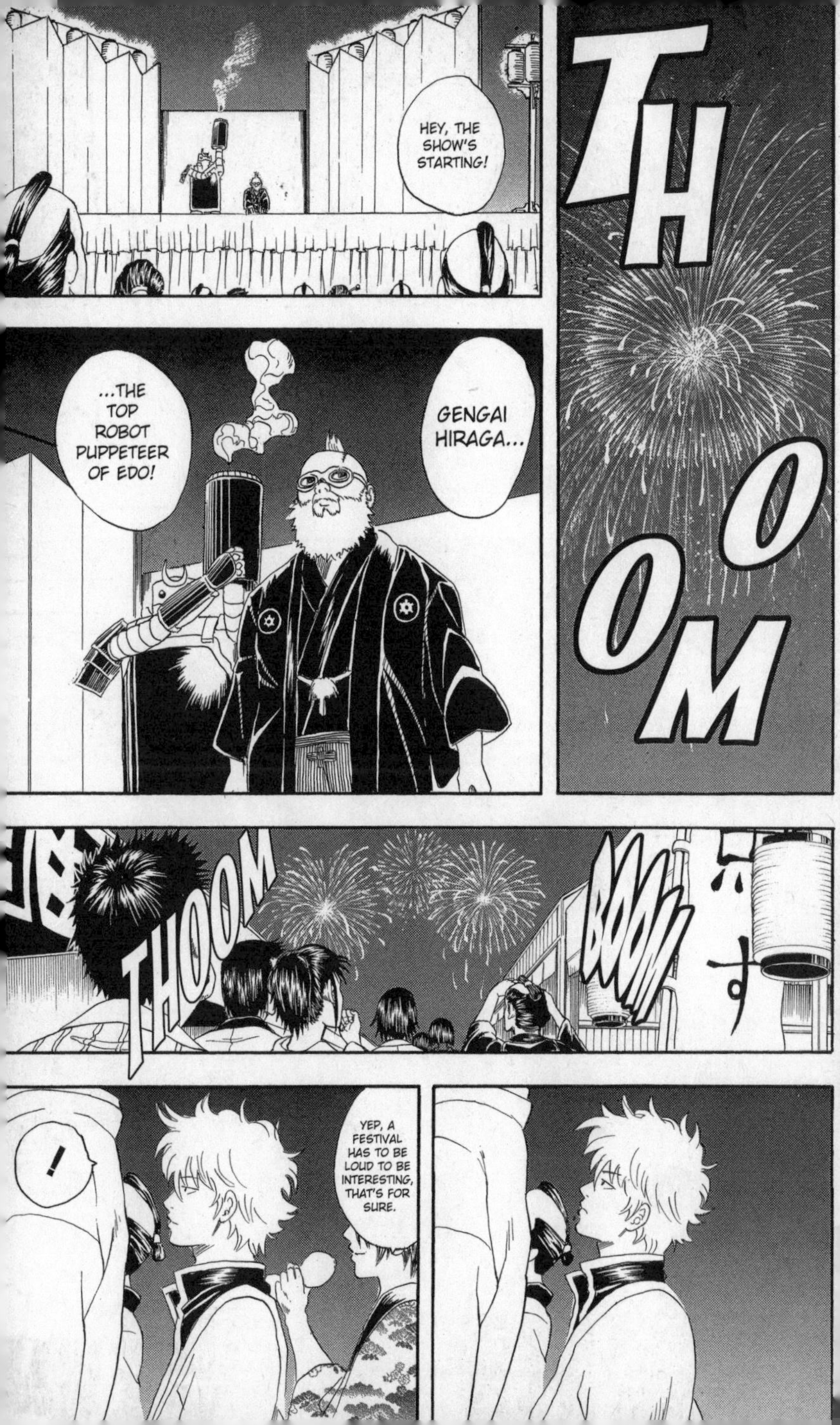
THOOOM
HEY, THE SHOW'S STARTING!
GENGAI HIRAGA...
...THE TOP ROBOT PUPPETEER OF EDO!
BOOM
THOOM
YEP, A FESTIVAL HAS TO BE LOUD TO BE INTERESTING, THAT'S FOR SURE.
!

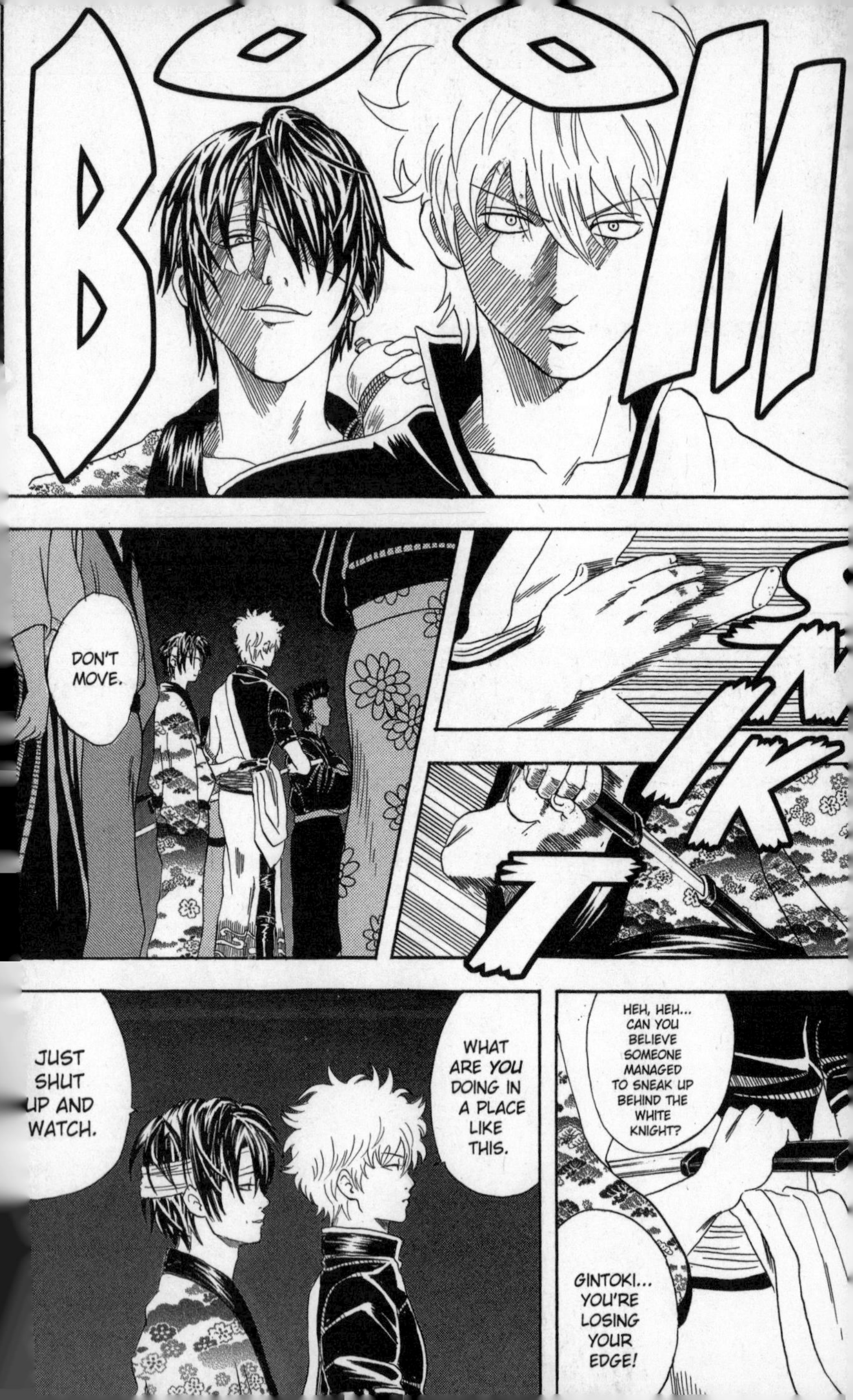
BOOM
DON'T MOVE.
HEH, HEH... CAN YOU BELIEVE SOMEONE MANAGED TO SNEAK UP BEHIND THE WHITE KNIGHT?
GINTOKI... YOU'RE LOSING YOUR EDGE!
WHAT ARE YOU DOING IN A PLACE LIKE THIS.
JUST SHUT UP AND WATCH.

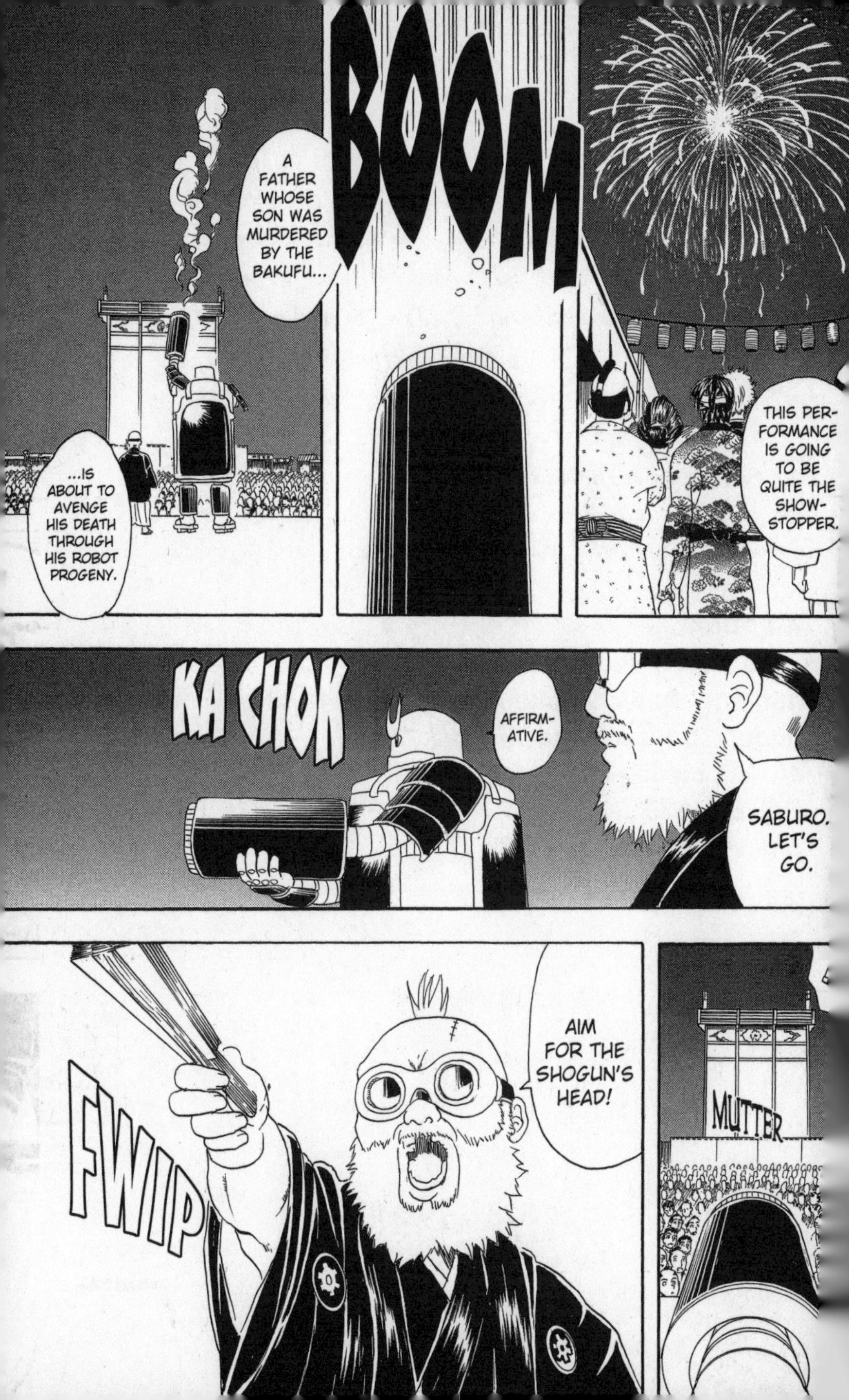

THIS PERFORMANCE IS GOING TO BE QUITE THE SHOWSTOPPER.
BOOM
A FATHER WHOSE SON WAS MURDERED BY THE BAKUFU...
...IS ABOUT TO AVENGE HIS DEATH THROUGH HIS ROBOT PROGENY.
SABURO. LET'S GO.
AFFIRMATIVE.
KA CHOK
MUTTER
AIM FOR THE SHOGUN'S HEAD!
FWIP

Ummm... So, how did you like the Q&A corner?
It sure is easier on me! Thanks to everyone for
your cooperation. Hey, you—over there.
If there's something you're burning to ask me,
give it a shot. I'm also looking forward to
receiving your opinions and requests.

We received a lot of complaints about the first
line of the address being too long, so I cut it down.
So go ahead, everyone, send in your letters to:

Attention:
SJA Gintama Volume 4:
"Thinking Up an Omake Freebie Page Is a Pain" desk
Shonen Jump Advanced/Gin Tama
c/o VIZ Media, LLC
P.O. Box 77010
San Francisco, CA 94107

So long, and see you in Volume 5!
Seeeee Youuuuu
 —Sorachi

空知

Lesson 31
Sons Only Take After Their Fathers' *Negative* Attributes

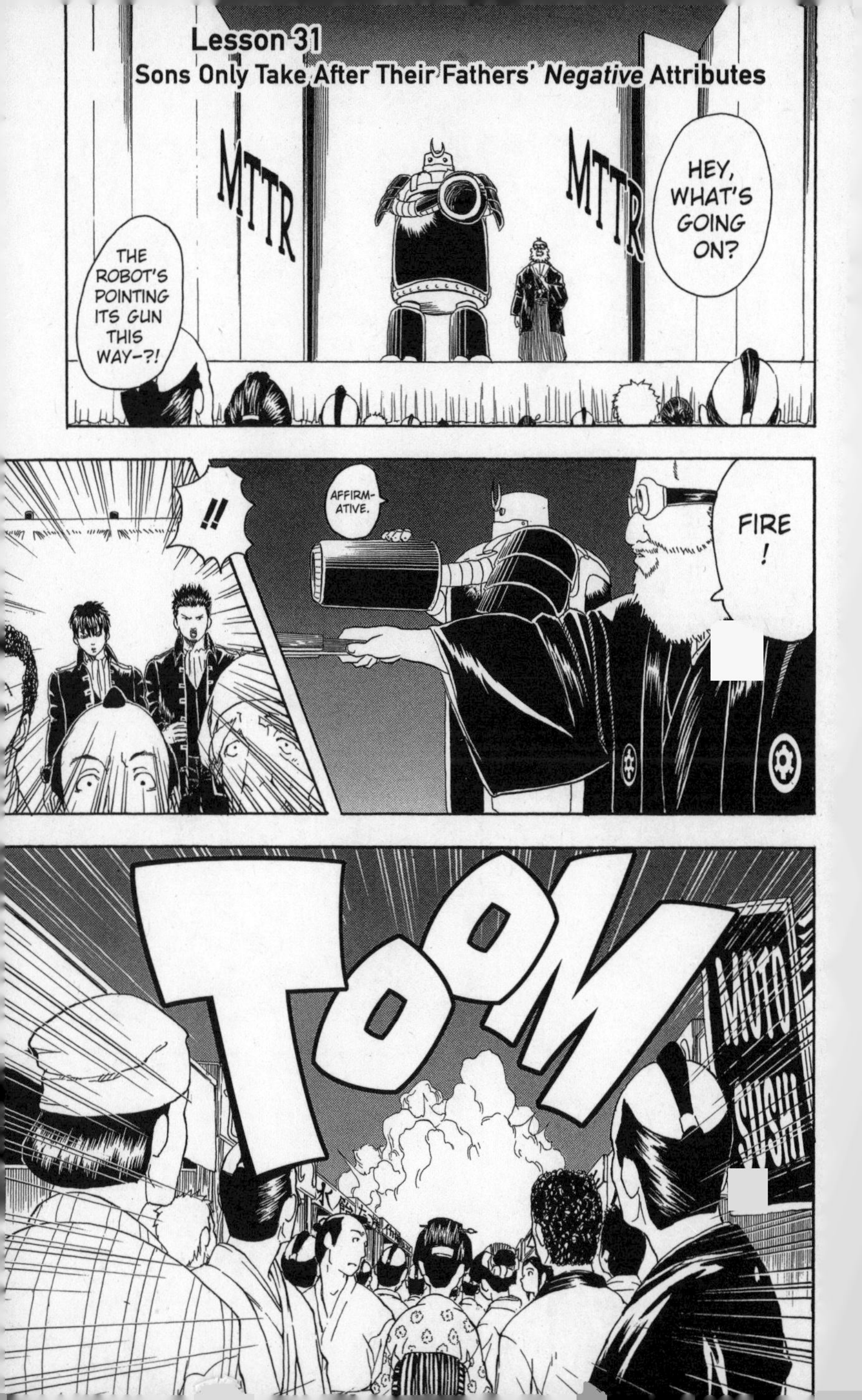
MTTR
MTTR
HEY, WHAT'S GOING ON?
THE ROBOT'S POINTING ITS GUN THIS WAY-?!
FIRE!
AFFIRMATIVE.
!!
TOOM
MOTO SUSHI

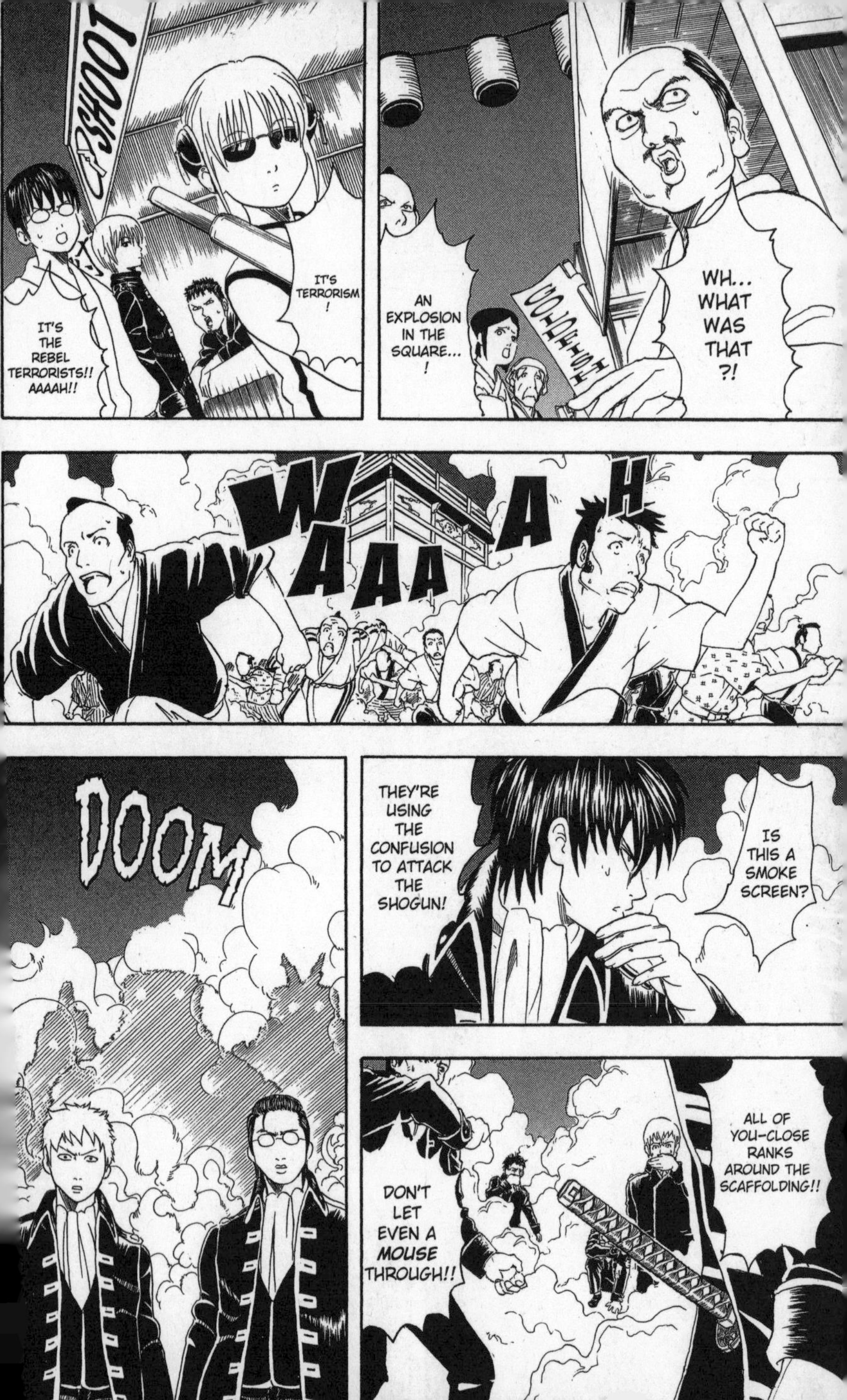
WH... WHAT WAS THAT ?!
AN EXPLOSION IN THE SQUARE... !
IT'S TERRORISM !
IT'S THE REBEL TERRORISTS!! AAAAH!!
WAAAAH
IS THIS A SMOKE SCREEN?
THEY'RE USING THE CONFUSION TO ATTACK THE SHOGUN!
ALL OF YOU-CLOSE RANKS AROUND THE SCAFFOLDING!!
DON'T LET EVEN A *MOUSE* THROUGH!!
DOOM

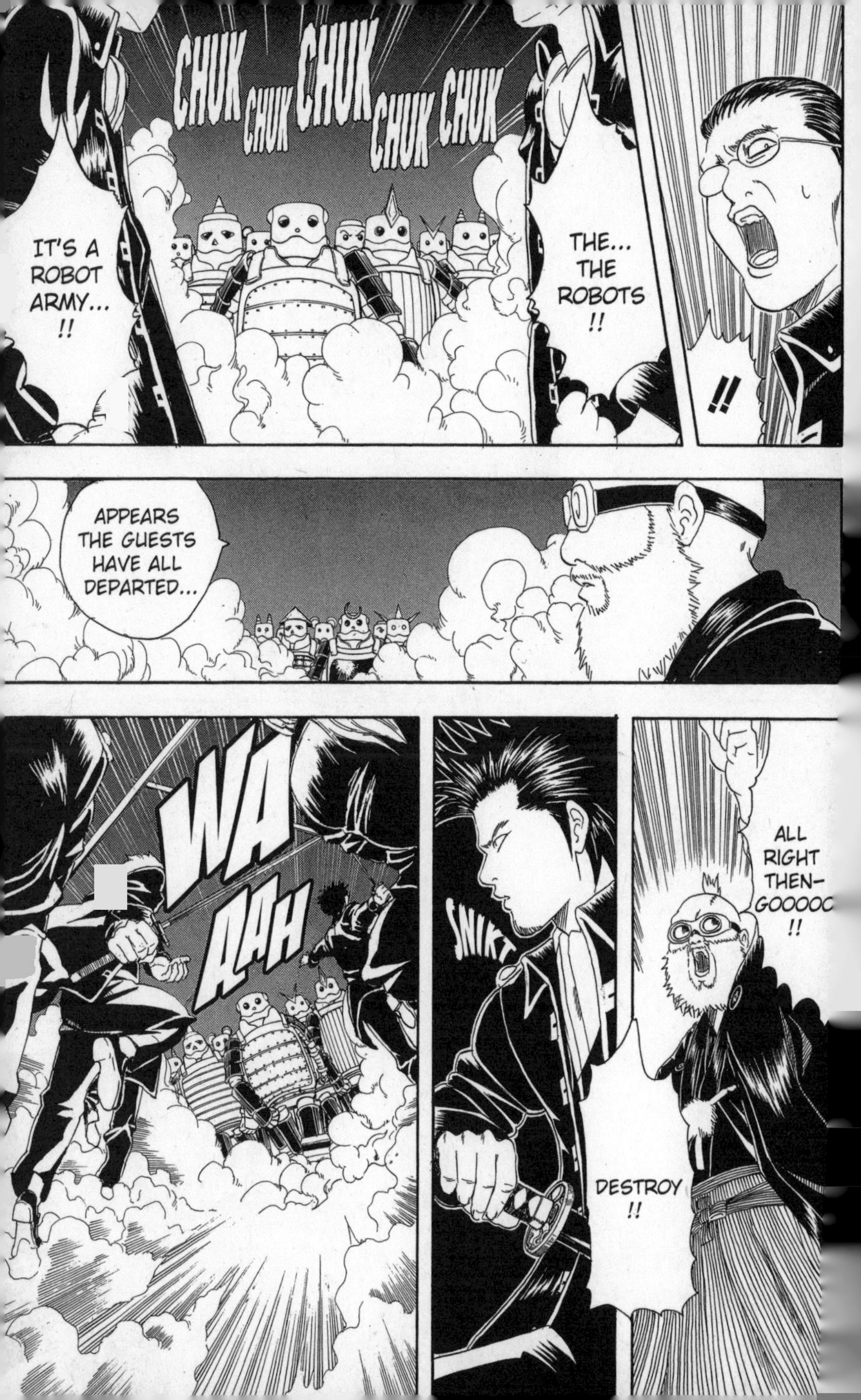
!!
THE... THE ROBOTS !!
CHUK CHUK CHUK CHUK CHUK
IT'S A ROBOT ARMY... !!
APPEARS THE GUESTS HAVE ALL DEPARTED...
ALL RIGHT THEN— GOOOOO
!!
DESTROY !!
SNIKT
WA AAH

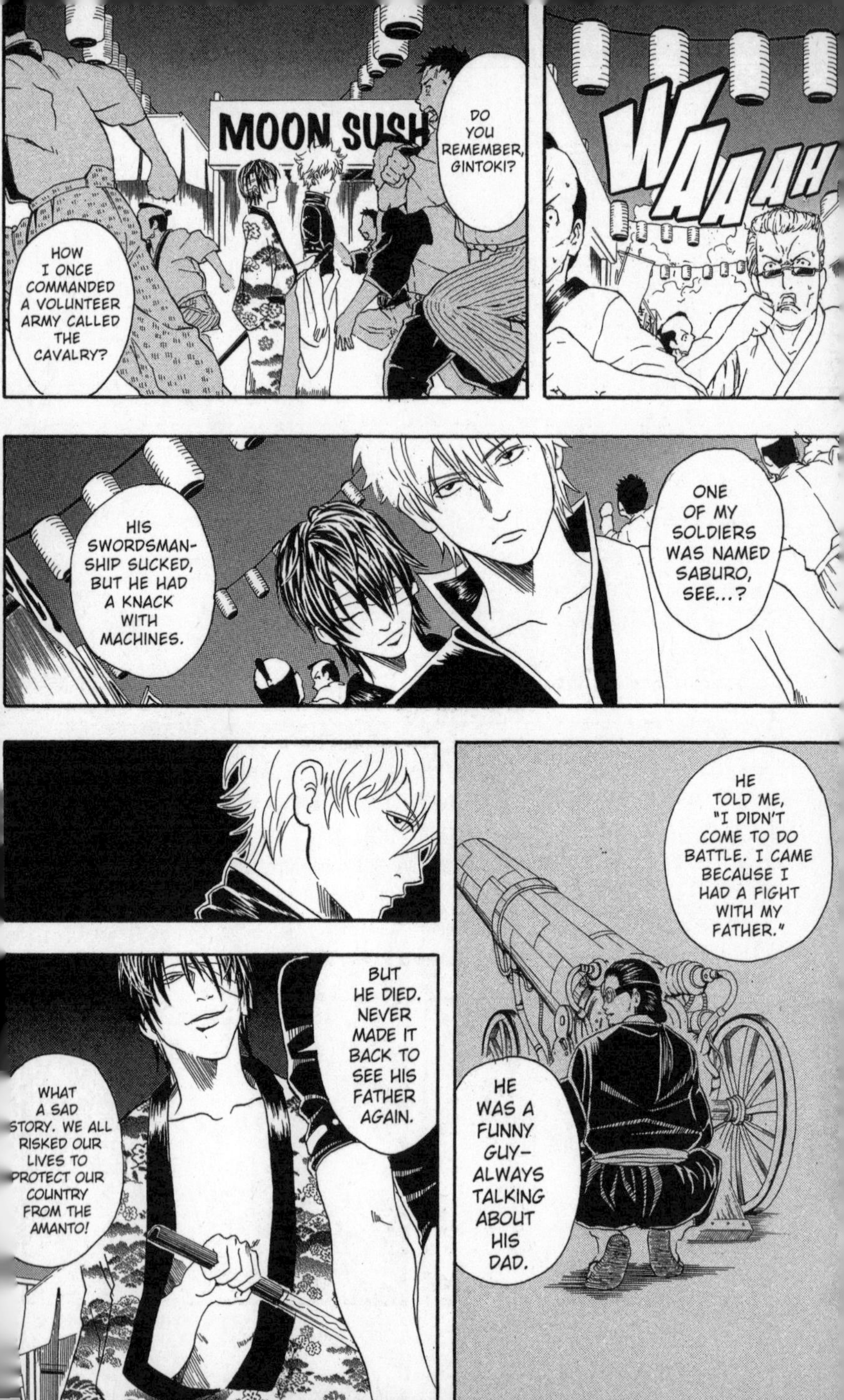
WAAAAH
DO YOU REMEMBER, GINTOKI?
HOW I ONCE COMMANDED A VOLUNTEER ARMY CALLED THE CAVALRY?
MOON SUSH
ONE OF MY SOLDIERS WAS NAMED SABURO, SEE...?
HIS SWORDSMANSHIP SUCKED, BUT HE HAD A KNACK WITH MACHINES.
HE TOLD ME, "I DIDN'T COME TO DO BATTLE. I CAME BECAUSE I HAD A FIGHT WITH MY FATHER."
HE WAS A FUNNY GUY—ALWAYS TALKING ABOUT HIS DAD.
BUT HE DIED. NEVER MADE IT BACK TO SEE HIS FATHER AGAIN.
WHAT A SAD STORY. WE ALL RISKED OUR LIVES TO PROTECT OUR COUNTRY FROM THE AMANTO!

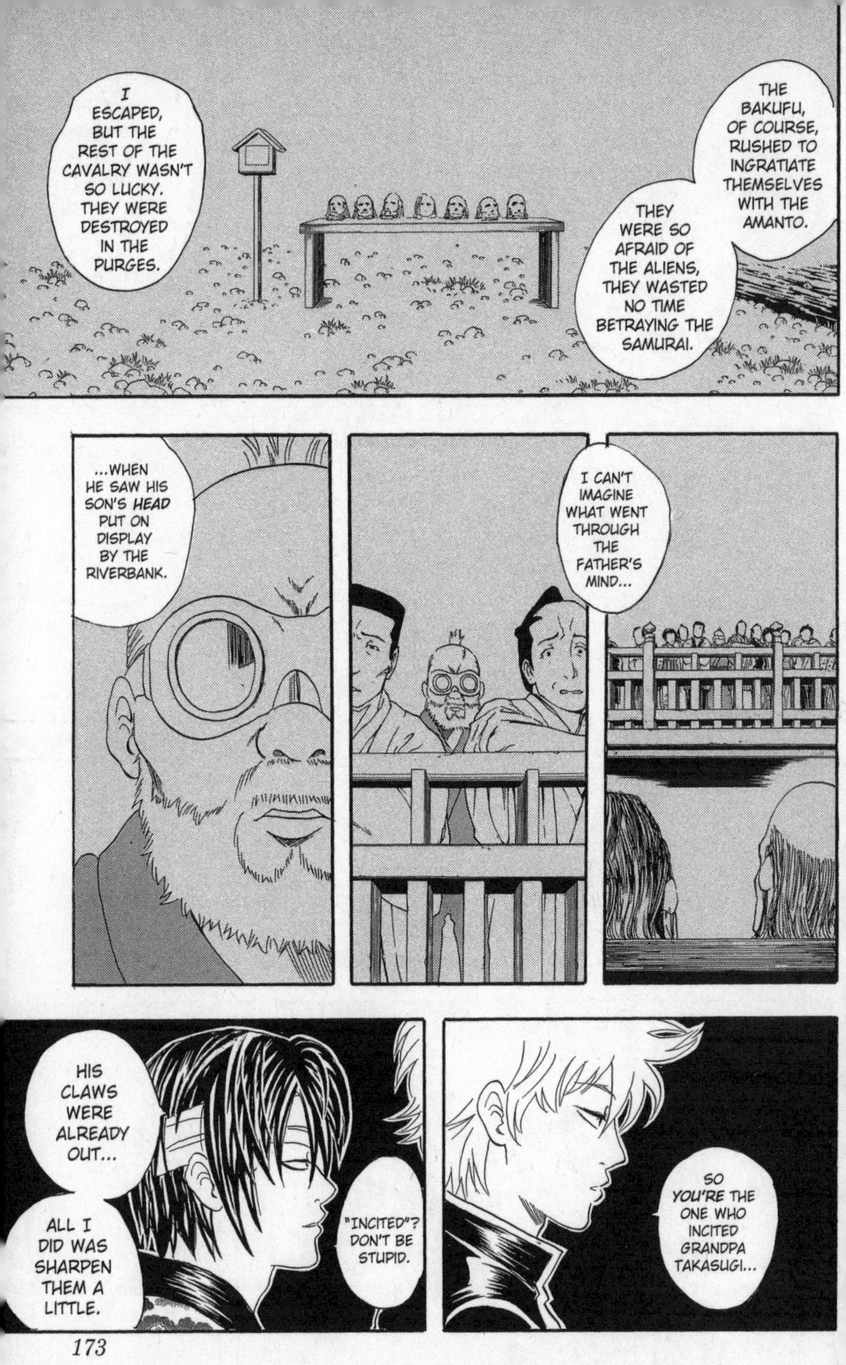
THE BAKUFU, OF COURSE, RUSHED TO INGRATIATE THEMSELVES WITH THE AMANTO.
THEY WERE SO AFRAID OF THE ALIENS, THEY WASTED NO TIME BETRAYING THE SAMURAI.
I ESCAPED, BUT THE REST OF THE CAVALRY WASN'T SO LUCKY. THEY WERE DESTROYED IN THE PURGES.
I CAN'T IMAGINE WHAT WENT THROUGH THE FATHER'S MIND...
...WHEN HE SAW HIS SON'S *HEAD* PUT ON DISPLAY BY THE RIVERBANK.
SO *YOU'RE* THE ONE WHO INCITED GRANDPA TAKASUGI...
"INCITED"? DON'T BE STUPID.
HIS CLAWS WERE ALREADY OUT...
ALL I DID WAS SHARPEN THEM A LITTLE.

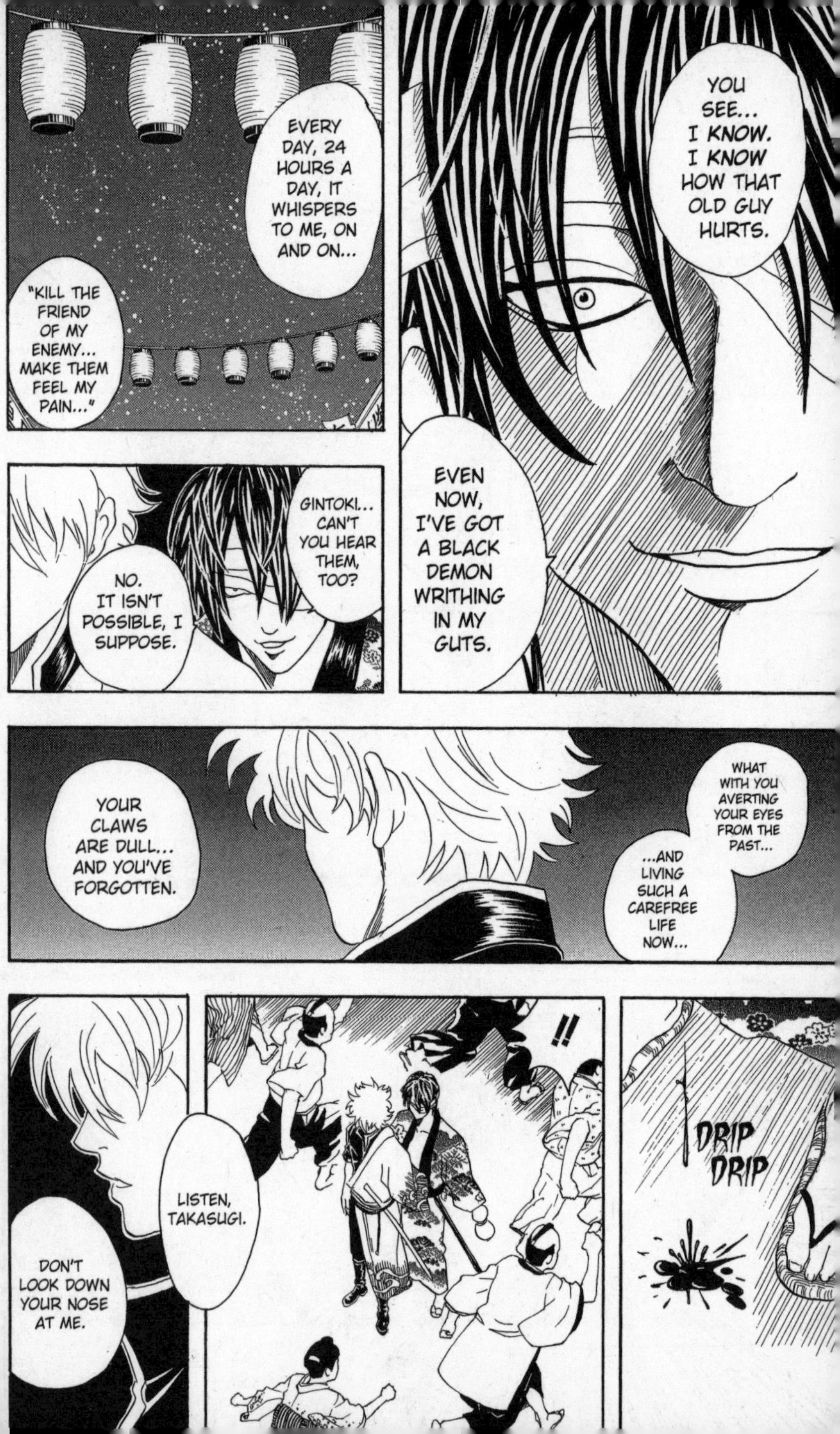
YOU SEE... I KNOW. I KNOW HOW THAT OLD GUY HURTS.
EVEN NOW, I'VE GOT A BLACK DEMON WRITHING IN MY GUTS.
EVERY DAY, 24 HOURS A DAY, IT WHISPERS TO ME, ON AND ON...
"KILL THE FRIEND OF MY ENEMY... MAKE THEM FEEL MY PAIN..."
GINTOKI... CAN'T YOU HEAR THEM, TOO?
NO. IT ISN'T POSSIBLE, I SUPPOSE.
WHAT WITH YOU AVERTING YOUR EYES FROM THE PAST...
...AND LIVING SUCH A CAREFREE LIFE NOW...
YOUR CLAWS ARE DULL... AND YOU'VE FORGOTTEN.
DRIP
DRIP
!!
LISTEN, TAKASUGI.
DON'T LOOK DOWN YOUR NOSE AT ME.

READ THIS WAY

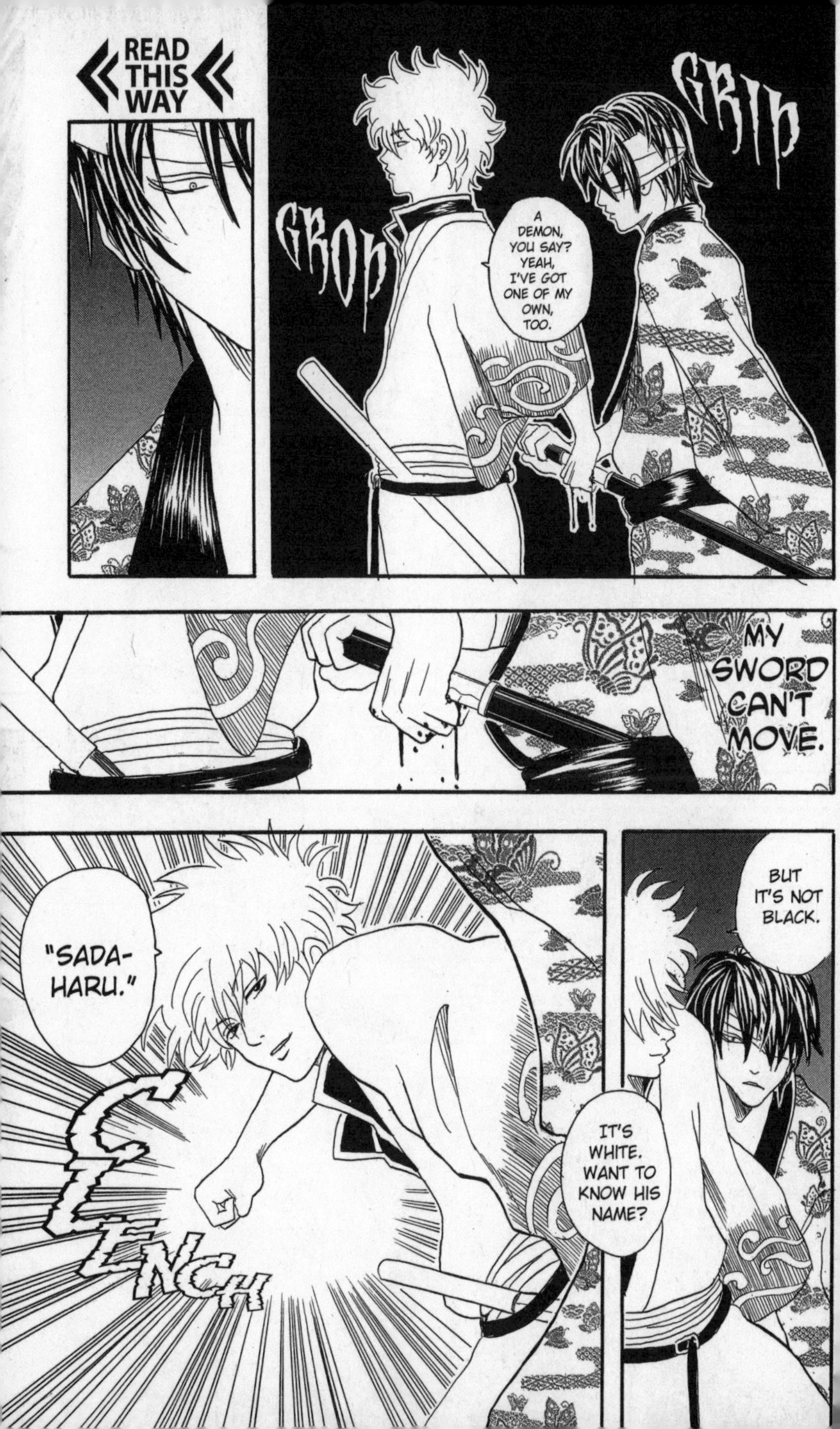
GRIP
A DEMON, YOU SAY? YEAH, I'VE GOT ONE OF MY OWN, TOO.
GROP
MY SWORD CAN'T MOVE.
BUT IT'S NOT BLACK.
IT'S WHITE. WANT TO KNOW HIS NAME?
"SADA-HARU."
CLENCH

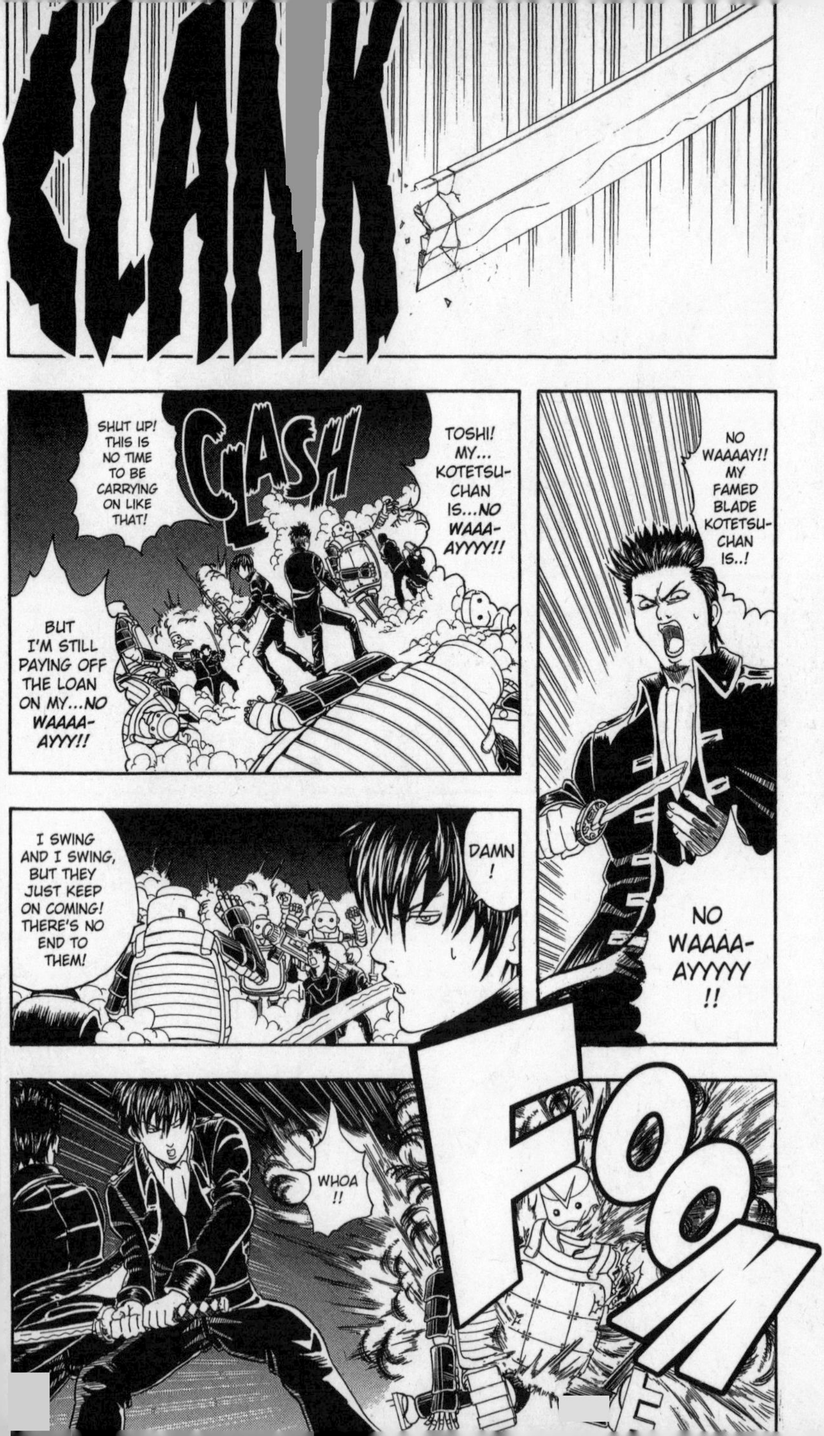
CLANK
NO WAAAAY!! MY FAMED BLADE KOTETSU-CHAN IS..!
NO WAAAA-AYYYYY !!
TOSHI! MY... KOTETSU-CHAN IS...NO WAAA-AYYYY!!
CLASH
SHUT UP! THIS IS NO TIME TO BE CARRYING ON LIKE THAT!
BUT I'M STILL PAYING OFF THE LOAN ON MY...NO WAAAA-AYYY!!
DAMN!
I SWING AND I SWING, BUT THEY JUST KEEP ON COMING! THERE'S NO END TO THEM!
FOOM
WHOA!!

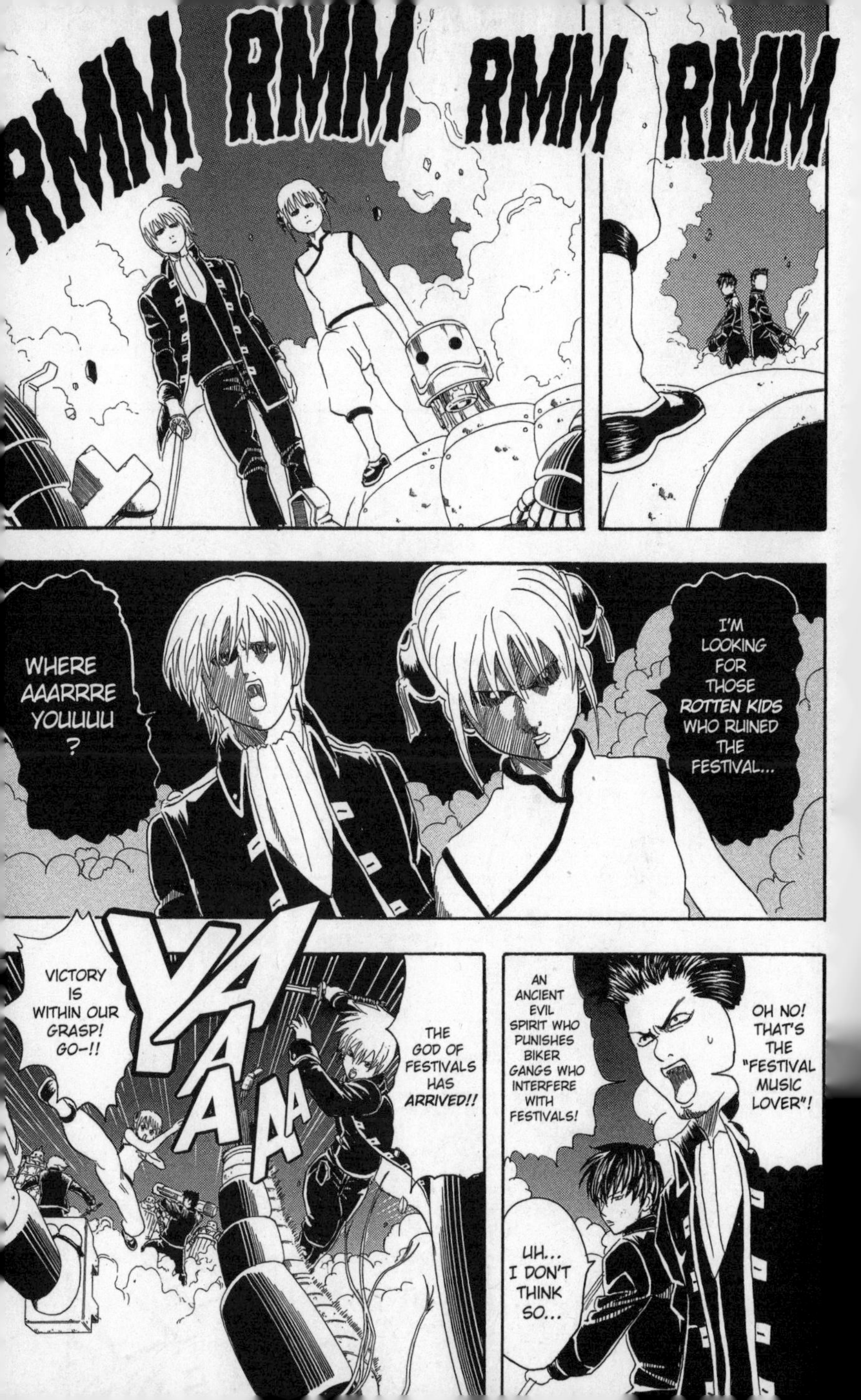
RMM
RMM
RMM
RMM
I'M LOOKING FOR THOSE ROTTEN KIDS WHO RUINED THE FESTIVAL...
WHERE AAARRRE YOUUUU?
OH NO! THAT'S THE "FESTIVAL MUSIC LOVER"!
AN ANCIENT EVIL SPIRIT WHO PUNISHES BIKER GANGS WHO INTERFERE WITH FESTIVALS!
UH... I DON'T THINK SO...
THE GOD OF FESTIVALS HAS ARRIVED!!
YAAAA
VICTORY IS WITHIN OUR GRASP! GO-!!

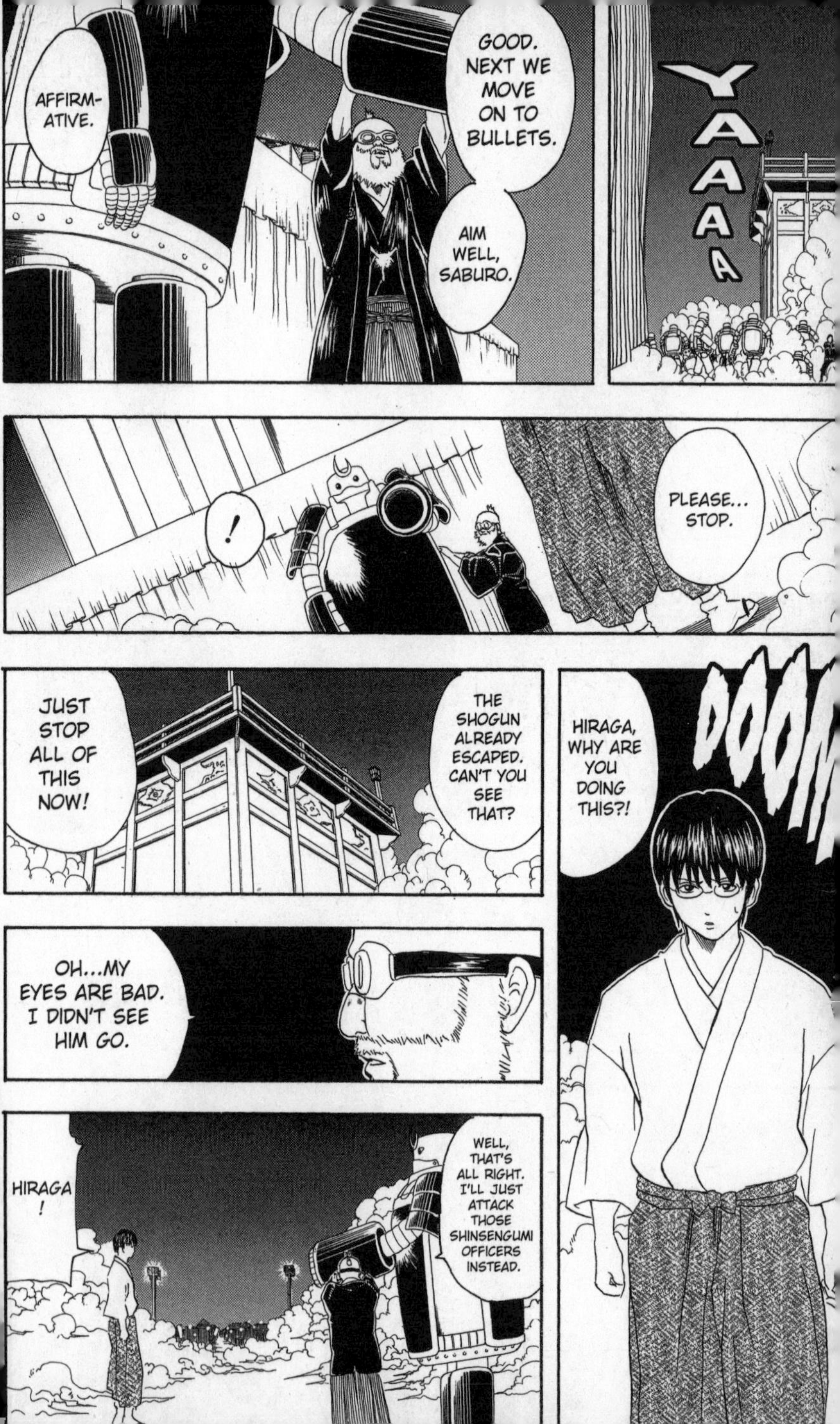
YAAAAA
GOOD. NEXT WE MOVE ON TO BULLETS.
AIM WELL, SABURO.
AFFIRMATIVE.
PLEASE... STOP.
!
DOOM
HIRAGA, WHY ARE YOU DOING THIS?!
THE SHOGUN ALREADY ESCAPED. CAN'T YOU SEE THAT?
JUST STOP ALL OF THIS NOW!
OH...MY EYES ARE BAD. I DIDN'T SEE HIM GO.
WELL, THAT'S ALL RIGHT. I'LL JUST ATTACK THOSE SHINSENGUMI OFFICERS INSTEAD.
HIRAGA!

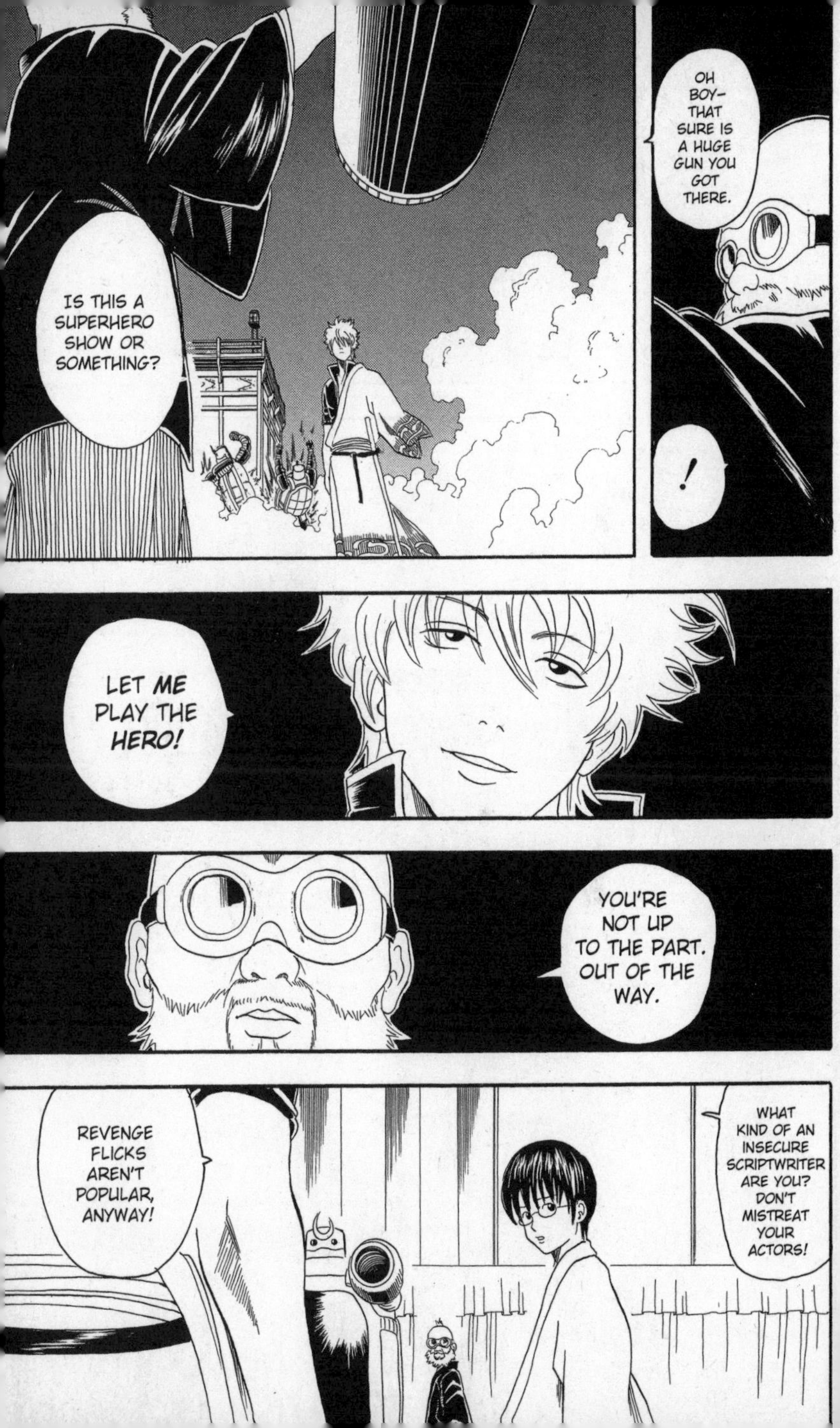
OH BOY— THAT SURE IS A HUGE GUN YOU GOT THERE.
!
IS THIS A SUPERHERO SHOW OR SOMETHING?
LET ME PLAY THE HERO!
YOU'RE NOT UP TO THE PART. OUT OF THE WAY.
WHAT KIND OF AN INSECURE SCRIPTWRITER ARE YOU? DON'T MISTREAT YOUR ACTORS!
REVENGE FLICKS AREN'T POPULAR, ANYWAY!

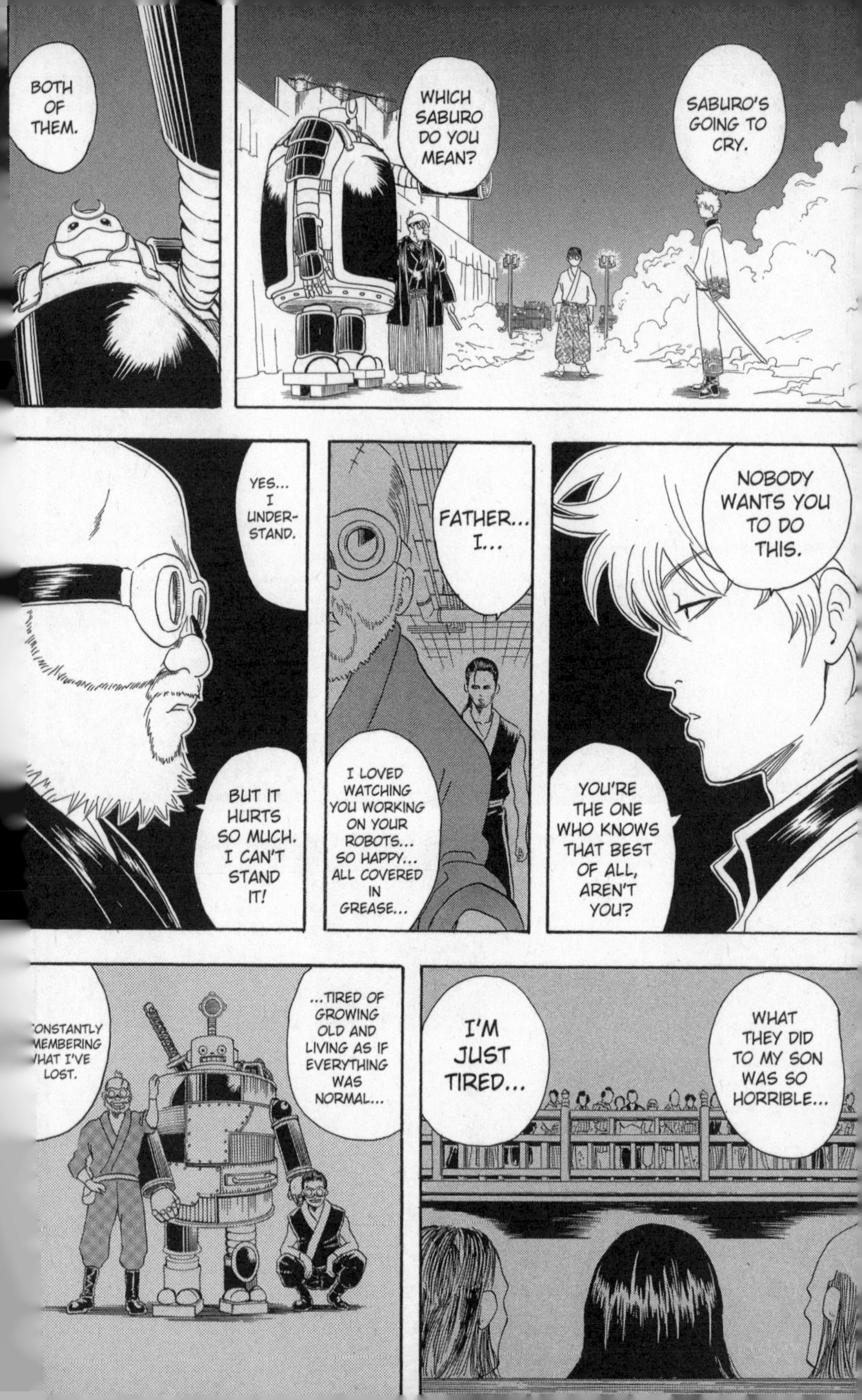
SABURO'S GOING TO CRY.
WHICH SABURO DO YOU MEAN?
BOTH OF THEM.
NOBODY WANTS YOU TO DO THIS.
YOU'RE THE ONE WHO KNOWS THAT BEST OF ALL, AREN'T YOU?
FATHER... I...
I LOVED WATCHING YOU WORKING ON YOUR ROBOTS... SO HAPPY... ALL COVERED IN GREASE...
YES... I UNDER-STAND.
BUT IT HURTS SO MUCH. I CAN'T STAND IT!
WHAT THEY DID TO MY SON WAS SO HORRIBLE...
I'M JUST TIRED...
...TIRED OF GROWING OLD AND LIVING AS IF EVERYTHING WAS NORMAL...
ONSTANTLY MEMBERING HAT I'VE LOST.

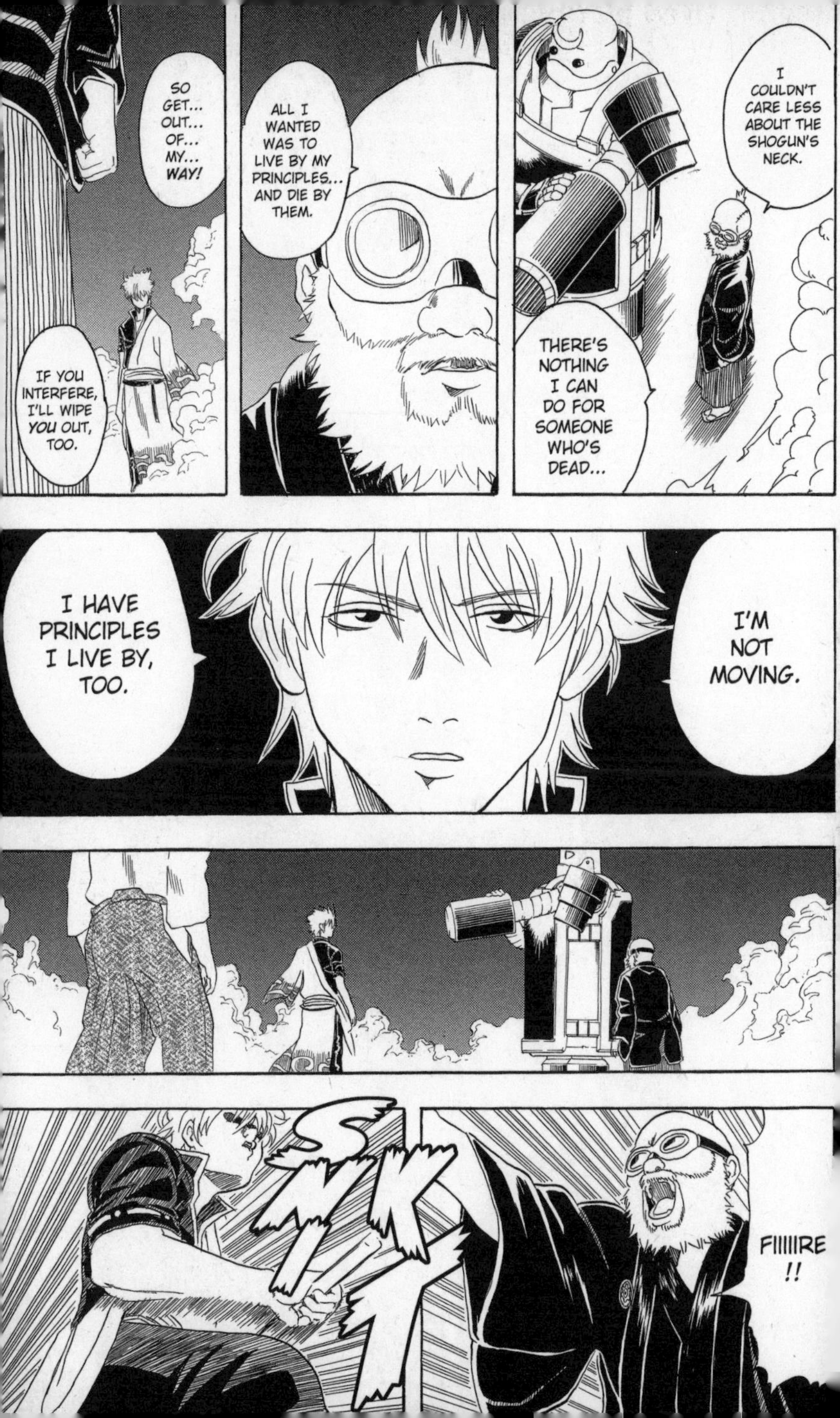
I COULDN'T CARE LESS ABOUT THE SHOGUN'S NECK.
THERE'S NOTHING I CAN DO FOR SOMEONE WHO'S DEAD...
ALL I WANTED WAS TO LIVE BY MY PRINCIPLES... AND DIE BY THEM.
SO GET... OUT... OF... MY... *WAY!*
IF YOU INTERFERE, I'LL WIPE *YOU* OUT, TOO.
I'M NOT MOVING.
I HAVE PRINCIPLES I LIVE BY, TOO.
FIIIIRE !!
SNK

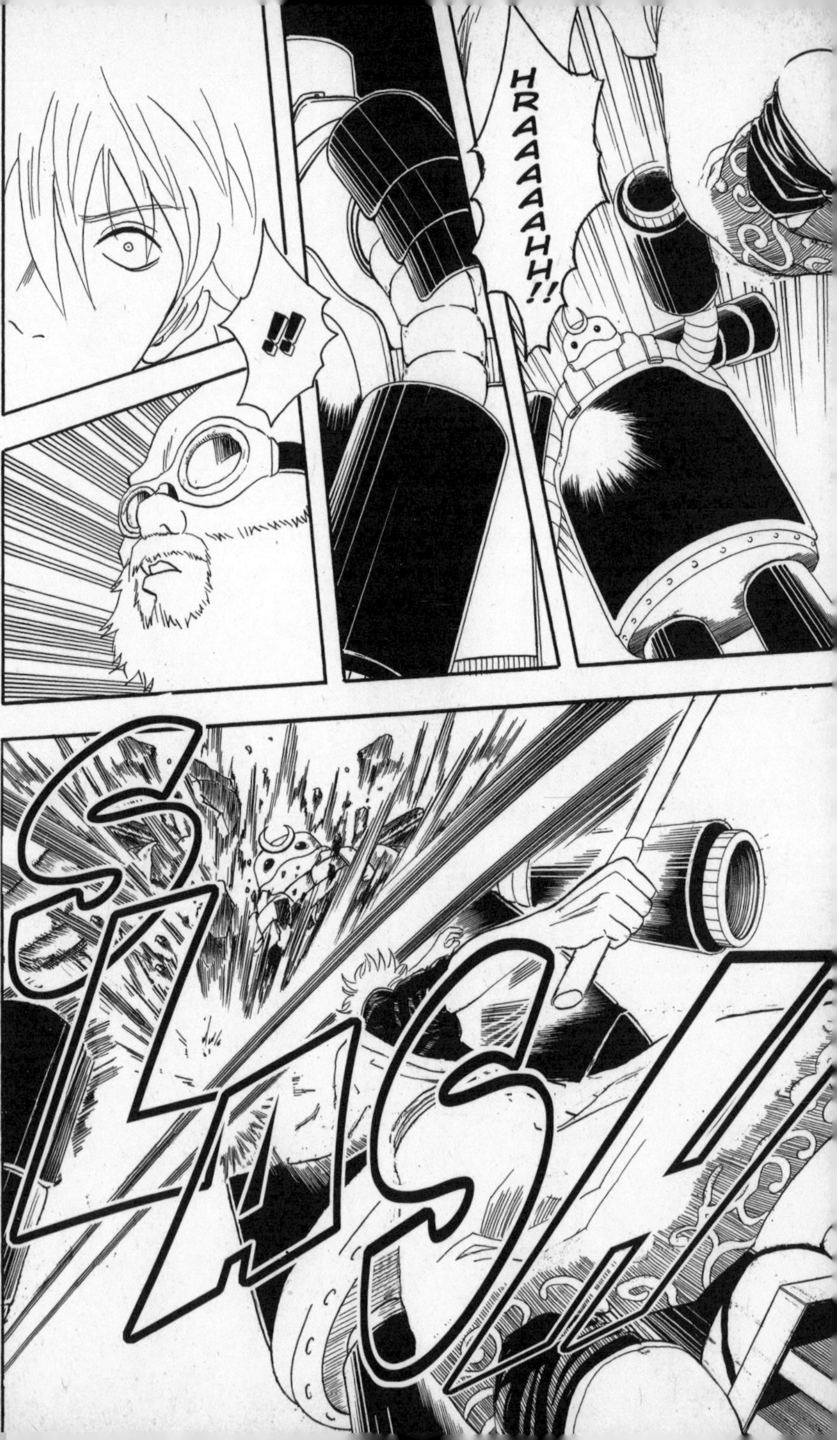
HRAAAAAAHH!!
!!
SLASH

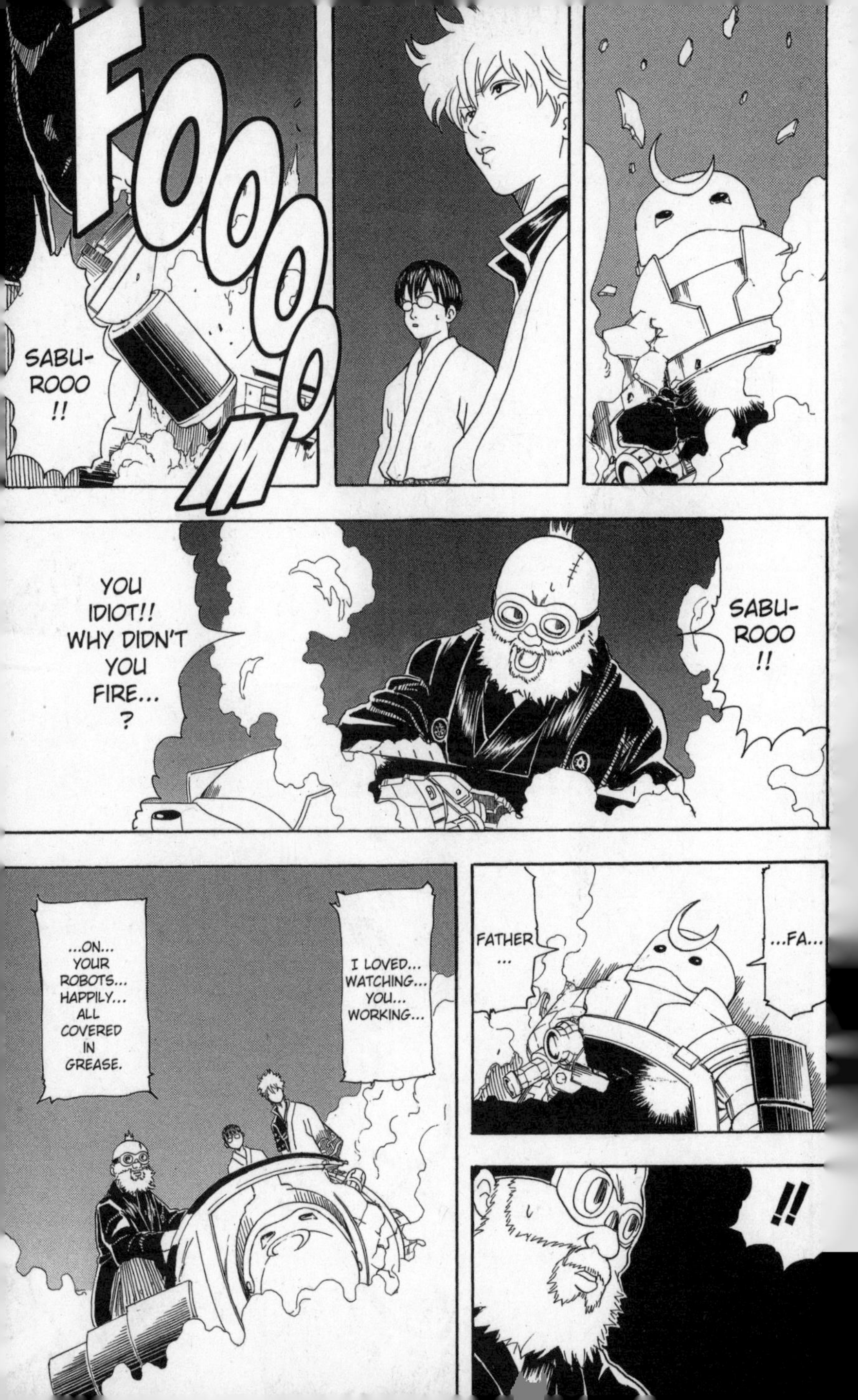
FOOOOOM
SABU-ROOO!!
SABU-ROOO!!
YOU IDIOT!! WHY DIDN'T YOU FIRE...?
...FA...
FATHER...
!!
I LOVED... WATCHING... YOU... WORKING...
...ON... YOUR ROBOTS... HAPPILY... ALL COVERED IN GREASE.

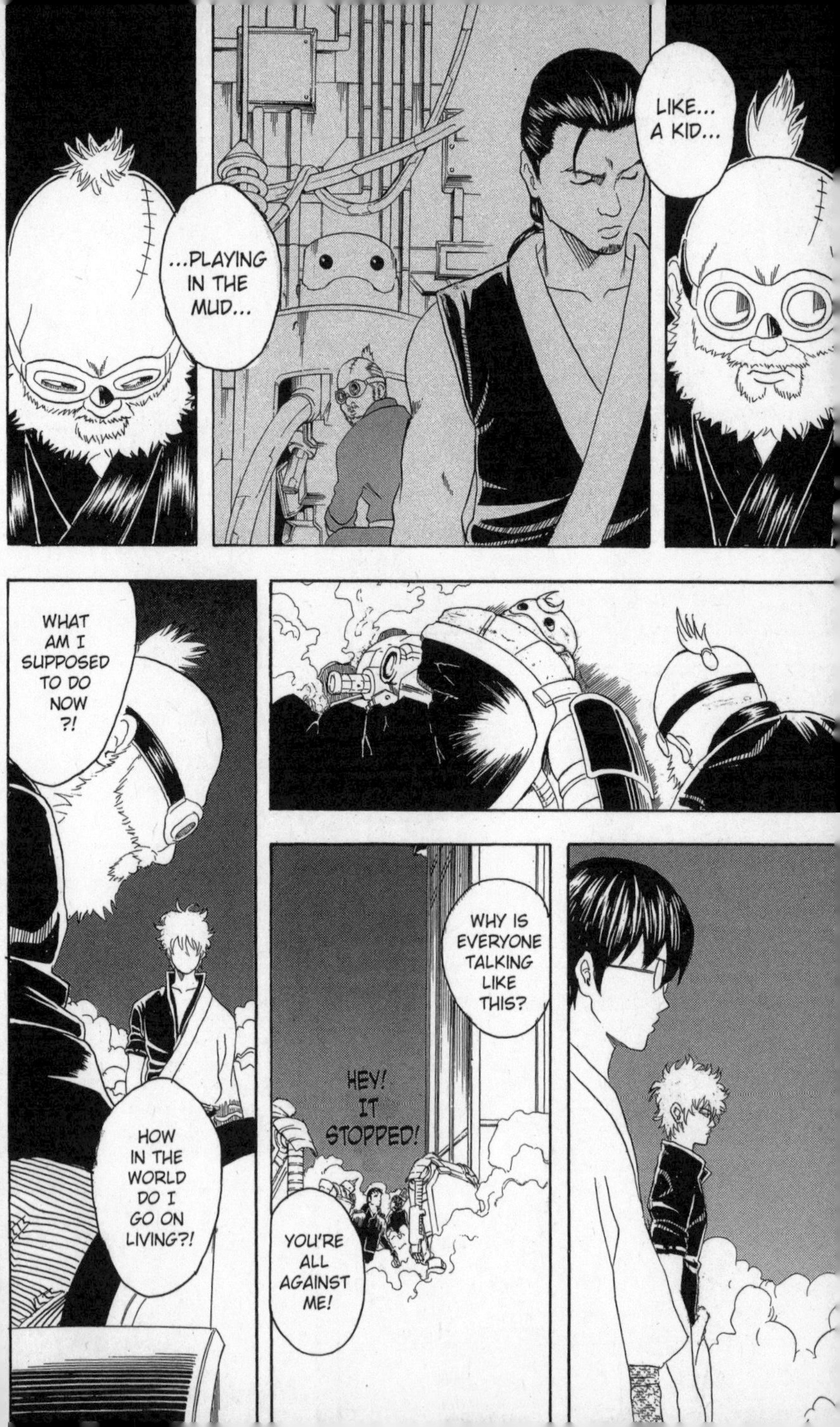
LIKE... A KID...
...PLAYING IN THE MUD...
WHY IS EVERYONE TALKING LIKE THIS?
HEY! IT STOPPED!
YOU'RE ALL AGAINST ME!
WHAT AM I SUPPOSED TO DO NOW?!
HOW IN THE WORLD DO I GO ON LIVING?!

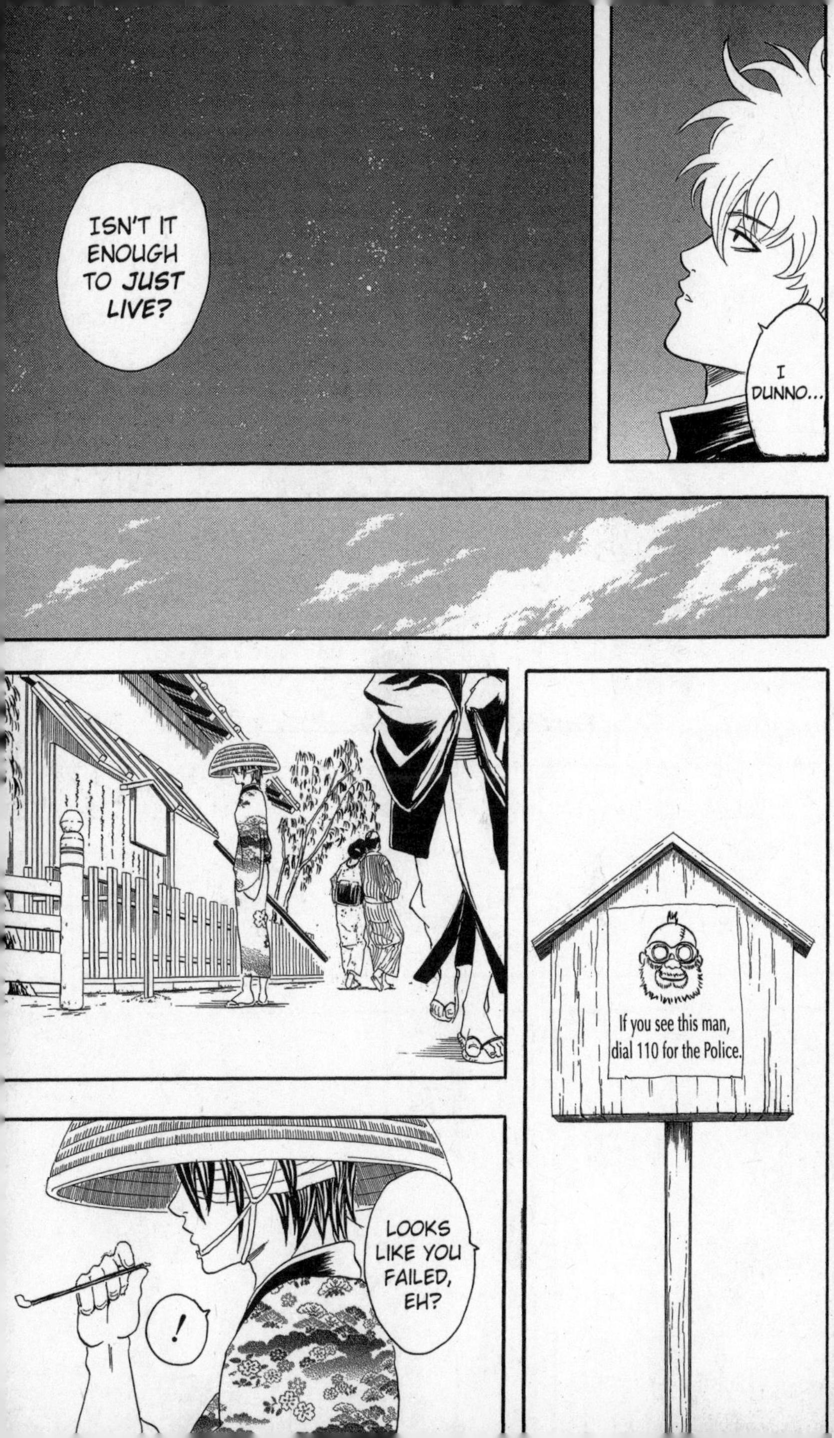
I DUNNO...
ISN'T IT ENOUGH TO JUST LIVE?
If you see this man, dial 110 for the Police.
LOOKS LIKE YOU FAILED, EH?
!

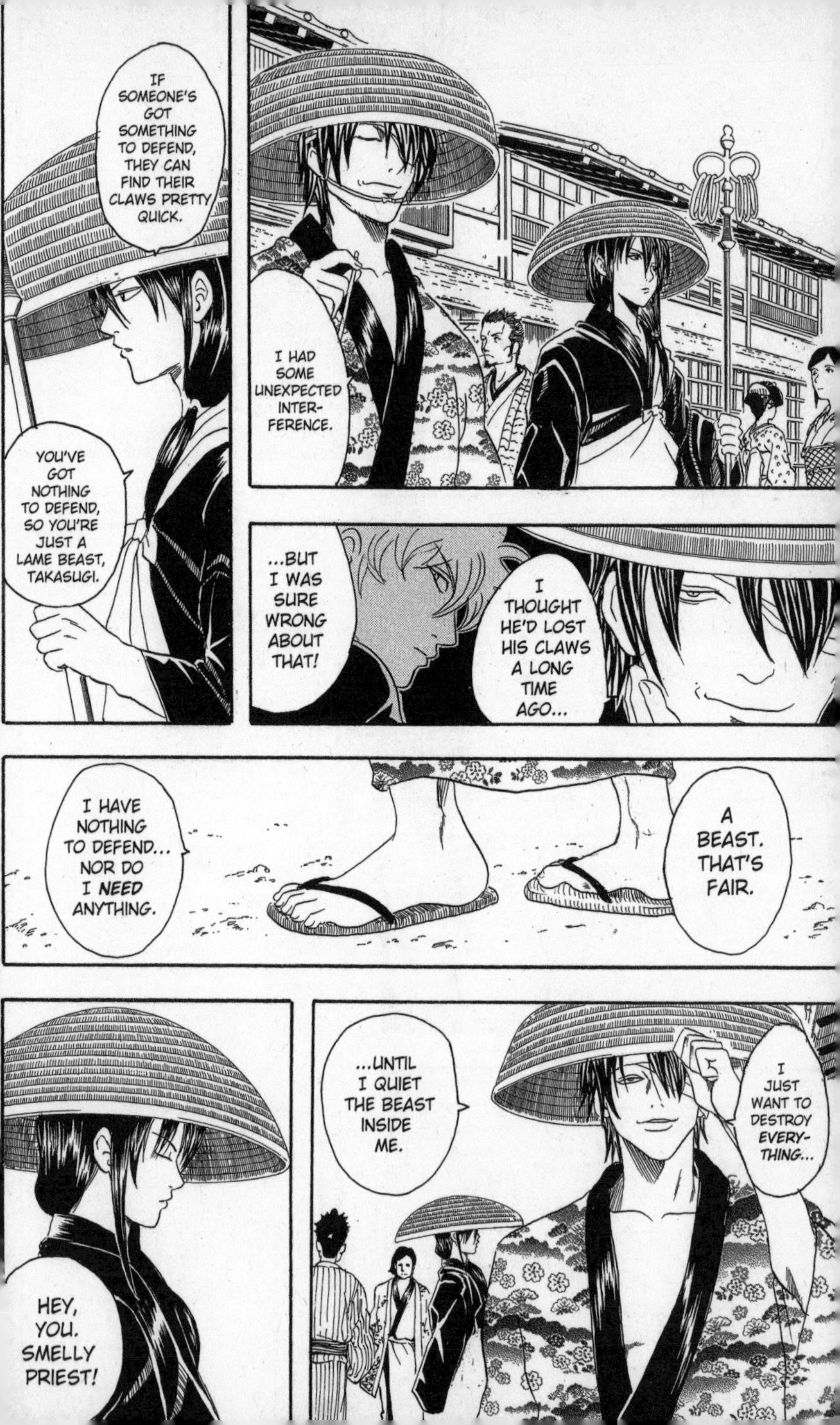
I HAD SOME UNEXPECTED INTERFERENCE.
I THOUGHT HE'D LOST HIS CLAWS A LONG TIME AGO...
...BUT I WAS SURE WRONG ABOUT THAT!
IF SOMEONE'S GOT SOMETHING TO DEFEND, THEY CAN FIND THEIR CLAWS PRETTY QUICK.
YOU'VE GOT NOTHING TO DEFEND, SO YOU'RE JUST A LAME BEAST, TAKASUGI.
A BEAST. THAT'S FAIR.
I HAVE NOTHING TO DEFEND... NOR DO I NEED ANYTHING.
I JUST WANT TO DESTROY EVERYTHING...
...UNTIL I QUIET THE BEAST INSIDE ME.
HEY, YOU. SMELLY PRIEST!

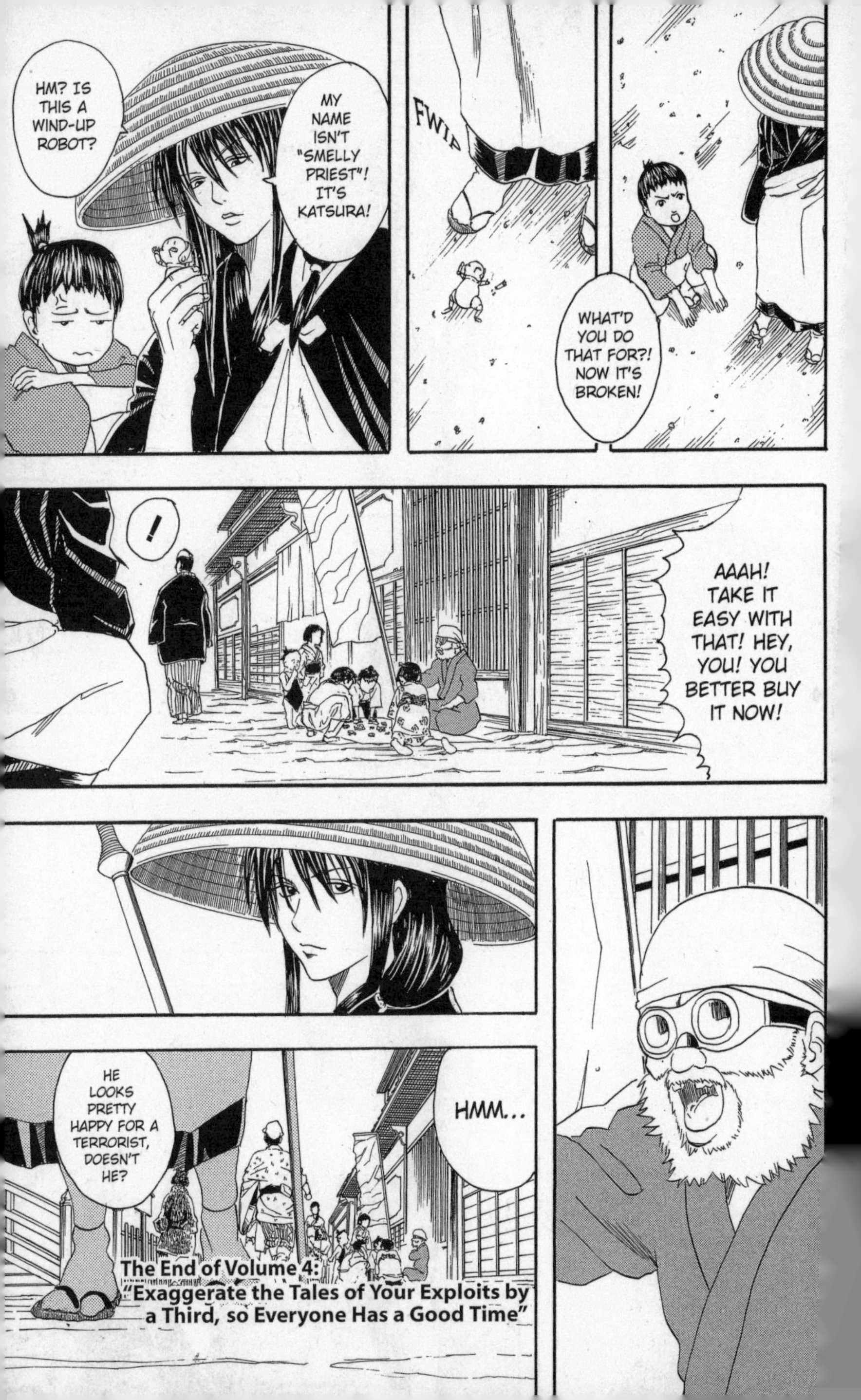
WHAT'D YOU DO THAT FOR?! NOW IT'S BROKEN!
FWIP
MY NAME ISN'T "SMELLY PRIEST"! IT'S KATSURA!
HM? IS THIS A WIND-UP ROBOT?
AAAH! TAKE IT EASY WITH THAT! HEY, YOU! YOU BETTER BUY IT NOW!
!
HMM...
HE LOOKS PRETTY HAPPY FOR A TERRORIST, DOESN'T HE?
The End of Volume 4:
"Exaggerate the Tales of Your Exploits by a Third, so Everyone Has a Good Time"

Next Volume, The Odd Jobs Trio gets down to business!

Yoruzuya Trio Will Work for Food
- Sea monster hunting
- Traveling exorcism
- Convenience-store sitting/ motorcycle gang thrashing
- Rescuing victims of kidnapping (willing and unwilling)

Special Skills
Pachinko, TV shopping, extricating self from shotgun weddings, etc.

AVAILABLE NOW

Black ✿ Clover

STORY & ART BY YŪKI TABATA

Asta is a young boy who dreams of becoming the greatest mage in the kingdom. Only one problem—he can't use any magic! Luckily for Asta, he receives the incredibly rare five-leaf clover grimoire that gives him the power of anti-magic. Can someone who can't use magic really become the Wizard King? One thing's for sure—Asta will never give up!

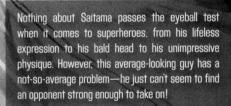

You're Reading in the Wrong Direction!!

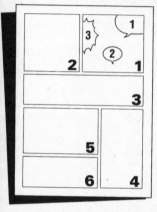

Whoops! Guess what? You're starting at the wrong end of the comic!

...It's true! In keeping with the original Japanese format, **Gin Tama** is meant to be read from right to left, starting in the upper-right corner.

Unlike English, which is read from left to right, Japanese is read from right to left, meaning that action, sound effects and word-balloon order are completely reversed... something which can make readers unfamiliar with Japanese feel pretty backwards themselves. For this reason, manga or Japanese comics published in the U.S. in English have sometimes been published "flopped"—that is, printed in exact reverse order, as though seen from the other side of a mirror.

By flopping pages, U.S. publishers can avoid confusing readers, but the compromise is not without its downside. For one thing, a character in a flopped manga series who once wore in the original Japanese version a T-shirt emblazoned with "M A Y" (as in "the merry month of") now wears one which reads "Y A M"! Additionally, many manga creators in Japan are themselves unhappy with the process, as some feel the mirror-imaging of their art alters their original intentions.

We are proud to bring you Hideaki Sorachi's **Gin Tama** in the original unflopped format. For now, though, turn to the other side of the book and let the wackiness begin...!

–Editor